Advances in International Law and Jurisprudence: Enhancing the Role of the Judiciary in the Rule of Law

Thomas Boudreau, Ph.D.
Juan Carlos Sainz-Borgo, Ph.D.
Brian Polkinghorn, Ph.D.

Editors

The Elias-Clark Law Series
Edited by
Dr Aron Ping D'Souza

The Elias Clark Group
www.elias-clark.com

GPO Box 5001
Melbourne, Victoria 3001
Australia

First Published 2017.

Typeset in Garamond.

Cataloguing-in-Publication entry

Series Editor:	D'Souza, Aron Ping, 1985-
Editor:	Boudreau, Thomas.
	Sainz-Borgo, Juan Carlos.
	Polkinghorn, Brian.
Title:	Advances in International Law and Jurisprudence: Enhancing the Role of the Judiciary in the Rule of Law
ISBN:	978-0-9925409-4-4 (pbk.)
Notes:	Bibliography.
Subjects:	Law.

CONTENTS

Notes on Editors

Thomas Boudreau is a Senior Research Fellow at the Institute for Resources and Security Studies at Cambridge University. Interdisciplinary Professor in Conflict Analysis and Resolution at Salisbury University.

Juan Carlos Sainz-Borgo is the Dean for International Cooperation and Professor in the Department of International Law, University for Peace, United Nations. He earned his Ph.D. in Juridical Sciences (with Honors) and is Doctor in Law by the Universidad Central de Venezuela and M.Sc. by Oxford University.

Brian Polkinghorn is an Associate Professor of Conflict Resolution and Executive Director of the Center for Conflict Resolution (CCR) at Salisbury University.

Aron Ping D'Souza is the editor of *The Journal Jurisprudence*. He read law at Oxford University and has a Ph.D. in law from the University of Melbourne.

Notes on Contributors

Baltasar Garzón is currently an advisor to the OEA (MAPP-OEA) Support Mission to the Colombian Peace Process. He has worked over the last 30 years as a magistrate. Advisor to the prosecutor at the International Criminal Court, Member of the Committee against Torture, lawyer, professor, author, and treatise writer.

Tara Helfman is an Associate Professor at Syracuse University College of Law; Yale Law School, J.D.; University of Cambridge, M.Phil., Political Thought & Intellectual History; University College London, M.A., Legal and Political Theory; Queens College, CUNY, B.A., History.

Joaquín González Ibáñez holds Doctorate in Law (SJD) from Madrid University Complutense. His post-graduate studies were in International Public Law at the International Institute of Law, The Hague at the Rene Cassin Institute of Human Rights, Strasbourg and holds a Diploma in European Law from Leuven University, Belgium. He has been a visiting scholar in China, Colombia and Costa Rica, and a visiting researcher in 2003-2004 at the European Law Center and Graduate School of Education in Harvard University. He is the recipient of the Fulbright-Schuman Award 2008-2009 and was a visiting scholar at American University Washington College of Law. Joaquín González is currently Co-director of the Human Rights Berg Institute and International Law professor at Madrid Alfonso X University.

Professor Mihir Kanade (India) is the Head of the Department of International Law and Human Rights at the United Nations mandated University for Peace (UPEACE) and is also the Director of the UPEACE Human Rights Center. He holds a LL.B from Nagpur University (India) and a Master degree and Doctorate from UPEACE. He is also an adjunct faculty at Universidad Alfonso XI El Sabio (Spain), Cheikh Anta Diop University (Senegal), and Long Island University (United States). His principal area of academic research and study is International Law, Human Rights and Globalization, covering several themes within that interface including trade and investment, sustainable development, forced migration, indigenous peoples' rights, public health, amongst others. He has extensive experience in training staff of intergovernmental, governmental and non-governmental organizations, as well as professionals, in the field of human rights. He acts as an advisor to several human rights organizations and corporations on issues related to international law and human rights. He serves on the International Advisory Board of the International Bar Association on the topic of Business and Human Rights. He also leads a project of the UN Office of the High Commissioner for Human Rights on promoting the Right to Development. Prior to his pursuit in academia, Mihir practiced for six years as a lawyer at the Bombay High Court and at the Supreme Court of India.

Professor Bernard Ntahiraja is the Dean for International Cooperation and Associate Professor at the Department of International Law at the University for Peace. He is a Professor of International Law. Master in International Relations: Dynamics of Co-operation, Conflict and Negotiation in International Relations and Diplomacy at Universidad Alfonso X. Madrid, Spain. He is also a researcher with the Associate Professor Rank. Instituto de Derecho Público de la Universidad Central de Venezuela.

Stephen J. Sfekas is an associate judge of the Circuit Court for Baltimore City, Maryland. He received a B.S.F.S. from the School of Foreign Service at Georgetown University in 1968, an M.A. in History from Yale University in 1972, and a J.D. from the Georgetown University Law Center in 1973.

CHAPTER 1

PROMISES TO KEEP: THE LAW OF NATIONS AND THE POST-WORLD WAR II INTERNATIONAL LEGAL ORDER

Thomas Boudreau

Acknowledgements

I want to thank Prof. Jose Alvarez, Prof. Michael Barkun, Prof. David Bennett, Michael Bersani Esq., Mrs. Terry Cardillo, Ms. Leesa Charlotte, Dr. Lowell Christie, Prof. Daniel Deudney, Ms. Filippa Ennerfelt, Dean Louis Goodman, Prof. Tara Helfman, Mr. Spencer Henderson, Ms. Amy Jones, Prof. Joseph Julian, Michael Kearney Esq., Prof. Ralph Ketcham, Mr. Edwin Njonguo, Frank Panopoulos Esq., Mr. Giandomenenico Picco, Dr. Aron Ping D'Sousa, Prof. Brian Polkinghorn, Ms. Susan Rojas, Christine Sabas, Esq.; Prof. Richard "Red" Schwartz, Prof. William Slomanson, Mark Thibodeau Esq., Gordon Thompson, Ph.D., and Anthony Yost, as well as Daniel Chou, a gifted student from the University of Pennsylvania, and other friends for reading earlier versions of this draft. Parts of this article are reprinted with permission from: *International Perspectives,* Spring 1994, vol. 5, No. 2 and *The Digest*, (forthcoming) both published by the Syracuse University College of Law. Responsibility for the ideas and possible mistakes in the following essay is, of course, my own.

Preface

This is a work of historically based jurisprudence concerning the actual origins of the modern law of nations during and immediately after World War II, which protects the basic "property" of peoples. In this regard, it is important to remember that Locke, in his *Second Treatise of Government*, defined "property" as people's lives, liberties, and possessions. Since the law of nations is a law of peoples, I am in debt to Locke's *Second Treatise* for providing the classical example of the fiduciary role that governments can assume as trustees of the rights of peoples throughout the world.

Dedicated

To Dean Guthrie Birkhead, combat veteran in Patton's Third Army in the European Theater (and my boss in graduate school); to Prof. Fred Goldie, an Australian Paratrooper (and, later, my Ph.D. dissertation advisor) who served in the Pacific Theater in World War II; to Mr. Don McCandless, combat decorated Marine in the Pacific Theater including Iwo Jima, and later Quaker Elder of Sandy Springs Meeting in Maryland; to Mr. Dee Paris, whose United States Army unit helped take the town and bridge of Remagen over the Rhine; to Col. David Sterling, Eighth Army in North Africa, a legend in all Allied Armies; and to countless others of their generation in American or Allied uniform who made the law of nations possible through their service and sacrifice.[1]

Origins of a Modern Law of Nations: Introduction and Summary

The operating axiom of this paper is that a new law of nations was created in international law due to the solemn promises made in good faith by the Allied powers during World War II to their own, neutral, conquered, and colonial peoples of the world. Specifically, this new law of nations emerged from the Atlantic Charter, the Declaration of [the] United Nations (UN) on January 1, 1942, the Moscow Declaration, and other promissory statements made by Allied governments, especially during the darkest times of the war.[2] These declarations contained solemn promises that, in essence, created fiduciary obligations, duties, interests, and norms that governments were to recognize on the international level and peoples of the world were to enjoy if the war was won.

This fiduciary law of nations now governs the relationship of governments to their own and other peoples and enunciates the rights of such nations to, among other things, human rights, self-determination, trusteeship, and collective security, as embodied in the Charter of the UN and other post-war documents. In particular, the modern law of nations limits and sharply curtails the unilateral violence that a government can legitimately use against its own or other peoples, as the Nuremberg Charter, the Convention on the Crime and Punishment of Genocide, or the subsequent international human rights regime attest. By doing so, the emergence of the law of nations resulted in a fundamental realignment of the legal relationship between the nation and the state,

[1] In alphabetical order.
[2] In the following essay, the terms law of nations and international law are regarded as synonymous.

terms that are usually conflated in the legal lexicon. In view of this, the analytic focus in the following essay preliminarily scrutinizes this increasingly important and problematic *legal relationship between a nation or nations and the state*, which actually does – or purports to – represent and protect its people under the relevant and respective domestic and international legal orders.

Specifically, the new law of nations reconfigures the legal relationship between the nation and state by recognizing the *international rights* of the people within the state and, in the case of Nuremberg Charter, the rights of the nation or a people *against the state*. These legal innovations have resulted in a profound shift in the fundamental and historically competing sources of legitimacy and sovereignty away from the state and towards the nation or people of the polity who are now the new *imperium et imperii* (sovereign within the sovereign) in international law.

Before World War II, the legal meaning of the "nation-state" was nearly always conflated with the legal definition of the "state." Yet, during and after the war, this simplistic shorthand for the "nation" ceased to be accurate—though the two terms have been and are continually used without critical reflection or review. Such linguistic and legal conflation simply does not do justice to the manifold promises made by the Allied governments to entire peoples during the war. In short, the "nations" of the world took on extraordinary significance during World War II as the Allied governments made solemn promises in good faith to peoples throughout the world in an ongoing attempt to mobilize the millions needed to defeat the Axis powers. These steps included the imparting of promissory declarations to millions of people under European colonial control in an effort to gain their supreme allegiance, or at least discourage them from supporting the Axis side.

The future fiduciary acts assured by the Allied governments included their promises to observe human rights, self-determination, systems of trusteeship, and collective security, when and if the peoples of the world helped defeat the mortal threat represented by the fascist Axis powers.

This not to claim that the development of the law of nations in the crucible of World War II was a deliberate war aim; on the contrary, it evolved as a result of complex, contested, and often convoluted interactions, interests, or compromises among the Allied powers fighting the war, some of whom had vast colonial holdings overseas and wanted to preserve these after the war, as well as those who detested colonialism, especially the Americans or Soviets. Specifically, the American government under Roosevelt sought termination of worldwide colonialism as one of the clear war aims to rally the conquered, colonial, neutral, and allied peoples of the world to join the anti-Axis coalition, or at the very least, refrain from joining the Axis cause at a time of mortal danger to the Allied nations.

These fiduciary norms render fully explicit a traditionally existing and often implicit international fiduciary legal order consisting of rights, duties, customs, and territories held *in common* by humanity. This traditional fiduciary legal order consists of the oceans and the "freedom of the seas," as illustrated in the Law of the Sea Convention, as well as other global commons. As this paper evidences, the United Nations General Assembly (UNGA) can monitor and maintain the global commons for future generations, beginning with the Earth's atmosphere, which has important implications for addressing global climate change. With the advent of the post-World War II fiduciary norms, duties, relationships, and interests, such as the observance of international human rights, this fiduciary legal order has become more robust and fully explicit, though still inevitably contested in international and national jurisdictions. *So, it is ultimately the role of present and future judges in national jurisdictions, international tribunals, and the International Court of Justice (ICJ) to decide the scope and extent of this still-emerging fiduciary international legal order.* The Pinochet indictment in Spain is a prominent, if not pioneering, example of this ongoing evolution in fiduciary international law that has its roots in legal developments during and after the most prominent war in human history.

This argument concerning the historical founding of an expanded *international* fiduciary legal order during World War II parallels John Lock's theoretical argument concerning the founding of government in the domestic sphere. In his classic *Second Treatise of Government*, Locke argued that after people have established a civil society through a social contract, they then proceed to create a government *as a trust* to protect people's rights. In Locke's scenario, governments are created simply to serve as trustees, while the people are both the true trustors *and* beneficiaries of this limited and fiduciary governmental power. As Prof. William Ebenstein of Princeton University has stated, the principal characteristic of a Lockean trust is that the government primarily assumes obligations, rather than rights. Ebenstein has stated that by claiming that government represents a fiduciary pact, Locke enunciated a sharp distinction between the state and society.

According to Locke, society is far more important and enduring than the government, which simply represents a trusteeship resulting from the limited fiduciary interests that the people have granted to it. Of course, Locke's theory on the formation of government has significant historical import. As Prof. Ebenstein has noted, by "committing themselves to Locke's theories of government the British supplied the case for the American Revolution and for the later—peaceful—independence of other colonies and India."

In the following essay, I posit that Locke's argument in his *Second Treatise* concerning the creation of government as a trustee on the domestic plane helps to explain, by analogy, the origins and evolution of an international fiduciary legal order out of the agony of World Word II. More specifically, I argue four key points concerning the creation of a fiduciary law of nations during the war.

First, as this paper establishes, governments made solemn declarations and promises to their own and other peoples concerning self-determination, human rights, trusteeship, and collective security, which would be recognized and respected by these promissory governments *when and if the war was won.*

Since many hundreds of thousands of soldiers were going to die to fulfill these solemn promises and pledges, these government declarations cannot be characterized as mere propaganda on the one hand, or as simple contractual statements between the living on the other. Instead, I propose in the following essay that these solemn pledges were made in good faith to the allied, colonial, conquered, and neutral nations of the world, creating fiduciary rights, duties, norms, and interests that *these peoples as a whole* would exercise and enjoy when and if they had first helped to win the war. Since people have always possessed these rights, these mortally threatened governments were making major assurances at the time *to recognize such rights and limits to their own governmental powers on an international level* after their own and other peoples helped to win World War II. In short, since these rights originate with the peoples of the world, and not their governments, each nation or peoples became the *trustors* and *beneficiaries* of these newly created or recognized fiduciary norms. This is precisely how Locke envisioned the relationship of the government as a *trustee* of the people or society's rights. From Locke's perspective, this relationship exists only within the context of an enduring trust.

These wartime promises, made and accepted in good faith, helped to mobilize the millions of people necessary to fight and defeat the mortal threat of global fascism. Their people's subsequent service can be easily construed as agreement and actual or tacit consent to the promises and goals of the Allied powers as stated throughout the war. In essence, using Locke's theoretical framework as an analogy to describe actual historical events, the governments that had made these promises during the war effectively became the trustees of this new fiduciary legal order, which includes their recognition binding legal norms concerning self-determination, international human rights, and strict limits on the state's unilateral use of international force.

Hence, this type of fiduciary pact essentially *begins below the threshold* of traditional interstate treaties. The Allied powers' original promises and solemn declarations in the early desperate days of World War II often resulted in eventual treaties after they won the war, and thus often became, like the Charter of the UN, hybrid agreements consisting of both state-centric or treaty and trust international law. Yet, the origins of the trusteeship relationship forged in the crucible of the world war began *within the state, as a matter between the mortally threatened government and its own and other peoples.* As such, the resulting trust – often consisting of contested fiduciary rights, interests, and relationships, such as human rights – are, or should be, self-executing *within* the nation's own borders and judiciary. This is currently an especially contested issue in the United States, despite its status as one of the prime architects of the new post-war legal order.

Second, this fiduciary law of nations is republican in scope in that it ultimately seeks to end, or legally limit, the traditional prerogatives and predations of states in the Westphalian system prior to World War II. As Prof. Daniel Deudney has indicated in his award-winning book, *Bounding Power*, republican security theory has been concerned since ancient times with the constraint of and limitations on unilateral political or military force. As such, republican security theory is useful in understanding the systems of restraints that resulted from World War II. The resulting regimes of human rights, Nuremberg, and the Charter's *outlawing of aggressive war can be viewed as legal systems of restraint* upon the once unfettered power of the state. In particular, under the law of nations, individuals can and must be held accountable for war crimes, crimes against peace, and crimes against humanity. In particular, under this fiduciary legal order, national jurisdictions have the responsibility to prosecute war criminals from their own and other states.

Such individual accountability for the commission of international crimes is a conceptual and legal anomaly in traditional public international law defined largely in terms of relations between states. Yet, in the emergent law of nations, the critical importance and World War II innovation of holding individuals internationally accountable for their crimes of state is fully consistent with a fiduciary legal order that recognizes both individual human rights and group rights, such as the right of a people to self-determination. A later section of this paper explores the profound significance of the modern law of nations in terms of creating further republican restraints upon the state once unilateral prerogatives and attempt to assert power, especially to wage war.

Third, this law of nations forged from efforts to win World War II is simply the most recent addition to the traditional fiduciary international legal order that has arguably existed since the time of Grotius, if not Justinian, and governs the freedom of the seas and the global commons, including the Earth's atmosphere, among other things.[3] The fiduciary norms, interests, duties, and relationships resulting from World War II are the newest elements in this traditional body of international trust law, which has generally been a largely recessed *legal order* within international law. With the advent of the post-World War II law of nations, this recessed (and thus often taken for granted) fiduciary order has become more fully developed and explicit in the modern (Post-World War II) law of nations, although it is certainly capable of further development and evolution in the future.

In particular, the Charter of the UN is described as a promissory document consisting of both treaty and trust law, and is founded in the Allied powers' fiduciary promises during World War II. Due to the policies and priorities of the Roosevelt Administration, legal trusteeship is central to the fiduciary foundations of the Charter. From this perspective, the legal responsibilities of trusteeship far surpass the stated goals of the Trusteeship Council, one of the original main organs of the UN. From the seed of these promissory declarations, especially the Moscow Declaration of 1943 (See Prof. Helfman's essay in this book), these fiduciary foundations are capable of evolution and expansion. As this paper illustrates, this has implications concerning ongoing international efforts to

[3] The legal reality of the global commons is also hotly contested by a small minority of states; yet, their claims are not recognized by the vast majority of governments throughout the world.

combat global climate change by monitoring and maintaining the Earth's atmosphere and oceans in order to preserve them for future generations.

Finally, this new law of nations is part of the now fully explicit fiduciary legal order: the public law of nations, which compliments, co-exists, and often is contested with the two other traditional legal orders recognized in the complex and pluralistic international legal order; the public law of states, which this paper defines as and largely limits to *treaties between states or state practice;* and private international law. In short, there are at least three major international legal orders that constantly interact and diffuse into one another, causing or threatening to cause contested and complimentary judicial decisions throughout the world (See Figure 1, below, Section IV). Hence, the new law of nations is part and parcel of the differing legal orders that constitute the newly emergent field of global legal pluralism. This has important implications for how courts interpret and apply the law of nations as part of the common and fiduciary heritage of humanity.

I

Promises Made: The Sources of the Modern Law of Nations

Because of the unprecedented scale of violence, suffering, and death experienced by human beings during World War II, the victorious nations of the world agreed during the war and in the war's immediate aftermath upon a series of declarations, treaties, and trials that literally transformed the very nature of international legal jurisprudence. Both the unmitigated violence of the Nazis against the Jews in the horrors of the Holocaust and the terror directed towards other European, Slavic, and Soviet peoples was unparalleled in human history. On the other side of the world, the slaughter and exploitation of the Chinese, Vietnamese, Korean, and Pacific peoples added millions more to the war's toll.[4]

Due to these terrible realities, a unique *corpus juris* or body of law was created in good faith to ensure, as far as possible, that the massive war against subject human

[4] See Peter Longreich, *Holocaust: The Nazi Persecution and Murder of the Jews* (Oxford Univ. Press Inc. 2010); see also Lamber M. Surhone, Miriam Timpledon and Susan F. Marseken, *World War II Casualties* (Betascript Publishing, 2010). Finally See, Gerhard L. Weinberg, *A World at Arms: A Global History of World War II* (Cambridge Univ. Press 2d ed. 2005) 894-921. (The last chapter of this excellent book is on the "cost and impact" of the war.)

populations—including both a state's own and others—would never happen again. Developed during and immediately after World War II, this *corpus juris* consists of the following: 1) the Atlantic Charter, the Declaration of [the] UN, and subsequent wartime or summit declarations by the Western Allies[5]; 2) the UN Charter[6]; 3) the Charter of the International Military Tribunal, hereafter referred to as the Nuremberg Charter, and the subsequent Nuremberg trials[7]; 4) the Universal Declaration of Human Rights, which contributed to the subsequent post-war explosion in international human rights law[8]; 5) the Convention on the Prevention and Punishment of the Crime of Genocide 1948)[9]; 6) the 1949 Geneva Conventions and the systematic elaboration of humanitarian law[10]; and

---

5 See, for example, the Declaration of Principles, known and cited hereafter as the Atlantic Charter, by the President of the United States and the Prime Minister of the United Kingdom, August 14,1941 [hereinafter Atlantic Charter] available at http://www.nato.int/cps/en/natolive/official_texts_16912.htm; see also *The Atlantic Charter* (Douglas Brinkley & David R. Facey-Crowther eds., St. Martin's Press 1994); Also, see "Declaration of United Nations," 6 Dep't State Bull. 3, 3-4 (1942). 1 January 1942.

6 See Leland M. Goodrich and Edward Hambro, *Charter of the United Nations: Commentary and Documents* (World Peace Found. 2nd ed. 1949); Jose E. Alvarez, *International Organizations as Law-Makers* (Oxford Univ. Press 2005) see also Charter of the United Nations [hereinafter UN Charter] available at http://treaties.un.org/doc/Publication/CTC/uncharter.pdf.

7 See Charter of the International Military Tribunal, Aug. 8, 1945, 59 Stat. 1544 [hereinafter Nuremberg Charter] available at http://avalon.law.yale.edu/imt/imtconst.asp; Judgement of the International Military Tribunal, Oct. 1, 1946 available at http://avalon.law.yale.edu/imt/judgen.asp. See also Quincy Wright, The Law of the Nuremberg Trial, 41 AM. J. INT'L L. 38 (1947). The Law of the Nuremberg Trial. The American Journal of International Law, Vol. 41, No. 1 (Jan., 1947), pp. 38-72. Also on line at: Published by: American Society of International Law. Stable URL: http://www.jstor.org/stable/2193853. Bradley Smith, *Reaching Judgement at Nuremberg: The Untold Story of How the Nazi War Criminals Were Judged* (Basic Books, 1977). Smith used the extensive Nuremberg Collection in the archival library at my *alma mater*, Syracuse University (SU), to research his book. I began using these archives, based upon the American judge Francis Biddle's personal diary and collection, at SU as a graduate student in the early 1980s, and have been using them ever since to understand the thinking behind events and the actual trial of the Nazi warlords.

8 See Universal Declaration of Human Rights, G.A. Res. 217A at 71, U.N. GAOR, 3d Sess, 1st plen.mtg., U.N. DOC A/810 (Dec. 12, 1948); *see also*: Johannes Morsink, *The Universal Declaration of Human Rights Origins, Drafting and Intent* (Bert B. Lockwood, Jr., ed., Univ. of Pa. Press 1999); *see* also: Mary Ann Glendon, *World Made New: Eleanor Roosevelt and the Universal Declaration of Human Rights* (Random House Trade Paperbacks, 2002). Finally, See, William R. Slomanson, *Fundamental Perspectives on International Law* (Wadsworth Publ'g Co, 1990, 2010 ed), which provides an excellent overview and analysis concerning the evolution of human rights law since World War II.

9 Convention on the Prevention and Punishment of the Crime of Genocide, Dec. 9, 1948, 78 U.N.T.S. 277 (entered into force Jan. 12, 1951) *available at* http://www.hrweb.org/legal/genocide.html; see also John Cooper, *Raphael Lemkin and the Genocide Convention* (Palgrave Macmillan 2008). Herbert Hirsch, *Genocide and the Politics of Memory* (Chapel Hill: University of North Caroline Press, 1995). Finally, See, Irving Louis Horowitz, *Genocide: State, Power and Mass Murder* (Transaction Books, 1976). Raphael Lemkin is a hero of humanity; the Genocide Convention is largely the result of his lifelong efforts to outlaw mass killings, an effort he began as a Polish lawyer under the League of Nations. He finally succeeded in 1948 at the United Nations, though in an unbelievably terrible and cruel irony, much of his own family perished in the Holocaust during World War II. He worked for the American government during World War II and at Nuremberg to account for Nazi war crimes. In tribute, I devote almost an entire chapter to this remarkable man in my forthcoming book, *Law of Nations, Legal Order in a Violent World.*

10 The Geneva Convention of 1949 and the two 1977 additional protocols are often referred to as the "Geneva Conventions," or as the "Law of Geneva." This now consists of the following: The Geneva Convention for the Amelioration of the Condition of the Wounded and Sick in Armed Forces in the Field, Aug. 12, 1949, 75 U.N.T.S. 31; (entered into force Oct. 21, 1950) *available at* http://www.umn.edu/humanrts/instree/y1gacws.htm; Geneva

7) the Reparations Case, which recognized the international personality of entities other than states, such as an international organization.[11] Subsequent to these developments was the gradual evolution of *erga omnes* obligations, *jus cogens* norms,[12] and the International Bill of Human Rights.[13] As Prof. Louis Henkin of Columbia has observed, the modern human rights movement is a key development of the "various articulations of the war aims of the Allies in World War II."[14]

The three charters – the Atlantic, the UN, and the Nuremberg, and their related declarations or documents – were critical factors in establishing the fiduciary foundations of the new international legal order.

This is because, beginning with the Atlantic Charter and the_Declaration by [the] UN, January 1 1942, the Allied wartime declarations contained specific *promises and commitments* by the Allied powers which created, as this paper argues, a *fiducia*, meaning a "pledge" in Latin or (later) a trust between the promissory government and its own people or nation, as well as with other peoples in the world. These promissory declarations, in essence, created legally binding *fiduciary duties, interests, or relationships* between the mortally threatened governments and the peoples or nations that they were trying to influence around the world.

Convention for the Amelioration of the Condition of the Wounded and Sick and Shipwrecked Members of the Armed Forces at Sea, Aug. 12, 1949, 75 U.N.T.S. 287 (entered into force Oct. 21, 1950) *available at* http://www.icrc.org/ihl.nsf/full/370?opendocument; see also Protocols I and II Additional to the Geneva Conventions of August 1949, June 8, 1977 (entered into force July 12, 1978).

[11] 1949 ICJ 174, *Reparations for Injuries Suffered in the Service of the United Nations*, International Court of Justice Advisory opinion, 1949. This ICJ recognized that entities besides states had standing under international law to bring claims against a state.

[12] See Maurizio Ragaszzi, *The Concept of International Obligations Erga Omnes* (Oxford Univ. Press, 2000). Also see see M. Cherif Bassiouni, 1998. International Crimes: *Jus Cogens* and *Obligatio Erga Omnes*, Law and Contemporary Problems, Law and Contemporary Problems, 59: 63-74. The concept of *jus cogens* predates World War II, yet events during the war gave it added urgency, even though it still suffers from legal imprecision. See, Christos L. Rozakis, *The Concept of Jus Cogens in the Law of Treaties* (North-Holland Publ'g 1976); see also Carin Kahgan, *Jus Cogens and the Inherent Right of Self Defense*, 3 ILSA J. INT'L & COMP. L. 767 (1997). Finally See, Vienna Convention on the Law of Treatises, May 22, 1969, U.N. Doc. A/CONF 39/27

[13] William Slomanson, above n 5. The first time that I heard this term was while reading the first version of Slomanson's text. I am in debt to Bill and his work. This preceding list is taken from my article: Thomas Boudreau, *Jus Gentium and Systematic Legal Order: New Paradigm for International* Law, 5 INT'L PERSP. (1994). Published at Syracuse University College of Law.

[14] Louis Henkin, *The International Bill of Rights: the Covenant on Civil and Political Rights*, (New York: Columbia Univ. Press, 1981).

The legal definition of the nation, unlike that of the state, has always been problematic and underdeveloped in international law.[15] For the purposes of this paper, the nation is legally defined as a jural community consisting of a distinctive people, some or most of whom occupy a specific territory, who share a sense of moral and legal obligation towards one another; as Michael Barkun has explained in his book *Law Without Sanction*, the concept of "jural community" means the "widest grouping within which there are a moral [or legal] obligation and a means of ultimately to settle disputes peacefully."[16] In this sense, the nation as a jural community exists as a legal pact and an ongoing normative narrative between the dead, the living, and the unborn, since it can keep legal obligations, such as public or private trusts, between preceding, present, and pending generations. According to Prof. Barkun, such jural communities can be found in so-called "primitive" societies, as well as in international law. As this paper evidences, because of legal developments during World War II, such nations had rights recognized prior to statehood, such as self-determination, and even against their own governments, as embodied in the Nuremberg Charter.

In short, the peoples or nations of the world assumed extraordinary significance during World War II, as the Allied governments made solemn promises to domestic populations throughout the globe in an ongoing attempt to mobilize the millions needed to defeat the Axis powers. Yet, in the early years of the conflict, especially during the summer of 1941, the Axis powers seemed to be winning the war.[17] The German Colossus stretched from Norway and the North Sea through Europe and Greece to the Mediterranean and North Africa. Hitler had just attacked the Soviet Union, and few observers thought at the time that the Russians could stand up to the Nazi onslaught.[18]

---

[15] For instance, Rawls has addressed this problem in his book; see John Rawls, *The Laws of Peoples* (Harvard Univ. Press 3rd ed. 2000) (which provides a non-historically based call for a law of the people.)
See also Robert J. Beck and Thomas Ambrosio eds, *International Law and the Rise of Nations: The State System and the Challenge of Ethnic Groups* (Chatham House Publications, 2002); J. Sammuel Barkin and Bruce Cronin, *The State of the Nation: Changing Norms and Rules of Sovereignty in International Relations*, 48 Int'l Org. 107 (1994). There are, of course, volumes written about what constitutes a nation; I am offering a legal definition here that will be inevitably contested; yet, I indicate that this definition, inspired by the work of Prof. Barkun, can be empirically measured and tested, especially in terms of the "nation(s)-State."

[16] Michael Barkin, *Law Without Sanction: Order in Primitive Societies and the World Community* (Yale Univ. Press, 1968). Prof. Barkun has been an invaluable teacher and colleague. Here, I am defining the nation or nations legally as a "jural community," usually in relationship to a state, a concept that can be empirically tested or falsified even though it is an admittedly elusive concept in daily discourse, or in the social sciences.

[17] Weinburg, above n 1; see William Shirer, *The Rise and Fall of the Third Reich: A History of Nazi Germany* (Simon and Schuster, 3rd ed. 1990).

[18] In the early years of the war, the British were particularly skeptical of the Soviet ability to hold out. See Elliot Roosevelt, *As He Saw It* (Greenwood Press, 1974).

On the other side of the globe, the Japanese had over a million men in China, and seemed intent on carving out its "Co-Prosperity Zone" without any serious opposition.[19]

In particular, there seemed to be nothing that could – or would – prevent the possible linkup of German and Japanese forces along the rim of the Indian Ocean, especially in 1940 until early June, 1942. Such a linkup would enormously complicate the Allies' capacity to win the war against their mortal enemies.

So, the outcome of the war was very much in doubt in the early 1940s, when the Allies began to make promissory declarations to their own and other peoples involving the international recognition of human rights, self-determination, and collective security to protect ensuing peace, if they first won the war.

The First Promises: The Atlantic Charter

The very first document in this regard, and one of the most important, was the Atlantic Charter, which explicitly reveals that the promises made by the governments of the United States and the United Kingdom were to the "peoples" or "nations" of the world. The choice of wording was deliberate; for instance, during the Atlantic Charter Conference in 1941, President Roosevelt told Prime Minister Churchill that "the peace cannot include any continued despotism. The structure of the peace demands and will get the *equality of peoples.*"[20] President Roosevelt meant both colonies and countries, and he never wavered from this position, which had the strong support of his civilian administration and military leadership. Accordingly, the Atlantic Charter mentions "peoples" or "nations" eight times, while it mentions the word "states" only once.

The Atlantic Charter was the culminating statement made by President Roosevelt and Prime Minister Churchill at their first meeting in Placentia Bay, Newfoundland in August, 1941.[21] At the outset of the meeting, the British undoubtedly wanted greater military involvement in the war against Germany by the neutral United States, which was

---

[19] Gaddis Smith, *American Diplomacy During the Second World War 1941-1945* (Newbery Award Records 2nd ed, 1985).

[20] Morton J. Frisch and Richard G. Stevens eds, *American Political Thought: The Philosophic Dimension of American Statesmanship* (Transaction Publishers, 3rd ed. 2011). (Emphasis added.) See also Edward A. Laing, The Contribution of the Atlantic Charter to Human Rights Law and Humanitarian Universalism. 26 WILLAMETTE L. REV. 113 (1989).

[21] Sumner Welles, *The Time for Decision* (Harper and Brothers. 1944). I am in debt to Welles' other books written during the war, but this was the first and main one on these events.

not yet a formal belligerent. President Roosevelt, who was worried about the domestic opponents of the war, such the isolationists, had the more subtle, focused, and far-reaching goal of agreeing to a set of fundamental principles that would guide the Allied cause in the future.[22]

Specifically, before the meeting of the two leaders, President Roosevelt made it clear to his private advisors that he wanted a concise statement of war aims from the very beginning that forcefully articulated that the goals of the war included self-determination for all peoples and nations, including the colonial and conquered nations of the world.[23] He thought the failure to issue such war aims, especially the failure of President Wilson to get all the Allies to sign off on the Fourteen Points prior to the United States' entry into World War I, partially contributed to the fiasco of the Versailles negotiations and treaty.[24] President Roosevelt strongly believed that President Wilson missed a prime opportunity to end European colonialism during the last World War, since Wilson did not require the Allied powers to agree to and sign off on his Fourteen Points as a price for America's decisive entry into the war. Ironically, when the Germans finally surrendered in November of 1918, they did so on the basis of President Wilson's nonbinding Fourteen Points.

Thus, President Roosevelt was determined not to repeat the same mistakes as his predecessor. According to memoirs of the meeting, which were written as the war in Europe continued, Undersecretary of State Sumner Welles wrote that President Roosevelt approached his first meeting with Prime Minister Churchill with a definite agenda in mind. Speaking of President Roosevelt, Welles stated:

> ... he [Roosevelt] felt it imperative to take up for consideration certain major political problems. Most important among the political problems which he desired to discuss with Mr. Churchill was the need for a general agreement between the

[22] Robert E. Sherwood, *Roosevelt and Hopkins, An Intimate History* (Enigma Books, rev. ed, 2001). See also Sumner Welles, *Seven Decisions That Shaped History* (Harper and Bros. Publishers, 1951); Welles, above n 18. For an intimate view of Roosevelt's first perceptions of Churchill, see Roosevelt, above n 15. In his book, Roosevelt's son Elliot, a U.S. naval officer at the time, also reveals his father's determination to raise the colonial issue within the delicate diplomacy of the looming war (for the US) Finally, see Foster Rhea Dulles & Gerald E. Ridinger, "The Anti-Colonial Politics of Franklin D. Roosevelt," 70 Pol. Sci. Q. 1 (1955).

[23] Welles, above n 18 and 19. See also Roosevelt and Sherwood, above, n 19 and, more generally, Foster Rhea Dulles & Gerald E. Ridinger, above n 19.

[24] Sherwood, above n 19; Welles, above n 19; Roosevelt (Elliot), above n 15. Finally, see Weinberg, above n 1, for how this issue between the Allies played out during the course of the war.

> two governments, while the United States was still at peace and the European war was still in its earliest stages, covering the major bases upon which a new world structure should be set up when peace finally came…The President rightly believed that the mere announcement of such an agreement would prove invaluable in giving encouragement and hope to the peoples now fighting for survival.[25]

A close aide of the president, Robert Sherwood, as well as Roosevelt's own son, who was present as a military officer at the summit, both later confirmed Welles' account concerning the planning and thinking behind the meeting. In short, President Roosevelt was determined to use this first summit between Churchill and himself to obtain a basic statement of the ultimate Allied war aims, including the enduring recognition of equality among all peoples.[26]

Due to the delicate diplomacy needed to forge an alliance that would survive the savagery of war, President Roosevelt did not seem to emphasize or constantly advertize his personally strong antipathy to colonialism or his administration's anti-colonial purposes during the summit. It seemed he simply wanted the words to speak for themselves; he especially seemed intent that any ensuing declaration resulting from the summit would represent a diplomatic demarche and clearly state that all peoples have the right to choose the form of government under which they live.

Unsurprisingly, President Roosevelt addressed the subject of issuing such a declaration of war aims immediately upon his first meeting with Prime Minister Churchill on the United States warship, the *U.S.S. Augusta*, and Churchill quickly agreed. In fact, in his memoirs, *The Hinge of Fate*, Churchill claimed to have written the "first draft" of the Atlantic Charter.[27] This is undoubtedly true; however, there is reliable evidence that Roosevelt already had a distinct idea of what he wanted the agreement to say. After expressing his enthusiastic approval for Churchill's proposal, President Roosevelt stated that "he would like to consider the precise text very carefully in order to be certain that

---

[25] Welles, above n 19, at 174. See also "Memorandum of Conversation from Sumner Welles, Under Sec'y of State" (Aug. 11, 1941) (on file with The Avalon Project at Yale Law School); Thomas H. Greer, *What Roosevelt Thought: The Social and Political Ideas of Franklin D. Roosevelt* (Mich. St. Univ. Press reprt. 1958).
[26] Sherwood, above n 19; Welles, above n 19; Roosevelt (Elliot), above n 15.
[27] Winston Chuchill, *Hinge of Fate* (Houghton Mifflin 1950).

all the points which he himself had already formulated, and which he regarded as essential, were amply covered."[28]

There is, in fact, further strong evidence that President Roosevelt had already written out "all the points…which he regarded as essential" while working with Welles in Washington, D.C. in the days before the first summit between the leaders. A key Roosevelt aide at the time, Robert Anderson, reported that then-acting Secretary of State Sumner Welles authored a working draft of President Roosevelt's personal ideas for a declaration while still in Washington, D.C. before the meeting, and took it to the summit. The president's son, who was with his father as a young naval officer throughout the summit, reported essentially the same facts and similar discussions.[29] Unsurprisingly, as soon as the president received Prime Minister's Churchill's proposal for such a joint declaration, he tasked Welles with working with the British to help create the first draft of the document. Welles continued to work with the prime minister and Sir Alexander Cadogan until the final draft was agreed upon at the conclusion of the summit.[30]

Examining the charter reveals not only its specific statements or implications, but also the important fact of to whom it is addressed—the "peoples" or "nations" of the world. United States statesmen repeatedly used these terms during the war in order to include colonial subjects, as well as the conquered populations living under the Axis yoke. However, even so, the charter itself is seemingly simple, and succinctly states:

The Atlantic Charter

> The President of the United States of America and the Prime Minister, Mr. Churchill, representing His Majesty's Government in the United Kingdom, being met together, deem it right to make known certain common principles in the national policies of their respective countries on which they base their hopes for a better future for the world.
>
> First, their countries seek no aggrandizement, territorial or other;

[28] Welles, above n 18, p 175 – 176. (Emphasis added.) Also see Sherwood, above n 19.
[29]ROOSEVELT (Elliot), above n 15.
[30]WELLES, above n 18, p 175-176; Also see SHERWOOD, above at note 19. ROOSEVELT (Elliot), above n 15.

Second, they desire to see no territorial changes that do not accord with the freely expressed wishes of the peoples concerned;

Third, they respect the right of all peoples to choose the form of government under which they will live; and they wish to see sovereign rights and self government restored to those who have been forcibly deprived of them;

Fourth, they will endeavor, with due respect for their existing obligations, to further the enjoyment by all States, great or small, victor or vanquished, of access, on equal terms, to the trade and to the raw materials of the world which are needed for their economic prosperity;

Fifth, they desire to bring about the fullest collaboration between all nations in the economic field with the object of securing, for all, improved labor standards, economic advancement and social security;

Sixth, after the final destruction of the Nazi tyranny, they hope to see established a peace which will afford to all nations the means of dwelling in safety within their own boundaries, and which will afford assurance that all the men in all lands may live out their lives in freedom from fear and want;

Seventh, such a peace should enable all men to traverse the high seas and oceans without hindrance;

Eighth, they believe that all of the nations of the world, for realistic as well as spiritual reasons must come to the abandonment of the use of force. Since no future peace can be maintained if land, sea or air armaments continue to be employed by nations which threaten, or may threaten, aggression outside of their frontiers, they believe, pending the establishment of a wider and permanent system of general security, that the disarmament of such nations is essential. They will likewise aid and encourage all other practicable measure which will lighten for peace-loving peoples the crushing burden of armaments

Franklin D. Roosevelt
Winston S. Churchill

August 14, 1941[31]

The heart of the charter is the section on the "certain common principles…on which they base their hopes for a better future for the world." From the perspective of the United States government and many colonized populations, the Atlantic Charter recognized first and foremost the rights of all peoples to self-government and, in essence, self-determination. President Roosevelt knew that the people of the United States, particularly the vocal isolationists, were not going to support a war effort that resulted, once again, in the triumph of European colonialism.[32]

Hence, at least for the United States government, the nations held under colonial control held precedence over states' once-sacred claims to the "right" of colonial domination as a domestic matter. The UN Charter later enshrined the right of peoples to self-determination, which is essentially the recognition of the nation or nations' rights on the international plane prior to statehood.[33] This was, perhaps, the most important element of the charter. In short, the Atlantic Charter, taken at its literal value, addresses the "peoples" or "nations" of the world, not simply "states."

For President Roosevelt, this distinction was critical, as he was convinced that people left in colonial servitude after the war was won would sow the seed of future wars. Such a belief directly clashed with British colonial and imperial policies.

As John J. Sebrega has stated, the "language of Point Three [of the Atlantic Charter] would cause much mischief in the Roosevelt-Churchill 'special relationship' during World War II."[34] Yet, at the time, Churchill was eager to forge an Anglo-American relationship, if not alliance, and thus agreed to the charter. He had strong incentives to do so; at the time, Churchill did not believe the Soviet Union could or would survive the

[31] See, Declaration of Principles, above n 2.

[32] See, for instance: Lynne Olson, (2013) *Those Angry Days: Roosevelt, Lindbergh, and America's Fight Over World War II, 1939-194, passim.* Manfred Jonas, *Isolationism in America 1935-1941* ([Paperback] imprint Pubns, 1989). Also: Wayne Cole, *Roosevelt and the Isolationists, 1932-1945* (Univ. of Nebraska Press, 1983) 698. The irony is of course that the United States had "colonies" as well, including the Phillipines, though Roosevelt promised its independence after he took office.

[33] "The purposes of the UN Charter are…To develop friendly relations among nations based on respect for the principle of equal rights and self-determination of peoples…" UN Charter, above n 3, ch. 1, art. 1.

[34] John J. *Sebrega*, "The Anti-Colonial Policies of Franklin D. Roosevelt: A Reappraisal," (1986) 101 Pol. Sci. Q. 65. Also see Louis, above n 29.

Nazi onslaught for much longer, and he did not want the United Kingdom to contend with the full fury and might of Hitler's legions largely alone again.

Even so, there is persuasive evidence that the British people, and indeed Churchill's own war cabinet, were not impressed with the summit statement or results, and many sought clarification concerning the Atlantic Charter's statements.[35] However, it was too late; the message, hopes, and promises of the charter were spreading worldwide.

As General Carlos Romulo of the Philippines soon stated:

> I toured the Asiatic territories and I learned from the leaders and the peoples of the flame of hope that swept the Far East when the Atlantic Charter was made known to the world. Everywhere these people asked the questions: Is the Atlantic Charter also for the Pacific? Is it for one side of the world, and not for the other? For one race and not for them too?[36]

President Roosevelt quickly answered the general's question. In a radio address to the people of the United States soon after the bombing of Pearl Harbor, President Roosevelt made the global scope of the Atlantic Charter fully explicit. In his "Broadcast to the World" on February 23, 1942, President Roosevelt stated:

> The Atlantic Charter applies not only to the parts of the world that border the Atlantic, but *to the whole world*; disarmament of aggressors, *self-determination of nations and peoples, and the four freedoms-freedom of speech, freedom of religion, freedom of want and freedom from fear.*[37]

As this paper reveals, the promissory origins of the fiduciary law of nations is found, in part, within the wording of the Atlantic Charter, addressed to the "peoples" or "nations" fighting (or conquered by) fascism, as well as in its recognition of a right that a people already possess prior to statehood, namely the right to self-determination. In fact, the charter's deliberate wording that it contains "certain common principles" contributed to

---

35 See Sherwood, above n 19, p. 362-363. Also, for another viewpoint, see Louis, above n 29.

36 Paul Gordon Lauren ed, *Diplomacy: New Approaches in History, Theory, and Policy* (The Free Press, 1979).

37 Franklin D. Roosevelt, President of the United States, Fireside Chat: Broadcast to the World, Feb. 23, 1942, http://www.mhric.org/fdr/chat20.html. (Emphasis added.)

the subsequent creation of fiduciary general principles of international law in the post-war world, especially within the Charter of the UN. (Much of the wording for the Preamble and Article 1 of the charter derives from this document, as well as the ensuing declaration written four months later.) In short, this was not simply a creative act of propaganda. Under threat of an imposing and seemingly growing mortal danger, the Allied governments endorsed the Atlantic Charter's norms as fiduciary "promises to keep" – if and when the war was won.

For instance, paragraph six of the Atlantic Charter states as a goal, after Allied victory, for a world in which "all the men in all lands may live out their lives in freedom from fear and want." This was the beginning of Roosevelt's pursuit of recognition of the four freedoms as explicit war aims.[38] This led, in turn, to the eventual acknowledgement of these freedoms as human rights in international law that belong to individuals and peoples as a whole.

Thus, President Roosevelt was recognizing on an international level the rights that the peoples of the world already possessed. States are not the sources of human rights, nor can a government provide what they do not own. According to John Locke, individuals and the nation, or people as a whole, inherently possess these rights naturally, and preserve these rights when they create a social contract to live together in a civil society.[39] In contrast, hypothetically speaking, there is no need to recognize human rights in a society of one. By agreeing to the Atlantic Charter, and to the subsequent wartime January 1, 1942 Declaration of UN (below), governments were simply acknowledging these rights for the first time on an international plane. This was not necessarily due to altruistic motives, but rather was a consequence of their mortal danger and subsequent need to mobilize the millions of people needed to serve, fight, sacrifice, kill, and possibly die in the war.

In this context, the telegram from Secretary of State Cordell Hull to John Winant, the United States Ambassador in Great Britain, which was sent immediately after the Atlantic Charter Conference, is revealing of this promissory intent. Hull was concerned

---

[38] Greer, above n 22; See also Edward Mortimer, *The World that FDR Built: Vision and Reality* (Charles Scribner's Sons 1988); Warren F. Kimball, *Forged in War: Roosevelt, Churchill and the Second World War* (Harper Collins reprt. 1998).

[39] John Locke, *Second Treatise of Government* (C.B. Macpherson ed., Hackett Publ'g reprt. 1980). See also A. John Simmons, *On the Edge of Anarchy: Locke, Consent, and the Limits of Society* (Princeton Univ. Press reprt. 1995). Finally, see William Ebenstein, *Great Political Thinkers: Plato to the Present 120* (Holt, Rinehart & Winston 4th ed. 1969).

that the press in London seemed uncertain about the meaning of the fourth principle of the Atlantic Charter. He bluntly warned Ambassador Winant:

> Actual and potential victims of the Axis powers will not take hope and do their upmost to resist aggression by joining forces with the United States, the United Kingdom and other like-minded nations if they gain the impression that the basic fourth point of the joint declaration is in reality an empty promise.[40]

Hence, this is immediate—though somewhat episodic—evidence that even the United States secretary of state considered the charter to be essentially a promissory declaration.

Furthermore, the promissory nature of the Atlantic Charter is evidenced by the formidable task to which paragraph six explicitly refers, the charter that was facing the two powers, namely "after the final destruction of the Nazi tyranny." In the summer days of 1941, long before Midway (a stunning United States naval victory only six months after Pearl Harbor, which allowed the Allies to focus their first priority on winning the war in Europe), El Alamein, Stalingrad, Rome, Normandy, or Remagen, this was not at all a foregone conclusion. In fact, in August 1941, the outcome of the war in Europe, China, and the Pacific was very much in doubt.

The savagery of the war soon became fully apparent to all those who had met at Placentia Bay. For instance, President Roosevelt and Prime Minister Churchill first met on the decks of the massive British battleship, the *Prince of Wales*, which was tragically lost with almost all crewmembers only four months later in a futile effort to support the besieged British garrison at Singapore. This terrible loss alone must have been a searing heartbreak to the statesmen and senior military leaders, who had enjoyed the hospitality, accommodations, and friendship of the officers and crew during the first summit between Prime Minister Churchill and President Roosevelt. However, more tragic news was yet to come, especially since the Allies would need to cross the oceans to fight their enemies. In addition to the losses that the United States sustained at Pearl Harbor, the four-month period between the historic meeting at Placentia Bay in August 1941 and the end of the year witnessed Allied losses of almost a dozen capital war ships or cruisers

[40] Telegram from Cordell Hull, Sec'y of State, to John Winant, Amb. I the U.K. 25 August 1941, <http://avalon.law.yale.edu/wwii/at11.asp>.

and scores of merchant ships with thousands of brave seamen to the Axis powers, a rate that simply could not be sustained if they had any hope of winning the war.[41]

Even so, the charter planted the seed that, as the war progressed, would grow into a highly developed system of promissory declarations to be fully redeemed, supposedly, in the post-war world. Yet, all of this was still uncertain and premature in August 1941. Unfortunately, events would quickly worsen in the dark days of late 1941 and early 1942.

The Promises Continue: The Declaration of [the] United Nations, January 1, 1942

The Atlantic Charter cannot be read in isolation from its immediate historical times, popular impact, or subsequent developments. This is because within four months of signing the Atlantic Charter, the United States was attacked by Japan at Pearl Harbor, and within days, Hitler declared war on the United States as well. Thus, in early December, the United States suddenly found itself embedded as a full combatant in a world war.[42] In the Pacific, the Japanese invaded the Philippines, Wake, Guam, and the Malay Peninsula, seizing the great naval base of Singapore to obtain access to the Indian Ocean and potentially link up with the Nazis. In Europe, Hitler's armies were poised to strike before Moscow; the Germans were also building up an army and air force to strike eastward in Africa towards the Suez Canal. In war theaters throughout the world, the Allied powers seemed to be in full retreat, while the victorious Axis powers were advancing. The fast and furious pace of events resulted in the United States quickly forming an alliance with the other countries at war with fascism and signing a joint declaration that reiterated the importance of the Atlantic Charter.

In his memoirs, *A Time for Decision*, Sumner Welles discussed the link between the Atlantic Charter and the declaration:

---

[41] See Churchill, above n 24. Also, see note below n 39 for specific Allied naval losses during this dismal time....

[42] Welles, above n 18, p. 178. During this time, (Aug.-Dec., 1941), the United States lost several battleships at Pearl Harbor, though some were recovered and used later in the war. The British Royal Navy suffered heavily as well, losing four battleships, a heavy cruiser, and an aircraft carrier, though the two battleships "sunk" in Alexandria Bay were later raised and used successfully in the war. Even the Australian Navy was fighting both the German and Japanese navies close to home, and lost the cruiser *HMAS Sydney* and its crew to a heavily armed German Raider disguised as a merchant ship, which was also sunk just off the coast of Western Australia in November 1941. At the same time, United States, British, and other Allied merchant ships were sinking at record rates on the high oceans.

> When the United States was forced into war less than four months later [after the Placentia Bay meeting] the Atlantic Charter became the agreement that was to bind together the United Nations. It linked them as allies during the war, and pledged them to continue their association after victory had been won. In January, 1942, the United Nations Declaration adhered to by all the governments at war with the Axis powers, and later signed by additional governments as they also entered the war for liberty, bound them all to support the principles set forth in the Atlantic Charter and committed each of them to make no separate peace with the Axis nations so long as the war continued.[43]

In a robust display of solidarity and alliance, the United States joined 25 other governments–8 of which were in exile–to make the Declaration of [the] UN on January 1, 1942, in Washington, D.C., which reads as follows:

> DECLARATION of [the] United Nations
> *A Joint Declaration by the United States, the United Kingdom, the Union of Soviet Socialist Republics, China, Australia, Belgium, Canada, Costa Rica, Cuba, Czechoslovakia, Dominican Republic, El Salvador, Greece, Guatemala, Haiti, Honduras, India, Luxembourg, Netherlands, New Zealand, Nicaragua, Norway, Panama, Poland, South Africa, Yugoslavia*
> *The Governments signatory hereto,*

This marked subscription to a common program of purposes and principles embodied in the Joint Declaration of the President of the United States of America and the Prime Minister of the United Kingdom of Great Britain and Northern Ireland, dated August 14, 1941, known as the Atlantic Charter.

They were convinced that complete victory over their enemies was essential to defend life, liberty, independence, and religious freedom and preserve human rights and justice in their own and other lands, and that they were now engaged in a common struggle against savage and brutal forces seeking to subjugate the world: (Emphasis added.)

> DECLARE:

[43] Welles, above n 18, p. 178.

(1) Each Government pledges itself to employ its full resources, military or economic, against those members of the Tripartite Pact and its adherents with which such government is at war.

(2) Each Government pledges itself to cooperate with the Governments signatory hereto and not to make a separate armistice or peace with the enemies. The foregoing declaration may be adhered to by other nations which are, or which may be, rendering material assistance and contributions in the struggle for victory over Hitlerism.

Done at Washington
January First, 1942[44]

In this historic declaration, the signatory governments announced their joint commitment to the "common programme of purposes and principles...known as the Atlantic Charter." They then expanded this to include the recognition of human rights, perhaps for the first time, as an international issue and norm "in their own lands as well as in other lands," and not simply within the domestic jurisdiction of the state.[45] Finally, each government pledged to cooperate with the other government signatories and not make a separate peace with the enemy. In short, the entire document takes the form of a promissory pledge between signatories, and to the watching world, to take every possible action to win the war, ensure life, liberty, independence, and religious freedom, and preserve human rights and justice. Therefore, the government signatories were undertaking solemn pledges among themselves, to their own people, and via the Atlantic Charter, to all other peoples of the world. These pledges are thus "promises." As noted, the Roman legal term "fiducia" can be defined as a "pledge," and is the basis of fiduciary interests, norms, and relationships that characterize the law of nations.[46]

---

[44] Declaration of United Nations, January 1, 1942. Dept. of State Bulletin, V I., p.3. See above n 2.

[45] Above n 41. To my knowledge, this is the first time in the context of World War II that governments explicitly recognize human rights as an international issue and responsibility i.e. "preserve."

[46] The term "law of nations" has a long and varied career in Western jurisprudence, beginning with the Romans, appearing in Blackstone, and even in the United States Constitution. For instance, see Thomas Boudreau, 'The Modern Law of Nations: Jus Gentium and the Role of Roman Jurisprudence in shaping the post World War II International Legal Order" (2012) 20, *The Digest,* 1. Also, see the prescient book by the distinguished jurist Phillip Jessup, *A Modern* (New York: Macmillan Company, 1948). Jessup has rejected the idea that this law is similar to the Roman idea of *Jus Gentium,* consisting of a "law common to the whole of humanity," which, in contrast, I accept, analyze, and defend in the *The Digest* essay. Also, see Gerhard Von Glahn's more recent book *Law Among Nations* (Macmillan, 1970), which is largely an excellent explanation and defense of state-centric public international law.

As stated, two governments originally signed the Atlantic Charter as representatives of their respective states. In contrast, the Declaration of United Nations expanded the number of signatory governments from the 2 in the Atlantic Charter to 26, and many of the signatories were not typical–or even legally speaking–sovereign states. This was, in part, an intentional design by President Roosevelt and his administration. In short, although this was just the beginning, President Roosevelt and his administration had a precise vision of the desired end result. More specifically, the United States administration was determined, at this early stage of the war, to clearly establish the end of European colonialism and freedom from fear for all "peace-loving peoples" as an explicit promise and goal of victory in the war.

For instance, India was a colony of Britain, and in fact, the British war cabinet initially seemed to flatly reject the idea that India might sign the declaration at all.[47] In contrast, President Roosevelt, urged by Harry Hopkins, was eager for India to sign the declaration, and Roosevelt even indicated in an extant working draft in his own hand the first ordering of India's place in the list of signatories.[48] In doing so, President Roosevelt was undoubtedly expressing his conviction that the Atlantic Charter, which was reaffirmed in the declaration, would apply to India and other colonies after the war was won.

Moreover, upon closer scrutiny, almost half the signatories of the historic yet often overlooked Declaration of [the] UN on January 1, 1942 were conquered, colonized, or "self-governing" countries. Unless one resorts to a legal fiction in such situations, the "state" in such signatories was often *de facto* governments or nations effectively severed from the full legal characteristics of statehood. Hence, President Roosevelt's personal decision to call the signatory powers the "United Nations" seems to be a highly accurate description of the alliance.[49]

Furthermore, several signatories were "dominions" of the British Empire, and thus did not seem to enjoy full control of their foreign relations, which was a legal requirement

---

[47] Sherwood, above n 19. Sherwood has quoted Lord Halifax's alarm at the inclusion of India in the declaration, so much so that Halifax wrote Churchill (then in Washington, D.C.) that "this is a mistake, and I would hope it might be reconsidered." P 447-448. The United States was insistent, and India was included. For Roosevelt's personal list, See Sherwood, above n 19, p. 450-453. Roosevelt personally listed India in the top 10, ahead of most other Allied signatories.

[48] Sherwood, above n 19

[49] Townsend Hoopes & Douglas Brinkley, *FDR and the Creation of the U.N.* (Yale Univ. Press reprt. 2000) (1997).

for full statehood. The government of Australia was then described by the British not as a "dominion," but as an independent "commonwealth" subject to King George VI, who was regarded as the sovereign.[50] There were similar arrangements with other dominions, in which the sovereign power of the king was apparently represented locally by a residing royal governor or governor–general. This led to some confusion over the sovereign powers and capacity of Australia; for instance, Churchill and Australian Prime Minister John Curtin were to have a famous dispute nearly half a year later over precisely who had the right to command Australian troops in the field.[51] Churchill ordered them to Burma and elsewhere in the spring of 1942, while the Australian prime minister ordered them home to defend the nation from possible Japanese invasion. Despite these political difficulties, the Australians provided stellar and incredibly heroic service in both the European and Pacific theaters throughout the course of the war.

Additionally, almost a third of the signatories–eight in all–were governments in exile. Due to Soviet occupation, some of these governments never effectively reasserted their control over their native homelands following the conclusion of the war. The presence of so many governments in exile presented the most extreme example of the distinction between the people or nation on the one hand, and the government on the other, since the state had literally been disemboweled by the war.[52] In short, this was *not* an example of international law making largely between states, which was traditionally done prior to World War II.

---

[50] King George VI demonstrated greatness as a wartime leader, staying in London with his family during the German bombing campaigns, visiting his dominions under German assault, such as Malta in 1943, and supporting the Anglo-American Alliance via his personal diplomacy, including visits to United States and other Allied troops in joint operation with their British counterparts in the field. Furthermore, in my judgment, he was a "behind the scenes" keen observer, if not supporter, concerning the idea of the "equality of nations" that Roosevelt publicly championed. For instance, in his speech to the first meeting of the United Nations held in London in 1946, the king expressed "our faith in the equal rights of men and women and of nations great and small." To demonstrate this, he then presided over the largely peaceful transition of the British Empire to the Commonwealth, and was entitled "Head of Commonwealth," a title that his daughter, Queen Elizabeth II, inherited and preserves. See Will Smith, *The Roosevelts and the Royals: Franklin and Eleanor, the King and Queen of England and the Friendship that Changed History* (John Wiley and Sons, 2004).

[51] See, for example, Exchange of Cablegrams between Mr. Churchill and Mr. Curtin, 1941-1942, NAA: A5954, 581/17. Also see biography on the Australian Prime Minister, David Day, *John Curtin: A Life* (Harper Collins Sydney, 1999). Finally, for Churchill's perspective, see e.g., Churchill, above n 24 at p. 10-19, 140-42. Part of the legal requirement for statehood is control of one's own foreign policy, including control of one's own troops. See Slomanson, above n 10, concerning the four legal criteria for defining a state.

[52] Governments in exile have often created perplexing problems of definition and appropriate powers in international law. See e.g., Richard Crawford Pugh, Oscar Schachter & Hans Smith, *International Law: Cases and Materials* (Louis Henkin ed., West Group 3rd ed. 1993), 283-285.

This is the reason the declaration does not say "The States signatory hereto." Rather, it simply says "The Governments signatory hereto." In short, this was patently not a source of state-centric law. As argued here, it is a promissory or fiduciary pact made *in solemn good faith* between governments and the allied, conquered, colonial, or neutral peoples of the world. The distinguished United States jurist Oscar Schachter has stated in this regard:

> [P]olitical texts which express commitments and positions of one kind or another are governed by the *general principles of good faith*. Moreover, since good faith is an accepted general principle of international law, *it is an appropriate and even necessary to apply it in a legal sense.*[53]

Elaborating upon this in the text *International Law*, co-authored by Louis Henkin, Richard Pugh, and Hans Smit, Schachter has continued:

> A significant practical consequence of the 'good faith' principle is that a party which committed itself in good faith to a course or conduct or to recognition of a legal situation would be estopped from acting inconsistently with its commitment or adopted position when the circumstances showed that other parties reasonably relied on that undertaking or position.[54]

Here, Schachter has identified another general principle of domestic and international law, namely that *unjust enrichment* based upon the failure to perform or deliver on a promise has legal consequences as well, especially when "other parties reasonably relied on that undertaking or position." Failure to fulfill promises gives rise to the "legal situation" that Schachter has discussed, and the courts can then address. Thus, the general principle of "good faith" can create a legal obligation in an ensuing "legal situation," especially when people rely upon such promises to the point of sacrificing their own lives, as they did in World War II.

---

[53] Oscar Schachter, *International Law in Theory and Practice*, 178 Rec.des Cours 120 (1982-V). Also, "unjust enrichment" is a general principal of international law, meaning that governments cannot make promises, win victories, and then enjoy the fruits of winning without first keeping their promises to their own and other peoples. (Emphasis added.)

[54] Schachter, above n 49, at 100. Prof. Oscar Schachter was one of the truly great international jurists of the 20th century, and it was my pleasure to know him as a wise counselor, unofficial mentor to my research projects, and friend while I worked at the Carnegie Council.

In other words, the making of solemn promises in good faith by governments to their own and other peoples *in times of mortal danger to all* is precisely such a "legal situation" that creates ensuing fiduciary duties and obligations that must be kept by the promissory parties, in this case the threatened governments. At the time that the Declaration to [the] UN was made on January 1, 1942, President Roosevelt and other Allied leaders seemed to realize that such promises must be made in good faith to the peoples of the world especially when, at the time, it seemed as though the Axis powers were winning the war.

Thus, the declaration, which incorporated the promises of the Atlantic Charter, was written as a solemn pact made in good faith, and became a source of trust law between governments and their own and others peoples, not simply a treaty between states. Specifically, the Atlantic Charter and the Declaration of [the] UN became significant sources of the most serious and solemn fiduciary obligations, duties, and rights that a government or peoples can incur. This is especially true since the profound purpose of these first promissory documents was to create a wartime alliance between nations and governments in a mortal struggle for their very existence. "Promises made" in such circumstances must become, legally speaking, "promises to keep," especially if the nations of the world do their critical part in fighting to reverse the tide of defeats, and through heavy sacrifices, finally succeed in winning the war.

Promises to Keep: The Crucible of World War II

At this bleak moment in the war, the declaration was addressed to neutral, conquered, or colonial peoples throughout the world, as well as to one anothers' domestic populations. Though historians might be tempted by hindsight to say that victory was certain in the war, the outcome was far from clear to the statesmen signing the UN declaration on a cold winter day in Washington D.C., at the very beginning of the new year in 1942.

In particular, the Allies had reason to fear that the conquered or colonial peoples, such as the Ukrainians, peoples of French Indochina, and the colonized peoples in India and Africa, might join the Axis cause. For instance, an outburst of anti-colonial sentiment or even an uprising anywhere along the rim of the Indian Ocean, which was covered then with European colonies, would give the Nazis and Japanese a natural point and strategic place to link up their forces, with devastating consequences for the Allies. For instance, during this time, the French Vichy government was actually in control of the colonized island of Madagascar and was allowing Japanese submarines to harbor and refuel, a potentially mortal threat to the British and Commonwealth armies that were then fighting Rommel in the Middle East. If reinforced by fascist naval forces, the Japanese and Germans could establish a linkup, destroy British supply lines, and thus control the oil routes of the Indian Ocean.

To prevent such a dangerous development in the Indian Ocean, Churchill personally ordered the invasion of Vichy-controlled Madagascar in early 1942, over the heated objections of his own military chiefs, in order to prevent a possible linkup and subsequent mortal threat to the Suez Canal and the critical British, Australian, and other North African military forces facing Rommel. He devoted an entire chapter in his volume, *Hinge of Fate*, to this ultimately successful assault.[55] In short, preventing a German-Japanese linkup in the Indian Ocean and keeping neutral and colonized peoples out of the war was a critical concern of the Allies, especially in the first desperate months of 1942. The balance of power at this time was extremely precarious; for instance, alignment of the Turkish or Spanish people alone with Nazi Germany might have made a decisive difference in the European war during the early 1940s, had they joined the Axis powers.[56] These dangers reinforced the reality of the dire Allied situation at the time. In order to confront these significant and growing dangers, the Allies signed the declaration as a promissory pact between governments and their own and other peoples throughout the world. A significant purpose of the declaration was, in effect, to give hope of independence to those millions still under European colonial control, and thus attract their allegiance so that they would not be tempted to join the Axis powers.

The Roosevelt Administration never lost sight of this collective audience. This is one reason that led Assistant Secretary of State Summer Welles to make the following statement a few months later at Arlington National Cemetery, on the solemn occasion of Memorial Day 1942:

[55] Churchill, above n 24. See, in particular, Chapter 13, "Madagascar." Also, Gerhard L. Weinberg is one of the very few modern historians who has recognized the strategic importance of the Indian Ocean in general, and potentially Madagascar, particularly during World War II. See Weinberg, above n 1. Fortunately, Churchill recognized it *at the time*.
[56] Weinberg, above n 1. Also see Welles' concern about Spain at: Welles, above n 18.

> This is a people's war. It is a war which cannot be regarded as won until *the fundamental rights of the peoples of the earth are secured.* In no other manner can a true peace be achieved.[57] (Emphasis added.)

These wartime promises, embodied in the Atlantic Charter and the Declaration of [the] UN (1942), undoubtedly aided in influencing millions of colonial subjects in Africa, the Middle East, and Asia to fight against, or at least not aid, the Axis powers. For instance, specific efforts by the United States and British governments immediately commenced, based upon the Atlantic Charter, to ensure that African colonies would remain on the Allied side (Committee on Africa, the War and Peace Aims, 1943).[58] These solemn declarations, such as the post-Moscow Four Power Summit Declaration (1943), could be described as an "Executory Trust," since later covenants and treaties, such as the Charter of the UN (1945), would be required to fulfill these wartime promises.[59] However, it would ultimately be up to the courts to decide if other characterizations of a trust may apply as well. The governments are simply the trustees of the promises made, figuratively written in the blood of the people who, together with their governments (including the governments in exile within the allied cause), fought this war on countless fronts throughout the world.

So, analysis of the January 1, 1942 declaration illustrates that, *in times of mortal danger*, governments, and not simply "states," can and do create binding international duties, interests, and norms–i.e., "Promises Made"–that are of a legal nature and must be kept after the danger has passed. Historically speaking, there are three key legal preconditions that comprise such international fiduciary obligations: the presence of a mortal danger to

---

57 Welles, Sumner, Under Secretary of State, Memorial Day Address at the Arlington National Amphitheater: World Leadership to Protect Peace, May 30, 1942, <http://www.ibiblio.org/pha/policy/1942/420530a.html>. Also, see Vital Speeches of the Day New York: The City News Publishing Company, Inc. Vol. III, Oct. 15-1941-Oct. 1, 1942.

58 Agnes Crawford, Leaycraft Donohugh, *The Atlantic Charter and Africa from an American Standpoint,* (Committee on Africa, The War, and Peace Aims, 1943). This was an ironically, heavily British-influenced publication that portended some possible post-war problems with keeping the promises of decolonization. The British honored their promises, but the same cannot be said for the French, who did not sign the original declaration, unlike some other European governments with occupied territories.

59 I argue that wartime declarations, such as the Moscow Summit's "Declaration of the Four Powers," essentially created an executory trust, since it promised and thus required a charter for an international organization and trials of the Axis warlords when and if the war was won. For authority on the construction of an executory trust, see City Bank Farmers Trust Co. v. The Charity Org. Soc'y, 265 N.Y.S. 267 (App. Div. 1933); Martling v. Martling, 55 N.J. Eq. 771 (1898); Carridine v. Carridine 33 Miss. 698 (1857); *In re* Fiar's Estate, 60 P. 442 (Cal. 1900). See also Hoopes Brinkley, above n 45. Such an executory trust is not mutually exclusive of other potential or actual fiduciary obligations, norms, duties, and trusts created by the promissory *corpus juris* of World War II. These will ultimately be for present and future courts to decide.

the current government and its people; resulting solemn promises by the government to their own *and other peoples* to overcome the threat; and successful mobilization indicative of explicit or tacit consent by the peoples, so promised to overcome the threat. Such subsequent mobilization and vast social support for the war effort after the establishment of these promises is, in essence, tangible evidence concerning the people's express or tacit acceptance of and consent to those promises. As the Allied leaders knew well, their peoples could not simply be coerced into fighting this war; they had to be motivated and mobilized by these now-fiduciary promises in order to make the supreme sacrifices necessary to defeat their mortal enemies.

So, current and future courts or judiciaries can find the key ingredients in these documents, declarations, and events—depending on the unique legal evolution and history of each jurisdiction—the legally binding elements of a binding express, implied, constructive, public, or other trusts, as well as ensuing fiduciary duties, obligations, and rights enjoyed by their own and others peoples. In view of subsequent sacrifices, costs, and consequences among the Allied peoples of the world, these solemn promises made in good faith by the Allied governments can only be construed as creating a binding fiduciary order, now consisting of the law of nations.

Traditional international lawyers may assert that only states can make international law; yet, the validity of such an assertion requires that the profound innovation, changes, and revolution in international law caused by World War II be ignored or reduced, wherever possible, to mere examples of state-centric law making. This insistence on the state-centric origins of international law is a "cookie cutter" or "one size fits all" approach to international law that simply does not reflect World War II and post-war legal developments, innovations, and realities. Because of this, the traditional framework is inadequate to analyze or explain the extraordinary legal developments that resulted from the Allies' ongoing solemn promises made during desperate times to win the war by appealing to almost all the peoples and nations of the world. In this sense, traditional lawyers who insist that only states can be sources of international law are like Dante's hapless geometer in the final Canto of the *Paradiso*, who "sets himself to measure the circle and who findeth not, think as he may, the principle he lacketh."

The Declaration of [the] UN was critically important because it set the *pattern for promissory declarations or statements between governments and their people throughout the war.* Unlike international treaties between states, this declaration was structured an intra-state, or even pre-state, pact (in the case of colonies, dominions, and the Australian Commonwealth) between a government and its own and other peoples. In view of this, Bentham's definition of international law as mainly consisting of agreements between sovereigns (states) is no longer controlling in many modern circumstances of international law. In particular, trustee obligations freely assumed by governments consisting of solemn promissory declarations or other government statements made in good faith intended for their *own and other peoples* result in enduring and evolving international legal obligations. Specifically, the creation of fiduciary obligations by a government and promised for its own and other peoples is a source of international trust law that must now also be recognized, especially by national or international courts when necessary, as the hard-earned and lasting legal legacy of humanity.

Therefore, these were the preliminary sources of an emergent international fiduciary legal order. In this regard, it is important to note that courts have historically stated that "intent" is *not* always a precondition of creating a trust or fiduciary obligations. The following section explores the origins of the fiduciary foundations of these new legal norms in more detail by first examining the meaning of "fiducia," or "fiduciary," as articulated by John Locke, and secondly, historical developments during and after World War II that directly led to a fiduciary law of nations.

Promises to Keep: The Fiduciary Foundations of the Law of Nations

> "Fides Servanda Est; Simplicitas Juris Gentium Praevaleleat"
> "Faith must be kept; the simplicity of the Law of Nations must prevail."

3 Burrows 1672

Under the extreme pressure of a mortal threat, such as World War II, a government of a state made "promises" to its own people and other nations in order to mobilize the millions of individuals necessary to serve, sacrifice, suffer, and perhaps even die so that that government and the people would survive. This fulfills the critical condition that Oscar Schachter (above) has stated concerning *good faith in legal situations*–namely, "[o]ther parties…concerned have reason to expect compliance and to rely on it."[60]

[60] See Schacter, above n 49 and n 50.

Even so, some might argue that any governmental promise or pledge made under such circumstances as a mortal struggle or declared war are made under duress and are purely propaganda, with no lasting political or *legal* significance. However, such a cynical interpretation makes a mockery of the subsequent service *of the millions and their families* who believed in their governments' statements concerning the ultimate purposes of the war. They believed in these promissory declarations to the significant extent that they left their homes and peacetime jobs and served honorably, often enduring much hardship and sacrifice until the war was won. Many who served never returned, having been killed on some distant shoreline, hilltop, or forgotten battlefield.

For instance, by the end of World War II, large United States cemeteries stretched from the Aleutian Islands in the North Pacific to North Africa, from the beaches of Normandy and Anzio to the frontiers of Germany, from Pearl Harbor and Guadalcanal to the blood-soaked sands of Iwo Jima. British cemeteries could be found from the home islands through France and to Germany, from Burma and Malaysia to Indochina, and not to mention the countless British, United States, and Allied sailors or soldiers lost at sea. Soviet cemeteries ranged from the steppes of old Russia deep into the Ukraine and Crimea, from the gates of Moscow and Leningrad to the Volga, the Don, and the center of Berlin. The Australians, Canadians, Chinese, French, and Poles, as well as many other nations, also had cemeteries scattered throughout war zones.[61] Most of these individuals were living, breathing human beings when their governments first articulated and promulgated the promissory aims of the war in 1941 and 1942.

In short, before these promises could be even partially redeemed or fulfilled, hundreds of thousands of people were going to be killed in the attempt to win the war. In view of this, these wartime promises cannot be construed or dismissed as simply *contractual* promises to specific individuals *or mere propaganda*; they essentially created fiduciary obligations, duties, relationships, and interests that further created an active, executory, or even involuntary (among certain Allied powers) trust between these governments and their own and other peoples who were struggling to be free of German and Japanese militarism. These promissory statements were solemn declarations to entire peoples, in their present and future capacities, to be redeemed after victory on countless battlefields

[61] In his monumental opus, *A World at Arms*, Weinberg detailed the horrific casualties and costs of the war. See Weinberg, above n 1.

across the globe. These promises made during the war constituted a lasting trust for domestic and international judiciaries to recognize once victory was finally achieved.

Locke's Argument: Government as a Trust

That law is based upon a fiduciary duty or interest and relationship with the people is a process and argument that is analagous, in limited ways, to those outlined by John Locke in his *Second Treatise on Government.* In his classic *Treatise*, Locke argued that the people create governments simply as trustees of the people's rights. Thus, the people are the original trustors, as well as the only true beneficiaries of the fiduciary trust so established. In Locke's scenario, the people who create governments to serve as trustees basically establish the fiduciary relationship.[62] It is a novel argument that helped inspire the American Revolution, and identifies civil society defined here as the "nation" prior to any particular government.

For Locke, the only basis of legitimate government and law was the consent of the people. In turn, Locke thought that there were two types of consent: either "express," in which individuals overtly consent through an oath or writing, or "tacit," in which people consent through their subsequent agreement or behavior, which indicates acceptance of government as a trust. A. John Simmons has noted:

> Tacit consent, by contrast, seems to be consent given without words or explicit signs ('expressions'), given rather by other behavior that constitutes the making of a morally significant choice in a clear, noncoercive choice situation.[63]

Given this, it would be unreasonable to claim that the behavior of millions who served to defeat the Axis powers, as well as the millions more back on the homefront who made the munitions, ships, and tanks necessary to win the war, were actually solely due to the government's *coercion.* The Allied peoples of the world knew the stakes and wanted to win the war, although they knew it would cost them dearly. Thus, they consented to their governments' policies and promises through their deeds and the consequent mass mobilization of entire nations needed to win the war. In short, express or tacit consent

---

[62] See Locke, above n 36. Simmons, above n 36. Eberstein, above n 36 (This is at least how, according to Locke, governments are supposed to operate; Locke, of course, was an optimist!)
[63] See Simmons, ibid.

are at the heart of the law of nations, though governments evidently used coercion as well through such methods as the draft and the execution of deserters. Regardless, the Allied governments knew they could not win the war through coercion alone. Hence, they began to make the solemn promises in good faith that resulted, however unintentionally, in the law of nations as a lasting legacy of the war.

Locke's distinction between express or tacit consent[64] in the formation of *government as a trust* is useful in analyzing the actual historical circumstances surrounding the creation of the fiduciary law of nations from governmental promises during World War II. Thus, a personal or even moral choice was made that was, in effect, in total agreement with and acceptance of the governments' promises and purposes concerning the war.

When millions of soldiers and their families accepted their duty to fight in the global war against fascism, they were essentially accepting their respective government's promises about the ultimate purposes of the war, and thus giving their express or tacit *consent* (depending on the *sui generis* circumstances), a key factor for Locke in the formation of binding political obligations. This includes the creation of a trust in which the people, in Locke's scenario, are both the trustees and the beneficiaries. In this sense, Locke echoed the original Roman use of the trust, in which the trustee and beneficiary were often one and the same.[65]

In short, from a Lockean perspective, a soldier's service could be construed in many cases, if not most, as an express or tacit agreement concerning the ultimate purposes and goals of the war as promised by his government. The risk that the soldier may not survive the subsequent tour of duty is an unfortunate but very real condition and possible consequence of his service; hence, the promises made by his government and accepted or "consented" to by millions of other soldiers do not create merely contractual obligations, as those accepting the contract may be required to die in its execution, which is hardly a recognizable condition of a legal contract. In contrast, the creation of a trust does not always require the survival of the trustees, nor does a trust's creation always

[64] Ibid. Also see Locke, above n 36.

[65] See James Hadley, *Introduction to Roman Law, In Twelve Academical Lectures 181* (D. Appleton & Co. 1873). See also Andrew Riggsby, *Roman Law and the Legal World of the Romans* (Cambridge Univ. Press 2010); Also, see the classic source: Henry Sumner Maine, *Ancient Law: Its Connection with the Early History of Society and Its Relation to Modern Ideas* (Beacon Press, Boston 10th ed. 1963) (1869). Also, see Gauis, above n 55. Finally, see Frankel, above n 55. Fiduciary Law (Oxford Univ. Press 2010).

legally require actual intent. However, a trust always demands that the promises made and agreed to must be kept in *good faith* to the beneficiaries.

Furthermore, for Locke, one's "property" consists of *one's life and liberties, including recognized or unrecognized natural rights*, as well as one's material possessions. So, in Locke's scenario, governments became the trustees of the newly recognized rights of the people. In this sense, the people create the ensuing trust by surrendering only those rights necessary to form a government dedicated to the common good, and as trustors and beneficiaries, the people retain the rest of their rights in perpetuity.

Yet, it is important to note here that unlike the theoretical account in Locke's *Second Treatise*, the governments in the actual historical circumstances of World War II essentially *created and accepted the ensuing fiduciary obligations*, duties, and norms as *trustees* of the ensuing law of nations, provided the peoples of their own and other countries first won the war. These fiduciary obligations, duties, and norms were mostly unintended, especially by governments that maintain the suppression of their own peoples, such as the Soviets, although they supported the anti-colonial policies of Roosevelt to a limited extent. Fortunately, as courts have ruled many times, "intent" is not a necessary condition for the creation of a trust. In contrast, in Locke's scenario, the people themselves as *trustors create government and the resulting fiduciary relationships as a trust.* Therefore, Locke's theoretical scenario within a domestic society is simply an analogous one, and not at all an exact explanation of the actual historical scenario that unfolded during World War II.

The key question remains: Who, then, are the beneficiaries? In the case of the promises made by governments during World War II, the Allied governments were making promises to their own and other Allied peoples, as well as to the conquered, colonial, and neutral nations of the world. The "nation" here includes families, relatives, and friends, since these promises undoubtedly made it "easier" for them to accept the mobilization of their sons, brothers, husbands, or friends and send them off to war. In short, these were incredibly serious and solemn commitments or promises made by the Allied powers to convince their nations to fight and win the war. Yet, as noted above, many of the people who received these promises were going to die in order for their governments to win the war. Basically, these were not contractual promises made, since–bluntly stated–many of the parties to whom such a "hypothetical" and poor "contract" was made would be dead before they could enjoy the benefits of the agreement. *So, as the peoples whom the Allied governments addressed, all these nations are the true heirs and beneficiaries of the Allies' promises*, unless one views these promises cynically and suggests that these pledges concerning the ultimate purposes of the war were mere propaganda.

This is especially true if the beneficiaries–including, at this point, the nations that actually took up arms against the Axis powers–indicate their faith in and reliance upon the solemn promises made by their own and other governments during a time of mortal danger to all by providing express or tacit consent.[66] Ensuring that such promises are honored has always been the traditional prerogative of the courts, especially if private or public parties—in this case, governments—*fail in their duties* as trustees of a fiduciary obligation or interest. In such cases, the national or international courts are responsible for recognizing and upholding the now-common fiduciary obligation, as embodied in the Charter or the UN and other human rights declarations resulting from the war, to protect, uphold, and observe the international "properties" of these peoples, including their lives, liberties, and freedom from harm. In short, these promises created legal obligations that must be kept, especially since the peoples of the world massively mobilized, with many nations fielding armies in the millions, in order to win the war over the Axis alliance.

In particular, national and international courts should construe and enforce the ensuing new duties, norms, and legal relationships that the Allies created during the war concerning human rights, self-determination, and *the legal limitations on a state power to unilaterally use force* as unquestionably fiduciary in nature. In short, trusts are now a source of international law, and it is ultimately the duty of national and international courts to review and decide whether or not a specific trust is executory, implied, public, special, or some other form of fiduciary obligation. This is especially true in view of the historical record and consequent legal developments in trust law and other legal areas during World War II. This paper returns to this issue below in the section entitled "The Nation and the State: The New Problematique?"

Hence, Locke's theoretical account differs from the actual historical scenario and significance of the UN Declaration of January 1, 1942, in which the governments–some of whom were in exile–largely initiated the legal process themselves, almost

---

[66] Locke, above n 36. Simmons, above n 36. Eberstein, above n 36.

unintentionally to be sure, leading to the international recognition of human rights, including self-determination.[67] Specifically, governments effectively became ***trustees*** of these wartime declarations and charters, essentially promissory notes, thus creating fiduciary obligations, interests, norms, and relationships to be redeemed between the individual government and the nation or the people within a specified territory, if they survived. These and other promises from the Allied governments during the war in a time of mortal peril became the *internationally recognized* fiduciary property of the nation or people for all time, if and once the war was finally won.

Ironically, although the French government's people had suffered from Nazi occupation, it would challenge this interpretation, especially after the war was over, and try to reassert its former control over its colonies. France almost immediately reoccupied its former overseas colonies, apparently uninhibited by its own suffering due to a brutal Nazi occupation during the war. In contrast, Great Britain gracefully accepted and acted upon its wartime promises and ultimately freed its colonial empire through a largely peaceful process. In particular, as argued above, King George VI played a critical role as the sovereign of the United Kingdom who oversaw and supported the transformation of the British dominions and colonies to the enduring Commonwealth through words and deeds. In my judgment, his extraordinary role in this process has never been fully appreciated and deserves further research and inquiry. In contrast, France's efforts in trying to reassert its colonial control and occupation of its overseas empire eventually culminated in bloody and costly wars in Vietnam and Algiers. The Vietnamese and Algerians had read these promises too, and expected them to honor what they had clearly stated—self-determination and human rights for all peoples.

Revisiting the Second Treatise: Locke's Understanding of "Property"

At this point in the analysis, it is important to remember that Locke defined "property" as a *person's life and liberties*, as well as his or her material possessions.[68] Locke emphasized that governments cannot take or enrich themselves at the expense of their people's

---

[67] According to Locke, and thus indirectly, the United States, people everywhere already possessed these rights. Roosevelt certainly believed this. See Carl Becker, *Declaration of Independence: A Study in the History of Political Ideas* (Vintage, 1958), in which he accurately states that as Americans, "we are all Lockeans." Also, see Bernard Nailyn, *Ideological Origins of the American Revolution* (Belknap Press, 1992). Above n 2, Declaration of United Nations, 6 Dep't State Bull. 3-4, (1942). Jan. 1, 1942.

[68] Ibid., Andrei. Also See Locke, above n 36. Simmons, above n 36. Eberstein, above n 36.

rights, lives, or natural liberties. According to Locke, this is especially true of a government's fiduciary duties. In stating this, Locke recognized a well-established principle of fiduciary law. The relevant law in Roman, medieval, and modern times unanimously agrees that the person *making the pledge cannot unjustly enrich himself or herself by virtue of false promises made in bad faith to the trustee or beneficiaries; in almost any current rule or system of law, such promises so made must be kept,* especially when the trustee risks so much because of his or her confidence in the promissory statements.[69] This duty led, in medieval feudal and English law, to the duty of *Fides Servanda Est*, which literally means "faith must be observed." Specifically, an agent as trustee must not violate the confidence reposed in him.

In short, in the historically grounded creation of the fiduciary law of nations during World War II, the peoples of the world essentially became both the trustors as the source of the "property" consisting of their lives and liberties and the beneficiaries of the enunciated rights, norms, and duties newly recognized by governments in response to their mortal peril. The Allied governments thus became trustees of their promises made in good faith to their own and other peoples. Other governments have assumed this role as trustee once they have signed the Charter of the UN, since it is a hybrid document and contains many of the war-era promissory obligations, duties, and norms concerning self-determination, human rights, and collective security.[70]

Yet, governments cannot provide what they do not possess; in such situations, they can only *recognize and respect* their solemn obligations to respect the rights, interests, or "property" of others that already exists within a civil society, although these liberties may

---

[69] Courts in multiple national jurisdictions, since Roman times and throughout the ages, have consistently held that promises made in "legal situations" (Schacther, above n 49 and 50) must be kept to the promisee, especially if those so promised have incurred costs in their commitment to the implicit or explicit agreement. See Reinhard Zimmerman, *The Law of Obligations: Roman Foundations of a Civilian Tradition* (Oxford Univ. Press, 1996). The idea of "trust" law probably entered English law via the Crusades and crusaders' encounters with Islamic law and culture. The concept of a "waqf," or a trustee relationship, was well-developed when the crusaders came to the Holy Land, yet to my knowledge was not yet used in medieval English law until around the 13th century. For a brief analysis of the waqf system in Islamic law, see T. Kuran, "The Provisions of Public Goods Under Islamic Law: Origins, Impact and limitations of the wafq system (2001) *Law and Society Review*. Also, see MW Leslie. "International Fiduciary Duty: Australia Trusteeship Over Nauru" (1990) *BU Int'l Lj*, which also reviews the history of the trust. Also, see Tamar Helfman, "Land Ownership and the Origins of Fiduciary Duty" (2006) 41, *Real Probate and Trust Journal*, 651. For its modern manifestation in Anglo/American business law, see e.g., Tamar Frankel, *Fiduciary Law* (Oxford Univ. Press, 2010). This is an excellent and encyclopedic treatment of the topic.

[70] Under Roman law, and from the perspective of Locke, it is possible to be both the trustor and beneficiary; this is still employed, though contested, in modern times. This argument is fully developed in my forthcoming book, Thomas Boudreau, *Law of Nations: Legal Order in a Violent World.* (A Manuscript).

be dormant and even unrecognized by the domestic government, especially at an international level.[71] As Locke has suggested, the people *already possess these rights*, which governments had promised during World War II to respect *on an international level* – i.e., to observe and enforce for their own and other peoples and to hold leaders or others accountable for violations. As such, in the promissory declarations and charters *supra*, governments recognized their new or fiduciary responsibilities to protect and respect the rights of all peoples to their lives, liberties, and land at the international level for the first time.

As evidenced, these promises were to become *internationally recognized and accepted* by governments as the *common property and possession* of all peoples when and if the war was won. In view of this, a government recognizes its own fiduciary responsibility as trustee of its new obligations, duties, and norms on at least three levels. First, the government as trustee, and especially its courts, must recognize that these duties and norms belong to the nation and its people as an independent jural community,[72] and it does not originate with the state. This means, first and foremost, that that the fiduciary duties that governments created and promised to their own and other peoples during the agony of World War II, such as their observance of human rights and crimes against humanity, are self-executing within the nation as an independent jural community. Specifically, these fiduciary obligations, duties, norms, and interests were created "below" the level of an interstate treaty, and *are already binding on a nation's judiciary as a pre-requisite for the lawful exercise of a sovereign or state power and authority.*

Second, a government signing the charter promises to recognize and respect these rights, which also *belong to other peoples or nations beyond its own borders.* This renders these fiduciary legal obligations, duties, and norms *international.* Hence, the observation, recognition, and respect of these rights by a government and its courts becomes the new basis of legitimate legal and political power. A government and state is legally legitimate, in the first instance, to the extent that it observes and respects its basic fiduciary legal obligations to its own and other peoples. Most importantly, the failure of governments

---

[71] Locke, above n 36, 64 and 65. Of course, the origins of human rights on the domestic level are always hotly contested. For a natural rights argument, see Leo Strauss, *Natural Right and History* (Univ. Of Chicago Press, 1999). For an innovative argument on human rights, see Loren E. Lomasky, *Persons, Rights and the Moral Community* (Oxford, 1987). Finally, see the work of Douglas Donoho, e.g. "Relativism Versus universalism in human Rights: The Search for Meaningful Standards." 27 Stan. J. Inter'l L. 345 (1990-91).

[72] Barkun, above n 13.

to observe and obey these binding obligations can give rise to a possible legal course of action to bring the violators to justice, as occurred at Nuremberg.

Such recognition and respect of binding legal obligations may, in the last instance, assume the form of prosecution of war criminals or other international criminals who violate the law of nations. This may require that national courts exercise universal jurisdiction much more often than has happened in the past.[73] This is because jurisdiction has value in terms of both *deterrence and enforcement*, so poor past state practice should not minimize its potential role in upholding the law of nations. In particular, the current state practice of *not invoking or using universal jurisdiction unless one of its own nationals is involved in the case is an extremely limited and unwarranted self-limitation* that only benefits potential or actual war criminals. As such, state practice must expand to include all states' common responsibilities to invoke universal jurisdiction when justified, i.e. when the home government or International Criminal Court (ICC) does not prosecute, in order to uphold the fiduciary law of nations as binding international law.

Because of the solemn wartime promises and subsequent massive response, especially by the Allied peoples around the world who relied and acted upon these promises at tremendous personal costs, the resulting fiduciary duties, norms, interests, and relationships following victory in the war became part of the very fabric of a legitimate government. As such, continual observance of these fiduciary obligations is a precondition for the legitimacy of its own sovereignty and state. In short, failure to do provides a legal cause of action that is actionable by other national or international courts. This is, after all, one of the reasons that universal jurisdiction exists even under current state-centric international legal order. This is a critical point to which this argument returns in the latter part of this essay.

Finally, these rights and protections of the people are adjudicated by the judiciary in the *nation's own courts* as the ultimate safeguard of these fiduciary norms and duties, such as human rights. Only if these internal institutions fail do the rights of jurisdiction accrue to

---

[73] See Princeton Univ., *The Princeton Project on Universal Jurisdiction, Program in Law and Public Affairs* (2001); See also Stephen Macedo (ed.) *Universal Jurisdiction: National Courts and Prosecution of Serious Crimes Under International Law* (Univ. of Pennsylvania Press, 2004); See also Kenneth Roth, "The Case for Universal Jurisdiction" (2001), September/October, *Foreign Affairs,* 150. Also, see Report of the Secretary-General, The Scope and Application of the Principle of Universal Jurisdiction. UN Doc. A/65/181(July 29, 2010). Finally, see Maximo Langer. "The Diplomacy of Universal Jurisdiction: the Political Branches and the Transnational Prosecution of War Crimes" (2011), 105, *American Journal of International Law*, 1-49.

international or other jurisdictions.[74] In fact, inspired by a gifted student, I would argue that the term "self-determination," which is often contested in legal literature, is an evolving phenomenon and process that is ultimately expressed in *a fully independent judiciary* that is the permanent protectorate of the peoples' rights and duties under the law of nations against potential governmental or state usurpations.[75] Thus, the ultimate expression of "self-determination" is a nation of laws, not of men, especially in judicial matters of respecting basic human rights and strict legal limitations on the legitimate use of force at home or abroad. In other words, the ultimate evolution of self-determination is that when the court decides, the nation abides.

Victory in World War II has led to the slow emergence of a fiduciary law of nations that consists of laws common to humanity. Yet, governments and national jurisdictions still inevitably contest many of these new norms, such as the observance of international human rights or individual responsibility for war crimes. Therefore, it is ultimately the role of present and future judges in national jurisdictions, international tribunals, and the ICJ to determine the scope and extent of this fully explicit fiduciary international legal order. Specifically, the role of the judiciaries across the world is not to *make* the law, but simply to *recognize and enforce* the fiduciary obligations, duties, and norms that governments accepted during the war to ensure that such lawless Leviathans, such as Nazi Germany, never threaten international peace and security again. The Pinochet indictment issued by Magistrate Garzón in Spain[76] is a prominent, if not pioneering, example of this ongoing evolution in fiduciary international law that developed during and after the most infamous war in human history.

The most accurate way to characterize this new fiduciary legal order that resulted from the Allied victory is to describe it as a "Law of Nations…common to humanity." This is a refinement of the ancient Roman idea of *Jus Gentium*, founded in Justinian *Institutes* and

---

[74] This is the legal basis of any jurisdiction by the ICC, established by the Rome Statute of the ICC, A/CONF.183/9., 1 July 2002.

[75] The student's name is Trevor O'Connor. I am grateful for the idea with which, upon reflection, I agree. Also, see Anne Marie Slaughter, *New World Order*, (Princeton University Press, 2000). I was particularly inspired by Anne Marie Slaughter's book, in which she discusses the enhanced role of judiciaries around the world. Reading this book made me realize that the nation's own judiciary could be the ultimate custodian of the law of nations, and as such, I pursued this idea to this current publication. Also, see "Judicial Globalization," (1999-2000) 40 *Virginia Journal of International Law* 1103.

[76] See Judge Garzon

elsewhere in the classical world.[77] This paper explores this classical idea in greater depth shortly; the point here is to focus on the profound shift in traditional international law caused by the World War II innovations, especially in terms of rights and recognition given to the peoples or entire nations of the world. Due to the new law of nations, the people are now the *imperium et imperia* (sovereign within the sovereign) of the newly legally limited state, at least implicitly.

The new law of nations does not necessarily favor the nation over the state; it simply makes explicit the legal tensions and contested nature inherent in the relationship between the people and statist structures, powers, and policies. As a result of the Allied victory in World War II, this law is available and common to all the peoples of the world as a way of recognizing human rights or providing universal jurisdiction[78] for war crimes or genocide that now legally constrain the once-absolute state prerogative to use unilateral force or commence war.[79]

Yet, it is important to note that in a pluralistic international legal order, a national jurisdiction may, depending upon its unique culture and historical evolution, choose to incorporate, emphasize, or reject different aspects of the law of nations based on possible misapplications or because of its *sui generis* circumstances. (This is poignantly pointed out and argued in Prof. Juan Carlos Sainz-Borgo's article later in this book.) Practically speaking, there is no single standard for uniform, or even universal, incorporation of the law of nations into each national jurisdiction, though the legal obligations and duties always exist. In fact, although these norms are self-executing, this does not always mean that these obligations will be politically or even judicially recognized or used. This partially reflects the inherent tension that almost always occurs between the nation and the government of the state. It is also an inevitable result of the differing legal cultures that have grown organically on their own native soil. The result will inevitably be a pluralistic international legal order, not a monotheistic "world law."

---

77 Caesar Flavius Justinian, *The Institutes of Justinian 4* (J.A.C. Thomas trans., North Holland Publishing Co, 1975). Also, see Arthur Nussbaum, *A Concise History of the Law of Nations 14-15* (The Macmillan Company, New York, rev. ed. 1962, 1947) Finally, see also Benedict Kingsbury and Benjamin Straumann, *The Roman Foundations of the Law of Nations* (Oxford Univ. Press, 2010).

78 See above, n 70.

79 Thomas Boudreau, "The Modern Law of Nations: Jus Gentium and the Role of Roman Jurisprudence in shaping the post World War II International Legal Order." (2012) 20 *The Digest*, 1. I like to think that the differences of definition concerning the law of nations and international law between Blackstone, Bentham, and those presented here represent the unique historical development and continuing evolution of the "nation" or the "state."

The Nation and the State: The New Problematique?

Prior to World War II, the state in international law had unquestioned rights of sovereignty in domestic and often international affairs. The epitome of such a state is the Nazi regime in Germany before and during the war, which became a lawless Leviathan towards its own and other peoples, resulting in the unparalleled and unprecedented tragedy of the Holocaust. After World War II, due to revulsion of Nazi atrocities—all of which were "legal" in the demented German legal system—this historical and highly evolved reification of state sovereignty began to erode as states recognized via the *Charter of the UN*, the *Convention for the Prevention and Punishment of Genocide*, and various human rights declarations and covenants that there were increasing legal limits on their once unchallenged powers to use violence, especially in domestic affairs. These new normative and legal obligations now regulate and legally govern the relationship of the state with its own and other peoples in international law. These legal limits were almost all promised or inspired by developments and declarations during the most significant war in human history.

Since the war, various courts throughout the world have clarified and elaborated upon their legal obligations to respect these new norms, even in the United States, which makes an often-strict delineation between domestic and international law. In a series of cases in the 1980s, specifically in the *Filartiga, Fernadez,* and *Forti* cases heard in United States federal courts,[80] the judges examined post-World War II developments in legal norms and used comparative legal research to reach their decision. In this way, the differential diffusion of fiduciary international norms created during and immediately after the war began to percolate through the once-impermeable barriers of domestic jurisdiction. Simultaneously, the domestic diffusion of municipal and constitutional law continued to spread to customary norms of international law, resulting in a "law… common to humanity."[81] The historical and current legal record explains this occurrence. Specifically, after the horrors of the Holocaust and unprecedented slaughter of World War II, states could no longer claim that their own nations or populations within their powers were merely a passive presence with no international status or standing, *subject*

[80] See *Filartiga v. Pena-Irala.* 630 F.2d. 876; *Fernandez v. Wilkinson.* 505 F. Supp. 787 (D. Kan. 1980); *Forti v. Suerez-Mason.* 694 F. Sup. 707.
[81] Boudreau, above n 76.

only to domestic jurisdiction. The international norms adopted during and immediately after the war represent nothing less than a radical repudiation of this previous impervious "domestic jurisdiction" doctrine of the state.

This inevitably leads to a legal distinction, if not an abrupt split, between the rights of the "nation" or the "people" united in a common jural community that is able to assert its rights on a legal plane and the responsibilities of a government. All too often, this results in the rarification, abstraction, and conflation of these two different realities into the simplistic political or legal construction of the "nation-state," or simply the "state."[82] Yet, after World War II, this is no longer is legally or politically accurate.

The Nuremberg Charter even recognizes a people's rights in relation to their own government, especially the right to exist free from arbitrary and overwhelming violence.[83] The entire thrust of these legal innovations was to limit and restrain the exercise of unilateral and illegitimate force by a state against its own or other peoples. These legal innovations have resulted in a profound shift in the fundamental and historically competing sources of legitimacy and sovereignty, away from the state and towards the nation or people of the polity. The people or nation are essentially the new *imperium et imperii*, or sovereign within the sovereign, of the now legally limited state. The result was the largely unintended, yet enduring creation of a new fiduciary law of nations that recognized that human rights, self-determination, and the right of protection, even from one's own government, were now an integral part of international law.

The apparent roots of *imperium et imperii* as an enduring legal concept were in the evolution of Roman law in the post-empire period.[84] Various kingdoms and principalities used Roman law to adjudicate their disputes and property rights throughout the so-called Dark and Medieval Ages of Europe. The first recognized use of *imperium et imperii* was evidently during this time to describe the idea of a divided sovereignty between the rulers

[82] For a refreshing exception to this oversight, see Franz Oppenheimet and John M. Gitterman, *The State* (BiblioBazaar, 2009). While I do not share the authors' faith in many of their libertarian beliefs or their Marxist conclusion in the "withering away of the state," they present the critical tensions between the nation or civil "society" versus the state.

[83] See above n 4. Also, see Theodor Meron, "International Criminalization of Internal Atrocities" (1995) 89 *American Journal of International Law*, 554-577. This article provides insights into post-war developments since Nuremberg.

[84] See Stephan Weiss, *Regum et Imperium* (Paris Institut Historique Allemand, 2008). This really is a concept that seemed to emerge in the Middle Ages, though it of course refers back to Rome. See T. Broughton, *The Magistrates of the Roman Republic Volume 3* (New York, American Philological Association, 1951-52) (describes this power as the Imperium, which was often delegated, but presumed to be exercised on behalf of the Roman people as a whole).

and the ruled. Yet, the term can also describe the ideal political arrangement of the early Roman republic between the Senate and the Roman people.[85] Even so, the idea of *imperium et imperii* was not fully articulated until the Medieval Ages in Europe, when Roman Law was increasingly utilized and sometimes conflicted with Canon law to describe and regulate the growing complexities of commerce, as well as the relationship between a people and their polity. In the late Medieval Ages, the idea of the *imperium et imperii* seemed to exist as more of an interrogatory, as progressively the church, the divine right of kings, and ultimately the people claimed to be the true basis of legitimate political authority.[86] With the Glorious Revolution in England, the American Revolution in the New World, and the French Revolution on the continent, the primacy of the people as the source of legitimate state authority seemed more assured, though still precarious. Yet, with the rise of fascism and communism in the 20th century, the people's role in politics–let alone as the legitimate source of political authority–seemed highly problematic, to say the least.

In the post-World War II period, the term *imperium et imperii* accurately describes the lasting significance of the new law of nations. Traditional, pre-World War II international law was and often still is defined solely in terms of state-centric law, or law made between sovereign states. In particular, before World War II, matters between the "nation" and the "state" were universally regarded as almost wholly within the domestic jurisdiction of the specific government in power, and hence untouchable by international law.[87] Due to profound legal innovations during and immediately after the war, such a "traditional" definition of international law is no longer historically plausible or legally possible.

Since World War II, the legal and political reality of the relationship between the nation and the state is now much more complex and problematic because of the fiduciary relationships, interests, and norms that governments created during the war. This has obviously established a dynamic tension between the fiduciary and other rights of nations, and the powers and authority of any particular regime. The people want to preserve their rights and security, and governments, qua governments, usually want to

[85] Ibid., Also see Boudreau, *Law of Nations* (Forthcoming manuscript).

[86] Ibid., Andrei.

[87] Of course, there were exceptions: piracy, slavery, and the Leagues' mandates. However, I would argue that these measures and mandates, especially the latter, were episodic, often un-enforced, and largely ineffective. Furthermore, slavery and piracy still persists today.

increase their power and control[88]; the result is an ongoing and sometimes contentious process of dynamic mutual definition or defiance, competing constructs, or contested powers, as the nation and state contend with each other for ascendancy in private law, public affairs, and political power. [89] In view of these conflicting claims, the courts of each national jurisdiction as an independent jural community must, in the first instance, adjudicate the controlling law of nations. The evolving doctrines, development of humanitarian intervention, and related yet distinct Responsibility to Protect (R2P) reflect this contested reality in the continuous and often-debated practices of states. This topic briefly factors in once again later in this essay.

II

After Victory: Promises to Keep

The new law of nations is at the heart of post-World War II domestic and international legal limits that bind the once-absolute and sovereign state. This law of nations was created by the declarations, conventions, charters, and treaties resulting from World War II, especially the Charter of the UN, which represent the latest developments in republican security theory concerning the constraint and control of unilateral political power, whether exercised by the individual, group, or state.[90] As mentioned in the beginning of this essay, *this law in particular limits and sharply curtails the unilateral violence that a government can legitimately use against its own or other peoples.*

In his award-winning book, *Bounding Power,* Daniel Deudney has indicated that *republican security theory* has been concerned with the restraint of centralized and unilateral or arbitrary political or military power since classical times.[91] From this useful theoretical perspective, the ultimate significance of the new law of nations can be found in the enduring republican structures that resulted from the fiduciary promises made by the

88 This is a truism that borders on a tautology. To demonstrate this, simply examine current headlines or read a reliable history book. Of course, the horrific ultimate example of this is the Nazi regime. See William Shirer, *The Rise and Fall of the Third Reich* (Simon & Schuster, 1990), which chronicles the seemingly endless gasping and predations for power of this lawless Leviathan.

89 See above n 10 .i.e. Thomas Boudreau, *Jus Gentium and Systematic Legal Order: New Paradigm for International Law*, 5 International Perspective (1994).

90 See Daniel Deudney, *Bounding Power: Republican Security Theory from the Polls to the Global Village* (Princeton: Princeton Univ. Press, 2007.

91 Ibid.

Allied powers to their own and others peoples during World War II. The so-called International Bill of Human Rights and other various human rights regimes that evolved out of wartime promises, such as the Declaration of [the] UN made by the Allies, can also be understood and explained as republican systems of security restraints upon the former, nearly absolute prerogatives of the state to use unilateral force, even against its own people.[92]

The Charter of the UN, and even the veto power that it establishes, can be cited as prominent, albeit imperfect examples of republican restraints upon political and military power.[93] The UN Charter has its origins in the same promissory declarations and agreements, such as the Moscow Declaration of 1943, as the fiduciary law of nations.

So, in many ways, the UN Charter represents a fiduciary pact by the Allied governments to fulfill their promises to millions of people in order to fight and win the war. The day that the drafting convention for the UN Charter commenced was the same day that advanced United States troops linked up with Russian troops on the Torgau River in Central Europe. In a remarkable development, the lead patrol of United States Army soldiers who were sent to Torgau, led by Lt. Kotzenbue [interviewed by the author in 1985 on the 40th anniversary of the linkup], were keenly *aware* that on the same day, the drafting convention began in San Francisco—indicating that the "promises made" by the Allied governments were of at least passing interest, even to the most advanced United States troops in Europe.[94]

For instance, Pvt. Joe Polowsky, a member of the Lt. Kotzenbue patrol, later wrote in almost poetic terms about that day:

> There was a tremendous burst of lilacs as we approached the Elbe River. This exaltation of being alive ...There were even jokes that we were approaching the

[92] See above n 2-10.

[93] Thomasn Boudreau, *Sheathing the Sword: The Preventive Role of the United Nations Secretary General* (Westport: Greenwood, 1991). In this book, I talk about the potential value of the veto to prevent action, and thus inhibit the exercise of force. In short, the power to prevent is the power to control. Hence, I think it provides an example of a negarchic restraint that Prof. Deudney so admirably articulates and develops in *Bounding Power* above n 87. Due to drastic editorial cuts, *Sheathing the Sword* (my first book) is basically a "Cliff-Notes," abbreviated and an inadequate version of my Ph.D dissertation (1985) "Watchman of the Peace" on the same topic; the latter is a much better document.

[94] Boudreau, 1991.

> River Jordan, crossing over into Canaan…*We also knew that the United Nations was being born in San Francisco on the very same day, twenty-fifth of April.* Can you imagine? The very same day that we linked up with the Russians at the Elbe River.[95]

On this historic day, these advanced troops had many *other concerns* to think about, such as staying alive, yet they were also thinking of the far-away founding conference for the drafting of the UN Charter. These developments reveal that the solemn promises made from the very beginning of the war were of at least minimal interest to a small group of the most advanced Allied soldiers in the West. An organization such as the UN was strongly inferred in the Atlantic Charter, then clearly enunciated by Undersecretary of State Sumner Welles in his speech at the Arlington National Cemetery Amphitheater on May 30, 1942. It became a full-fledged war aim among all the Allies in 1943 in the Moscow Declaration.

To fulfill the promise of a "world organization,"[96] the governments drafting the charter defined and developed a trusteeship system and collective security obligations, institutions, sanctions, and legal norms that were intended to limit the unilateral legitimization of political violence by a sovereign state. These norms and principles provide legal preconditions for the legitimate existence and exercise of hereafter-limited state sovereignty, especially in the use of force. In other words, the UN Charter has profound fiduciary foundations in the wartime promises and declarations of the Allied powers to their own and other peoples. In the end, even the "enemy states" of the war agreed upon the new legal and fiduciary legal order once they requested membership in the newly established UN.

The UN Charter and Republican Restraints on State Power

Due to the egregious examples of Nazi Germany and Japan, the soldiers and statesmen who drafted the charter were determined that such unilateral powers of aggression would

[95] See quote by Pvt. Joe Polowsky in dedication to my book, *Sheathing the Sword: The UN Secretary-General and the Prevention of International Conflict* (Greenwood Publishers, 1991). Lt. Kotzenbue's patrol was the first to link up with the Soviet forces; however, he apparently submitted the wrong map coordinates, and a second United States patrol further north received the majority of the subsequent press. Even so, his men received the Bronze Star for bravery for driving through about 30 miles of enemy-held territory to ensure the linkup with the Russians. (Emphasis added.)

[96] Welles, 1942.

never be lawfully used again. Hence, the charter specifically prohibits the unilateral use of force in international affairs, except in cases of armed attack against a member (Article 51). In such a situation, a member state of the UN has the inherent right of self-defense. This is an almost unprecedented repudiation of the use of force in international affairs that had been largely accepted as "legal" since the Treaty of Westphalia. This is a singular, though often unobserved, new restraint in international relations.

The veto power of the permanent members of the UN Security Council (UNSC) can also be described as a republican restraint. Though often overlooked, the veto power can *prevent* a course of action, including military adventurism. As described elsewhere, the veto power provides the "power to prevent," as well as to enable, and thus can be characterized as a mechanism of international or republican restraint.[97]

Finally, the charter's recognition of human rights, even in the abstract (as critics note), is a significant source of potential restraint among states. Since the adoption of the charter, there has been unprecedented activity by scholars, diplomats, and policymakers alike in pursuit of a workable human rights regime that is global in scope. One result of these efforts is the International Bill of Rights, consisting of several declarations, treaties, and conventions that have been increasingly cited in domestic jurisdictions around the world.[98] While far from perfect, the ensuing human rights standards and legal regimes are a marginal, yet increasingly important system of restraint in international affairs, especially when coupled with developing global telecommunication technologies that add transparency and provide instant communication of violations or atrocities throughout the world.

The victors of World War II accepted these restraints, however inchoate, though only after much internal debate at the drafting convention of the UN Charter in San Francisco. Such an interpretation is consistent with that put forward by G. John Ikenberry in his ground-breaking book, *After Victory*, which asserts that the most successful and enduring political orders that emerge from war are those that include voluntary restraints on power by the victors.[99] As evidenced, this process of imposing

---

[97] Ibid., Above n 90 Boudreau.

[98] Above n 10, 11, 12.

[99] G. John Ikenberry, *After Victory: Institutions, Strategic Restraint and the Rebuilding of Order After Major Wars* (Princeton Univ. Press, 2001).

legally binding self-restraints on state power began *at the very beginning* of World War II in an attempt to mobilize the millions of allied, conquered, colonized, commonwealth, and neutral peoples of the world in order to win the war. When this effort succeeded, the victorious governments recognized during the drafting of the UN Charter in San Francisco (and afterwards) a system of self-restraints, such as self-determination, human rights, war crimes against one's own and other peoples, and the legal commitments to collective security against an aggressor that have been described elsewhere, as a new law of nations common to the whole of humanity. *Hence, the ultimate measure of a state's own legitimacy as a sovereign power is its recognition and respect for these new fiduciary norms and relationships, described here as the modern law of nations* that includes human rights and collective security, solemnly promised by the Allied governments during World War II to their own peoples and the conquered, colonized, or neutral nations of the world after victory in the war. Therefore, significant state departure from these new norms, such as initiating a war, war crimes, or genocide, justifies a serious legal cause of action that can be prosecuted via universal jurisdiction, when possible, in any national, transnational (regional), intergovernmental, or global court.

The Nuremburg Charter: The Nation vs. The State

By signing the Declaration by [the] UN under mortal duress, the signatory governments, including several governments in exile, reaffirmed the principles of the Atlantic Charter and, in doing so, simply recognized that the conquered, colonial, and other democratic peoples already possessed the right to human rights and self-determination.

The Nuremberg Charter, which was written *after* the drafting of the UN Charter had begun, took the *a priori* existence and rights of the nation *one step further, and stated that no government has the right to effectively wage war against its own peoples or the peoples of other nations under its control.* In short, groups and the nation or nations were recognized as possessing certain rights at the international level, which they can claim even against their own government. Hence, there has been a *significant expansion in terms of the subjects in international law*, both regarding recognition on the international plane of these nations' rights, and subsequent state responsibilities.

The Nuremberg Charter and subsequent trials, discussed in detail in the following chapters by Prof. Tara Helfman and Judge Stephan J. Sfekas, reinforced and expanded upon these legal limitations.[100] By acknowledging crimes against peace and crimes against humanity and codifying customary law concerning war crimes, the Nuremberg Trials further limited sovereign states hitherto absolute rights to legitimate, unilaterally political violence. This even included violence directed at a state's own domestic population, an area once considered untouchable by international law. Finally, the Nuremberg Trials held *individuals* responsible, and sentenced several German warlords to death for the crimes committed by the Nazi regime. Henceforth, in a truly revolutionary development, individuals were held accountable under international law for crimes they committed while "serving" their government. Thus, new limits to unilateral legitimating of political violence involved explicit individual and state responsibilities as an inherent part of international law.

This development was clearly intentional, as Telford Taylor, the United States' chief legal counsel at Nuremberg, has stated:

> The United Nations and the Nuremberg trials were initially twin offspring of the Allied negotiations and agreements with respect to the peace that would follow victory... Different as the twins were, they shared the same two basic purposes: promoting peaceful rather than warlike settlements of international disputes, and humanitarian governmental policies.... Essentially, the Nuremberg trials were intended to bring the weight of law and criminal sanctions to bear in support of the peaceful and humanitarian principles that the United Nations was to promote by consultation and collective action.[101]

These "twin offspring" of World War II deeply question the previous state-centric legal order. Specifically, they sharply curtailed the sovereign state's once-absolute legal right to decide the preeminent issue of war in favor of international recognition of human rights, the illegality of unilateral force except in cases of self-defense against armed attack, and collective security. The advent of such a system involved, at the time, the near-universal

[100] Above n 4. Also See Telford Taylor, *The Anatomy of the Nuremberg Trials: A Personal Memoir* (Little, Brown & Co., 1993).

[101] See Telford Taylor, *Nuremberg and Vietnam: An American Tragedy* (Chicago: Quadrangle Books, 1970). Also see Taylor, above n 94.

recognition of human rights, collective norms, rights, obligations, and sanctions contained within the UN or Nuremberg Charters. This development marked a virtual revolution in the international legal order. The full weight of domestic or international adjudication should now equally apply to those, including state or substate actors or individuals that commit terrorist acts involving the killing of innocents, either through disproportionate or excessive use of force or wanton disregard for innocent civilian life. The terrible era of state or individual impunity for killing innocent civilians and other war crimes is over, and should forever remain in the past.

After their experiences with Germany and Japan, the Allied governments of World War II were simply not content to leave the ultimate question of war solely to the unilateral decision of the sovereign state. Because of this, the existing legal order was largely replaced, or supplanted, by a new order, which placed legal limits on a sovereign state's once-absolute right to legitimate and wage war for the first time. In short, ever since the development of the UN and Nuremberg Charters, governments or states no longer possess legitimate unilateral authority to initiate or wage war, as the United States had done in its invasion of Iraq in 2003, unless they are under or have suffered from an armed attack. If such unilateral and illegitimate force is used, then the leaders of the state or states initiating the attack are guilty of war crimes and crimes against peace. This is one of the most prominent lessons and legal legacies of the Nuremberg Trials.

Nuremberg was necessary because of the unparalleled horrors of the Holocaust,[102] including Hitler's war against his own nation, which targeted other Germans, especially German Jews, some of whom served honorably in World War I, as well as gypsies and civilians in other occupied territories. Hitler's war against entire civilian populations made it evident that nations as legally distinct entities need protection from states, including their own.

The following Nuremberg Trials, which fully documented and presented the horrors of the Holocaust and other Nazi wartime atrocities in a courtroom setting, had significantly contributed to the development of subsequent declarations, conventions, and treaties, such as the Universal Declaration of Human Rights, Convention on the Crime and

---

[102] See Peter Longerich above n 1. Also, see Michael Marrus, "The Holocaust at Nuremberg," (1998) 26 *Yad Vashem Studies,* 5-41.

Punishment of Genocide, and the revised Geneva Conventions of 1949.[103] In this regard, the solitary work and efforts of Raphael Lemkin, who tirelessly advocated for the adoption of the Genocide Convention, stands out as a beacon of inspiration and deserves a special mention here. A Polish lawyer from a Jewish family, Lemkin prophetically began his efforts to prevent mass murder in the 1930s at the League of Nations, prior to the outbreak of World War II.[104] The "Great Lemkin" even coined the term "genocide" to refer to the killing of an entire group or contributing to conditions leading to its demise. He continued his tireless work to protect entire peoples throughout World War II, during which he lost most of his family in the Holocaust. Lemkin persevered despite his devastating losses, and successfully achieved the adoption of the convention in 1948. As such, he is a true hero of humanity and provides an enduring inspiration to work for a lawful world for generations to come.

The new emphasis in international law on legally protecting entire groups of peoples first emerged from the Nuremberg Charter, and subsequently from the Convention on the Prevention and Punishment of Genocide, which criminalized genocide. It was the first instance of recognition on an international plane that individuals, groups, and entire nations have essential innate and legal rights against their own government or other states.

Never Again? The ICC and R2P

The importance of protecting civilians from an assault by their own or other governments, especially genocidal assaults aimed at destroying part or all of a population of peoples, is a main reason for the initiation of negotiations for the ICC in the late-1990s. The Rome Statute that created the ICC went into force on July 1, 2002 following ratification by 60 countries.[105] The creation of the ICC is a watershed event in international affairs in general, and international law in particular.[102] This is because, by its mere existence, the ICC may help deter leaders from embarking on devastating unilateral wars. As such, it certainly embodies some of the key characteristics of

---

103 See above n 1- 11 for this wartime and post-war *corpus juris.*

104 John Cooper, *Raphael Lemkin and the Struggles for the Genocide Convention* (Palgrave Macmillan, 2004). Also, see Lemkin's own book written, during World War II: Raphael Lemkin, *Axis Rule in Occupied Europe* (The LawBook Exchange, Ltd., 2005). Finally, see Dirk Moses, (2010) "Raphael Lemkin, Culture, and the Concept of Genocide" in Donald Bloxham and A. Dirk Moses (eds.) *The Oxford Handbook on Genocide Studies* (Oxford Univ. Press, 2010), 19-41.

105 Rome Statute, ICC-ASP/2/Res.3, U.N. Doc. A/CONF.183/9 (July 1, 2002) (is the legal bias of any jurisdiction by the ICC).

systematic restraint that Daniel Deudney has described as essential to a negarchic world order that is characterized by inhibition of illegitimate use of force. The ICC is the court of last resort that holds individual leaders accountable for launching war and for guilty parties' subsequent war crimes. The indictment of Pinochet as a former head of state has now been duplicated by the ICC, which has even indicted a sitting head of state, Al-Bashir of the Sudan. The message seems clear: if you commit war crimes or crimes against humanity, "you can run, but you can't hide." The potential deterrence value of the ICC is difficult to measure, but one can anticipate that this value will become more tangible, especially after other present or future (as well as active or retired) heads of states and their advisors are indicted by the ICC and tried for their crimes. However, the ICC needs to extend beyond its Afrocentric focus of indictments and encompass the whole world, including the most developed states. In this way, a truly global system of criminal justice can be activated to enhance the protection of peoples around the world. This would be inconceivable without the legal legacy of the Nuremberg Charter and Trials after World War II.

The Two-Edged Sword? Humanitarian Intervention

The evolving and contested doctrines of humanitarian intervention and R2P recognize that if a domestic government fails in its primary responsibility to protect its own civilians, then other governments may have a legal responsibility to act and intervene to stop massive bloodshed.[106] Such doctrines can admittedly be a dangerous and double-edged sword, as Hitler himself demonstrated in Czechoslovakia and Poland. In both cases, Hitler cited the supposed dangers to Germans living in these countries as a main reason to invade and essentially initiate World War II.[107] Thus, humanitarian intervention can easily be used to overstep the boundaries of civilian protection to include conquest and fundamental regime change. As a later article in this volume by Bernard Ntahiraja suggests, the destruction of the sitting government of Libya and the subsequent bloody chaos illustrates once again the dangers of so-called humanitarian intervention that grossly oversteps its legal boundaries or mandate to inhibit and even destroy the chances of a diplomatic settlement.

---

[106] See Secretary-General's Report: "In Larger Freedom: Towards Development, Security and Human Rights for All" A/59/2005, which outlines the doctrine and criteria for the R2P.
[107] See Weinberg, Shirer, above n 14.

Yet, precisely due to Hitler and the horrors the Nazi state had unleashed, the necessity of such international intervention, especially in genocidal situations, has finally been legally recognized after World War II. Unfortunately, in my judgment, protecting people from genocidal assaults has been a major failure of the UNSC and international society as a whole in the post-World War II era, as the situations in Bosnia, Rwanda, and Darfur have illustrated.[108] These three examples alone reveal a massive failure of national or international will and purpose on the part of all watching governments, especially those with the power to intervene. The UN, and specifically the UNSC, were created in part to prevent such genocidal assaults against innocent peoples. However, the UN's failure to intervene effectively in Bosnia, Rwanda, and Darfur has left a legacy of infamy that should haunt sitting diplomats and their governments for their failure to act in time. These terrible episodes contributed to the creation of the ICC in 2002.

The ICC was founded because states simply cannot or will not protect their own or other civilian populations adequately, despite the terrible lessons of World War II. If states or the UN do not prevent such assaults against civilians, *then the legal and juridical emphasis must be focused, in the short term, on capturing and punishing all those suspected of or complicit in the commission of war crimes and crimes against peace or humanity.* In short, the configuration of legal relationships surrounding the concept of the "nation-state" and its population has become much more complex, distinct, and separate since the post-World War II revolution in international law. This is due in large part to assault by the state on its own or other peoples. In the first instance, domestic courts in national jurisdictions can serve in a critical role in this regard by enforcing the fiduciary law of nations that emerged out of World War II. Only if these domestic courts cannot or do not act does the adjudication by the ICC then become necessary and ideally inevitable.

III

Historical Background: Roman Jurisprudence and the Law of Nations

[108] See Daniel Reiff, *Slaughterhouse: Bosnia and the Failure of the West* (Touchstone, 1996). Also, see Jan Willem Honig and Norbert Both, *Srebrenica: Record of a War Crime* (Penguin Books, 1997).

This new law of nations resembles, but does not completely correspond to, the classical conception of *Jus Gentuim*, or a "law of nations…common to the whole of humanity."[109] In this section, I argue that the modern law of nations can be defined and described largely in terms of the Roman and Justinian concept of *Jus Gentium*, or a law of nations… held in common with other nations or juridical communities in the world. Because each jural community is unique, I also argue that this is not the same argument found in the monist approach that the "law of nations and the law of each nation form an integrated, universal legal order." The reality is much more complex and pluralistic.

A full understanding of the scope and significance of modern legal developments emanating from World War II first requires comprehension of the classical roots of *Jus Gentium* in Roman jurisprudence. This necessitates resorting to legal archeology or, in essence, an exercise in historical jurisprudence in order to thoroughly grasp the origins of the law of nations.

The *Institutes* of Justinian define *Jus Gentium* as "[t]he law of nations…common to the whole human race."[110] This seemingly simple sentence presents significant definitional and conceptual complexities. As Arthur Nussbaum has noted, the meaning of *Jus Gentium* in classical times evolved as Rome expanded from a peninsular republic to a vast empire.[111] At first, as a distinctive body of law, *Jus Gentium* represented the Roman republic's attempt to provide foreign merchants with a more equitable court of justice in which to pursue mercantile claims using comparative legal analysis of local laws and customs held in common with the Romans. As the empire grew, the Roman conception of *Jus Gentium* evolved under the influence of stoic philosophy as a body of law that ideally governed the legal affairs of humanity as a whole.[112] The former definition reflected the origins of *Jus Gentium* in the Roman practice of using what might be described as comparative legal analysis of the local laws and customs of societies beyond the republic to ascertain the controlling law in a particular case. The latter characteristics of *Jus Gentium* were influenced by stoic philosophy, and during the days of the empire,

---

[109] The terms law of nations and international law are regarded as synonymous and interchangeable in the following sections. In contrast, the term "intergovernmental law" is used synonymously with public law of states, or law made solely between states.

[110] Caesar Flavius Justinian, *The Institutes of Justinian 4* (J.A.C. Thomas trans., N. Holland Publishing Company, 1975).

[111] See Arthur Nussbaum, *A Concise History of the Law of Nations 14-15* (The Macmillan Company, rev. ed. 1962, 1947).

[112] Id. See also Henry Sumner Maine, *Ancient Law: It's Connection with the Early History of Society and Its relation to Modern Ideas* (Boston: Beacon Press, 10th ed. 1963).

they emphasized the universal nature of the legal norms that governed "the whole human race."[113] The meaning of *Jus Gentium* derives from the Latin *Gentium*, which is the genitive case for the Latin word *gentes* meaning "peoples" or "nations," and *Jus*, meaning "law." Because of the precision of the Latin language, the phrase *Gentium* leaves no doubt that Roman jurists were referring to "peoples" or "nations" in the genitive case. There is no hint here of the concept of law *between* (or *inter gentes* in Latin) nations, peoples, or governments.

With excellent precision, the Romans described the juridical concept of a law that originates from different peoples and nations themselves, rather than a law that derives from relations between governments or nations, or *jus inter gentes*, which is an entirely different concept.[114] In view of this, the law of nations as the Romans originally intended it becomes at first a question of evaluating the domestic law of each nation or people, and then of trying to determine commonalities between this law and all other nations and peoples. The sources of the law of nations are a nation's customs and "necessity."[115]

In the first instance, the origins of *Jus Gentium* were found within the common customs and law of the nation, not law created between nations. As the concept evolved and stoic philosophy exerted an influence, *Jus Gentium* under Justinian rule eventually became a composite and potentially universal law that reflects the similar contributions of the "whole human race."[116] Thus, it is the law within a nation to be found "in common" with all other nations that is properly regarded in later Roman jurisprudence as the "law of nations." The phrase "the whole human race" reflects the influence of stoic philosophy and its basic belief in the universal brotherhood of mankind. A notable irony of the period of Pax Romana is that a political order based upon the sword, iron discipline, and military skills of the Roman Legions also gave birth, by the sheer success of the empire, to innovative and prescient belief in the universal human family, a true "brotherhood of mankind."[117]

113 See Nussbaum, above n 76; See also Justinian, above n 75.
114 See also Benedict Kingsbury and Benjamin Straumann, *The Roman Foundations of the Law of Nations* (Oxford Univ. Press, 2010.
115 See Nussbaum, above n 76.
116 Boudreau, above n 73.
117 Boudreau, above n 73.

Of course, in the late Roman era, such universality could only be a philosophical longing or a juridical concept and legal pretense, since the whole of the Earth–let alone the entire human family–was unknown and largely unexplored. Even at the height of empire, the Roman world encompassed a relatively limited, though historically significant section of the globe. Thus, the idea of a legal order based upon laws common to the whole of humanity remained largely a legal fiction and a lingering echo from the classical human heart for a more just and peaceful world–that is, until the bloodiest war in human history occurred, resulting in a profound legal revolution concerning the newly limited legitimate powers of the state.

Not until after the Holocaust and other horrors of World War II were the legal, political, and even geographical preconditions for a modern *Jus Gentium* fulfilled. From a legal perspective, the important feature of the post-war period is that nearly all governments at the time expressly consented to UN Charter, which is perhaps the hybrid treaty and fiduciary foundation stone of the new law of nations. After the war, new signatories continued to join the UN Charter from around the world as decolonization proceeded. Thus, for perhaps the first time in human history, the sociolegal and political preconditions for a law of nations common to the whole of "humanity" are actually being fulfilled. In this regard, it is important to note that the UN Charter and the new fiduciary law of nations were not written by hypothetical individuals living alone in the Lockean state of nature, but by actual governments attempting survival during a Hobbesian state of war. Yet, even in modern times, the "whole human race" in a legal sense does not require *de facto* universality among all peoples as nations of the world.

For instance, the drafting of the concept of *jus cogens* after World War II, which culminated 20 years later in the Vienna Convention on the Law of Treaties, illustrates this point. Article 53 of the Vienna Convention states that a *jus cogens* norm is one endorsed by the whole.[118] Yet, in extensive discussions among drafters of the convention, it is quite clear from the record that they did not mean by this article that universal agreement by all states was necessary to be a universal norm. This would essentially provide the aggressor state or states with a veto power that would violate and

[118] See *Vienna Convention on the Law of Treaties article. 53*, May 23, 1969, 1155 U.N.T.S. 331.

even void the meaning or purpose of such a norm.[119] In view of this, a distinction can be made between *de facto* universality and *de jure* universality that is implicit within the now-accepted principle of *jus cogens* embodied in the Vienna Convention. Hence, the term "whole of humanity" is misleading. For this reason, I simply use the word "humanity" when describing the law of nations. The challenge is to find which laws *are held in common within the various jural communities of humanity*, and not necessarily to seek the consent of all human beings.

In particular, by virtue of the bloody victory by the Allies in World War II, the fiduciary duties, norms, interests, and relationships—many of which are embodied in the Charter of the UN—are the common birthright of humanity and all subsequent generations. In this sense, the Charter of the UN is a hybrid document that consists of both fiduciary norms from the law of nations and positive international law involving states. Hence, any state that signs the Charter of the UN agrees also, by necessity, to the basic norms of the fiduciary law of nations, such as self-determination, recognition, and respect for basic human rights, as well as legal restraints on the unilateral use of force in international affairs. These fiduciary norms recognized within the charter existed prior to and now independently of it as well, in the sense that jurisdictions around the world have almost universally recognized and accepted the law of the charter. These slight modifications of the original meaning of *Jus Gentium* seem fully consistent with the classical intent of its ancient authors and practitioners, who were primarily concerned with the practical application of comparative laws.[120]

Defining this law of nations in terms of the classical Roman and Justinian concept of *Jus Gentium* requires the exploration and explanation of the meaning of the key word "common." The latter task of defining the word "common" appears deceptively easy, but on the contrary, it has multiple and often the most uncommon of meanings. Since World War II, treaties, conventions, customary law, and general principles of international law sometimes partake in the law of nations, and they often reach deep into domestic jurisdictions for their origins, formulation, and use. In fact, as evidenced below, I argue that the only true law between states is treaty law or other subsequent

[119] See Rozakis, above n 10. Also, see M. Cherif Bassiouni above n 9, "International Crimes: 'Jus Cogens' and 'Obligatio Erga Omnes'" (1996) 59(4) *Law and Contemporary Problems, Accountability for International Crimes and Serious Violations of Fundamental Human Rights* 63-74.
[120] See Henry Sumner Maine, *Ancient Law*, above n 77.

agreements; other sources, such as custom or general principles, originate and have always originated in the law of nations, and many of these are held in "common." Yet, the word "common" may be misleading, since it has far more than one meaning or application. Rather, this seemingly simple word has manifold legal meanings depending on the shared norms and recognized legal obligations of often highly disparate and *sui generis* jurisdictions.

Defining *jus gentium* as "Laws Common to Humanity"

Using the term "Law of Nations" largely in terms of the ancient Roman juridical concept of *jus gentium* first requires a definition of the various modern meanings of the term "common," i.e., "[t]he law of nations…common to humanity." Due to space limitations, this paper can only highlight the commonality of certain laws, though the following list is obviously not exhaustive. Such "common" laws include:

(1) The series of treaties and conventions created during and after World War II, partly in response to fiduciary promises made by the Allied governments to their own and other peoples. This is basically state-centric law, though it now interpenetrates and overlaps with the fiduciary law of nations (see Fig. 1 below). For instance, the Charter of the UN is one such state-ratified treaty, though as this paper has already argued, it is actually a hybrid document that recognizes fiduciary rights and legal norms, such as self-determination or human rights, under the law of nations as well. (2) Customary law, including those laws common to domestic legal orders;[121] the decisions of domestic courts that are or become common to most of humanity through the domestic diffusion of customary law or differential diffusion of non-consensual or fiduciary general principles of international law. In short, customary law has always been more appropriately categorized under the law of nations. Because of this, domestic courts and judiciaries have a critical role in interpreting and upholding the customary norms in the law of nations. (3) General principles of international law that differentially diffuse into widespread state practice and domestic acceptance;[122] these include the new fiduciary legal norms as a new class of general principles in international law created as a result of World War II. (4) Universal obligations or common and shared jurisdiction concerning

121 See Roozbeh (Rudy) B. Baker, "Customary International Law in the 21st Century: Old Challenges and New Problems" (2010) 21 *European Journal of International Law*, 173 (providing a recent comment on customary law).
122 See Schachter, above n 50.

legal obligations in wartime or military occupations, including war crimes and crimes against humanity; the pioneering "Martens Clause" is one example. More recently, the shared obligations of the high contracting parties found in common Article 1 of the 1949 Geneva Conventions are further key examples of such joint or "common" obligation that can be adjudicated in national courts.[123] (5) The so-called global commons or other public trusts held in common by the whole of humanity, such as the high seas, Antartica, the atmosphere, or near outer space.[124] These areas belong to everyone as a common fiduciary possession of the peoples or nations of the world.

As such, they are part and parcel of the fiduciary law of nations. This far older and established international fiduciary order concerning the global commons and the freedom of the seas are the legal precedents of the modern law of nations as a legal order. It is interesting to note in this regard that the Atlantic Charter refers to the "freedom of the seas" as one of the fundamental rights of the international legal order. (Grotius, the Father of the Law of the Sea would be proud!)[125] The new fiduciary norms consisting of the law of nations is easily grafted onto a far older, but often implicit fiduciary legal order. As such, this is one of the most promising areas for the development and evolution of a fiduciary international legal order in the future, especially in contending with global climate change.

(6) Other *pre-state* (Westphalia 1648) legal and diplomatic customary and treaty norms, principles, and practices that have survived a succession, not only of governments, but of consecutive states presiding over a given territory. Often these norms—such as the inviolability and immunity of the ambassador—have begun in ancient customary practice and thus eventually became binding legal obligations of international law that were subsequently embodied in treaties and are therefore "hybrid" law, such as customary diplomatic privileges and immunities.[126] (7) Universal jurisdiction as a common basis for exercising international or national jurisdiction over crimes "so harmful to international

123 See Theodor Meron, 'The Martens Clause, Principles of Humanity and the Dictates of Public Conscience' (2000) 94 *American Journal of International Law*, 78. Also, see above n 7, the "Law of Geneva." I believe this law should be enforced, if necessary through judicial review, indictments, and trials, as a further way to "ensure" its increasing respect. The age of impunity for war crimes and other atrocities must end...

124 See Christopher C. Joyner, "Legal Implications of the Concept of the Common Heritage of Mankind" (1986) 35 *International and Comparative Law Quarterly* 190-199. (providing an example of the debate on the legal status of the global commons.) Of course, some contest the status of the polar caps.

125 See *The Atlantic Charter*, at ¶7, above n 3.

126 See Thomas Boudreau, "A New International Diplomatic Order," 24 *Occassional Paper* (Stanley Foundation of Iowa, 1980). (Published when I was a graduate student at the Maxwell School at Syracuse University.)

interests that states are entitled—and even obligated—to bring proceedings against the perpetrator…Human right rights abuses widely considered to be subject to universal jurisdiction include genocide, crimes against humanity and torture."[127] (8) In addition, the manifold domestic laws making social life possible, such as outlawing murder, robbery, and the like that are found in common across many, if not most, national or local jurisdictions in the world.[128] Specifically, as evidenced, the fiduciary promises made by governments, especially during wartime when such governments are in mortal danger, essentially create public, resulting, implied, or even executory fiduciary norms, interests, or relationships to their own and other peoples concerning the (government's) legal obligations to act or fulfill a ***legal*** promise in the future. However, this is dependent on the specific circumstances of their founding or subsequent applications by domestic courts. (9) Jurisprudence and the writings of jurists or scholars that courts throughout the world *commonly accept* as descriptive or definitive. These are only some of the main areas where common or shared international legal duties, norms, and fiduciary interests exist under the law of nations. The important point here is that in keeping with the classical, yet largely aspirational concept of *jus gentium* in ancient times, there is now a historically grounded law of nations *common to humanity* that orginated out of the agony of World War II, which has developed and is still evolving in courtrooms and jurisdictions across the globe.

IV

The Law of Nations and a Fiducary International Legal Order: Climate Change and the Atmosphere as a Common Trust

Of course, a fiduciary international legal order common to humanity is not a new phenomenon. Since at least after the time of Grotius and the publication of his *Mare Nostrum* (1609), the principle of freedom of the seas has been recognized as part of

---

127 See Princeton Univ., *The Princeton Project on Universal Jurisdiction, Program in Law and Public Affairs* (2001); See also Stephen Macedo, (ed.), *Universal Jurisdiction and the Prosecution of Serious Crimes Under International Law* (Univ. of Pennsylvania Press, 2006).

128 See Thomas Boudreau, *Law of Nations: Legal Order in a Violent World.* (Unpublished, forthcoming)

international law.[129] Since Grotius, the idea that *the global commons belongs to everyone*—including of the oceans, atmosphere, Antarctica, and near outer space—has been increasingly recognized, though also hotly contested. The modern law of nations simply expands upon and makes fully explicit this traditional and implicate fiduciary international legal order, which seeks to recognize, maintain, and even restore some of the most powerful forces on or above Earth—the global commons, especially the Earth's atmosphere—for present and future generations.

In this regard, it is important to note that the law of nations, like the doctrine concerning freedom of the seas, is capable of evolution and growth within this traditional fiduciary legal order. This is especially true of the Charter of the UN and the legacy principles of human rights, self-determination, trusteeship, and collective security that it contains. For instance, the practice of UN peacekeeping that is not mentioned in the charter is an accepted outgrowth of its primary mission to maintain international peace and security. In short, normative evolution as the outcome of experience is the life of the law.

The importance of such evolution is due to increasing and significant threats to international peace and security that are emerging from potentially catastrophic climate change, as the International Panel on Climate Change (IPCC) has documented.[130] Space limitations here do not permit a thorough review of scientific evidence for human contributions to climate change, nor do they allow for a detailed review of the legal argument that the UNGA might possess the legal power to monitor and maintain the global commons, beginning with the Earth's atmosphere. I argue this in my forthcoming book, entitled the *Law of Nations: Legal Order in a Violent World.* Even so, a few words on this critical topic facing the world should be ventured, especially in view of growing droughts and dangers posed by climate change worldwide. For this reason, this section is probably the most important of the essay.

As argued above, the Charter of the UN was a direct result of promises made to Allied peoples during World War II, especially the Moscow Declaration (1943). As such, it is a

[129] Hugo Grotius, *The Free Sea* (Liberty Fund, Inc., 2004). Also, see Christopher C. Joyner, *Antarctica and the Law of the Sea* (Martinus Nijhoff Publishers, 1992) Robin Churchill and Vaughan Lowe, *Law of the Sea* (Juris Publishing, Inc. 3rd ed. 1999).

[130] See, e.g.: *Intergovernmental Panel on Climate Change (IPCC)* (2014) Contribution of Working Group III to the Fifth Assessment in 2014. Some political or economic pundits disagree with the emergent worldwide scientific consensus concerning human contributions to global climate change. Such politically inspired denial is simply ideological fiddle playing while the world burns. See <http://www.ipcc.ch/news_and_events/outreach.shtml>, passim.

hybrid document consisting of treaty and trust law. The idea of trusteeship was in fact central to the founders of the UN, especially since many of the founders and colonized subjects anticipated the end of European colonialism under the tutelage of the new organization.[131]

To achieve this, the charter established an international trusteeship system and the Trusteeship Council, which is one of the six main organs of the UN.[132] Although decolonization occurred largely outside the auspices of the UN, the fiduciary foundations of the UN Charter may provide an unanticipated basis for addressing global climate change, especially if the global commons are involved. The legal argument for doing so is summarized and inevitably simplified as follows. First, the UNGA could make specific recommendations (Article 13) to "promote the progressive development of international law and its codification" concerning the need to monitor, maintain, and restore the Earth's atmosphere as a global trust for present and future generations.[133] Specifically, based on Articles 16 and 85 of the UN Charter, the UNGA can pass a nonbinding resolution explicitly recognizing the "area" of the Earth's atmosphere as a *global trust* and establishing the principle concerning the *proportionate responsibility* of all states to ensure *its timely restoration* to a minimum of 350 Parts Per Million (PPM) levels of carbon dioxide (CO^2). In short, such a resolution should contain the following three basic legal principles of fiduciary law to guide subsequent UNGA deliberations and possible ensuing treaty negotiations on climate change that could make this resolution into binding law. The first principle represents what already exists, though in an implicate form:

1) *Recognize the Earth's atmosphere as a global trust belonging to all.* The Earth's atmosphere as a global commons is essential to all life on the planet; yet, its legal status as a global trust still needs to be recognized and reaffirmed in order to allocate proportionate

---

131 This was clearly President Roosevelt's idea and intent. See above n 35 and 46. For a personal account of American efforts to establish a trusteeship system at the San Francisco Convention, see Brian Urquhart, *Ralph Bunche: An American Odyssey* (W.W. Norton & Co., 1993). Mr. Ralph Bunche was clearly aware of the aspirations of colonial subjects for freedom and self-determination, which were promised during the war, and tirelessly worked as part of the United States delegation for the trusteeship system during the drafting of the charter in San Francisco. For the Moscow Declaration, see *US Department of State Bulletin* (1943) 9, 308, Avalon Project, <http://avalon.law.yale.edu/wwii/moscow.asp> at Aug. 16, 2012.

132 See above n 3.

133 Boudreau et. al, "The Earth Atmosphere as a Global Trust: A New Role for the United Nations Environmental Trusts (UNETs)" (2013) *Publication of Global Trust Project.* Circulated to UN Diplomatic Community, 2013-15.

responsibility concerning its restoration and preservation for present and future generations, as part of the common heritage of humanity.

2) Second, the resolution simply recognizes that *all member states have a proportionate responsibility to monitor, maintain, and restore the atmosphere as a global trust for present and future generations. Member states that historically contributed the most greenhouse gases (GHG) to the atmosphere have the greatest proportionate responsibility to remove these from the common global atmosphere used by all and develop the technologies or green methods to do so.* In this sense, governments are trustees, while the peoples of the world are both trustors and beneficiaries of the Earth's atmosphere as a global trust.

The global commons, such as the Earth's atmosphere, belongs to all, and no one state has the right to abuse it for its own purpose or profit. In particular, proportionate responsibility requires that the "Most Industrialized Or Polluting States" (MIOPS) that have historically contributed the majority of GHGs to the global atmosphere must *be the first* to take immediate steps and act collectively *to restore the Earth's atmosphere to 350 PPM.*[134] The MIOPS, which have collectively and *historically* placed over 50% of CO^2 in the global atmosphere owned by all, are the following nations: the United States, China, Russia, and Germany.[135] The MIOPS can each use their own uniquely tailored portfolio of mitigation methods to restore the atmosphere and accomplish this urgent and historic priority of humanity.

3) *Third, the UNGA resolution should call for the RESTORATION of the Earth's atmosphere as a global trust to 350 PPM of CO^2 as the most urgent and immediate challenge facing humanity.*[136] The immediate challenge is to reduce the amount of CO^2 in the atmosphere until it is below the recently "achieved" benchmark of 400 PPM. The peoples of the world can do this if mobilized through UNGA leadership, though the collective ability of peoples to achieve such an immediate reduction is likely to degrade quickly over time as the impact of climate change and economic or political instability increase during the coming years. Thus, there is an overwhelming need for immediate action in all possible fronts and

---

134 Boudreau, above n 130.

135 Duncan Clark, "Which Nations are the Most Responsible for Climate Change?" *The Guardian* (UK), Apr. 21, 2011.

136 James Hansen et al, "Doubling Down on Our Faustian Bargain." *The Huffington Post* (online), Mar. 31, 2013. < http://www.huffingtonpost.com/dr-james-hansen/doubling-down-on-our-faustian-bargain_b_2989535.html>; James Hansen., et al., "Target atmospheric CO^2: Where should humanity aim?" (2008) 2 *Open Atmospheric Science Journal.*, 217-231.

forums, including in the UNGA, until the danger has been successfully addressed and overcome.

Based upon Articles 16 and 85 of the UN Charter, the UNGA can achieve the goals of this resolution by also approving a single trusteeship agreement that recognizes the "area" (Article 85) of the Earth's atmosphere as a global trust. This would initiate the United Nations Ecological Trusts (UNETs). Once created, the UNGA as a whole can administer UNETs or can delegate this responsibility to a subsidiary organ, as provided by the UN Charter. Although the ability to restore the atmosphere still exists, it is likely to rapidly degrade in coming decades as the result of the rampaging impacts of climate change

At the same time, all member states share this proportionate responsibility and must become fully engaged in ongoing efforts to ultimately restore the Earth's atmosphere to the stable levels of 350 PPM of CO^2. Simply stated, there will probably be little to no sustainable development possible in the future if member states, starting with the MIOPS, fail to reverse climate change by restoring the Earth's atmosphere to sustainable levels for life in the future.

Current United Nations Framework Convention on Climate Change (UNFCCC) talks to cut carbon emissions are important and must continue. At the same time, successfully addressing different issues requires different forums in order to avoid the hopeless intertwining of complex issues. Hence, the UNFCCC should focus on carbon cuts and UNETs should focus on carbon sequestration and other mitigation methods designed and developed to remove CO^2 from the global atmosphere. Moreover, restitution efforts could be pursued through the ICJ. Naturally, there is potential legal and political overlap between these three potential spheres of action; in view of the urgency of the hour, all three forums should be tried simultaneously until one or all are proven to work effectively.

Such restoration efforts, broadly defined to include necessary research and development and subsequent implementation, can also create thousands of jobs throughout the world.

So, the UNGA can lead the world in efforts to restore the global atmosphere, which will require the sequestration or capture of carbon, which is already in the atmosphere in concentrations of well beyond 400 PPM. There are many promising carbon sequestration techniques, such as carbon capture using the common mineral olivine, carbon farming, or the proven "iron hypothesis," which should be integral parts of any country's overall portfolio of carbon cuts, carbon sequestration, reforestation, and conservation. No single method is going to accomplish all necessary achievements in this critical regard if the world is to act in time.[137]

One promising development is the growing social and political movement to keep fossil fuels in the ground. However, enormous economic interests and global demands for energy make this approach rather precarious if used alone. Therefore, trying *all possible and practical approaches* is imperative to avert catastrophic climate change. Acting independently as the *only* global forum addressing climate change, the periodic and slow-moving UNFCCC may not be equipped to accomplish this increasingly daunting task at the necessary pace. If so, there is a pressing need to rapidly develop other options and forums to compliment UNFCCC negotiations and the Paris Agreement (2015). The UNGA and UNETs are two such options that could be swiftly employed in a move that Gandhi might have called truly imperative "Experiments with Truth."

No Second Chances: Annual UNETs Meetings on Climate Change

One such "experiment" could be employing continuous UNETs diplomacy until the danger of climate change is finally overcome. For instance, consistent with Article 20 of the UN Charter, the UNGA should meet in yearly emergency sessions every spring until it has achieved goals for sustainable development by reversing human-induced climate change.[138] Furthermore, in accordance with the powers of the UNGA provided by Article 13 of the UN Charter concerning its responsibility to promote the "progressive development of international law," the UNGA can continually encourage compliance and the needed innovation in carbon conservation or sequestration by drafting the appropriate treaties necessary to allocate short- and long-term legal proprietary responsibility for cleaning, monitoring, and maintaining the global atmosphere by all member states. As a global organization with the largest diplomatic community in the world, the UNGA can help mobilize the necessary research and development of policies,

137 For olivine sequestration, see http://www.ldeo.columbia.edu/gpg/projects/carbon-sequestration. For carbon farming, see http://www.marincarbonproject.org/carbon-farming. For ocean sequestration, see http://earthobservatory.nasa.gov/Features/Martin/martin_4.php. Plus-Caroline Dopyera, "The Iron Hypothesis" *Earth Magazine*, Oct. 1996. http://www.palomar.edu/oceanography/iron.htm.

138 IPCC, 2014, above n 127.

programs, and technologies during these special sessions to accomplish greater efficiencies in all possible mitigation methods, including healthy carbon *sequestration and possibly "in stratosphere" and space-based solar screening.* The IPCC stated in 2014 that carbon sequestration could now be considered part of the process; if so, the apparent rule in this regard that should guide the subsequent development of legal norms and policies is that *no such technologies should be deployed if the damage that they cause to the global environment is greater than that of continuing, unabated climate change.* In view of the dangers the world population collectively faces, this clearly leaves a large and growing amount of room for experimentation and leverage, and thus even controversial steps should be immediately tested and implemented, when practical, to help curtail the rising threat.

Another possible Gandhian "Experiment with the Truth" is to reconstitute the Trusteeship Council consisting of all member states of the UNGA (Art. 86) to administer UNETs during such special sessions. If this occurs, the reconstituted Trusteeship Council would presumably have legal powers determined by a specific trusteeship agreement (Article 87, Para. D) to help enforce its policies and decisions.

So, given the advancing danger, the increasingly empty arguments that carbon sequestration is unethical must be measured by the unabated and ongoing damage to the Earth as a whole, including its ecological systems and species, that is likely to occur *if nothing changes or nothing is done* to arrest the upward climb of CO^2 and other GHGs in the global atmosphere. In short, using purist moral arguments against carbon sequestration are simply too late, and should be measured against *complete inaction.* After all, given the reality of increasing CO^2 and other GHGs in the atmosphere, disaster is likely to follow if these GHGs are not stabilized and reversed before more irreversible damage is done to the Earth's ecology. The answer is not to avoid new approaches, but rather to test and use the ***protean possibilities*** available via the UN Charter. Failing to do so in view of the oncoming danger seems surreal at best, and grossly negligent at worst; the problem of climate change is not going to go away with wishful thinking or disgraceful denial.

In view of this dramatically increasing danger due to advancing climate change, the real ethical question becomes whether or not *everything* that is morally responsible and legally possible is being done to stop and reverse global climate change. It is already late in the process to be taking action, and much has already been lost or is likely to be lost soon. Thus, reversing climate change and *restoring* the Earth's atmosphere as a global commons that belongs to all is a great moral and legal challenge of the present age.

Humanity as a whole, as represented by the UNGA, can meet this historic challenge of reversing global climate change by acting now to mobilize global resources, reverse climate change, and restore the Earth's atmosphere as a global trust. If no action is taken now, there will not be a second chance.

NFCCC and UNETS: Dual-Track Climate Negotiations

Creating a fiduciary legal framework for the Earth's atmosphere is complementary to, not competitive with, ongoing UNFCCC negotiations to cut carbon emissions, which have been continuing since Rio (1992). Yet, in an alarming development, levels of CO^2 in the atmosphere have now surpassed 400 PPM, despite over 20 years of post-Rio conferences on carbon cuts. Thus, there is an urgent need to try a new diplomatic track as well.[139] Specifically, the UNGA can initiate a sustained, "in-place" second track or set of climate negotiations. By initiating UNETS, the UNGA can create an important new structure and process for reversing human-induced global climate change, which the IPCC has recently recognized as a growing imperative for collective survival.

From a legal point of view, these critical steps aboveare fully consistent with the relevant articles of the UN Charter.[140]As presented, the Charter of the UN has its fiery origins in the same fiduciary promises made to the peoples of the Allied powers during World War II. Essentially, it is part and parcel of the fiduciary foundations of modern international law. Because of this legacy, the charter provides a legal basis for the formation of UNETs to help preserve and perpetuate the Earth's atmosphere as a global trust.

Such are some of the *protean possibilities* revealed by the promises the UN made to peoples around the globe to cultivate a peaceful world after World War II. The Charter of the UN has its foundations in the promises made to the Allied and other peoples of the world during World War II. Thus, it is fully consistent with the fiduciary foundations of the charter to preserve and perpetuate the common heritage of humanity in the future. Even so, diplomats, politicians, and scholars continue to think in terms of an outdated

---

139 David Biello, "400 PPM: Carbon Dioxide in the Atmosphere Reaches Prehistoric Levels," *Scientific American*, May 9, 2013. Also, see, <http://www.ipcc.ch/news_and_events/outreach.shtml>, passim.
140 IPCC, 2014, *above*, ftnote, 127. Also, see, <http://www.ipcc.ch/news_and_events/outreach.shtml>, passim.

mindset that originated when the world was thought to be flat. So, thinking and acting anew is desperately necessary in order to help preserve the Earth for future generations.

V

Conclusion: The Leviathan and the Law

> "People like myself want not a world in which murder no longer exists…but rather one in which murder is not legitimate."
>
> Albert Camus, Nobel Laureate
> *Neither Victims nor Executioners*

This essay has examined the origins of the new law of nations in promissory declarations and wartime charters, beginning with the Atlantic Charter, that the Allied powers agreed to in their initially desperate and eventually successful effort to defeat the Axis powers. These documents were critical in establishing the new law of nations out of the crucible of the bloodiest war in human history because World War II was a time of unprecedented mortal danger to Western democracies. The war began in 1939, and the Axis powers seemed to be winning almost worldwide for the first few years. In response to unique historical, political, and military forces interacting as the war unfolded and grew in fury, especially in late 1941 and early 1942, a new fiduciary law of nations began to emerge in response to mortal threats to the Allied cause due to the aggression, atrocities, and early military successes of the Axis powers.

This is not to say that the creation of a law of nations was an intentional or deliberate war aim; rather, the emergence and development of the law of nations was due to these several significant forces that engaged with and reinforced one another as the war progressed. President Roosevelt and his administration were particularly determined to articulate a set of war aims from the very beginning, even before the official entry of the United States into the war, indeed promising that which President Wilson was only able to deliver in word—namely, self-determination and human rights for all peoples. President Roosevelt even tried to incorporate his four freedoms into the Declaration of [the] UN, signed in Washington, D.C. on January 1, 1942 at a time when it appeared that the Allied powers were losing the war. The Allies, including the Soviet Union, were eager for United States participation in the war in Europe, and thus agreed to these principles, which set the stage for the subsequent emergence and evolution of a modern law of nations. Allied leaders and peoples hoped that these legal innovations or declarations would help prevent the emergence of another lawless Leviathan, like the devastating Nazi regime in Germany, from emerging in the future. In particular, the law of nations and two hybrid treaty and trust documents—the UN Charter and the Nuremberg Charter—embodied many of the promises made to the peoples of the world, though in vague terms, like an executory trust to be fully redeemed in the future. Even so, the UN Charter clearly intended to outlaw, prevent, or punish the unilateral use of violence by a state against its own or other peoples.

I have argued in the preceding pages that the very fabric of a state's legal legitimacy is determined by its observance of the law of nations, especially fiduciary or *erga omnes* norms. This applies not only to interactions with other states, but first and foremost to its own people as well. In fact, in view of the horrors of the war, human costs around the world, and the unparalleled Holocaust of World War II, *it must be emphatically argued that observance and promotion of this new law of nations is the basic legal precondition for the existence and exercise of legitimate state authority or power. This is especially true of the post-World War II legally binding ban on the unilateral use of force by the state against its own or others peoples, except in cases of self-defense against armed attack*. Failure to observe this fundamental ban, such as the United States' unprovoked invasion of Iraq in 2003, should result in legal action against state leaders and civilian advisors in the executive branch. Thus, it is ultimately the responsibility of a nation's judiciary to ensure that its government and state respect and observe the law. This is admittedly a rare and difficult task. However, failure to do so passes this right and responsibility to other national or international judiciaries, who are then obliged to bring to justice those who are guilty of violating the law of nations and other *erga omnes* norms or committing war crimes and crimes against peace or humanity.

Yet, governments can sometimes act tenaciously, so the progression of human rights law as part of the law of nations is likely to always be tenuous and problematic, especially at first. If the past is precedent, states may unquestionably seek to maximize their own unregulated power. If so, each unique jurisdiction of a people will struggle tremendously in the coming years between preserving the unchecked power of the state or recognizing anew the fiduciary and international rights of the human being. As part of this, even the mere existence of a new law of nations could be hotly contested, or even denied. As such, this struggle—which has already commenced—could continue far into the future, as states seek to escape legal limits that the World War II revolution has imposed in the international legal order. Meanwhile, the people or nation of each jurisdiction would attempt to reaffirm and recognize anew the rights that they possess in common with all other nations on the planet.

So, a contest between raw power and the rule of law could be waged, even as the world faces unprecedented challenges due to climate change and the other "converging crisis" of the 21st century.[193] As this paper has evidenced, the judiciary of national and international jurisdictions has a critical role in deciding the ultimate scope and significance of the law of nations. In particular, the national courts of each unique jurisdiction and its people as distinct jural communities must uphold the law of nations in their own and other lands. Thus, current and future judges in national, transnational, or intergovernmental jurisdictions represent the world's final, strongest hope, and may be solely capable of victory in the ongoing struggle between the ageless Leviathan and the law.[141]

[141] See James Howard Kunstler, *The Long Emergency*, (Grove Press, 2005).

CHAPTER 2

FRANCIS BIDDLE AND THE NUREMBERG LEGACY: WAKING THE HUMAN CONSCIENCE

Tara Helfman

Introduction

On October 1, 1945, former United States Attorney General Francis Biddle embarked for Europe on the *Queen Mary*.[1] The weather was unseasonably hot and the boat was filthy, covered in graffiti left by soldier transports. Only the day before, Biddle was being fêted in Washington, D.C., where he had been sworn in as the United States member of the International Military Tribunal for the Trial of German Major War Criminals, the Nuremberg Tribunal.[2] Now, he was venturing to war-ravaged Germany to help oversee what President Harry S. Truman would call "the first international criminal assize in history."[3] Biddle was accompanied by his advisors, Assistant Attorney General Herbert Wechsler and Quincy Wright of the University of Chicago.[4] The men were already vigorously discussing the difficult task at hand. Wright was concerned that the legitimacy of the tribunal would be undermined by claims that the legal principles to be applied were generated *ex post facto*.[5] "It seems to me," Biddle wrote:

---

[1] Francis Biddle Collection of International Military Tribunal Nuremberg Trial Documents and Related Material, Syracuse University, New York (Biddle Collection) Box 1, Journal, 2 October 1945. Two works identify the ship as the *Queen Elizabeth*. See e.g. Joseph E. Persico, *Nuremberg: Infamy on Trial* (Penguin Books, 1994) 77; Ann and John Tusa, *The Nuremberg Trial* (Atheneum, 1984) 116. However, in his own journal, Biddle identified it as the *Queen Mary*.

[2] Biddle Collection, above n 1, Box 1, Journal, Oct. 2, 1945.

[3] *US Department of State Bulletin*, Vol. 15 (Oct. 27, 1946) 755.

[4] From 1944 to 1946, Wechsler served as Assistant Attorney General in charge of the war division. He was a member of the Columbia faculty throughout his career, also serving as director of the American Law Institute for 21 years. In Memoriam: Herbert Wechsler, 1909-2000, *American Law Institute Reporter* (2000), American Law Institute, <http://www.ali.org/ali_old/R2204_Wechsler.htm>, at Aug. 16, 2012; Tamar Lewin, "Herbert Wechsler, Legal Giant, Is Dead at 90," *New York Times*, Apr. 28, 2000. During World War II, Quincey Wright served as an advisor on international law to the Department of State and the Foreign Economic Administration. "Dr. Quincy Wright, 79, Is Dead; Authority on International Law," *New York Times*, Oct. 18, 1970, 92. He subsequently served as president of the American Society of International Law from 1955 to 1956. The American Society of International Law Presidents Gallery, <http://www.asil.org/asilpresidents.html>, Aug. 18, 2012.

[5] Biddle Collection, above n 1, Box 1, Journal, Oct. 2, 1946.

> …that we can state that we are bound by and cannot examine the instrument under which we are acting, particularly after we have taken an oath so to act – but that we are not thereby excluded from pointing out the large body of international law existing in 1939. Our opinion must at least have its roots in the past even if its fruits are to ripen in the future.[6]

This chapter offers new insights into the legal and historical significance of the Nuremberg Tribunal as gleaned from Biddle's personal papers. It is well known that Nuremberg serves as the juridical touchstone of modern international criminal law. Nearly every work on the subject mentions the tribunal's significance for the development of international criminal law.[7] Drawing on primary sources, particularly the papers of Francis Biddle and meeting notes of the tribunal,[8] this chapter reveals that the members were acutely aware that the proceedings at Nuremberg represented an important pivot point in the history of international law, and that they managed the proceedings accordingly.[9] Biddle knew that far more was at stake at Nuremberg than the fate of the 22 Nazi defendants on trial. The future of international criminal law was also in the tribunal's control.

It was in this vein that, while sailing to Europe, Biddle asked Wright "to let [Biddle] have, briefly, the principles of international law [Wright] would like to see established"[10] by the tribunal. Wright responded as follows:

---

6 Ibid. Hans Kelsen took the stance that [t]he judgment rendered by the International Military Tribunal in the Nuremberg Trial cannot constitute a true precedent because it did not establish a new rule of law, but merely applied preexisting rules of law defined by the International Agreement concluded on August 8, 1945, in London[.] "Will the Judgment in the Nuremberg Trial Constitute a Precedent in International Law?" (1947) *International Law Quarterly* 153, 154.

7 Ruti G. Teitel has noted that the period immediately following World War II was the heyday of international justice. "Transitional Justice Genealogy" (2003) *Harvard Human Rights Journal* 73. See also Michael J. Kelly and Timothy L.H. McCormack, "Contributions of the Nuremberg Trial to the Subsequent Development of International Law" in David A. Blumenthal and Timothy L.H. McCormack (eds), *The Legacy of Nuremberg: Civilising Influence or Institutionalised Vengeance?* (Martinus Nijhoff Publishers, 2008) 101, 103 (It is hardly surprising, then, that as the first champion of the principle of individual criminal responsibility for violations of international law, Nuremberg retains an exalted status.).

8 The Special Collections Research Center of the Syracuse University Library in New York houses the Francis Biddle Collection of International Military Tribunal Nuremberg Trial Documents and Related Material. The collection consists of 19 boxes of documents, including personal notes and correspondence, meeting minutes and notes, draft opinions, photographic evidence, and scrapbooks.

9 M. Cherif Bassiouni, "The 'Nuremberg Legacy'" in Guénaël Mettraux (ed), *Perspectives on the Nuremberg Trial* (Oxford Univ. Press, 2008) 577, 583.

10 Biddle Collection, above n 1, Box 1, Journal, Oct. 3, 1945.

1. The definition of crimes in Article VI of the protocol is declaratory of pre-existing international law.
2. Individuals are subjects of international law in the sense that international law confers upon them certain rights and holds them liable for certain crimes.
3. The individual cannot avoid responsibility for his acts on the ground that they were authorized by a government of the State for which the government purporting to act lacked power under international law to give such an authorization.
4. States lack power under international law to authorize the exercise of rights of war except in necessary self defense or as permitted by appropriate international procedures.[11]

In exploring Biddle's role on the Tribunal, this chapter also examines how Nuremberg fulfilled Wright's ambitions for international law.

Release, Summary Punishment, or Trial?

Even before the war was over, the Allies were preparing to address the systematic atrocities that Nazi Germany had perpetrated. The question was not whether those responsible for the war and its atrocities should be held accountable for their conduct; rather, the question was how to do so. "There were three different courses open to us when the Nazi leaders were captured: release, summary punishment, or trial," wrote Henry L. Stimson, Roosevelt's Secretary of State. "Release was unthinkable; it would have been taken as an admission that there was here no crime."[12] Thus, the remaining options were summary punishment or trial. The United States Office of Strategic Services (OSS), which was the precursor to the Central Intelligence Agency, was ready for either course. Throughout the war, OSS personnel had been on the ground to collect evidence of Nazi repression, murder, torture, rape, persecution, concentration camps, and a litany of other Holocaust-era horrors in anticipation of a post-war reckoning.[13]

---

[11] Ibid.

[12] Henry L. Stimson, "The Nuremberg Trial: Landmark in Law," *Foreign Affairs*, Jan. 1947, 179.

[13] Michael Salter, *US Intelligence, the Holocaust and the Nuremberg Trials: Seeking Accountability for Genocide and Cultural Plunder*, (Martinus Nijhoff Publishers, Vol. 1, 2009) 161-220. The other Allied powers shared in this project. In January 1942, the very month that top SS brass were meeting at Wansee to discuss the Final Solution, Allied leaders declared their intention to place among their principal war aims the punishment, through the channel of organized justice, of those guilty and responsible for these crimes, whether they have ordered them, perpetrated them, or in any way participated them. *Resolution by the Allied Governments Condemning German Terror and Demanding Retribution*. Jan. 12, 1942. British and Foreign Papers, 1940-42, 144 (Her Majestys Stationery Office, 1952). The following year, the Allies established the

This section demonstrates that the path to Nuremberg was by no means a certain one. Persistent arguments regarding the legitimacy of Nuremberg have long antedated the decision to establish the war crimes tribunal; yet, adjudication was ultimately viewed as the best course of action. This section explains this decision.

In the Joint Declaration of Four Nations on General Security (Moscow Declaration), the Allies made clear their commitment to bringing war criminals to justice.[14] Issued on November 1, 1943, the declaration officially acknowledged Nazi "atrocities, massacres and executions,"[15] and pledged that the Allies would pursue those responsible "to the uttermost ends of the earth and... deliver them to their accusers in order that justice may be done."[16] In cases in which a specific territorial nexus with crimes could be established, the perpetrators would "be brought back to the scene of their crimes and judged on the spot by the peoples whom they ha[d] outraged."[17] If possible, such crimes would be dealt with in municipal legal jurisdictions.[18] Meanwhile, in cases in which offenses had "no particular geographical localization," perpetrators would "be punished by joint decision

United Nations Commission for the Investigation of War Crimes, a body that bore the name of the United Nations two years before the charter of the organization had even come into force. Timothy L.H. McCormack, "From Sun Tzu to the Sixth Committee: The Evolution of an International Criminal Law Regime," in Timothy L.H. McCormack and Gerry J. Simpson, (eds), *The Law of War Crimes: National and International Approaches* (Martinus Nijhoff Publishers, 1997) 33, 57; *United Nations War Crimes Commission: 1943-1949*, United Nations Archives, Predecessor Archives Group, PAG-3/Rev. 1, 1987, i-iii, United Nations, <http://archives.un.org/ARMS/sites/ARMS/uploads/files/Finding%20Aids/Predecessors/ag-042%20UNWCC.pdf>, Aug. 16, 2012.

14 *US Department of State Bulletin*, Vol. 9, (1943) 308, Avalon Project, <http://avalon.law.yale.edu/wwii/moscow.asp> Aug. 16, 2012.

15 Ibid.

16 Ibid.

17 Ibid.

18 From 1947 to 1949, the United Nations War Crimes Commission reported on the more significant war crime proceedings of World War II. The result was a 15-volume series, *Law Reports of Trials of War Criminals Selected and Prepared by the United Nations War Crimes Commission* (1947-49). Most of the reported trials were held in military tribunals convened by the occupying powers. Others were held in the municipal courts of liberated states (see eg *Trial of Kriminalsekretär Richard Wilhelm Hermann Bruns and two others*, Eidsivating Lahmannsrett and the Supreme Court of Norway (29 March and 3 July 1946) Vol. III 15 (torture as a war crime); *Trial of Wilhelm Gerbsch*, Special Court in Amsterdam, First Chamber (28 April 1948) Vol. XIII, 131 (defendant intentionally committed terrorism against Netherlanders and persons through whom the interest of the Netherlands was or could be harmed.) Ibid 132. The series also reported on domestic legislative measures passed for the purpose of trying war criminals (e.g. *Norwegian Law Concerning Trials of War Criminals*, Vol. III, p. 81.) According to one estimate, almost 10,000 persons had been tried for war crimes in domestic legal fora by 1950. M. Cherif Bassiouni, *International Criminal Law* (Martinus Nijhoff Publishers, 3rd ed, Vol. III, 2008) 307. By 1988, over 91,000 individuals had been tried in German courts for World War II war crimes. About 6,500 of them were convicted. Axel Marschik, *The Politics of Prosecution: European National Approaches to War Crimes* in Timothy L.H. McCormack and Gerry J. Simpson (eds), *The Law of War Crimes: National and International Approaches* (The Hague, 1997) 66, 74-5.

of the government of the Allies."[19] The question then became how that joint decision could be be made.

At the Second Quebec Conference (1944), Churchill and Roosevelt agreed that summary punishment was the appropriate course of action against high officers of the Third Reich. No trials were necessary; Germany had perpetrated unprecedented atrocities during the war, and the Allies considered the fact that the principal criminals possessed the authority to order and orchestrate them to be sufficient proof of guilt. Churchill wrote, "these persons should be declared, on the authority of the UN, to be world outlaws."[20] As such, the Allies would determine a suitable punishment. Trials were both unnecessary and inappropriate for Nazi leadership because, as Churchill argued, "the question of their fate is a political and not a judicial one."[21] According to Roosevelt's advisor Henry Morgenthau Jr., punishment ought to be exemplary and severe.[22]

The Soviet Union was an early and vigorous advocate of adjudication, not because it was committed to fair judicial processes, but because of the propagandist ends to which it could utilize a show trial on so grand a scale.[23] By January 1945, President Roosevelt had

---

[19] Above n 14.

[20] Winston Churchill, "Draft of a Suggested Telegram to be Sent by the President and the Prime Minister to Marshal Stalin" in *Foreign Relations of the United States: The Conference at Quebec, 1944*, (1972) 489 (hereinafter *Draft Churchill Memorandum*). See also Memorandum by the British Lord Chancellor (Simon): Major War Criminals, Sept. 4, 1944, in ibid 91-93. The Draft Churchill Memorandum adopts the position for which the lord chancellor advocated in his memorandum on major war criminals.

[21] *Draft Churchill Memorandum*, above n 20, 489. There was also a strategic element to this argument. By treating high-level Nazi officials differently from the majority of war criminals, he hoped to isolate the upper echelons of Nazi leadership from the masses of German foot soldiers. If the average German soldier knew that he would be afforded a fair trial in his home country, as opposed to swift and summary punishment, he would be less likely to fight as desperately as his superiors, thus preventing the prolongation of the war. Ibid 490.

[22] Morgenthau advocated for the summary execution of major war criminals by a firing squad composed of United Nations soldiers. "Memorandum from Henry Morgenthau Jr. to President Roosevelt, 5 Sept. 1944" in Bradley F. Smith (ed), *The American Road to Nuremberg: The Documentary Record* (Hoovr Inst Press, 1982) 27-28.

[23] The Soviet member of the tribunal, Major General Nikitchenko, Vice-Chairman of the Soviet Supreme Court, had presided over numerous show trials in Russia during the 1930s. Michael J. Bazyler, "The Role of the Soviet Union in the International Military Trial at Nuremberg" in Herbert R. Reginbogin and Christoph J.M. Safferling (eds) *The Nuremberg Trials: International Criminal Law Since 1945* (K. G. Saur München, 2006) 45. Indeed, Robert Jackson commented of Soviet participation, "This is not an ordinary trial. Some of the proprieties went by the way when General Nikitchenko... was made a member of the Tribunal." Biddle Collection, above n 2, Box 1, Meeting in Mr. Biddles Residence, Sunday, Oct. 21, 1945, p. 2. As early as 1942, the Soviet government was pledging to bring major Nazi leaders to trial when the war was over. Interestingly, the stated purpose of adjudication was to provide the Soviet public with the retribution they demanded through public trial and harsh punishment. Letter from V. Molotov, Soviet Commissar
for Foreign Affairs, to M. Z. Fierlinger, Czech Minister, Oct. 14, 1942, Avalon Project, <http://avalon.law.yale.edu/imt/jack01.asp#2> at 16 August 2012. One of the most startling moments at

begun leaning toward adjudication, albeit for different reasons. His advisors cautioned that summary executions of top Nazi brass would ensure their immediate martyrdom in Germany and convey that the Allies were no more respectful of law and justice than the Nazis had been. Furthermore, adjudication "would make available for all mankind to study in future years an authentic record of Nazi crimes and criminality."[24] There were lessons to be learned from the past, and a trial would preserve them for posterity. Britain remained skeptical of the propriety of a trial. Sir Alexander Cadogan wrote, "If the method of public trial were adopted, the comment must be expected from the very start to be that the whole thing is a 'put-up-job' designed by the Allies to justify a punishment that they have already resolved on."[25]

However, summary execution would have been even more distressing to public opinion. In a memorandum to the Allies on April 30, 1945, the United States made the case for adjudication.[26] It argued that "[n]o principle of justice is so fundamental in most men's minds as the rule that punishment will be inflicted by judicial action."[27] While the legal right to summarily execute war criminals existed under the laws of war, the possibility of public adjudication was preferable to the isolation of the firing squad. The war had been public; thus, the reckoning that followed ought to be public as well. A trial would serve as a deterrent for future crimes and raise international standards of conduct. By revealing the scope and scale of German atrocities and aggression, a fair public trial would underscore the moral rectitude of the Allied cause, as well as discredit totalitarianism.[28] Most importantly for the immediate future, a fair and expeditious trial would develop legal and judicial institutions in Germany, while also "bring[ing] home the truth to those Germans who remain[ed] incredulous about the infamies of the Nazi regime."[29] To

Nuremberg (and certainly the most discreditable) came when the Soviet prosecutor attempted to blame the Soviet-led massacre of nearly 15,000 Poles at the Katyn Forest on the accused. Persico, above n 1, 358-9.

24 Memorandum from Henry Stimson, Francis Biddle, and Edward R. Stettinius, Jr. to President Roosevelt, Jan. 22, 1945, Avalon Project, <http://avalon.law.yale.edu/imt/jack01.asp#2> at Aug. 16, 2012.

25 Sir Alexander Cadogan, Aide-Memoire from the United Kingdom to the United States, Apr. 23, 1945, Avalon Project, <http://avalon.law.yale.edu/imt/jack02.asp>, at Aug. 16, 2012. The British alternate for the tribunal, Sir Norman Birkett, later remarked in a different spirit that the proceedings at Nuremberg were intended to be a world object lesson, and anything which brought the importance of the trial home to the world at large, or the English public in particular, would have a positive effect on public opinion. Biddle Collection, above n 1, Box 1, Notes of Tenth Organizational Meeting (Oct. 14, 1945, 3:00 p.m.) 17.

26 Memorandum of Proposals for the Prosecution and Punishment of Certain War Criminals and Other Offenders, April. 31, 1945, Avalon Project, <http://avalon.law.yale.edu/imt/jack05.asp>, at Aug. 16, 2012.

27 Ibid.

28 Ibid.

29 Ibid.

pursue retribution for its own sake would be to squander the many opportunities that a fair trial presented for the cultivation of law, reconciliation, and peace.[30]

In the April 30 memorandum, the United States anticipated many aspirations of the system of international criminal law to which the Nuremberg Tribunal was a precursor:[31] deterrence of future crimes;[32] the expression of the world community's condemnation of criminal conduct;[33] the allocation of individual guilt;[34] the establishment of a historical record of atrocities;[35] the cultivation of a rule of law in post-conflict society;[36] and, indeed, retribution.[37] The memorandum succeeded in its immediate objective of persuading Britain to support and participate in an international war crimes trial.[38] From

---

30 Benjamin Ferencz, Chief Prosecutor of the largest murder trial in history (that of the *Einsatzgruppen*, Hitler's killing squads), framed the problem of retribution as follows: Deciding to shoot people leads to the argument of who to shoot and when to stop shooting. 'Nuremberg, A Prosecutors Perspective' in Belinda Cooper (ed), *War Crimes: The Legacy of Nuremberg* (TV Books, 1999) 33.

31 For a rich discussion of the Nuremberg Tribunal and the objectives of international criminal law, see Gerry J. Simpson, "War Crimes: A Critical Introduction" in Timothy L.H. McCormack and Gerry J. Simpson (eds) *The Law of War Crimes: National and International Approaches* (Martinus Nijhoff Publishers, 1997) 5-30.

32 Kathryn Sikkink, *The Justice Cascade: How Human Rights Prosecutions Are Changing World Politics* (W. W. Norton & Company, 2011); Payam Akhavan, "Beyond Impunity: Can International Criminal Justice Prevent Future Atrocities?" (2001) *American Journal of International Law* 7; David Wippman, "Atrocities, Deterrence, and the Limits of International Justice" (1999) *Fordham International Law Journal* 473; Johannes Andenaes, *Punishment and Deterrence* (Univ. of Michigan Press, 1974).

33 Mirjan Damaska, "What is the Point of International Criminal Justice?" (2008) *Chicago-Kent Law Review* 300.

34 Gary Jonathan Bass, *Stay the Hand of Vengeance: The Politics of War Crimes Tribunals* (Princeton Univ. Press, 2000); Steven R. Ratner and Jason S. Abrams, *Accountability for Human Rights Atrocities in International Law: Beyond the Nuremberg Legacy* (Oxford Univ. Press, 1997).

35 Lawrence Douglas, *History and Memory in the Courtroom: Reflections on Perpetrator Trials*, in David A. Blumenthal and Timothy L.H. McCormack (eds), *The Legacy of Nuremberg: Civilising Influence or Institutionalised Vengeance?* (Martinus Nijhoff Publishers, 2008) 95; Susan Haack, "Epistemology Legalized: Or, Truth, Justice, and the American Way" (2004) *American Journal of Jurisprudence* 43 (on the perils of judicial historiography); Mark Osiel, *Mass Atrocity, Collective Memory, and the Law* (Transaction Publishers, 1997). Notwithstanding the lofty aspirations of the 30 April memorandum, the French alternate for the Nuremberg Tribunal, Judge Robert Falco, objected on one occasion to the length of the tribunal's draft judgment, saying, "we are judges and not historians." Biddle Papers, Box 14, *Notes of Third Conference on Opinion* (July 17, 1946).

36 Erik G. Jensen, "Justice and the Rule of Law" in Charles Call (ed), *Building States to Build Peace* (Lynne Rienner Publishers, 2008) 119; Mark A. Drumbl, "Punishment, Postgenocide: From Guilt to Shame to *Civis* in Rwanda" (2000) *New York University Law Review* 1221.

37 Graham T. Blewitt, "The Importance of a Retributive Approach to Justice" in David A. Blumenthal and Timothy L.H. McCormack (eds) *The Legacy of Nuremberg: Civilising Influence or Institutionalised Vengeance?* (Martinus Nijhoff Publishers, 2008) 39.

38 British Memorandum, May 28, 1945, Avalon Project, <http://avalon.law.yale.edu/imt/jack06.asp>, at Aug. 16, 2012 (the United Kingdom government had become convinced of the desirability of proceeding along the general lines outlined in the American proposal). Aide Memoire from the United Kingdom, June 3, 1945. Available at <http://avalon.law.yale.edu/imt/jack07.asp> at Aug. 16, 2012 (His Majesty's Embassy are instructed to inform the State Department that His Majesty's government has now accepted in principle the United States' draft as a basis for discussion by the representatives appointed by the Allied governments to prepare for the prosecution of war criminals.).

June to August 1945, representatives of the Four Powers (the United States, the United Kingdom, the Soviet Union, and France) convened an international conference in London for the purpose of deciding the law and procedure to apply to major German war criminals. Unprecedented criminality demanded unprecedented justice.

Ex Post Facto Law?

At the heart of the offenses to confront at Nuremberg was, as Winston Churchill called it, "a crime without a name."[39] Rafaël Lemkin named it "genocide."[40] This atrocity, along with the crime of waging an aggressive war, became one of the focal points of the Four Powers' efforts in developing the International Military Tribunal. Sir David Maxwell Fyfe, then Attorney General for England and Wales, made it clear from the outset of the London Conference that legal clarity was essential to the adjudication of the crimes: "What we want to abolish at the trial is a discussion as to whether the acts are violations of international law or not. We declare what the international law is so that there won't be any discussion on whether it is international law or not."[41] Article 6 of the resulting Charter for the International Military Tribunal attempted to do precisely that, declaring that the tribunal had jurisdiction over the following offenses, for which there would be personal responsibility:

> (a) Crimes Against Peace: namely, planning, preparation, initiation or waging of a war of aggression, or a war in violation of international treaties, agreements or assurances, or participation in a common plan or conspiracy for the accomplishment of any of the foregoing;
> (b) War Crimes: namely, violations of the laws or customs of war. Such violations shall include, but not be limited to, murder, ill-treatment or deportation to slave labor or for any other purpose of civilian population of or in occupied territory, murder or ill-treatment of prisoners of war or persons on the seas, killing of

39 Quoted in William Schabas, *Genocide in International Law* (Cambridge Univ. Press, 2000) 14.

40 Lemkin was a Polish Jew who fled his homeland in 1939. He was a tireless campaigner for the development of international rules prohibiting genocide, and advised the secretary-general of the United Nations on the drafting of the Genocide Convention. Ibid at 24-30. In addition to the 6 million Jews (two-thirds of European Jewry) murdered by Nazi Germany, it is estimated that between 200,000 and 250,000 disabled, 3 million ethnic Poles, between 250,000 and 1.5 million Gypsies (250 of which were children used in a Zyklon-B experiment at Buckenwald), and 3,000 to 9,000 homosexuals were killed. Steven Lipman, Hitlers Other Victims, *Jewish Week*, May 2, 1997, 30. *See also* Gunnar Heinsohn, "What makes the Holocaust a uniquely unique genocide?" (2000) *Journal of Genocide Reseach* 411.

41 International Conference on Military Trials, Minutes of Conference Session of 29 June 1945, Avalon Project, <http://avalon.law.yale.edu/imt/jack17.asp>, at Aug. 16, 2012.

> hostages, plunder of public or private property, wanton destruction of cities, towns or villages, or devastation not justified by military necessity;
> (c) Crimes Against Humanity: namely, murder, extermination, enslavement, deportation, and other inhumane acts committed against any civilian population, before or during the war; or persecutions on political, racial or religious grounds in execution of or in connection with any crime within the jurisdiction of the Tribunal, whether or not in violation of the domestic law of the country where perpetrated.[42]

The category of war crimes was not particularly contentious during the London Conference, as it had precedents in customary international law and treaty law – namely, the Hague Convention Respecting the Laws and Customs of War on Land (1907)[43] and the Geneva Convention relative to the Treatment of Prisoners of War. (1929).[44] Under these treaties, the person, property, and dignity of civilians and prisoners of war alike were to be treated with all due care and respect. Thus the substantive content of the offense did not undergo substantial revision during the conference.[45]

When the defendants objected to the category of war crimes as *ex post facto* law, the tribunal ruled:

> With respect to War Crimes, ... the crimes defined by Article 6, section (b), of the Charter were already recognized as War Crimes under International Law [by 1939]. They were covered by ... the Hague Convention of 1907, and... the Geneva Convention of 1929. That violations of these provisions constituted crimes for

42 Agreement for the Prosecution and Punishment of the Major War Criminals of the European Axis Powers and Charter of the International Military Tribunal, Aug. 8, 1945, art. 6, 59 Stat. 1544, 82 U.N.T.S. 279 [hereinafter IMT Charter]. Available at Avalon Project, <http://avalon.law.yale.edu/imt/jack60.asp>, at 16 August 2012.

43 Convention Respecting the Laws and Customs of War on Land, 18 October 1907, 36 Stat 2277. Available at International Committee of the Red Cross, <http://www.icrc.org/ihl.nsf/full/195>, at 16 August 2012 (hereinafter, Hague Convention).

44 Geneva Convention relative to the Treatment of Prisoners of War, 27 July 1929, 118 LNTS 343. Available at International Committee of the Red Cross, <http://www.icrc.org/ihl.nsf/full/305?opendocument>, at Aug. 16, 2012.

45 An early draft proposal defined war crimes as violations of the laws, rules, or customs of war. Such violations shall include murder and ill-treatment of prisoners of war, atrocities against and violence towards civil populations, the deportation of such populations for the purpose of slave labor, the wanton destruction of towns and villages, and plunder, as well as other violations of the laws, rules, and customs of war. Redraft of Charter Submitted by British Delegation, July 23, 1945, Avalon Project, <http://avalon.law.yale.edu/imt/jack45.asp>, at Aug. 16, 2012.

> which the guilty individuals were punishable is too well determined to admit of argument.[46]

The tribunal also rejected the defendants' argument that the Hague Convention did not apply because not all the belligerents had been parties to the treaty, as required by Article 2.[47] The tribunal quickly dismissed this argument, noting, "by 1939 these rules laid down in the [Hague] convention were recognized by all civilized nations, and were regarded as being declaratory of the laws and customs of war which are referred to in Article 6(b) of the Charter."[48] In other words, by 1939, the Hague Convention's rules had crystallized into independent norms of customary international law binding on all states when the war began. Article 6(b) of the Nuremberg Charter did nothing more than incorporate war crimes *jure gentium* into the jurisdiction of the tribunal.

The category of crimes against peace was more contentious, even though it had an indirect precedent in international law under the 1928 Kellogg-Briand Pact. Parties to that treaty, including Germany, had pledged to "condemn recourse to war for the solution of international controversies, and renounce it, as an instrument of national policy in their relations with one another."[49] The pact had outlawed recourse to war unless in self-defense, effectively making warfare an unlawful method by which to execute state policy. In addition, the prohibition of wars of aggression had deep roots in customary international law, from the concern of Scholastic lawyers with just war theory to Grotian and Vattelian writings on *jus ad bellum*.[50] However, the Nuremberg Charter did not define a war of aggression and this was deliberate. The Soviets knew that they themselves might be considered guilty of crimes against peace as a result of the

---

46 Judgment of 1 October 1946, *The Trial of German Major War Criminals. Proceedings of the International Military Tribunal sitting at Nuremberg, Germany*, Part 22 (Aug. 22, 1946 to Oct. 1, 1946) 467 (hereinafter, Nuremberg Judgment).

47 Article 2 of the Hague Convention stipulates, "The provisions contained in the regulations (Rules of Land Warfare) referred to in Article I as well as in the present convention, do not apply except between contracting Powers, and then only if all the belligerents are parties to the convention." Above n 44.

48 Nuremberg Judgment at 467.

49 Treaty between the United States and other Powers Providing for the Renunciation of War as an Instrument of National Policy (Kellogg-Briand Pact), Aug. 27, 1928, 46 Stat 2343. Also available at Avalon Project, <http://avalon.law.yale.edu/20th_century//kbpact.asp>, at Aug. 16, 2012. See also J. L. Brierly, *The Law of Nations: An Introduction to the International Law of Peace* (6th ed. 1963) 406-12.

50 Stephen C. Neff, *War and the Law of Nations: A General History* (Cambridge Univ. Press, 2006) 49-82, 314-56; Richard Tuck, *The Rights of War and Peace: Political Thought and the International Order from Grotius to Kant* (Oxford Univ. Press, 1999) 51-108; William C. Bradford, "International Legal Regimes and the Incidence of Interstate War in the Twentieth Century: A Cursory Quantitative Assessment of the Associative Relationship" (2001) *American University International Law Review* 647, 666-721; John F. Murphy, *Crimes against Peace* in George Ginsburg and Vladimir Nikolaevich Kudriavtsev (eds), *The Nuremberg Trial and International Law* (1990) 121.

Ribbentrop-Molotov Pact, a secret non-aggression agreement wherein the two states divided Europe into spheres of influence.[51] So, for the sake of the charter, the Four Powers were content to compensate for gaps in the category of crimes against peace with the hazy notion of "wars of aggression."[52]

The tribunal did little to elaborate on the definition of crimes against peace, and its legal analysis of the offense is conspicuously thin. Rather than elaborate on the elements that compromise crimes against peace, the judgment left Nazi aggression to speak for itself. In a painstaking account of the course of the war, the tribunal concluded that "the aggressive designs of the Nazi Government were not accidents arising out of the immediate political situation in Europe and the world; they were a deliberate and essential part of Nazi foreign policy."[53] In almost 50 pages, the tribunal scrupulously detailed the ideological and military course of German expansionism, starting with the publication of *Mein Kampf* and proceeding through the invasions of Austria, Czechoslovakia, Poland, Denmark, Norway, France, Belgium, the Netherlands, Luxembourg, Yugoslavia, Greece, and the U.S.S.R.[54] The tribunal was careful to note the carnage that the Nazis left in their wake: the soil of Greater Germany was scarred with the ashes of the millions burned in Nazi crematoria.[55]

The charter also introduced an altogether new category of offense into international law: crimes against humanity. In order to constitute a crime against humanity, "murder, extermination, enslavement, deportation, and other inhumane acts committed against any civilian population" had to have occurred before or during the war.[56] However, the necessity of this category may not be clear.[57] Although it initially seems redundant in light

---

[51] Henry Kissinger, *Diplomacy* (1994) 359-68. For Soviet views of the definition of aggression under the Charter of the Tribunal, see Minutes of Conference Session, July 25, 1945, Avalon Project, <http://avalon.law.yale.edu/imt/jack51.asp>, at Aug. 16, 2012.

[52] In discussing the draft judgment of the tribunal, Judge de Vabres urged his colleagues to abstain from any definition because the notion of aggressive war was too dependent on the precise context in which hostilities occurred. Biddle Collection, above n 2, Box 14, Notes of Third Conference on Opinion (July 17, 1946). Biddle himself resisted elaborating on the definition of aggression on the grounds that it was dangerous, academic, and poor international law. Ibid.

[53] Nuremberg Judgment at 422.

[54] Nuremberg Judgment at 421-466.

[55] Nuremberg Judgment at 465-66.

[56] For discussion, see Antonio Cassese, *International Criminal Law* (2003) 69-71. The temporal nexus between war and crimes against humanity has begun to disappear. See text beginning at n 103 below.

[57] Ian Brownlie has written of the two, "The category of war crimes was certainly orthodox law in 1945, and crimes against humanity were to a great extent war crimes writ large." *Principles of Public International Law* (Clarendon Press, 5th ed. 2001) 566.

of the Article 6(b) prohibition of war crimes, the category was far from superfluous. Rather, it was intended to fill two jurisdictional gaps in international law. The first gap was the lack of a robust legal regime protecting civilians from deliberate harm in wartime. The second concerned the singular nature of crimes against German nationals. The category of crimes against humanity enabled the Allies to address the horrors perpetrated by Germany, within Germany, against German citizens, and in compliance with German law. It would not be enough for a Hermann Göring to defend himself by saying, "[T]hat was our right! We were a sovereign State and that was strictly our business."[58] Crimes against humanity had become the business of all states because they were proscribed by transcendent "laws of humanity, and from the dictates of the public conscience."[59]

This category of offense was most vulnerable to the charge of *ex post facto* lawmaking, and the members of the tribunal appear to have known it. It was difficult to assert that the charter was simply declaratory of existing international law while it elaborated so novel a criminal category.[60] Yet, the Allies expressed concern throughout the war that prevailing norms might not suffice to hold the enemy accountable for atrocities committed against his own people.[61] The notion of crimes against humanity represented the tribunal's most significant challenge to traditional conceptions of state sovereignty. Conduct by a state towards its own citizens within its own borders that was thoroughly permissible and, in fact, *required* by domestic law could be declared criminal under international law, and its perpetrators held to account in an international legal forum.

Antonio Cassese has suggested that this approach discomforted the judges of the Nuremberg Tribunal, as in the judgment, they shied away from addressing whether crimes against humanity constituted an *ex post facto* legal category, focusing instead on the

---

58 G. M. Gilbert, *Nuremberg Diary* (Perseus Books Group, 1961) 39.

59 Draft Showing Soviet and American Proposals (in Parallel Columns), 1945, Avalon Project, <http://avalon.law.yale.edu/imt/jack23.asp>, at Aug. 16, 2012. The phrase appears to be patterned after language in Preamble of the 1907 Hague Convention (above n. 44), which stipulates that the "belligerents remain under the protection of the rule of the principles of the laws of nations, as they result from the usages established among civilized peoples, from the laws of humanity, and the dictates of public conscience."

60 Shortly after the trial, one scholar characterized the category as a legal innovation of the first magnitude. F.B. Schick "The Nuremberg Trial and the International Law of the Future" (1947) *American Journal of International Law* 770, 785.

61 See discussion in Egon Schwelb, Crimes Against Humanity in Mettraux, 120 at 125-26. Philosopher Jean François Lyotard wrote of the Holocaust: suppose that an earthquake destroys not only lives, buildings, and objects, but also the instruments used to measure the earthquake. Cited in Marion A. Kaplan, *Between Dignity and Despair: Jewish Life in Nazi Germany* (Oxford Univ. Press, 1998) 229. In the aftermath of that earthquake, the Four Powers had to develop a juridical framework within which to make legal sense of the horrors that had just transpired.

antiquity of the category of crimes against peace.[62] Yet, memoranda that members of the tribunal had exchanged suggests otherwise. In notes recorded on March 16, 1946, Biddle wrote:

> The maxim of *nullum crimen nulla poena* is not a limitation of sovereignty and in certain circumstances and particularly in International Law it may be just for the sovereign power to treat some acts as crimes which had not been designated as crimes at the time they were committed.[63]

He was agreeing with a memorandum circulated by the French member of the tribunal, Donnedieu de Vabres, Professor of Law at the University of Paris. After an exhaustive review of the principle *nullum crimen nulla poena sine lege* from Roman antiquity to the modern era, de Vabres concluded that it was *a doctrine unique to domestic legal systems*, a doctrine that found its articulation only during periods of legal codification as a check on the power of the sovereign. If the international community wished to recognize an analogous doctrine for international law, it would have had to do so explicitly before the trials began.[64] In the meantime, to insist on applying the principle to the defendants at Nuremberg would be to disregard the higher interests of justice and the common interest of states that the tribunal was meant to serve.[65]

---

62 For discussion, see Antonio Cassese, *International Criminal Law* (2003) 69-71; ibid, *International Law* (2002) 248-49. To Henry Stimson, the notion of *ex post facto* law was an ill fit for defendants like those before the tribunal. That concept is based on the assumption that if the defendant had known that the proposed act was criminalized, he or she would have refrained from committing it. Nothing in the attitude of the Nazi leaders corresponds to that assumption; their minds were wholly untroubled by the question of their guilt or innocence. "The Nuremberg Trial: Landmark in Law" (1947) *Foreign Affairs* 179, 183.

63 Biddle Collection, above n 1, Box 14. See also the views of American alternate John J. Parker in the meeting of Aug. 19, 1946 (Maxim *nulla crimen* is not a limitation on sovereignty and does not apply here) in ibid.

64 Biddle Collection, above n 1, Box 14, Note by Donnedieu de Vabres. De Vabres went so far as to encourage the international community to codify international criminal law as soon as possible so as to remove any confusion about its substantive content. *Nous souhaitons vivement que, dans le plus bref delai possible, il s'institute une codification du droit penal international.*

65 Ibid. *Mais attender pour châtier les grands criminels de guerre que cette codification sit vu le jour, ce serait sacrificier a un scrupule, sans fondement historique ni rationnel, les exigencies supérieures de la justice et lintérêt commun des Etats.* The Russian member was far less rigorous in his approach. In a two-hour peroration to the other members of the tribunal, Nikitchenko argued that the charter of the tribunal introduced many new things in [the] field of international law, such as criminal responsibility for actions that were previously announced, but not made punishable... "[The] Tribunal [is] not an institution to protect old law and to shield old principles from violation." Biddle Collection, above n 1, Box 15, Notes from Session on Opinion, Aug. 15, 1946. In a letter to Wechsler on July 10, 1946, Biddle confided, "for all the Members arguments about *nullum crimen*, I find no improvement in the vagueness of the English mind, nor in the tight logic of the French. I sometimes feel that the Russians understand what it is all about better than any of us." Biddle Collection, above n 1, Box 1. This comment suggests a cynical approach to the issue of *ex post facto* law, but it is notable that Biddle penned the letter to Wechsler more than a week before becoming receptive to de Vabres' position. See above n 58.

Article 6(c): The Connective Clause

Article 6(c) *famously includes* the following clause: (c) "Crimes Against Humanity: ... or persecutions on political, racial or religious grounds *in execution of or in connection with any crime within the jurisdiction of the Tribunal*." This connective clause clearly intended to limit the potential scope or application of Article 6(c) to individuals who were also guilty of crimes against peace or war crimes. For the Nuremberg Tribunal, this appeared to be a determining factor in distinguishing it from any potential accusation of *ex post facto* law, since the connective clause would ensure that its application was in strict relationship to clearly established acts of aggression or war crimes. In this sense, the tribunal saw Article 6(c) as an inferential extension and elaboration of pre-existing criminal categories, since before the war, no one could have anticipated the sheer size and scope of the collective crimes of the Nazis against entire states and their peoples. In view of the vast scale of such Nazi criminal enterprizes, such an elaboration and extension was needed, though its potential application was legally limited by the Article 6(c) connective clause; specifically, only if 6(a) or 6(b) were first established in the Nuremberg Tribunal's "courtroom" could 6(c) then be applied. This provided procedural due process in the law since the factual presence and sheer magnitude of the criminal behavior had to be established before the connective clause could allow for application of the subsequent category of crimes against humanity as well. This rigorous application of the connective clause was a controlling consideration in nearly every case before the original Nuremberg Tribunal, although the necessity of the connective clause in establishing subsequent "crimes against humanity" has evolved and eroded after World War II.

Interpreting Article 6(c) appears to have been no less challenging than determining whether to apply it in the first place. In fact, the two offenses are addressed jointly throughout the ruling, which makes no meaningful attempt to distinguish them from each another. Acts categorized under the single heading of "War Crimes and Crimes Against Humanity" included: enslaving prisoners of war and civilians;[66] official

[66] Nuremberg Judgment (Hermann Göring) at 485; Nuremberg Judgment (Wilhelm Keitel) at 493; Nuremberg Judgment (Alfred Rosenberg) at 496-97; Nuremberg Judgment (Hans Frank) at 498; Nuremberg Judgment (Walther Funk) at 503; Nuremberg Judgment (Fritz Sauckel) at 515-16; Nuremberg Judgment (Arthur Seyss-Inquart) at 520; Nuremberg Judgment (Albert Speer) at 521-23; Nuremberg Judgment (Martin Bormann) at 527-28

persecution of the Jews;[67] official persecution of Poles;[68] the murder of prisoners of war;[69] orchestrating the mass deportation and extermination of Jews;[70] orchestrating the mass deportation and execution of Poles;[71] looting cultural property;[72] plunder and destruction of private property;[73] forced euthanasia of the insane, sick, and aged;[74] and the deportation and execution of political opposition.[75]

Only two defendants, Jules Streicher and Baldur von Schirach, were accused of committing crimes against humanity and not war crimes.[76] However, this did not concern the nature of their conduct, but rather that they initiated their crimes prior to the outbreak of war in 1939.[77] It was in this vein that the tribunal explained:

> With regard to Crimes Against Humanity, there is no doubt whatever that political opponents were murdered in Germany before the war, and that many of them were kept in concentration camps in circumstances of great horror and cruelty. The policy of terror was certainly carried out on a vast scale, and in many cases was organized and systematic. The policy of persecution, repression and murder of civilians in Germany before the war of 1939, who were likely to be hostile to the Government, was most ruthlessly carried out. The persecution of Jews during the

67 Nuremberg Judgment (Hermann Göring) at 487; Nuremberg Judgment (Rudolf Hess) at 488-89; Nuremberg Judgment (Alfred Rosenberg) at 496; Nuremberg Judgment (Wilhelm Frick) at 500; Nuremberg Judgment (Walther Funk) at 503; Nuremberg Judgment (Arthur Seyss-Inquart) at 520; Nuremberg Judgment (Konstantin von Neurath) at 524; Nuremberg Judgment (Martin Bormann) at 527-28

68 Nuremberg Judgment (Rudolf Hess) at 488-89; Nuremberg Judgment (Wilhelm Frick) at 500

69 Nuremberg Judgment (Joachim von Ribbentrop) at 490; Nuremberg Judgment (Ernst Kaltenbrunner) at 494;.

70 Nuremberg Judgment (Joachim von Ribbentrop) at 490-91; Nuremberg Judgment (Wilhelm Keitel) at 492-93; Nuremberg Judgment (Ernst Kaltenbrunner) at 494; Nuremberg Judgment (Alfred Rosenberg) at 496; Nuremberg Judgment (Wilhelm Frick) at 500; Nuremberg Judgment (Arthur Seyss-Inquart) at 520; Nuremberg Judgment (Martin Bormann) at 527-28

71 Nuremberg Judgment (Hans Frank) at 497; Nuremberg Judgment (Wilhelm Frick) at 500

72 Nuremberg Judgment (Wilhelm Keitel) at 492; Nuremberg Judgment (Alfred Rosenberg) at 496.

73 Nuremberg Judgment (Alfred Rosenberg) at 496; Nuremberg Judgment (Walther Funk) at 503; Nuremberg Judgment (Alfred Jodl) at 516

74 Nuremberg Judgment (Wilhelm Frick) at 500

75 Nuremberg Judgment (Wilhelm Keitel) at 492-93; Nuremberg Judgment (Hans Frank) at 497; Nuremberg Judgment (Konstantin von Neurath) at 524.

76 Streicher, the Nazi propagandist known as "Jew-Baiter Number One," was convicted of crimes against humanity for his rabid incitement of the murder and extermination of Jews, all with the knowledge that his exhortations were coming to fruition. Von Schirach was convicted of crimes against humanity for his role as the Reich's Governor of Austria in the deportation of Austrian Jewry to the ghettoes and death camps of the East. Nuremberg Judgment (Jules Streicher) at 501-2; Nuremberg Judgment (Baldur von Schirach) at 512-13.

77 For discussion, see Matthew Lippman, "Crimes Against Humanity," (1997) *Boston College Third World Law Journal*, 171 at 193-95.

> same period is established beyond all doubt. To constitute Crimes Against Humanity, the acts relied on before the outbreak of war must have been in execution of, or in connection with, any crime within the jurisdiction of the Tribunal. The Tribunal is of the opinion that revolting and horrible as many of these crimes were, it has not been satisfactorily proved that they were done in execution of, or in connection with, any such crime. The Tribunal therefore cannot make a general declaration that the acts before 1939 were Crimes Against Humanity within the meaning of the Charter, *but from the beginning of the war in 1939 War Crimes were committed on a vast scale, which were also Crimes Against Humanity;* and in-so-far as the inhumane acts charged in the Indictment, and committed after the beginning of the war, did not constitute War Crimes, they were all committed in execution of, or in connection with, the aggressive war, and therefore constituted Crimes Against Humanity.[78] (Emphasis added.)

To the tribunal, crimes against humanity and war crimes seemed to be synonymous, partially due to the legal requirement of the connection clause in Article 6(c). Crimes against humanity that occurred outside the context of an armed conflict could not constitute war crimes. However, crimes against humanity that occurred during an armed conflict might also constitute war crimes. As Section V discusses below, subsequent generations would attempt to further define and clarify the distinction between the two categories under international criminal law.

Individual Responsibility: "the very essence of a positive and moral international law"[79]

Essential to justice at Nuremberg was the establishment of individual criminal responsibility for violations of international law. Reflecting on his work on the tribunal, Biddle wrote,

> There is a moral value in fixing responsibility in a field of anonymous responsibility. A state, after all, like a corporation, is a fictitious body... Of course

[78] Nuremberg Judgment at 468.

[79] Biddle, The Nürnberg Trial in Mettraux 200, 207 (referring to the tribunal's ruling that the very essence of the charter is that individuals have international duties that transcend national obligations of obedience imposed by the individual state.)

> the representatives of a state under certain circumstances are protected under the doctrine of international comity. But authors of acts criminal under international law cannot shelter themselves behind their official positions. If the state moves outside of its competence under international law the authority to act cannot create immunity.[80]

Thus, it should not have been altogether surprising when Robert Jackson told the Americans at Nuremberg that the defendants were being cooperative. Jackson remarked, "They did not dispute the fact that crimes had been committed." He also presented a particular line of reasoning: "Their defense would be that a particular individual did not participate. They would attempt to lay everything on Hitler."[81] Holding the defendants individually accountable for their illegal conduct during the war would require the tribunal to pierce the veils of command responsibility and the act of state doctrine. Biddle was thoroughly prepared to engage with and progress such an important legal development. The following section briefly examines Biddle's role in doing precisely this, beginning with the way his experience as attorney general for the United States influenced his views on individual responsibility for violations of international law.

The Road to Nuremberg: Biddle's Decisive Wartime Contribution

Francis Biddle had served as Attorney General under President Roosevelt from 1941 to 1945. Only a few weeks after he was sworn into office, the Japanese attack on Pearl Harbor launched the United States into World War II. As Attorney General, Biddle was responsible for representing the United States government in some of the most controversial causes of the day, not least of which was the *Nazi Saboteurs* case, *Ex parte Quirin*.[82] The case involved seven German-born men who landed secretly on United States shores in 1942. German submarines had dropped them off the coasts of New York and Florida. The men made their way ashore wearing German Marine Infantry uniforms, armed with explosives, and carrying maps of strategic facilities. Disguising themselves as civilians, they set out to fulfill their orders from the German High Command: to destroy war industry facilities in the United States.[83] However, one of the

---

[80] Ibid 207.
[81] Biddle Collection, above n 1, Box 1, Notes of Meeting in Mr. Biddles Residence, Sunday, Oct. 21, 1945.
[82] 317 US 1 (1942).
[83] Ibid.

saboteurs informed the Federal Bureau of Investigation (FBI) of the plot. Ten days after the men landed, they were rounded up and taken into custody by the FBI.

The attorney general found himself in a bind. If he tried the men in federal court, he might not be able to prove the charge of attempted sabotage because the defendants were not close enough to undertaking the planned attack to meet the elements of the offense under federal criminal law.[84] Perhaps worse, he might also be required to disclose that the plot had not been foiled through capable investigative work on the part of the FBI, but through the sheer luck of one of the saboteurs becoming an informant on the others.[85] After consulting with President Roosevelt and the Department of Defense, Biddle decided to transfer the men to military custody for trial outside the regular courts. On July 2, President Roosevelt appointed a special military commission to try the men swiftly and secretly, with the trial beginning as early as the next week. Biddle would serve as prosecutor alongside Major General Myron Cramer, Judge Advocate General of the United States Army.[86]

Seven of the eight accused sought writs of *habeas corpus* from the Supreme Court of the United States, arguing that they could not be tried by a military commission while the regular courts of the United States were still open.[87] The court rejected their argument on the grounds that the accused were combatants and were therefore subject to trial by military authorities. It reasoned:

> By universal agreement and practice, the law of war draws a distinction between the armed forces and the peaceful populations of belligerent nations and also

---

84 Francis Biddle, *In Brief Authority* (Doubleday, 1962) 328.

85 The New York Times reported, "Praise for the swift and sure work of the Federal Bureau of Investigation was heard on all sides... FBI officials maintained their customary silence, refusing to comment on reports that their agents had infiltrated into the German secret service or had stationed men to watch the landing of the saboteurs." Saboteurs Face Military Justice; Inquiry Widens: Biddle Statement is Taken to Mean that Army Will Try at Least Six Invaders, *New York Times*, June 30, 1942, 1.

86 Lewis Woods, "Army to Try 8 Nazi Saboteurs: President Names 7 Generals on commission to Hear Case Beginning Wednesday," *New York Times*, July 2, 1942, 1; "Secrecy Shrouds Saboteurs Trial: Comment is Refused on the Procedure, Set by Order to Be Started Today," *New York Times*, July 7, 1942, 25.

87 This argument had its basis in the Civil War case of *Ex parte Milligan*, 71 U.S. (4 Wall.) 2 (1866), in which the U.S. Supreme Court granted the writ to a civilian in Indiana who had been sentenced to death by a military commission for subversive activities. The Supreme Court held that as long as the regular civil courts were open, Milligan, a civilian, was entitled to trial in them. The Constitution of the United States is a law for rulers and people, equally in war and in peace, the court held, and covers with the shield of its protection all classes of men, at all times, and under all circumstances. Ibid 71 U.S. 120-121.

> between those who are lawful and unlawful combatants. Lawful combatants are subject to capture and detention as prisoners of war by opposing military forces. Unlawful combatants are likewise subject to capture and detention, but in addition they are subject to trial and punishment by military tribunals for acts which render their belligerency unlawful.[88]

It is worth noting here that the military commission appointed by the president had jurisdiction over the defendants by merit of their status as combatants in time of war. The commission applied the international law of war as codified in treaties and enshrined in customary law. To Biddle, the Nuremberg Tribunal was convened in this vein:

> In the *Saboteur* case as Attorney General I was assigned to take charge of the prosecution. My mail was filled with hundreds of indignant letters suggesting that the saboteurs should be immediately shot and not tried. So too in the Nürnberg case it was urged that what is loosely termed 'political' treatment would have been appropriate – i.e. execution or expulsion to some convenient Elba, without trial... Yet all standards of justice required some measure of trial even where 'political' methods are used.[89]

The policy arguments for the trial of the German saboteurs mirror those made for the trial of Nazi war criminals at Nuremberg.[90] More importantly, though, the trial of the saboteurs was an instance in *which individuals were held judicially accountable for violations of the international laws of war.* It was a fitting prelude to Nuremberg, and perhaps one of the reasons that President Truman appointed Biddle to the tribunal.[91]

---

[88] *Ex parte Quirin*, 317 US at 31.

[89] Biddle, The Nürnberg Trial in Mettraux 200, 207 (referring to the Tribunals ruling that the very essence of the Charter is that individuals have international duties which transcend the national obligations of obedience imposed by the individual state.)

[90] Above Section I. However, while domestic due process requirements obligated the United States government to try the saboteurs, the laws of war would have permitted the Allies to summarily execute the Nuremberg defendants if they so wished.

[91] Joseph Persico has suggested that Truman chose Biddle because he felt regretful about having demanded Biddle's resignation from his position as attorney general over the phone rather than in person. While in that position, Biddle had opposed Truman's candidacy for vice president, so it was logical for Truman to appoint a more loyal person to lead the Department of Justice. Persico, above n 2, 61-63. This interpretation seems overly simplistic given Biddle's ample qualifications to serve the United States on the tribunal.

A great achievement of the Nuremberg Tribunal was signaling to the society of states that the time had come to consider regulating states' conduct toward their nationals – not only in times of war, but in times of peace as well.[92] Notwithstanding the United States' efforts to secure convictions for pre-war atrocities through conspiracy charges,[93] the tribunal declined in its judgment to hold the defendants responsible for crimes against humanity committed prior to the outbreak of the war.[94] Provided an individual's conduct occurred in time of international war, he could be held criminally liable for his conduct. Beyond that, the veil of sovereignty would remain drawn over the face of human rights violations, at least for the Nuremberg Trials.

The decades following the tribunal's efforts have become what one scholar has termed "The Age of Rights."[95] Immediately following the tribunal's judgment, the UNGA issued Resolution 95 (I), Affirmation of the Principles of International Law recognized by the Charter of the Nürnberg Tribunal,[96] directing the International Law Commission:

> To treat as a matter of primary importance plans for the formation, in the context of a general codification of offences against the peace and security of mankind, or of an International Criminal Code, of the principles recognized in the Charter of the Nuremberg Tribunal and in the judgment of the Tribunal.[97]

Consistent with the connective clause discussed above, the resultant Nuremberg Principles limited crimes against humanity to acts undertaken in conjunction with crimes against peace.[98] Nevertheless, the Nuremberg Principles would become central to the

---

92 Ratner and Abrams, above n 35, 6.

93 Biddle Collection, above n 1, Box 14, Secret Memorandum to Attorney General Tom C. Clark from Herbert Wechsler, 29 December 1944. For discussion of the crime of conspiracy at Nuremberg, see Jackson Nyamuya Maogoto, *State Sovereignty and International Criminal Law: Versailles to Rome* (Transnational Publishers, 2003) 90-95.

94 To constitute crimes against humanity, the acts relied on before the outbreak of war must have been in execution of in connection with any crime within the jurisdiction of the tribunal. The tribunal was of the opinion that, as revolting and horrible as many of these crimes were, it had not been satisfactorily proven that they were done in execution of or connection with any such crime. The tribunal therefore could not make a general declaration that the acts before 1939 were crimes against humanity within the meaning of the charter. Judgment of the Nuremberg Tribunal, above n 46, 254.

95 Louis Henkin, *The Age of Rights* (Columbia Univ. Press, 1990) 13-15.

96 G.A. Res. --95 (I), U.N. GAOR, 1st Sess., pt. 2, at 1144, U.N. Doc. A/236 (1946).

97 Ibid.

98 Report of The International Law Commission, 5 U.N. GAOR, Supp. No. 12, at 14, U.N. Doc. A/1316 (1950). M. Cherif Bassiouni has explained the relationship between these categories of offense. [T]hree charges were set forth in the Nuremberg Charter: crimes against peace, crimes against humanity, and war crimes. Crimes against humanity emerge from war crimes. The drafters were very careful in making sure that they were deemed to be an outgrowth of

progressive development of international criminal law and international human rights law after the most infamous war in human history.[99]

The Legacy of Nuremberg

In assessing the legacy of any tribunal, it is tempting to let the privilege of hindsight obscure the difficult context in which decisions were made. Too frequently, the tribunal's decision is examined for the totality of its jurisprudential achievement. So, it is hoped that this article has helped enrich the reader's appreciation of the turbulent context from which the Nuremberg Tribunal emerged, as well as the troubled context in which it operated. In particular, this article has demonstrated the seriousness with which the members of the tribunal considered the controversial issue of *ex post facto* law in applying the law of the charter to defendants. It has illustrated the energy with which the members challenged one another's views, as well as some of the compromises that resulted from this process of engagement. It has also revealed that Francis Biddle, like his counterparts on the bench, was acutely aware that the tribunal's function was not simply to adjudicate the recent past; it was also to serve as a model for the future, to progressively develop existing norms of international law, and to lay the foundation of a body of international criminal law that would enforce accountability for perpetrators of war crimes and related atrocities.[100] In this sense, the work of the tribunal was as much prospective as it was retrospective, fulfilling Biddle's vision of the tribunal as having roots in the past and fruits that would ripen in the future.[101]

---

war crimes because of their concern with the principles of legality. This is why Article 6(c) states that crimes against humanity are those crimes that were committed in connection with one of the other two crimes within the jurisdiction of the court. Although the language seems somewhat confusing, its purpose was to establish a connection with the war. "The International Criminal Court in Historical Context" (1999) *Saint Louis-Warsaw Transatlantic Law Journal* 55, 60.

99 Rich discussions of Nuremberg's effect on the development of international criminal law can be found in Ratner and Abrams, above n 35 and Reginbogin and Safferling, above n 24.

100 Hans-Heinrich Jescheck, "The Development of International Criminal Law after Nuremberg in Guénaël Mettraux" (ed), *Perspectives on the Nuremberg Trial* (Oxford Univ. Press, 2008) 408, 409. The Soviets initially (and understandably) resisted these ambitions, lest the principles enshrined at Nuremberg be turned against Stalin's own policies. The members of the tribunal were particularly cautious about the potential ends to which the Soviet Union might use the trial. Biddle wrote in his diary, "Many difficult problems. If we hold these organizations [i.e., the Gestapo and the SS] to be criminal it opens the door to the Russians – to everyone in fact – to shoot on proof of membership, referring to our judicial approval – not a very desirable result." Biddle Collection, above n 1, Box 1, Journal (Oct. 4, 1945).

101 Biddle Collection, above n 1, Box 1, Journal (Oct. 2, 1946). See discussion above at n 7.

In the decades following the Nuremberg Trials, individual responsibility for crimes against humanity expanded well beyond the limits of international armed conflict, if only due to the seemingly boundless human capacity for atrocity.[102] The category of crimes against humanity is no longer firmly tethered to the other offenses of the Nuremberg Principles. The first significant step in this direction was the Convention on the Prevention and Punishment of the Crime of Genocide, which provides that genocide, "whether committed in time of peace or in time of war, is a crime under international law which [states] undertake to prevent and to punish."[103] Subsequent treaties have stipulated that policies of apartheid and forced disappearance are likewise crimes against humanity, regardless of whether or not they accompany a state of war.[104] Both customary international law and treaties have recognized the independent character of crimes against humanity. In 1995, the International Criminal Tribunal for the Former Yugoslavia notably held the following:

> It is by now a settled rule of customary international law that crimes against humanity do not require a connection to international armed conflict. Indeed... customary international law may not require a connection between crimes against humanity and any conflict at all.[105]

This principle lies at the heart of Article 7(1) of the Rome Statute of the ICC. The statute stipulates that crimes against humanity consist of certain acts undertaken "as part of a widespread or systematic attack directed against any civilian population, with knowledge

102 Since the post-war period, states have been grappling with the Nuremberg Charter's tangled categories of "war crimes" and "crimes against humanity." See Lippman, above n 78.

103 Dec. 9, 1948, 78 U.N.T.S. 277, Art. 1.

104 International Convention on the Suppression and Punishment of the Crime of Apartheid, Nov. 30, 1973, 1015 UNTS 243; Inter-American Convention on the Forced Disappearance of Persons, June 9, 1994, OEA Doc. AG/RES. 1256 (XXIV-0/94). See also, *Draft Code of Crimes Against the Peace and Security of Mankind Seventh Report*, Mr. Doudou Thiam, Special Rapporteur, (1989) II Year Book of the International Law Commission 81, 86, ¶ 38, U.N. Doc. A/CN.4/419/Add.1 ("First linked to a state of belligerency ,.. the concept of crimes against humanity gradually came to be viewed as autonomous and is today quite separate from that of war crimes. Thus, not only the 1954 draft code but even conventions which have entered into force (on genocide and *apartheid)* no longer link that concept to a state of war.")

104 Dec. 9, 1948, 78 U.N.T.S. 277, Art. 1

105 *Prosecutor v. Dusko Tadić*, Decision on the Def. Motion for Interlocutory Appeal on Jurisdiction, Case No. IT-94-1-AR72, Oct. 2, 1995, ¶ 151. See also Guénaël Mettraux, "Crimes Against Humanity in the Jursiprudence of the International Criminal Tribunals for the Former Yugoslavia and for Rwanda," (2002) *Harvard International Law Journal* 237; Beth Van Schaak, "The Definition of Crimes Against Humanity: Resolving the Incoherence" (1999) *Columbia Journal of Transnational Law* 787.

of the attack."[106] The "attack" need not be part of a broader war; it is sufficient that civilians be unlawfully targeted by any government, be it a foreign state's or their own. The provenance of Article 7 can be directly traced to the work of the Nuremberg Tribunal. It is then fitting that Benjamin Ferencz, who prosecuted a case before the Nuremberg Tribunal when he was 27 years old,[107] remarked before the ICC last year, "The most significant advance I have observed in international law has gone almost unnoticed; it is the slow awakening of the human conscience."[108] Ferencz, by then 92 years old, was delivering the closing arguments in the case against Congolese war criminal Thomas Lubanga Dyilo.[109] The Nuremberg Tribunal was instrumental in rousing the human conscience from its wartime slumber. It has been the project of international criminal law ever since to keep that conscience attentive, responsive, and engaged. Once awakened, this collective human conscience, represented by such courts, will hopefully never slacken or slumber in the future.

---

[106] 2187 U.N.T.S. 90 (entered into force on July 1, 2002).

[107] See above n 31.

[108] "Ferencz Closes Lubanga Case for ICC" (Aug. 25, 2011) Benjamin J. Ferencz: Law Not War, http://www.benferencz.org/index.php?id=5&media=38 at Aug. 19, 2012.

[109] *The Prosecutor v. Thomas Lubanga Dyilo*, ICC-01/04-01/06, Mar. 14, 2012.

CHAPTER 3

TAMING THE FURIES: THE JUSTICE TRIAL AT NUREMBURG 1947

Stephen J. Sfekas

'Therefore, O Citizens, I bid you bow in awe to this command,
"Let no man live uncurbed by law nor curbed by tyranny,"
Thus, I ordained it now, a court, pure and unsullied...'

The Eumenides
Aeschyleus

Introduction

Between 1945 and 1949, a series of 13 trials of former German officials, officers of the German armed forces, and business leaders took place in Nuremberg, Germany. The first and most famous of the trials was the International Military Tribunal (IMT), which tried 22 men who had been identified as major Nazi war criminals, including Herman Goering, Marshalls Keitel and Jodl, Albert Speer, Hans Frank, and others. The tribunal consisted of four judges and four alternate judges from each of the major Allied powers: the United States, Great Britain, France, and the Soviet Union. In addition, 17 countries authorized the proceedings, and many sent observers.[1]

Less well known are the 12 trials known as the Nuremberg Military Tribunals (NMT), which consisted only of American judges and prosecutors.[2] These trials were structurally and procedurally different in many ways from the IMT at Nuremberg that Prof. Tara Helfman so ably analyzes and discusses in the preceding chapter. Yet, they shared the

[1] There are a number of excellent accounts of the IMT, including most notably Telford Taylor's *The Anatomy of the Nuremberg Trials: A Personal Memoir* (Random House, 1991) and Ann Tusa & John Tusa, *The Nuremberg Trial*, (Skyhorse Publishing, 2010).

[2] The best overall treatment of the 12 NMT trials are Kevin Jon Heller's *The Nuremberg Military Tribunals and the Origins of International Criminal Law*, (Oxford University Press, 2011), and Telford Taylor's *Final Report to the Secretary of the Army on the Nuremburg War Crimes Trials Under Control Council Law No. 10*, 1949. Taylor's Trial Report is an excellent near-contemporary account of the trials by the chief prosecutor in the NMT trials.

same goals of the IMT in seeking to ensure a procedurally fair and substantively just legal foundation for prosecuting individuals who have been accused of committing the most serious crimes in international or domestic legal jurisprudence.

The tribunals came into existence only for the purposes of the trial and disbanded thereafter. The judges were largely recruited from United States state courts.[3] The prosecutors were American lawyers, of whom a large number were women.[4] The rules of procedure were created for the sole purpose of these trials, although they borrowed heavily from the IMT experience.[5] Thus, in a sense, 1945 served as "year zero" in the establishment of a new legal system.

The prosecution was led by Brig. General Telford Taylor, who had been chief deputy to Justice Robert Jackson, the leader of the prosecution team in the IMT, while on leave from his duties on the Supreme Court. General Taylor and his staff had the responsibility of selecting charges and choosing defendants for the NMT cases.

Early on, Taylor decided that each trial would focus on a particular group of elites in German society, rather than on particular events or subject matters.[6] Thus, Trial I was the Doctor's Trial, which concerned medical officials who had authorized or undertaken medical experiments of doubtful scientific value or engaged in involuntary euthanasia of so-called undesirable populations. In addition, there were trials of high-ranking German officers (High Command Trial), German commanders in the Balkans (Hostages Trial), industrial leaders (Krupp Trial, I.G. Farben Trial, and Flick Trial), the senior professional civil service (Ministries Trial), special police units (Einsatzgruppen Trial), and, of course, the trial of German judges and justice officials (*United States v. Alstötter et al.*, more commonly referred to as the Justice Trial), which is the subject of this chapter.[7]

---

3 Ibid, 41–42. Federal judges were not permitted to serve. Chief Justice Vinson apparently felt that the federal judiciary had too heavy a workload to permit the diversion of federal judges to a trial overseas.

4 Ibid, 34. 10 of the 94 prosecutors were women. Sadie B. Arbuthnot, Esq., was the only woman assigned to the Justice Trial.

5 See Rules of Procedure for Military Tribunal III, February 19, 1947.

6 Taylor, above n 2, 76-77. Heller, above n 2, 47–49. As an example, no single trial focused on the Holocaust or the use of slave labor, although the Holocaust and slave labor was a factor in many of the cases (see discussion *below*). Taylor felt that by structuring each trial around a particular group, such as judges and justice officials, he could explore the degree of culpability more deeply, expose problems in German society more clearly, and simultaneously simplify the conduct and proof of the case.

7 Heller, above n 2, 85-107. The 12 trials produced 132,855 pages of transcript, from 1,300 witnesses and 30,000 documents. The judgments in the 12 trials run to 3,828 pages. Heller, above n 2. Taylor felt strongly that the record of

Taylor felt that the Justice Trial would be of particular interest to judges and lawyers because of the anomaly that judges and prosecutors of one country were trying judges and prosecutors from another country for crimes committed within the judicial process.[8] Indeed, German judges and justice officials were tried on German soil, in many cases for crimes against German citizens for acts of injustice apparently sanctioned under German law.[9]

The trial permits an exploration of the problem of what constitutes justice from the perspective both of the Americans conducting the trial and the Germans who were on trial in their capacities as judges or justice officials. Indeed, this trial can best be interpreted as an attempt to establish universal standards of justice, which would both govern the conduct of the trial and serve as a basis for accountability for the German judicial officials.

The trial poses three questions. First, was the trial procedurally fair? As the court's opinion implicitly set forth the minimum criteria for a fair trial, the trial itself establishes the test for the fairness of its own processes. This question is of particular interest because the IMT and NMT trials took place before the landmark equal protection, due process, and criminal law decisions of the Warren Court. Second, was the trial substantively fair? That is, were the defendants charged and convicted of crimes recognized as such under international law? Third, regardless of legal culpability, was justice done? Of particular interest are arguments in mitigation raised by the defendants and the subsequent impact of the NMT trials.

The thesis of this chapter is that the NMT trials in general and the Justice Trial in particular were procedurally and substantively fair. Indeed, the German defendants were, in some cases, afforded procedural protections that would not be constitutionally required under United States law until the criminal law decision of the Warren Court

---

the cases should be readily available to document the proceedings of the court; however, the sheer volume of material made it impractical to publish the entirety of the trials. Therefore, after completion of the trials, his staff combed through the transcript to compose an edited version of the most important components of the transcript, the key documents, and the final opinion. The transcripts were then published in a series entitled *Trials of War Criminals Before the Nuremburg Military Tribunals Under Control Council Law No. 10*. Volume III of the series consists of 1,250 pages excerpted from the record of the Justice Trial. All citations to the transcript of the trial come from Volume III.

8 Taylor, above n 2, 169.

9 Ibid.

almost two decades later. Similarly, the substantive charges were justified under international law despite the novelty of the charge of crimes against humanity. Finally, despite the early termination of sentences, justice was achieved.

Part II describes the development of the international war crimes program under the London Charter, Allied Control Council Law Number 10 (ACC10), and OMGUS 7. Part III recounts the trial and its aftermath. Part IV addresses the three questions posed in this introduction.

I

The London Charter, Allied Control Council Law No. 10, and Office of Military Government- Germany, U.S. No. 7 (OMGUS 7)

> "You must put no man on trial before anything that is called a court under the laws of judicial proceeding if you are not willing to set him free if not proven guilty."
>
> Justice Robert H. Jackson

The London Charter

In 1942, the governments-in-exile of nine German-occupied nations meeting at St. James Palace in London issued a call for the punishment of persons committing war crimes in their respective countries by means of "organized justice." This Declaration of St. James received little notice, but was the first call for a trial of war criminals rather than summary justice.[10]

Subsequently, the Western Allies organized the UN War Crimes Commission to investigate war crimes, including the "... bestial policy of extermination of the Jewish people in Europe."[11]

---

[10] Taylor, above n 1, 25.

[11] Ibid, 26. The term "United Nations" became the preferred term for describing the Allied powers during the war. The commission was not an arm of the modern day United Nations organization, which was created after the war. This commission would be superseded by the IMT and NMT trials and various other national tribunals, and did not play a role in the investigation of war crimes. However, under the leadership of a notable British jurist, Lord Robert

In November of 1943, the foreign ministers of Great Britain, the United States, and the Soviet Union met and issued the Moscow Declaration. This declaration provided that Italian Fascist chiefs and generals suspected of war crimes would be "... arrested and handed over to justice," and that Austria would be treated as a victim nation, not a participant in German aggression.

With respect to German war crimes, there were two provisions of note. The declaration provided the following:

> At the time of granting of any armistice to any government which may be set up in Germany, those German officers and men and members of the Nazi party who have been responsible for or taken a consenting part in the above atrocities, massacres, and executions will be sent back to the countries in which their abominable deeds were done in order that they may be judged and punished according to the laws of those liberated countries and free governments which will be erected therein.... The above declaration is without prejudice to the case of German criminals whose offenses have no particular localization and who will be punished by joint decision of the governments of the Allies.[12]

This declaration established a basic framework for war crimes trials. First, crimes committed by identifiable Germans in occupied countries would be returned to these countries for trial. Second, there would be a subset of major criminals, such as Hitler himself, whose crimes affected all of Europe, and whose fate would be settled by the major powers. As the war drew to a close, the question of what to do with the major criminals became acute. Several options were considered: (1) summary execution of up to 50,000 German offenders, a proposal Stalin offered at a dinner at the Yalta Conference, perhaps jocularly, and which Churchill strongly objected and Roosevelt did not take seriously;[13] (2) exile of the major leaders; (3) summary execution of the leading Nazis, which would remain the favored British position until the end of the London

---

Anderson Wright of Durley, the commission collected and published law reports on all of the major international and national war crimes trials after the war, including the 13 Nuremburg trials. Lord Wright wrote excellent analyses of the war crimes trials, including an overview of all the trials in the 15th volume of the series. See Law Reports of Trials of War Criminals Selected and Prepared by the United Nations War Crimes Commission, 1947-1949, vol. 1-15.

[12] Nuremburg, above n 7, Preface XX.

[13] Taylor, above n 1, 29-30.

Conference in August 1945;[14] (4) do nothing and release them; and (5) an international tribunal for the major offenders.[15]

The issue was crystallized for the Allies when word of the so-called Morgenthau plan leaked to the public. This proposal by Secretary of the Treasury Henry Morgenthau, initially endorsed by Roosevelt and Churchill, would have called for the deindustrialization of Germany and transformation of the country into a pastoral and agricultural economy. This proposal was heavily criticized, and ultimately rejected.[16] It did, however, result in intensified post-war planning. Two key developments tipped the balance towards an international trial.

The first was a memorandum proposed by Colonel Murray Bernays, Chief of the Special Projects Branch of the War Department, which proposed a trial of major war criminals but would also include a trial of criminal organizations, such as the SS. If an organization were found to be a criminal enterprize, further proceedings could take place against former members of the organization, which could be limited to disposition, as guilt would have been established by mere membership.[17]

The second key development was an appointment by Harry Truman, who became president after the death of Franklin D. Roosevelt on April 12, 1945, of Robert H. Jackson, Justice of the Supreme Court of the United States, to be the chief United States prosecutor at the war crimes trials. Truman's appointment occurred on May 2, 1945 and was one of his earliest and most inspired appointments.

Justice Jackson had experienced an extraordinary career. He met Franklin D. Roosevelt while Roosevelt was still the governor of New York, and he followed Roosevelt to Washington, D.C. after the latter assumed the presidency. Jackson held an increasingly significant number of government jobs, culminating in his service as solicitor general in 1938 and attorney general of the United States in 1940. He was appointed to the

---

14 Ibid, 29-33.

15 Ibid, 27-42.

16 See Taylor, above n 1, 29-33; Tusa and Tusa, above at location 386-465.

17 See Bernays memorandum, January 20, 1945. Truman Library website. The Bernays memorandum set forth what would be viewed as a practical way to try the massive numbers of Nazi war criminals. Although the memo would convince the United States government of the need for war crimes trials, Bernays himself played no role at Nuremburg.

Supreme Court in July 1941.[18] Most relevant was Jackson's role in *Korematsu v. United States*, 323 U.S. 214 (1944), which upheld the military order that resulted in the internment of loyal Japanese citizens of the United States in internment camps without any semblance of due process or indication of wrongdoing. Jackson wrote an eloquent and scathing dissent, denouncing the denial of due process and the use of racial and ethnic categories in the internment order.[19]

On April 13, 1945, shortly before his appointment, Jackson gave a speech before the American Society of International Law, in which he stated:

> I am not troubled as some seem to be over problems of jurisdiction of war criminals or of finding existing and recognized law by which standards of guilt may be determined. But all experience teaches that there are certain things you cannot do under the guise of judicial trial. Courts try cases, but cases also try courts.... There is no reason for a judicial trial except to reach a judgment on a foundation more certain than suspicion or current rumor.... But further you must put no man on trial if you are not willing to hear everything relevant that he has to say in his defense and to make it possible for him to obtain evidence from others.... You must put no man on trial before anything that is called a court under the laws of judicial proceeding if you are not willing to set him free if not proven guilty.[20]

In 1945, representatives of the major Allied powers – the United States, Great Britain, France, and the Soviet Union – met to determine a course of action regarding the major Nazi war criminals. The resulting charter set the tone and parameters for the IMT and NMT trials that followed, including the Justice Trial. The London Conference dealt with three categories of issues: the logistics of a trial; the charges to be brought; and the procedures, including rules of evidence to be used.

---

[18] Justice Jackson would be the last and possibly only Supreme Court justice in the 20th century who did not attend college and never completed law school. He left Albany Law School after one year, but was able to pass the New York State Bar Exam.

[19] 323 U.S. at 242.

[20] Justice Robert H. Jackson, "The Rule of Law Among Nations" (Speech delivered at American Society of International Law, April 13, 1945) <https://www.roberthjackson.org/speech-and-writing/rule-of-law-among-nations/>.

Logistics

The logistics issues were difficult, but readily resolved. The trial would be held in the Palace of Justice at Nuremberg, Germany, primarily because, unlike most German cities, Nuremberg had an intact courthouse that was connected to an intact jail and offered sufficient housing and office space to support the personnel associated with the trial. Furthermore, Nuremberg was in the United States zone of occupation. Therefore, the United States, which was the wealthiest of the Allied countries, would provide support services for the trial.[21] Additionally, Nuremberg had strong symbolic power as the site of annual Nazi Party rallies and the announcement of the Nuremberg racial laws.[22]

Language issues would bedevil all of the proceedings, particularly the IMT, as all documents and testimony had to be translated into English, French, German, and Russian from the respective language of the original. Colonel Leon Dostert of the United States Army and IBM solved the language problem by developing the technologies of simultaneous interpretation and creating the listening and recording technologies by which each participant could hear the trial in his or her own language through earphones.[23] Throughout the 13 trials, the United States Army maintained a massive staff of interpreters to translate documents into the respective languages. Telford Taylor noted in his Final Report that, at its peak, the NMT trials required a support staff of over 1,300 persons.[24]

The Charges

Although the logistics issues were complex, they were not a subject of major division among the Allies. In contrast, the choice of charges and trial procedures caused major difficulties and required weeks of negotiation to resolve. Jackson came to the conference convinced that the greatest evil, which subsumed all others, was the waging of aggressive war itself. The war crimes, Holocaust, slave labor, displacement of populations, starvation of civilians, mass destruction of property, theft of art treasures, and sexual abuse of civilians all derived from or were part of preparation for aggressive war.

---

21 Tusa & Tusa, above n 1, ch. 5; Taylor, above n 1, 61.
22 Taylor, above n 1, 61.
23 Tusa & Tusa, above n 1, 218-219. Dostert later founded what was formerly the School of Languages and Linguistics at Georgetown University. His system is in use in international proceedings to this day.
24 Taylor, above n 2, 69.

Accordingly, Jackson insisted that one charge be crimes against the peace, and the other parties agreed. (As this was not one of the charges in the Justice Trial, this shall not be discussed further.)

However, Jackson also insisted on the inclusion of a separate charge of conspiracy to wage aggressive war, as well as charges of war crimes and crimes against humanity. The conspiracy charge would be a controversial component of all of the trials. The difficulty with conspiracy as an independent charge is that although conspiracy is incorporated into the common law tradition of the United States and the United Kingdom, it is not part of the civil law tradition of France, Germany, the Soviet Union, and most of the other belligerent powers. The French in particular argued that conspiracy was not an element of the customs or usages of war or of customary international law, as it was not accepted as law by the legal system used by the majority of affected countries.[25] This issue was important because charges of crimes against the peace required the actual invasion of a country. Thus, the charge would only apply to events immediately leading up to September 1, 1939, the day that Germany attacked Poland, and the events and persons directly involved in planning and implementing the invasion.

Jackson's conception was much broader. In his view, everything leading up to the beginning of the war – including the Nazi seizure of power, the rearmament of Germany, the expansion of the army, and the persecution of Jews and political opponents in Germany – were all part of a plan leading to the initiation of war. Furthermore, subsequent war crimes were a continuation of the same conspiracy. The British shared Jackson's perspective on the law of conspiracy, but the French and Soviets strongly opposed it. The issue was resolved by an agreement that the charge of conspiracy would be limited to crimes against the peace, but would not extend to war crimes or crimes against humanity.[26]

The second problem with the charges arose out of limitations to the traditional notion of a war crime. Unlike the other charges in the indictments, war crimes related to a body of law that had developed by 1945. Prior to 1863, war crimes were primarily a matter of customary international law based on the "customs and usages of war by civilized nations." During the American Civil War, Abraham Lincoln commissioned Franz

25 Tusa, above n 1, 1761-1771, 1831-1841; Taylor, above n 1, 35-36.
26 Taylor, above n 1, 75-76.

Lieber, a legal scholar, to develop a code of conduct for Union armies to deal with Confederate armies and the hostile civilian population. The resulting code, known generally as "Lieber's Code" and more recently and appropriately as "Lincoln's Code," was incorporated into General Order Number 100.[27]

This code attempted to clarify and dictate the law of war for the first time. The code was viewed as a significant success, and European countries gradually adopted it to govern the conduct of their armed forces in times of war.[28] Lincoln's Code thereafter became one of the primary sources for the Hague Conventions on the Laws of War of 1899 and 1907.[29] Prior to World War II, there was a further modification of the code in the Geneva Convention of 1929. The laws of war as defined by these treaties had a number of important limitations, which complicated efforts to bring the defendants to justice. First, the laws of war require a war, and second, that the war be between belligerent powers.[30] Thus, the laws of war as declared in the conventions would not apply at all before September 1, 1939, nor would they apply to offenses committed by Germany in Germany or German allies. Thus, the persecution of Jews from Czechoslovakia or Austria would not be considered a war crime because both countries had been absorbed by Germany prior to September 1, 1939 and the international community had not contested the absorption. Similarly, the persecution and extermination of Hungary's Jews after April 1944 would not have been a war crime, as Hungary technically was an ally of Germany until the end of the war.

To navigate this issue, the London Conference concluded that certain offenses of a sufficiently substantial nature associated with war crimes or the waging of war would constitute crimes against humanity. Indeed, the Hague Convention notes in its preamble to the convention:

> Until a more complete code of the laws of war is issued, the High Contracting Parties think it right to declare that in cases not included in the Regulations adopted by them, populations and belligerents remain under the protection and

---

27 See John Fabian Witt, *Lincoln's Code*, (Free Press, 2012) for an excellent account of the development of General Order 100.

28 Ibid, 342-345.

29 Ibid, 349-350.

30 Hague Convention of 1899, Article II. The provisions contained in the regulations mentioned in Article I are only binding on the contracting parties in case of war between two or more of them.

> empire of the principles of international law, as they result from the usages established between civilized nations, from the laws of humanity and the requirements of the public conscience.

Thus, the conventions were not intended as a comprehensive declaration of all rules of war or "the laws of humanity, and the requirements of the public conscience." The London Conference therefore concluded that international law encompassed the offense of "crimes against humanity." However, the London Charter included an important limitation to this charge, which would change significantly in Allied Control Council Law No. 10 and OMGUS 7, which covered the NMT trials. The London Charter defined a crime against humanity as the following:

> ... murder, extermination, enslavement, deportation, and other inhumane acts committed against civilian populations, *before or during the war*; or persecutions on political, racial or religious grounds *in execution of or in connection with any crime within the jurisdiction of the Tribunal, whether or not in violation of the domestic law of the country where perpetrated.*

Thus, a crime against humanity within the contemplation of the charter could be committed before the war or in Germany or its ally countries, regardless of the domestic law of Germany, if it were "... in execution of or in connection with any crime within the jurisdiction of the Tribunal." A crime against humanity was therefore predicated on the commission of a separate crime within the tribunal's jurisdiction, i.e., war crimes, crimes against the peace, or conspiracy to commit crimes against the peace. Since Jackson's conception of the conspiracy charge incorporated acts that occurred as early as January 30, 1933, a crime against humanity could include acts committed in Germany, Greater Germany, or German-allied countries in or after 1933.

Procedures

Differences between civil law and common law traditions presented a major problem in designing the procedures to be used in the IMT. Common law criminal trials, such as those of the United States and Great Britain, rely on the prosecution to present evidence to prove the defendant guilty beyond a reasonable doubt. Therefore, the indictment is brief and intended to provide notice of the charge only. The defendant has the right to cross-examine or present his or her own evidence. The judge's involvement is limited to rulings on the law and admissibility of evidence and asking clarifying questions. Before the decision in *Brady v. Maryland*, 373 U.S. 83 (1963), defendants in United States courts had extremely limited discovery, so trial by surprise was routine.

In the civil law tradition, the prosecutor prepares a lengthy and detailed indictment, which is attached to any documents that the prosecutor believes are relevant. It also includes witness affidavits, which summarize the testimony of each witness to be called. The defense may suggest additional witnesses and documents, but the defense receives complete discovery when it obtains the indictment. The trial is conducted before a multi-judge panel. One of the judges reviews the indictment and materials and decides whether or not the case should proceed. The judges then determine which witnesses will be heard in person, and the court conducts the questioning. Thus, lawyers in this tradition are relatively passive, and judges assume the most active role in prosecuting the case.[31]

The charter authorized judges to develop rules of procedure to govern the IMT. The Rules of Procedure in civil law practice at the time provided for the following: (1) the right to counsel of the defendant's choice; (2) the appointment of counsel if the defendant did not have one; (3) the right of the defendant to compulsory process; (4) the right of the defendant to receive copies of all documents made a part of the indictment and have access to other documents in the prosecution's possession, translated into German. It should be noted that these rules of procedure were adopted prior to the United States Supreme Court decisions in *Mapp v. Ohio*, 367 U.S. 643 (1961), *Miranda v. Arizona*, 384 U.S. 436 (1966), *Gideon v. Wainwright*, 372 U.S. 335 (1963), or *Brady v. Maryland*, so the defendants were accorded more rights than the then-existing constitutional minimum in United States law.

In practice, the IMT employed a hybrid approach between civil and common law principles for the presentation of cases. Notably, the case did not rely on strict rules of evidence. Rather, the prosecution relied heavily on captured German documents that were organized into evidence books, with covering affidavits explaining where and when the documents were discovered and certifying the accuracy of translation. The practice of having the prosecutor read portions of the document into the record and make an oral presentation of the significance of the document packet was also developed. Much

[31] Taylor, above n 1, 63.

of the testimony in both cases was by way of affidavit. However, the parties had the right to require a party to call a witness who had rendered an affidavit. A version of this practice was to be used in the NMT trials.[32]

The trial lasted from November 1945 through July 1946. Nineteen of the twenty-two defendants were found guilty. Twelve received death sentences, three received life sentences, four received a significant sentence, and three were acquitted.

Allied Control Council Law No. 10

It had been understood from the outset that the IMT would be the first trial of major Nazi war criminals, but that others would likely follow. However, the logistical, cultural, and legal difficulties of conducting a lengthy and complex trial in four languages and with hybrid procedures and law derived from two different systems of law caused widespread reluctance regarding the prospect of repeating the experience.[33] Justice Jackson ultimately decided that the United States would not participate in a follow-up trial under the same circumstances.[34]

The Allied Control Council, which consisted of the commanders of the four occupying armies in Germany, issued ACC10 to establish a new process for trying the remaining major war criminals. Under ACC10, the respective occupation zones would be responsible for future trials. The occupying authority in each zone would have the ability to convene a military tribunal to try German defendants within its custody according to the general framework of ACC10, which set forth a number of general principles regarding subsequent trials:

1. The occupying authorities other than the occupying zone conducting the trial would give full cooperation in transferring defendants, serving subpoenas, and producing witnesses and documents. [ACC10, Articles 3, 4, and 5].
2. The principles and provisions of the Moscow Declaration and the London Charter were incorporated by reference into the directive. [ACC10, Article I].

---

32 Tusa & Tusa, above n 1, 1821-1826.
33 Taylor, above n 2, 26-27.
34 Ibid.

However, most importantly, ACC10 clearly defined the scope of jurisdiction of subsequent trials in Article II and specified the crimes with which defendants could be charged.

Article IIa established "crimes against the peace" and used the same definition as the London Charter.

Similarly, Article IIb defined war crimes in the same manner as the London Charter.

However, Article IIc addressed the third crime – crimes against humanity – in a manner that differed significantly from the definition in the London Charter. The definition of the crime in the London Charter included:

> …murder, extermination, deportation, and other inhumane acts…in execution of or in connection with any crime within the jurisdiction of the Tribunal." However, the corresponding language of ACC10 reads "atrocities and offenses, including but not limited to murder, extermination, enslavement, deportation, imprisonment, torture, rape or other inhumane acts… [and dropped the limiting clause] …in connection with any crime within the jurisdiction of the Tribunal…

The definition of ACC10 is therefore substantially broader than the definition of the London Charter in some important respects. First, the list of acts constituting crimes against humanity was broadened to include enslavement, imprisonment, torture, and rape. The inclusion of rape is noteworthy given the massive number of sexual assaults by the Red Army during its invasion of Germany, and to a lesser extent by the French Army.[35]

The specific reference to imprisonment also made it clear that the acts of German judges, prosecutors, and other justice officials would fall within the jurisdiction of the court. The definition by inclusion of the term "…including but not limited to…" also

---

35 See Richard Bessel, *Germany 1945: From War to Peace* (Harper, 2009), 152-159; Tony Judt, *Postwar: A History of Europe Since 1945* (Penguin Books, 2006), 20-21. Lowe estimates that two million German women may have been raped in the Russian invasion of Germany. Keith Lowe, *Savage Continent: Europe in the Aftermath of World War II* (St. Martin's Press, 2013), 50, 53.

evidenced that the offenses that followed were intended as examples of crimes, rather than as a comprehensive list of the elements of the crime.

The deletion of the reference to "…in execution of or in connection with…other crimes…" represented an evolution of thinking as to what would constitute crimes against humanity. There had been concerns at the London Conference regarding crimes against humanity. One interpretation was that they were simply a logical extension of war crimes, and therefore within the tradition of international law. Another was that they were in fact a new crime. If the latter was true, defendants might have a strong argument about the *ex post facto* application of the law. The "in connection language" therefore emphasized that this was a natural extension of existing law, rather than a new law.

ACC10 conveyed greater comfort with the concept of a crime against humanity as an extension of existing law. Just as in the definition in the London Charter, crimes against humanity in ACC10 applied to any civilian population, including offenses against German civilians, "…whether or not in violation of the domestic laws of the country where perpetrated." The directive also states in ACC10, Article II, 4(a) that the defendant's official position would not free the defendant from criminal responsibility, and the fact that a defendant was following orders did not constitute a defense to charges, but might be considered in mitigation.

From the perspective of judges and defense counsel, the definitions of the crimes created serious problems. The defendants might have had defenses against the charge of war crimes, as that crime requires that there was a war and applies only to offenses committed against belligerent populations. By September 1, 1939, the day that the war began, Austria and Czechoslovakia had already been incorporated into Greater Germany. After the conquest of Poland, portions of Poland known as the "Incorporated Eastern Territories" were formally incorporated into Germany. Since offenses committed in former Austria, Czechoslovakia, and incorporated portions of Poland were therefore arguably taking place in Germany, they were not war crimes. In fact, most actions of the defendants took place in Germany according to this definition.

However, crimes against humanity did not have limits regarding location, as the definition applied to any population. The offense did not require the existence of a war, so acts before September 1, 1939 could arguably warrant charges. Finally, the exclusion of reliance on the domestic law as an excuse eliminated an additional defense.

The definition of a crime against the peace included a specific statement that "...a participation in a plan or conspiracy for the accomplishment of the foregoing would also be an offense." There is no such reference in the definition of war crimes or crimes against humanity.[36]
The final potential charge was membership in any organization that the IMT had deemed a criminal organization. However, liability would be established only if the defendant was aware of the criminal nature of the organization.

ACC10 did not establish trial procedures, nor did it require occupying authorities to take any particular action. As an example, the British issued a royal warrant in response that limited further prosecutions to trials of war crimes, especially those associated with British citizens.[37] Similarly, the French conducted trials in their zone for crimes committed in France during the occupation period.[38] The Russians engaged in aggressive proceedings against Nazi leaders, but also against the non-communist opposition. It is not clear whether they relied on ACC10 for their authority.

The United States, however, decided to continue the prosecution of major war criminals under ACC10. In response to ACC10, the Office of the Military Government- Germany, United States issued OMGUS 7, which established procedures for the conduct of the NMT to be held in the American zone.[39]

OMGUS7 was intended to implement ACC10, but not to make substantive changes in its provisions. However, the ordinance altered ACC10 in its first sentence in Article I: "The purpose of this Ordinance is to provide for the establishment of military tribunals which shall have power to try and punish prisoners charged with offenses recognized as crimes in Article II of Control Council Law No. 10, including conspiracies to commit any such crimes."

36 ACC 10, II a, b and c.
37 Taylor, above n 2, 254-57.
38 Ordinance of the French Commander, Number 36 (1946) Article 11, United Nations War Crimes Commission Law Reports
39 Nuremburg, above n 7, Preface XXIII.

However, ACC10 and the London Charter recognized conspiracy only with respect to crimes against the peace, not as part of war crimes or crimes against humanity. The balance of the ordinance would then be less controversial.

Article II established the tribunals, which would consist of three judges and one alternate judge. Each judge would need to be a member of the bar in good standing of any United States jurisdiction and have at least five years of experience. As a practical matter, the vast majority of these judges were current or retired judges of state appellate courts.[40]

Article IV sets forth basic precepts of the trials:

1. The defendant would receive copies of the indictment and of relevant documents at a reasonable time, translated into German;
2. The trial would be conducted in or translated into German;
3. The defendant would have the right to counsel of his own choice, and the court would appoint counsel for anyone unrepresented. The counsel would be compensated by the occupying forces;
4. The defendant would have the right to be present at all stages of the proceeding;
5. The defendant would have the right to present evidence on his own behalf and cross-examine prosecution witnesses;
6. The defendant would have the right to request the tribunal to produce witnesses or documents.

Additionally, the tribunal would have the power to issue subpoenas, administer oaths, or impose sanctions for contempt of court. Article XIV sets forth the order of proceedings. In general, the trial would be conducted in accordance with proceedings in American or British courts.

Article VII is of particular interest, as it presents the rules of evidence. This article states that the tribunal would not be bound by the technical rules of evidence, and that it shall admit any evidence into the record that it has deemed to have probative value. The tribunals were specifically authorized to admit "...affidavits, depositions, interrogations

---

[40] Heller, above n 2, 39-42. Heller includes brief biographical material for each participating judge. Ibid, 85-105.

[the term 'interrogations' likely refers to interrogations performed by military intelligence] and other statements, diaries, letters, the records, findings, statements and judgments of the military Tribunals..." However, the opposing party would need to be given an opportunity to question the affidavit or probative value of such evidence.

In most respects, the procedure outlined in OMGUS7 closely resembles the procedures typical of federal and state administrative hearings.

II

The Trial

> "But a court is far more than a courtroom; it is a process and a spirit. It is the house of law. This the defendants know, or must have known in times past. I doubt that they ever forgot it."

Opening Statement of Brigadier General Telford Taylor, Nuremburg, above n 7, at 31.

The Defendants, Lawyers, and Judges

The sixteen defendants were largely judges and prosecutors of the People's Court and Special Courts, and the balance were officials of the Ministry of Justice:

1. Judges of the People's Court: Karl Engert, Gunther Nebelung, Oswald Rothaug, Hans Petersen;
2. Prosecutors of the People's Court: Paul Barnickle, Ernst Lautz;
3. Judges of the Special Court: Hermann Cuhorst, Rudolph Oeschey, Oswald Rothaug (who also served as a Judge of the People's Court);
4. Prosecutors of the Special Courts: Gunther Joel;
5. Ministry of Justice: Josef Alstotter, Wilhelm Von Ammon, Karl Engert, Gunther Joel, Herbert Klemm, Wolfgang Mettgenberg, Curt Rothenberger, Franz Schlegelberger, Carl Westphal.

The People's Court and Special Courts were established after the Nazi takeover of Germany in 1933 as courts that were parallel to the existing German judicial system. The People's Court had concurrent jurisdiction over internal subversion, and the Special

Courts over external threats. Both courts were staffed by loyal Nazis and functioned primarily as tools for maintaining party control. As time progressed, and particularly after the war began, there was a substantial migration of cases, including ordinary criminal cases, from the regular German courts to the People's or Special Courts.

After a reorganization of the legal system after the Nazi takeover, the Ministry of Justice was the central organization of the legal system. The ministry included all courts and prosecutors, and issued all laws and decrees relating to criminal justice.

All defendants were charged with war crimes, crimes against humanity, and conspiracy to commit war crimes and crimes against humanity. Additionally, Alstotter, Cuhorst, Engert, Joel, Nebelung, Oeschey, and Rothaug were charged with membership in a criminal organization for their roles in the leadership ranks of the Nazi Party or SS.

None of the defendants was charged with crimes against the peace or conspiracy to commit crimes against the peace.[41] The most prominent defendant and primary target of the prosecution was Franz Schlegelberger, who had been an internationally known legal scholar and a pillar of the German legal establishment. In 1941, after a long and illustrious career, he became the acting minister of justice. In that capacity, he participated in some of the most notorious abuses of the German legal system under Nazi rule.

OMGUS7 ensured defendants the right to counsel of their own choice. By the time the NMT trials commenced, there was a group of 50 German lawyers who had experience in the proceedings, were ruled acceptable to the tribunal, and were recommended to defendants.[42] It was also determined that although an attorney with a significant Nazi past would not be recommended to the defendants, such a lawyer might be acceptable to the tribunal if the defendant chose someone who was not on the recommended list. Some of the counsel did in fact have a history of participation in Nazi activities.[43]

The German attorneys, however chosen, were paid by the United States Army and provided housing in Nuremburg at no cost. They were also supplied with cigarettes, low

[41] Ibid, Appendix A for a listing of all the defendants, their charges, and the results for all NMT trials.
[42] Taylor, above n 2, 30.
[43] Ibid, 46-47. Ultimately, over 200 attorneys represented defendants in the 12 NMT trials. *Id.*

cost meals, office space, and staff.[44] In the prevailing conditions of immediate post-war Germany, the inclusion of cigarettes, housing, and food provisions was likely as important as the actual monetary payment.

In accordance with OMGUS7, a panel of three judges and one alternate were chosen. Covington Marshall, the Chief Justice of the Ohio Supreme Court, was intended to be the presiding judge in the Justice Trial, but withdrew from the tribunal for health reasons. He was replaced by Justin W. Harding, who had served as a Judge Advocate General (JAG) officer during the war but had also been a federal judge in the then-territory of Alaska from 1929 to 1933. Harding was the only federal judge to serve in any of the NMT trials. James T. Brand, an Associate Judge of the Supreme Court of Oregon, became the new presiding judge. Mallory Blair, an Associate Justice of the Court of Civil Appeals of Texas, was the third judge.

The prosecutors assigned to the case included following: Former Republican Congressman Charles LaFollete, the lead counsel; Robert King; Alfred Wooleyhan; Arnold Buchold; Rudolph Auerbach; and Sadie Arbuthnot, who was one of several women attorneys on the prosecution team. However, Telford Taylor himself delivered the initial portion of the opening statement.

Preliminary Motions

The defendants in the first three trials – the Medical trial, the Milch trial, and the Justice Trial – all moved to dismiss Count I of the indictment relating to conspiracy to commit crimes against humanity and war crimes. Egon Kuboshok, the attorney for Schlegelberger and Von Ammon in the Justice Trial, argued the motion on behalf of all defendants in each of the three trials. Telford Taylor argued for the prosecution. The three tribunals heard the motion together and issued three opinions that were separate, yet essentially identical.[45]

As previously noted, the conspiracy count had been problematic throughout the entire Nuremburg war crime program. At the London Conference, the American and British

[44] Ibid, 49.

[45] Heller, above n 2, 275-280. The United Nations War Crimes Commission, *Law Reports of Trials of War Criminals Vol. VI* (1948), 104.

representatives had argued for the inclusion of a conspiracy count, while the French and Russian delegates had strongly opposed its inclusion in the charges (see discussion supra). The compromising solution was to include a count for conspiracy to commit crimes against the peace, but war crimes or crimes against humanity. Neither ACC10 nor OMGUS7 had clarified matters. Indeed, ACC10 specifically included language related to conspiracy in Article 2a while describing crimes against the peace, but not in Article 2b or 2c in discussing war crimes and crimes against humanity. Meanwhile, OMGUS7 recognized conspiracy as applicable to all counts.

The decision in the IMT was not helpful to the prosecution, as the tribunal gave a narrow interpretation of the conspiracy charge. No defendant was found guilty of conspiracy unless he had also been found guilty of crimes against the peace. The defendants argued strenuously that conspiracy was a feature unique to Anglo-American law and had no counterpart in the civil law system, which in turn meant it had none in international law.[46]

General Taylor argued on behalf of the prosecution that although conspiracy as such was a part of British and American practice, civil law systems all contain prohibitions on aiding and abetting or attempting to commit a crime. Therefore, the issue was not whether a person could have participated in the commission of a crime without pulling the trigger, as all legal systems recognize closer and farther circles of accountability. Rather, the prosecution argued that the inclusion of the charge of conspiracy with respect to crimes against the peace resulted from the fact that crimes against the peace was a newer offense. Thus, unlike the other offenses, it had not developed an analog in domestic law, so there was greater need to specify that the offense was a collective one.

Taylor also argued that the London Charter did not intend to limit the application of conspiracy law to the other crimes when it included it in the definition of a crime against the peace. ACC10, which was adopted before the IMT rendered its decision with its narrow interpretation of conspiracy law, was intended to give an expansive, rather than restrictive, application of the law.[47]

---

[46] Ibid, 105-106.

[47] Ibid, 106-109; Heller, above n 2, 278-280.

The importance of this issue lies in the use of the conspiracy count in the IMT. Justice Jackson had used the conspiracy count as the core of the entire prosecution. From his viewpoint, the conspiracy had commenced in 1933, and all that followed was included in the overall conspiracy. Thus, for him and the American prosecutors in general, the conspiracy charge allowed the prosecution to explore all participants, events, and aspects of the Third Reich, from its inception in 1933 through its termination in 1945.[48]

This broad interpretation of conspiracy in the Justice Trial would have allowed the prosecution to build strong cases against defendants whose modest involvements in offenses might otherwise have resulted in acquittals or light sentences. It would also have recognized the liability of each defendant for wrongful acts of other defendants.

The three tribunals ultimately ruled in favor of the defendants, dismissing the conspiracy counts on the basis that ACC10 had established their jurisdiction and only referred to conspiracy with respect to crimes against the peace.[49]

A major implication of the ruling was that the defendants could not be found guilty of war crimes or crimes against humanity for any act committed before September 1, 1939. However, the prosecution could cite acts committed before that date to prove motive, knowledge, or intent with respect to acts committed after September 1, 1939.[50]

Opening Statements

Telford Taylor, Charles LaFollette, Alfred Wooleyhan, and Robert King delivered the opening statement for the prosecution. Taylor's eloquent address established key principles in the trial of this group of defendants. Most notably, Taylor made clear that the judges in particular were not being prosecuted for being incompetent judges. Indeed, early in his argument, Taylor noted:

---

48 Taylor, above n 2, 226-227.
49 Ibid.
50 As a result of this temporal restriction, several important allegations of crimes against humanity, including euthanasia, compulsory sterilization, and persecution of the Catholic church and Confessing church (protestant dissidents), could not be fully explored, as most of the offenses took place prior to September 1, 1939. *See* Charles LaFollette, Speech before the International Conference of Lawyers and Justice Officials, June 3, 1948 at 18-19 (Digital Commons of the University of Georgia Law School).

> The "trials" they conducted became horrible farces, with vestigial features of legal procedure which only served to mock the helpless victims. This conduct was dishonor to their profession but the defendants are not now called to answer for violating Constitutional guarantees or withholding due process of law.
>
> On the contrary, the defendants are accused of participating in and responsibility for the killings, tortures, and other atrocities, which resulted from, and which the defendants knew were the inevitable consequences of the conduct of their offices as judges, prosecutors and ministry officials.[51]

Thus, the prosecution theorized that the German legal system actually ceased being a legal system, and the judges and prosecutors were utilizing the legal system to commit crimes. Taylor described in detail the degeneration of the German legal system during the Nazi era.[52] LaFollette then took command of the opening, arguing at length that the tribunal was authorized to make its own interpretation of the London Charter and ACC10 and was free to interpret them more broadly than the IMT had. He particularly emphasized that the definition of crimes against humanity in ACC10 was broader than that in the London Charter, as it did not require that crimes against humanity be in association with other crimes.

He then noted that the evidence would fall into three categories. The first category included offenses that clearly resembled traditional notions of war crimes, specifically violations of the Hague Convention of 1907 and the Geneva Convention of 1929. These offenses included two of the major categories in the trial, the Night and Fog Decree, and the extension of German law to the Incorporated Eastern Territories and deprivation of rights to Poles and Jews in that extension.

The second category encompassed the extensive cooperation of the judiciary with the Gestapo and SS in persecution of Germans and non-Germans alike.

The third category contained the systematic denial of fair trials to political and ethnic minorities so that trials would be tantamount to murder.[53]

---

51 Nuremburg, above n 7, 31-32.
52 Ibid, 40-62.
53 Ibid, 62-71.

King refined these categories to focus specifically on the Law Against Poles and Jews and the Night and Fog Program.[54]

Wooleyhan presented the facts in some detail that would be proven for each individual defendant, including descriptions of the most notorious cases tried by the various judges.[55] Finally, LaFollette resumed the podium to discuss questions of evidence and provide additional arguments concerning the perversion of the legal profession under Nazi rule.[56]

Kuboshok, Schlegelberger's attorney, assumed the role of lead counsel for all defendants in the opening statement. The other defense counsel presented additional arguments with respect to their specific clients. Kuboshok essentially made two points. First, unlike the American or British common law systems, judges in the German civil law system essentially apply law codes adopted by competent authorities. Before Hitler, law would have been adopted by the Reichstag. However, after passage of the Enabling Act in 1933, legal authority to legislate transferred to Hitler personally. Thus, after 1933, Hitler was the duly constituted supreme legislative authority under the Weimar Constitution, which, it should be noted, was never abrogated. As the German legal tradition dissociated morality and law, it was not the role of the judiciary to ignore valid law, regardless of the ethical implications.[57]

Second, many of the specific provisions subject to complaint had pre-Nazi antecedents or were legitimate exercises of power in wartime conditions. Thus, in 1936, law by analogy was intended to introduce the flexibility of the common law system into the civil law.[58]

---

54 Ibid, 71-78; see discussion below.

55 Ibid, 78-89.

56 Ibid, 89-100.

57 The defense called Prof. Jahrreiss as an expert on the German legal system and constitutional law, who testified: "On the continent of Europe, in the course of four centuries, a development had taken place by which law and morality in legislative thought are separated sharply; and so as the question of morality arises, the lawyer on the continent of Europe says as a lawyer, '[t]hat has nothing to do with me.'" Nuremburg, above n 7, 257.

58 A penal law adopted by decree in 1936 dictated that if a German judge believed a legislatively adopted law was too lenient, the judge could apply the penalty in an analogous criminal offense. For example, if a Jew had sex with a German at night, as in the Katzenberger case, and the judge felt that the two-year term was too light, he could adopt the penalty for an analogous crime, such as the commission of a crime taking advantage of wartime conditions, e.g. nighttime blackout regulations, the penalty for which happened to be death. Katzenberger was sentenced to death for

There was precedent in Weimar Germany for use of Special Courts and People's Courts. Under the customs and usages of war, many acts that might otherwise have been viewed as war crimes could possibly be excused on the grounds of military necessity. For example, the offensive components of the Night and Fog Decree stemmed from the military necessity of secrecy in judicial proceedings involving the resistance. Kuboshok also noted that the judiciary was in a constant struggle with the SS, the Gestapo, and the Nazi party over control of the judicial process and maintenance of judicial independence.[59]

Of the remaining arguments, the one of most interest was by Erich Wandschneider, the counsel for Rothenberg. Schneider highlighted that his client was operating within the climate of a totalitarian state. The average citizen tends to adopt a general attitude of passivity in response to dictatorship because, unlike in a democracy, any display of initiative requires a high degree of personal commitment and courage. It is false, therefore, to examine a course of conduct retrospectively without taking into account the pressures and climate of a dictatorship. Acts that might be culpable under normal circumstances might be readily excusable under the special circumstances of Nazism. Thus, Rothenberger's notorious memorandum on the reorganization of the German judiciary on national socialist lines was actually an effort to preserve some remnants of judicial independence. The tribunal therefore had to view the evidence in the case in light of the circumstances with which the defendants were faced.[60]

Testimony

Arraignment took place on February 17, 1947. The trial began on March 5, 1947 and ended on October 18, 1947. There were 140 live witnesses, 2,093 exhibits and 10,964 pages of trial transcript.[61]

---

a crime with a two-year prison term. See discussion below. Law by analogy also permitted the judge to find someone guilty of a crime even when no law governed the offense by finding the person guilty of an analogous offense. 1935 Reichsgosetzblatt, Part 1, p. 899; Nuremburg, above n 7, 177-78.

[59] Nuremburg, above n 7, 108-126.

[60] Nuremburg, above n 7, 146-47.

[61] Nuremburg, above n 7, 5.

The trial proceeded in a manner similar to a conventional common law court. The prosecution presented its case first, the defense responded with its case, and the prosecution had opportunity for rebuttal. The prosecution had to prove its case beyond a reasonable doubt through the use of sworn testimony and documents, which were subject to defense cross-examination and confrontation. The defense had a full opportunity to present its witnesses and documentation, and in fact presented substantially more testimony and documents than did the prosecution. All prosecution documents had to be translated into German or English and provided to the defense prior to introduction.[62]

However, there were significant modifications from the typical proceedings of a criminal trial in the United States during that era. Either side could present evidence by affidavit, subject to the opposing side's request for cross-examination of the witness. In fact, the bulk of testimony in the trial was taken by affidavit. The United States Army created a document center that produced affadavits for the introduction of documents in order to certify the authenticity and place of origin of the document.

As in the IMT, the prosecution chose to rely heavily on documentary proof of wrongdoing so that the proof of guilt would be by the defendants' own words. By contrast, the defense relied more heavily on oral testimony, and most of the defendants actually testified in the trial. The prosecution did minimal cross-examination of defense witnesses.[63]

Although substantial evidence was introduced with respect to a number of issues, such as the failures to prosecute civilians for lynching Allied flyers who had been shot down, members of the Gestapo or SS for abuse of prisoners of war or political prisoners, or a German Catholic priest for officiating at a Polish laborer's funeral, the heart of the case against all defendants was their participation in either or both of the Night and Fog Program or actions taken in accordance with the Law Against Poles and Jews and other anti-Semitic laws.

After the invasion of Poland on September 1, 1939, the country's territory was partitioned between the Germans and Soviets. Part of German-occupied Poland was

---

[62] Rules of Procedure for Military Tribunals I and III.
[63] Nuremburg, above n 7, 1-6.

organized into the "Government General," where military law would apply. The parts of Poland contiguous to Germany were annexed to Germany and became known as the "Incorporated Eastern Territories." The Law Against Poles and Jews was issued to provide a legal framework for the administration of the Incorporated Eastern Territories.

The law had two major themes. First, in the new regime, Poles would be reduced to a docile permanent underclass that would support the spread of German settlement in Eastern Europe and, over time, be eliminated. Thus, the law regarding Poles would be applied harshly to break spirits and establish German domination, but would not seek short-term elimination of the Polish population.[64] Second, the goal would be to eliminate the massive Jewish population of Poland.

The law itself provides substantively that Poles and Jews would be subject to the death penalty for any of the following activities:

1. Any act of violence against a German;
2. Manifesting any anti-German sentiment by making anti-German comments or defacing or removing official notices or lowering the prestige of the German people.

The sentence would be death or imprisonment for any of the following:

1. Any act of violence against any member of the German armed forces, police, or any agency of the Nazi Party whether the victim was German or not;
2. Causing damages to any installation of the German government or the Nazi Party;
3. Soliciting any person to disobey any decree or regulation;
4. Conspiring with or aiding or abetting anyone in the violation of this decree;
5. Possession of any weapon;
6. Committing any other act contrary to "fundamental principle of German law" or contrary to the interest of the German state.

[64] Letter, Schlegelberger to Lammers, April 17, 1941, Nuremburg, above n 7, 611-13.

The death penalty was made mandatory for any act for which death was the only penalty. A schedule of prison terms ranging from 3 months to 10 years was prescribed for cases in which imprisonment was an option. However, it was determined "... in those cases where the law does not provide for the death penalty, it shall be imposed if the act shows a particularly base attribute or is particularly serious for other reasons...."

The minimum penalties could not be reduced unless the crimes were committed against a fellow Pole or Jew. The law also changed the procedures available to a Polish or Jewish defendant:

1. The cases would be brought before the Special Courts in most cases.
2. All sentences, including the death penalty, would be carried out without delay.
3. The prosecutor could appeal a decision, but the defendant had no right to appeal.
4. Poles and Jews had no right to lodge a criminal complaint.
5. Poles and Jews had no right to ask for recusal for bias of a German judge.
6. Poles and Jews could not be sworn in as witnesses. However, even if unsworn, they could be prosecuted for perjury or false statements.[65]
7. Although proceedings would be conducted in accordance with the German Law of Civil Procedure, the court was free to depart from the established rules when appropriate for the rapid and efficient conduct of proceedings.

The law allowed the governor of the Incorporated Eastern Territories to impose martial law and try Poles and Jews before civilian court-martials, or otherwise defer trial indefinitely and refer the case directly to the Gestapo.

Finally, Poles and Jews were forbidden to file civil cases.[66] In January 1942, a subsequent decree was issued over Schlegelberger's signature that made this law retroactive.[67]

---

65 The provision of this law forbidding the swearing in of Poles or Jews as witnesses while retaining penalties for perjury would seem to be contradictory. However, the purpose of the provision was to discourage the calling of Poles or Jews in any case involving a German, and to receive such testimony only with the utmost caution. Letter from Reich Ministry of Justice to Presidents of District Courts of Appeal, August 7, 1942, signed by Freisler. Nuremburg, above n 7, 668.

66 See 1941 Reichsgesetzblatt Part I at 759 (Nuremburg, above n 7, 632–36), issued December 4, 1941.

67 See 1942 Reichsgesetzblatt, Part I at 52, January 31, 1942.

On July 1, 1943, a new decree was issued that deprived Jews of any right to a trial at all and demanded that any Jew accused of a crime be turned over to the police for processing. The individual's property would be confiscated upon his or her death. Thus, the Law Against Poles and Jews would no longer apply to Jews.[68] This change in the law reflected the official adoption of the so-called Final Solution, i.e. the systematic murder of the entire Jewish population in the occupied territories of Europe.

By 1941, resistance movements had sprung up in a number of occupied countries, and the German Army was struggling to maintain control of occupied territories. Hitler instructed the German Army to implement a program whereby suspected resistants would disappear into the "night and fog."

Field Marshal Wilhelm Keitel, the Chief of the Supreme Counsel of the Armed Forces, issued the Night and Fog Decree on December 7, 1941 at Hitler's direction. Keitel himself would be tried by the IMT and found guilty of war crimes, crimes against humanity, crimes against the peace, and conspiring to commit crimes against the peace. He was executed in 1946.

The decree provided that in circumstances in which the trial of a member of the resistance could not be arranged within one week of arrest, the resistor would be transferred to Germany for trial. The defendant's family and acquaintances would not be informed of his or her fate or location and would be denied contact or correspondence with the person. If the person died, either by natural causes or execution, the family members would not be informed. If the defendant wrote a will or a farewell letter, the document would not be delivered until the war's end. As no foreign witnesses would be allowed to testify in court to preserve secrecy, the defendant essentially had no ability to call witnesses on his or her own behalf. The defendant would have the right to counsel in capital cases, which comprised the majority of cases, but the court would choose the counsel with he permission of the prosecutor. The proceedings would be conducted in German, with no provision for interpreters.[69] The decree was made applicable in all cases involving:

---

[68] See 1943 Reichsgesetzblatt Part I at 372.

[69] See Night and Fog Decree, December 7, 1941. (Nuremburg, above n 7 at 774–81). See also Secret Instructions of Reich Ministry of Justice to Prosecutors and Judges concerning measures to maintain secrecy in Night and Fog cases. March 6, 1943 (Nuremburg, above n 7 at 794–97).

1. Assault with intent to kill;
2. Espionage;
3. Sabotage;
4. Communist activity;
5. Crimes liable to create disorder;
6. Favoring of the enemy by smuggling people into a country, enlisting in an enemy army, or support of members of an enemy army such as by harboring parachutists; and
7. Illegal possession of weapons.[70]

Although the decree was applicable to all occupied territories, it in fact was primarily directed at Western European occupied countries, with the exception of Denmark – i.e., France, Belgium, the Netherlands, Luxemburg, and Norway.[71]

The case against Schlegelberger focused on his roles in drafting the Law Against Poles and Jews and implementing the Night and Fog Decree, which he kept in the judiciary rather than leaving with the Wehrmacht, where it more likely should have been kept. The testimony indicated that the Wehrmacht was reluctant to participate in the program because of doubts as to its legality. [72]

The prosecution introduced Schlegelberger's draft of the Law Against Poles and Jews, which revealed that he had played a pivotal role in producing that policy and overseeing its implementation. The prosecution produced many documents signed by Schlegelberger that indicated his complicity in the overall degradation of German justice in the Nazi period. Two particularly damaging pieces of evidence were a memorandum removing two notaries from office for having bought postcards from a Jewish street vendor[73] and his proposal that Jews in mixed marriages not be deported to the East if they consented to sterilization.[74] The defense, for its part, produced Schlegelberger in his own defense. He noted that throughout the entire period of Nazi rule, the Ministry of

[70] Ibid, 778–79.
[71] See Memorandum of Defendant von Ammon to Defendant Rothenberger December 9 and 26, 1942, concerning Night and Fog cases. (Nuremburg, above n 7, 788–89.)
[72] Nuremburg, above n 7, 806-807.
[73] Nuremburg, above n 7, 363.
[74] Nuremburg, above n 7, 270.

Justice and the judiciary were in a constant struggle against the SS, Gestapo, and Nazi Party for control of the judicial process. Therefore, many of his actions actually served to protect judicial independence and protect defendants.[75] Even the Law Against Poles and Jews offered some limited procedural rights to victims, and was therefore superior to laws that the SS, Gestapo, or Nazi Party might have proposed.

He also testified that he agreed to support the Night and Fog Program because the alternative, given the Werhmacht's reluctance, would have been to turn defendants over to the Gestapo or SS for immediate disposition without trial.[76] Schlegelberger also noted that many of the harsh measures adopted in the Law Against Poles and Jews were intended to stave off harsher measures. He further asserted that after resigning as Minister of Justice in 1942, he was replaced by Thierack, a Nazi zealot, and all semblance of judicial independence and adherence to legal norms disappeared after his departure.[77]

The prosecution introduced testimony that in addition to Schlegelberger, Klemm, Rothenberger, Lautz, Mettgenberg, Van Ammon and Joel were also involved in the Night and Fog Program. Additionally, there was substantial evidence against Rothaug, Lautz, and Joel for actions under the Law Against Poles and Jews.

Of greatest interest was the testimony against Rothaug and Oeschey, two People's Court judges, which consisted of case reports and testimony of multiple trials in which Poles and Jews had been deprived of all semblance of a fair trial, ultimately found guilty, and executed. Many of the most widely known incidents of the trials occurred in their courtrooms. Perhaps the most famous aspect of the case was evidence from the Katzenberger-Seiler case.[78]

Katzenberger Case

Leo Katzenberger was a 68-year-old Jewish man who was a leader in the Jewish community. He had befriended Irene Seiler, the daughter of one of his tenants, and the two had maintained a friendly relationship for years. On one occasion, she was seen

---

[75] Nuremburg, above n 7, 292-96.
[76] Nuremburg, above n 7, 807-811.
[77] Nuremburg, above n 7, 720-731.
[78] This case was recounted in the movie *Judgment at Nuremburg* as the "Feldenstein case."

sitting on his lap, which led to Katzenberger being charged with violating Nuremburg race laws that prohibited sexual relations between Jews and non-Jewish Germans. Evidence revealed that Rothaug had prejudged the case and privately disclosed prior to the trial that Katzenberger would be found guilty and receive the death penalty, even though there was no evidence that he had actually had sexual relations with Seiler.

Seiler denied any sexual contact with Katzenberger, so Rothaug decided that she should be tried for perjury in the same trial as Katzenberger. Thus, her denial was discredited. The minimum penalty for violation of the Nuremburg laws was two-and-a-half years imprisonment. However, Rothaug noted that the alleged offenses occurred at night. Using law by analogy, he concluded that the sexual relationship was analogous to a violation of the wartime blackout restrictions, for which the death penalty was available. Rothaug sentenced Katzenberger to death, and Seiler to two years imprisonment.[79]

Kaminska-Wdowen Case

Sophie Kaminska was a 37-year-old Polish woman who was the mother of three children. Her husband was killed in the German attack on Poland in September 1939. Thereafter, she arrived in Germany to work on a German farm. Wasyl Wdowen was a 20-year-old Ukrainian farm worker who resided in Poland at the time of the German invasion. Kaminska and Wdowen developed a romantic attachment and had a child together while working on the farm. At some point, a dispute erupted between Kaminska and the German farmer over compensation. Wdowen joined the dispute in support of Kaminska and reportedly shoved the farmer. A German soldier on leave heard the commotion and joined the dispute. He later gave a statement that Kaminska had slapped him, and he slapped her back. She was also alleged to have picked up a hoe and threatened him. The soldier then pulled out a bayonet and ordered Kaminska and Wdowen to leave. As the soldier left on his bicycle to call the police, Kaminska threw a stone at him.

Kaminska's account differed in that she testified that the soldier slapped her first. The soldier's account came from a statement he had given at the police station. As he was missing in action in North Africa, he did not testify. Kaminska gave unsworn testimony,

---

79 Nuremburg, above n 7, 653, 1150-1155.

in accordance with the law. The court credited the soldier's testimony and discredited hers.

When the police came to arrest her, she resisted arrest. Wdowen tried to help her, but was ordered to stay away. He followed her to the jail and took her hands as she was being put into jail.

Kaminska was convicted of using a knife or thrusting weapon against a German soldier on the grounds that she had thrown a stone at him as he rode away. Using the doctrine of decision by analogy, the judge concluded that the purpose of throwing the stone was to injure the soldier. If the stone had hit by him, he might have died. As a soldier, he was essential to the German war effort. Therefore, the stone must be considered equivalent to a knife. According to this logic, she was deemed guilty of a serious violent crime. By invoking the Law Against Poles and Jews, the judge imposed a death sentence on Kaminska.

Wdowen was found guilty of insulting German honor by pushing the German farmer. In addition, by holding Kaminska's hands while a police official tried to put her in jail, he offered forceful resistance to an official in performance of his official duty. As these crimes were only possible because the war called most able-bodied men to the army, he was also found to be taking advantage of wartime conditions to commit his crimes. As a result, he was also sentenced to death. The presiding judge in this case was defendant Oeschey.[80]

Stefanowicz-Lenczewski Case

In another case that was typical of many cited in the opinion, two Polish farm workers – 20-year-old Paul Stefanowicz and 18-year-old Franz Lenczewski – left a farm to which they were committed and attempted to cross the border into Switzerland. However, border control apprehended them at the border. The court noted that although it could not be proven that they intended to join the Polish army (indeed, the court noted that both men appeared to be "effeminate"), "[n]evertheless, as Poles, both of them have hurt the German Reich by their conduct. For they were assigned to work in the Reich,

80 See Opinion and Sentence of the Nuremburg Special Court, October 20, 1943; Nuremburg, above n 7, 705–12.

and in total warfare any loss in this regard harms the interest of the Reich." Under the Law Against Poles and Jews, both were sentenced to death.[81] It should be noted that although neither had ever been a German citizen, they were both charged with treason, thereby vesting the People's Court with jurisdiction.[82] The prosecutor in this case was defendant Lautz.

Two Unidentified Polish Girls

A final case concerned 17- and 18-year-old Polish girls who had worked in a munitions factory. Both were accused of setting a fire at the factory, and one was alleged to have confessed. Their trial was held the same day as the arrest and the fire. Their attorney was given two hour's notice of the trial, and his request for postponement was denied. The girl who reportedly confessed recanted her confession at the trial. The presiding judge, defendant Rothaug, found both girls guilty and sentenced them to death. They were executed three days after the trial.[83] In each of these cases, the trappings of a trial were present, but the reality of a fair trial was not.

Opinion

> "Woe to those who make unjust laws, to those who issue oppressive decrees, to deprive the poor of their rights and withhold justice from the oppressed of my people."
>
> Isaiah 10:1-2.

On December 3 and 4, 1947, the tribunal issued a thorough and comprehensive 243-page opinion. It began with a review of its jurisdiction and authority to proceed under the London Charter, ACC10, and OMGUS7. The tribunal then presented detailed analyses of the crimes charged in the indictment, focusing particularly on Count III: crimes against humanity.

As noted, the charge of crimes against humanity was first specifically identified in the London Charter and modified by the requirement that such an offense be in association

81 See Secret Judgment of the First Senate of the People's Court, May 21, 1943; Nuremburg, above n 7, 702-704.
82 Nuremburg, above n 7, 1123.
83 Nuremburg, above n 7, 1146-1147.

with some of the other crimes identified in the charter, such as crimes against the peace and war crimes. Despite the opinion of the IMT, which found a number of defendants guilty of crimes against humanity, the difference in text between the definitions of crimes against humanity in the London Charter and ACC10 left many questions about the application of the charges. The tribunal set about to answer these questions.

First, the tribunal clearly distinguished between a war crime and a crime against humanity, and in doing so, established a definition used in subsequent cases of international law. The tribunal noted that a war crime was an offense committed during war time against the population of a belligerent enemy power. Treaties such as the Hague and Geneva Conventions as well as the traditional customs and usages of war had established the specific type of offense constituting a war crime. A war crime could be committed against a single person.

The defendants had argued that an offense committed against civilians in the Incorporated Eastern Territories could not be a war crime because they had become part of Germany. The tribunal concluded that because there were Polish armies still fighting in the field[84] and a Polish government-in-exile had existed throughout the war, the administrative decision to incorporate Polish land into the German Reich did not convert any part of pre-war Poland into German territory.

Crimes against humanity, particularly as ACC10 defines them, served as a complement to war crimes. Under ACC10 §2(b), a crime against humanity is an offense against any civilian population, not just that of a belligerent power. Thus, German officials could be guilty of a crime against humanity even in cases where the offense was against German civilians or on German soil.

The tribunal recognized that not all offenses against German civilians would constitute crimes against humanity, a crime under international law. For example, the court concluded that the imposition of seemingly excessive harsh penalties on certain

[84] Subsequent to the conquest of Poland, substantial numbers of Polish soldiers were released by the Soviet Union to fight for the Western Allies. Polish army units had a distinguished combat record during the war, including the capture of Monte Cassino in the Italian campaign, and played a major role in the breakout from the Normandy bridgehead. A Polish parachute brigade fought at Arnhem. There were two armed revolts in Warsaw during the war, including the revolt of the Warsaw Ghetto and the revolt of the Polish Home Army. Polish flyers had also served in the Royal Air Force during the Battle of Britain. See Atkinson, the Day of Battle, at 511, 531-33; Keegan, Six Armies in Normandy, at 262-282.

categories of offenders, such as habitual criminals or violators of laws concerning hoarding and black markets, were not crimes against humanity as long as the prosecution or penalty was not based on racial, religious, or prohibited discrimination.[85] Similarly, references in ACC10 to offenses "against any civilian population" had to be interpreted to mean that any offense against an individual, regardless of how serious, would not be a crime against humanity.[86] The tribunal therefore agreed upon the following interpretation:

We hold that crimes against humanity, as defined in CC law 10, must be strictly construed to exclude isolated cases of atrocity or persecution, whether committed by private individuals or by governmental authority.

As we construe it, that section provides punishment for crimes committed against German nationals only where there is proof of conscious participation in systematic government organized or approved procedures amounting to atrocities and offenses of the kind specified in the Act and committed against populations, or amounting to persecutions on political, racial or religious grounds.[87]

Although the opinion, in deciding the fate of individual defendants, especially the Judges on trial, relied heavily on particular incidents of miscarriage of justice, the opinion made clear that the specific cases were being cited to demonstrate a pattern of wrongdoing against populations, rather than constituting offenses in their own right.[88]

The defendants in all of the NMT cases argued that the charge of crimes against humanity was an ex post facto law, as the crime was first officially identified in the London Charter. All the tribunals concluded that, as their jurisdiction was established by the London Charter and ACC10, they accepted the inclusion of crimes against humanity as binding.

This tribunal, however, was the only one to consider whether the offenses also violated fundamental justice as an ex post facto law.[89]

---

[85] Opinion, Nuremburg, above n 7, 1027.
[86] Ibid, 973.
[87] Ibid, 982.
[88] Ibid, 984-985.
[89] Heller, above n 2, 377-378.

The tribunal first noted that, unlike legislation in the United States or other constitutional countries, there was no constitutional limit or superior law by which to challenge the London Charter or ACC10.[90] Thus, there was no basis for a legal challenge to the offense.

However, the tribunal concluded that the ex post facto rule was based on notions of justice and that there was no injustice in the application of ACC10. First, the ex post facto principle is primarily applied to statutory provisions, but is generally not applied in decisions under the common law, that is decisions which typically deal with novel situations. International law is comparable to the common law in that it grows by accretion. Thus, a rigid application of the ex post facto principle would "strangle common international law in its crib."[91]

Moreover, the tribunal noted:

> As a principle of justice and fair play, the rule in question will be given full effect. As applied in the field of international law, that principle requires proof before conviction that the accused knew or should have known that in matters of international concern he was guilty of participation in a nationally organized system of injustice and persecution, shocking to the moral sense of mankind and that he knew or should have known that he would be subject to punishment if caught.[92]

The opinion then indicated that, as part of the Versailles Peace Conference, the Commission on Responsibility of Authors of the War had specifically stated that persons who had violated "... the laws and customs of war or the laws of humanity, are liable to criminal prosecution."[93]

The opinion also recounted a number of prior incidents in which countries had intervened in Ottoman Turkey to protect its Christian minorities, with Russia and Romania on behalf of their Jewish minorities and Spain on behalf of its Cuban

[90] Nuremburg, above n 7, 974-975.
[91] Nuremburg, above n 7, 975.
[92] Nuremburg, above n 7, 971-78.
[93] Ibid, 978.

population.[94] Finally, and ironically, Hitler himself had justified his intervention in Czechoslovakian internal affairs on behalf of the allegedly persecuted Sudeten Germans, an incident that triggered the notorious Munich Agreement dismembering Czechoslovakia.[95]

Thus, the defendants had to have known that if they had engaged in massive acts of injustice, even against their own people in war time, they might very well be found criminally liable. There was no unfairness or injustice in trying the defendants for crimes against humanity.[96]

The tribunal disposed of several other defenses of the defendants. First, the tribunal concluded that the defendants were charged with using German law as an instrument for the commission of war crimes and crimes against humanity. Since ACC10 specifically rejected compliance with domestic law as a defense, the defendants could not use compliance with German law as a defense.[97]

Additionally, the tribunal noted that the doctrine of judicial immunity that was applicable in United States courts would not be available to German judges, as this immunity was only available to judicial officials who were acting independently and judicial independence had ceased to exist in Germany.[98]

Although there was a great deal of testimony on a number of issues, the opinion focused on two general categories of offense: acts associated with the Night and Fog Decree and acts of racial persecution, particularly in relation to the Law Against Poles and Jews.

The IMT ruling that found Field Marshals Keitel and Jodl guilty of war crimes and crimes against humanity for their role in the Night and Fog Program simplified the tribunal's task with respect to the Night and Fog Decree. There was therefore binding precedent that the Night and Fog Program could not be justified on the basis of military necessity. Indeed, the tribunal noted in a number of cases that victims of the Night and Fog Program were acquitted or given light sentences for posing little threat, yet were

---

[94] Ibid, 981-982.
[95] Ibid.
[96] Ibid, 979-983.
[97] Nuremburg, above n 7, 984.
[98] Ibid, 1024-25.

sent to concentration camps anyway to prevent them from returning home and revealing the nature of the program.[99]

The tribunal further noted that the program violated the laws of war, particularly Article 4 of the Hague Convention relating to the treatment of prisoners of war, Article 3 regarding maintainance of the civilian courts of occupied countries, Article 43 concerning the preservation of order and enforcement of the law, and most importantly, Article 46 addressing the protection of family honor and rights and safeguard of the lives, property rights, and religious practices and convictions of persons in occupied territories.[100]

An important aspect of the decision was the tribunal's conclusion that the secrecy of the Night and Fog Program was intended to terrorize and intimidate victims' families and members of the occupied population, whether they were engaged in resistance activities or not, thereby violating international law. Thus, intentional infliction of emotional harm to third parties could constitute a crime.[101]

The tribunal also addressed the nature of the Night and Fog court proceedings as well. Even if the trials provided under the Night and Fog Program had been conducted fairly, the program would still likely have been perceived as a war crime or crime against humanity, although the crimes would have been highly mitigated. However, the tribunal noted:

> ... the trials of the accused NN persons did not approach even a semblance of fair trial or justice. The accused NN persons were arrested and secretly transported to Germany and other countries for trial. They were held incommunicado. In many instances, they were denied the right to produce evidence, to be confronted by witnesses against them, or to present witnesses on their own behalf. They were tried secretly or denied the right of counsel of their own choice, and occasionally denied the aid of any counsel. No indictment was served in many instances and the accused learned only a few moments before the trial of the nature of the alleged

[99] Nuremburg, above n 7, 1058.
[100] Ibid.
[101] Nuremburg, above n 7, 1061.

> crime for which he was to be tried. The entire proceeding from beginning to end was secret and no public record was allowed to be made of them.[102]

It is clear that the systematic denial of these rudiments of a fair trial – whether under common law, civil law, or courts martial to persons in occupied countries – could itself constitute a war crime and crime against humanity. Each defendant indicted for participation in the Night and Fog Program as a drafter of the decree, a judge, or a prosecutor was found guilty of war crimes and crimes against humanity.

The second broad category of offense the opinion discussed was racial persecution, particularly of Poles and Jews. A majority of the cited cases concerned Poles rather than Jews, as Jews were effectively barred from the court system in early 1943 upon implementation of the Final Solution.

This portion of the opinion focused on the impact of the Law Against Poles and Jews and the trials of Polish citizens for high treason against Germany. Schlegelberger and others drafted the Law Against Poles and Jews to extend German law, including its racial laws, to the newly annexed Polish land. As previously noted, this law dramatically reduced the rights of Poles and Jews in the legal system. When coupled with provisions of German law, such as law by analogy, it effectively made it impossible for a Pole or Jew to even know which conduct might constitute a crime under new German laws.

Schlegelberger, as primary draftsman, and Oeschey and Rothaug, as judges applying the law, were the principle targets of this segment of the case. Although the tribunal meticulously reviewed the various defendants' individual acts of cruelty and injustice, the defendants were not found guilty because of the conduct of any particular trial. Rather, the tribunal determined that the overall policy of the government was the extermination of Jews and Poles from Germany and throughout Europe. The defendants participated in this policy of extermination through various actions, including enacting laws for the persecution and extermination of Poles and Jews, attempting to enforce those laws, and presiding over the adjudication of alleged violations of such laws by means of sham trials.[103]

---

[102] Nuremburg, above n 7, 1046-1047.
[103] Nuremburg, above n 7, 1063-1064.

The policy of extermination constituted a war crime despite the purported annexation of portions of Poland because, as previously noted, a Polish government-in-exile was still in operation and a Polish army was continuing to engage in resistance against Germany. The tribunal concluded that the annexation should not be recognized, and that it would be improper to allow a country to evade responsibility for war crimes through the simple expedient of annexing occupied territories.[104] Therefore, the Law Against Poles and Jews and actions taken under it could constitute war crimes. Additionally, because German policy consisted of atrocities and persecutions by the German government against racial and religious minorities, the law would constitute a crime against humanity in any event.[105]

The opinion's discussion of charges against the defendants Oeshey and Rothaug are of particular interest. The tribunal concluded that Oeshey and Rothaug had conducted their trials in a manner that failed to meet even minimal levels of due process or fairness to such an extent that they could not be considered trials at all. The tribunal recognized the then-recently coined term "genocide" to mean the deliberate murder of members of a defined group in order to eliminate the group's existence.[106] Given that the only purpose of these trials was the judicial murder of Jews and Poles in accordance with the overall eliminationist government policy, Rothaug was one of the first persons in history found guilty of genocide, a subset of crimes against humanity.[107]

The tribunal also considered a bizarre feature of German law during the war. Polish laborers from the annexed areas were brought into Germany, whether voluntarily or involuntarily, to work on German farms. On a number of occasions, workers fled their farms to escape to Switzerland. These escaped farm hands were captured, tried for high treason against Germany, and sentenced to death, even though they had no allegiance to Germany. Between 150 and 200 Polish workers were prosecuted under this theory.[108]

---

104 Nuremburg, above n 7, 1058.

105 Nuremburg, above n 7, 1080-1081.

106 Nuremburg, above n 7, 983. Raphael Lemkin coined the term "genocide." Lemkin was a Jewish refugee lawyer who lobbied successfully for this United Nations Resolution and the subsequent genocide convention. See Samantha A. Power, *Problem from Hell: America in the Age of Genocide* (Harpperen, 2003), 40-60.

107 Nuremburg, above n 7, 1156. Lautz, the prosecutor who brought the high treason cases against the Polish farmworkers, was also found to have participated in genocide. Nuremburg, above n 7, 1128.

108 Nuremburg, above n 7, 1121.

The tribunal found this program to be a crime against humanity and a war crime because the finding of guilt for treason required the imposition of the death penalty. [109]

Regarding the Night and Fog portion, the opinion describes the manner in which Oeshey and Rothaug failed to meet minimum standards of justice in their courts. Specifically, they refused to permit the Poles and Jews tried before them to present witnesses on their own behalf. They denied defense counsel time to prepare a defense or even be present, and were neither fair nor impartial. Indeed, in a number of cases, these judges met with prosecutors to advise them on the presentation of their cases or come to an agreement about the punishment before the trial was even held. Both indicated from the bench that they would not believe the testimony of a Jewish or Polish witness.[110]

One conclusion of this opinion is that the systematic denial of a fair trial could constitute a war crime or crime against humanity.

Verdict and Sentences

Schlegelberger was found guilty of crimes against humanity and war crimes arising out of his involvement with the Night and Fog Decree and the Law Against Poles and Jews. The tribunal seriously considered Schlegelberger's argument that the judiciary was under constant challenge from the SS, the Nazi Party, and the Gestapo, that his actions were intended to ward off even harsher actions, and that anyone who would have succeeded him would have been worse. It acknowledged that his actual successor, Thierack, was in fact worse, and that Schlegelberger may have mitigated some measures.[111] However, the tribunal noted that by attempting to hold off the SS and Gestapo, Schlegelberger and the other defendants had created a system of which more extreme successors would take advantage.[112] The court concluded:

> Schlegelberger is a tragic character. He loved the life of the intellect, the work of the scholar. We believe that he loathed the evil that he did, but he sold that

[109] Nuremburg, above n 7, 1027-1028.
[110] Nuremburg, above n 7, 1155-1156.
[111] The tribunal noted one such "mitigation." When German authorities issued an order that all remaining German Jews be evacuated to the East and certain death, Schlegelberger suggested that half-Jews be given the alternative of sterilization, rather than evacuation. The tribunal noted that this alternative itself was hardly humane. Nuremburg, above n 7, 1084.
[112] Nuremburg, above n 7, 1086.

> intellect and that scholarship to Hitler for a mess of political pottage and for the vein hope of personal security.[113]

Schlegelberger was sentenced to life imprisonment.

In addition to Schlegelberger, Von Ammon, Engert, Klemm, Lautz, Mettgenberg, and Rothenberger were convicted of crimes against humanity and war crimes. Joel and Oeschey were convicted of crimes against humanity, war crimes, and membership in a criminal organization. Rothaug was convicted of crimes against humanity, but was acquitted of war crimes. Alstotter was convicted of membership in a criminal organization, but was acquitted of war crimes and crimes against humanity. Barnickle, Cuhorst, Nebelung, and Petersen were acquitted. Westphal died before trial and Engert was granted a mistrial due to illness.

In addition to Schlegelberger, Klemm, Oeschey, and Rothaug received life sentences. The rest received sentences ranging from 5 to 10 years.

One group of verdicts is of particular interest. Seven of the defendants were tried for offenses committed in their capacity as judges. A mistrial was declared in Engert's case, and the tribunal acquitted Nebelung and Petersen with no explanation or review of evidence.[114]

The opinion describes at great length its conclusion with respect to Oeschey, Rothaug, and Cuhorst. In each case, the tribunal described the actions of the defendants in harsh terms. For example, Cuhorst is described as: "... a fanatical Nazi and a ruthless judge. There is also much evidence as to the arbitrary, unfair, and unjudicial manner in which he conducted his trials."[115]

However, the tribunal also noted that some of the records of his cases had been destroyed in an air raid, with the result that "... the tribunal does not consider that it can say beyond a reasonable doubt that the defendant was guilty of inflicting the punishment which he imposed on racial grounds, or that it can say beyond a reasonable doubt that he

[113] Nuremburg, above n 7, 1087.
[114] Nuremburg, above n 7, 1156-1157.
[115] Nuremburg, above n 7, 1158.

used discriminatory provisions of the Law Against Poles and Jews to the prejudice of the Poles to be tried."[116]

Thus, although Cuhorst may have been an agent of injustice, it had not been proven that he committed a crime against humanity, one element of which was atrocity or persecution based on racial, religious, or political grounds.

There was no such problem of proof with respect to Oeschey and Rothaug. Their convictions were based on many examples of sham trials and harsh sentences given to defendants specifically because they were Jews or Poles.[117]

Aftermath

The story does not end with the imposition of sentences. Both during and after the 12 NMT trials, pressure to stop the trials or mitigate the sentences developed in Germany and the United States. Opposition in the United States was led by a group of conservative Republican senators, notably Senators Joseph McCarthy and Robert Taft.[118]

In Germany, a number of groups sought the release of the NMT defendants, including church groups and the Adenauer government of the newly formed Federal Republic of Germany. While the United States was negotiating for German accession to the North Atlantic Treaty Organization (NATO) alliance and German support in the Cold War, the High Commissioner for Germany, John McCloy, set processes in motion that resulted in the release of all NMT defendants, including the Justice Trial defendants. Schlegelberger received a medical release in 1951. The last Justice Trial defendants to be released were Oeschey in 1955 and Rothaug in 1956.[119]

IV

Conclusion

116 Ibid.
117 Nuremburg, above n 7, 166. See discussion above.
118 Heller, above n 2, Appendix A.
119 Heller gives an excellent account of this process in his book, above n 2, 331-369.

> I myself was a criminal judge. One single murder occupied our time for 2 to 3 weeks, and it was a terrible thing. Two murders by one person- that was horrifying. If someone had eight to ten murders on his conscience, then he was described as a mass murderer in the press of Europe, and people asked themselves whether this was something that could be handled by means of the penal code at all.
>
> When, last year, in the courtroom of the big trial I listened to Hoess, of Auschwitz, when he answered the question of the prosecutor as to how many people he had killed, he answered he didn't remember exactly whether two and a half or three million. At that time it was quite obvious to me that this had anything to do anymore with legal considerations because, Mr. Prosecutor, no matter what a state regulates concerning the question of review of a law the state has to think of normal conditions. These occurrences and matters cannot be measured by any order of the world at all.
>
> Professor Hermann Jahrreiss, Nuremburg, above n 7, at 281.

> "The arc of the moral universe is long, but it bends toward justice."
>
> Martin Luther King Jr.

The introduction to this article posed three questions: Was the trial procedurally fair? Was it substantively fair? Was justice done?

Was the Trial Procedurally Fair?

The opinion in the trial provides the appropriate measure of its fairness. In discussing the Night and Fog Program in particular, the tribunal set forth a number of criteria defining a fair trial under international law.

A fair trial would have to be public, with a record of proceedings. The defendants could not be held incommunicado. They would be entitled to counsel of their own choice and would receive adequate notice of the charges against them with sufficient time to prepare for their case. They would have an opportunity to confront witnesses against them and present witnesses and documents on their own behalf. There would need to be interpreters available for those unable to understand the language or proceedings, and the finder of fact and law would be fair and impartial. [120]

The Nuremburg Trials in general, and the Justice Trial specifically, met this international standard well. The defendants not only had counsel of their own choosing, but unlike in pre-Gideon American practice, the United States government paid for their counsel. They received copies of the indictments long before the trial, and were given copies of all documents the prosecution intended to introduce prior to their introduction.[121] The defendants were allowed to present witnesses on their own behalf, as well as exhibits. Indeed, the defense submitted more witnesses and exhibits than did the prosecution. Guilt had to be established beyond a reasonable doubt.

Given the hybrid nature and logistical problems of the proceedings, much of the evidence was presented by affidavit rather than live witnesses. However, the defense had the ability to require the prosecution to call any person whose affidavit the prosecution had produced for purposes of cross-examination. The defense also benefitted from the availability of simultaneous interpreters. As noted, supra, Justice Jackson offered as a standard rule for determining the fairness of a proceeding that the result could be the acquittal of defendants. In the Justice Trial, the tribunal granted the defense motion striking the conspiracy count. It also acquitted four of the defendants. Most significantly, it acquitted Cuhorst; although the tribunal found that he was a reprehensible judge, they could not find him guilty beyond a reasonable doubt of the charge of war crimes because it had not been proven that he had discriminated against Poles and Jews on the basis of race.

On the one hand, if this trial is said to have established a universal standard of procedural fairness, it is of note that United States law did not constitutionally mandate many of the protections afforded to the defendants, such as provision of counsel at public expense or full discovery, until several years later. Additionally, although the United States legal system was well regarded at the time, the standard of justice for

120 Nuremburg, above n 7, 1046-1047. UN War Crimes Commission Report, above n 45, Vol. VI, 103-104.

121 *Brady v. Maryland,* 373 U.S. 83 (1963), which ensured criminal defendants the right to exculpatory materials, was decided 16 years later.

African Americans, particularly in the American South, did not meet the standard set forth by the Justice Trial tribunal.[122]

On the other hand, other elements of American and British practice were not recognized as universally binding. As an example, the trials made no use of a lay jury. They easily admitted hearsay in the form of affidavits, and concomitantly did not require the confrontation of witnesses. However, the defendants were allowed to challenge affidavits and require that the preparer of the affidavit make the witness available for cross-examination and confrontation.

On balance, it appears that the trial was conducted fairly.

Was the Trial Substantively Fair?

This is a more difficult question than procedural fairness. The entire Nuremburg project has been criticized from its inception for serving as "victors' justice" and trying defendants *ex post facto*.

In a sense, most international criminal trials could be viewed as victors' justice. Generally, trials can only take place when the suspect is in custody and witnesses and documentation are available. In the case of high government officials or war lords, these conditions only occur after military defeat or the overthrow of a government.[123] Thus, there was no prospect for trial of Nazi leaders until the Allies had defeated Germany, captured its leaders, and seized German archives. To this extent, the charge of victors' justice is of no weight. The Nuremburg project could have constituted victors' justice if the trials had been show trials or if the Allies had accepted the British suggestion at the London Conference to simply shoot the Nazi leaders. It should be noted that in some circumstances in post-war Europe, victors' justice did in fact occur. Resistance forces summarily executed Mussolini and other fascist leaders, female collaborators in France and Italy underwent public humiliation, and German populations were summarily expelled from Czechoslovakia for collaboration.

---

122 See, e.g., the Scottsboro cases; *Powell v. Alabama*, 267 U.S. 45 (1932); *Patterson v. Alabama*, 294 U.S. 600 (1935); *Norris v. Alabama*, 294 U.S. 587 (1935). It appears also that the trial and execution of Japanese general Yamashita did not meet the international standard recognized in the Justice Trial. See In re Yamashita, 327 U.S. 1 (1946) (see dissents of Justice Rutledge and Justice Murphy).

123 The experience of the ICC with respect to Darfur and Kenya demonstrates this problem.

Some critics have suggested that the trial should have included at least one German judge, or perhaps a judge from a neutral country. Given the failure of the Leipzig trials after World War I and the very discrediting of the German judiciary that led to the convening of the Justice Trial, it would have been profoundly inappropriate to have included German judges. Similarly, there were few European neutrals in World War II: Spain and Portugal, which both had authoritarian governments[124]; Sweden, which had cooperated with the Germans in the military occupation of Norway and sold iron and weapons to Germany[125]; Ireland, which exhibited intense anti-British sentiments that led it to refuse all cooperation with the Allies[126]; and Switzerland, which sold war materials to the Germans until late in the war, despite Allied pressure.[127]

More importantly, based on their failure to enter the struggle against Nazism and frequent collaboration with the German war effort, none of these countries had earned the moral stature to participate in the trials.[128] It is not clear if the participation of neutral governments would have been acceptable to any of the belligerent powers, or if their participation would in any way have contributed to the real or perceived justice of the proceedings.

The *ex post facto* charge was a defining moment. None of the defendants in the Justice Trial was charged with crimes against the peace, and the charges of conspiracy to commit war crimes and conspiracy to commit crimes against humanity were dismissed, as international law did not recognize those charges.

The IMT recognized the charge of belonging to a criminal organization, but viewed it as problematic even in that proceeding. The charge required proof that voluntary participation in a criminal organization, such as the SS, at a sufficiently high level with knowledge would constitute a crime. Only Alstotter was found guilty on that count alone. This count, while not technically one of conspiracy, certainly is related. There was little to no precedent for this charge apart from the IMT trial itself, and the charge was

124 Additionally, Franco's Spain, while neutral, favored the Nazis. See Gerhard Weinberg, *A World at Arms: A Global History of World War II* (Cambridge University Press, 2005), 396-397.
125 Ibid, 174-75, 394-95.
126 Ibid, 372-73, 146.
127 Ibid, 399-400.
128 Ibid, 174, 397-98.

essentially residual from the Barney's Memorandum. This count is the most doubtful of the counts in the case, and Alstotter's conviction the only questionable conviction in the trial.

By contrast, the war crimes count was based on centuries of customary law and, since General Order 100 and the subsequent Hague and Geneva Conventions, codified law. All defendants were convicted of war crimes, with the exception of Alstotter and Rothaug, who were acquitted.

The charge of crimes against humanity was the most prominent and substantive innovation of the Nuremburg Trials. In each of the NMT trials, the defendants moved to dismiss this count. However, in 11 of the 12 trials, the tribunals declined to dismiss the count on the basis that ACC10 had defined the tribunals' jurisdiction to include crimes against humanity.[129] The tribunal in the Justice Trial went further and addressed the fairness of the charges, as evidenced. The London Charter defined the crime as a crime in association with one of the other offenses, such as crimes against peace or war crimes. In fact, many crimes against humanity also constituted war crimes. Of course, ACC10 eliminated the "in association" language, and thus seemed to reflect greater confidence in the charge.

In the IMT and NMT trials, the argument was made that crimes against humanity should be recognized as a natural extension of existing offenses, such as war crimes. As international criminal law should grow similarly to common law through the application of existing principles to new situations, there was no *ex post facto* application. Furthermore, and fundamentally, the defendants knew or should have known that their actions were wrong and that they would be held liable should Germany lose the war. Interestingly, in *The Anatomy of the Nuremburg Trials: A Personal Memoir*, at page 629, Telford Taylor seems to agree that at least the offense of crimes against the peace was *ex post facto*, but argues that the injustice would have been greater had the charge not been brought. The tribunal made a strong showing that whether the charge was *ex post facto* or not, there was no injustice in applying the charge to these defendants.

[129] Heller, above n 2 125-126.

The defendants all argued in their defense that they were acting in accordance with German domestic law and did not have the option of disobeying or holding the law invalid. This defense of dealing with unjust Nazi laws has generated a veritable cottage industry among legal philosophers debating the nature of law.[130] In an article in the *Harvard Law Review*, "*Positivism and the Separation of Law and Morals*," 71 Harv. L. Rev. 593 (1958) that was later expanded into the book *The Concept of Law* (1961), Prof. H.L.A. Hart discussed a case in which a German court tried a German woman for the offense of having informed on her husband for violating Nazi law, knowing that he would likely be convicted and executed. Hart argued from a positivist perspective that although German law in the Nazi era was unjust and violated moral norms, it was nevertheless law; therefore, it was unjust to convict her for making use of it. He acknowledged that although the unjust law might have a claim of obedience over her, she would have had a moral imperative to disobey.

In the same edition of the *Harvard Law Review*, professor and modern natural law philosopher Lon Fuller published a response, arguing that German law under the Nazi regime violated basic norms for the recognition of the validity of the law, e.g. the *ad hoc* application of rules.[131] Thus, at a certain point, Germany ceased to have a legal system at all. Therefore, the wife should not be able to claim the protection of the law. This article was expanded into *The Morality of Law*, also in 1961.

Ronald Dworkin, the leading interpretivist philosopher, criticized Hart and the positivists in his book *Law's Empire*, Harvard University Press, 1986, for their semantic focus on the word "law." It certainly is correct that Nazi Germany had laws, which the government expected its subjects to obey and most Germans did willingly obey. However, Hart was wrong in rejecting the notion based on a deeper understanding of German law as lacking the fundamental characteristics of a flourishing legal system; therefore, it lacked the moral basis to command obedience.

Fuller and Dworkin seem to have presented a sounder argument. Certainly, the enactment of law by analogy in 1936 eliminated all certainty from the law. Henceforth,

---

130 Richard Primus, "A Brooding Omnipresence: Totalitarianism in Post-war Constitutional Thought" (1996) 106(2), *The Yale Law Journal*, 423 gives a illustrative description of the impact of the Nazi experience on legal theory.

131 Lon L Fuller, "Positivism and the Fidelity to Law- A Reply to Professor Hart," (1958) 71(4) *Harvard Law Review* 630.

judicial decisions were at the complete discretion of judges, whose decisions were motivated by national socialist ideology. Among the defendants, Ministry of Justice officials such as Schlegelberger could not claim Hart's approach as defense, as the ministry officials were the drafters of the unjust laws. Prosecutors and judges, to the extent that their trials were shams intended only to give a pretextual legality to discriminatory and lethal conduct, had departed from any reasonable concept of the law.

One irony regarding the development of the law under Nazism was that law by analogy negated the basic positivist basis of German jurisprudence. By relying as it did on the "sound sentiments of the people," this law in effect established a perverse form of natural law. Traditional natural law theories assumed the existence of a fundamental, transcendent structure of law found in nature and ordained by God (although Fuller's version of natural law does not have a theological basis). National socialist ideology, however, posited that the fundamental law of nature was a struggle for existence on the basis of race, in which the fittest race would survive. The "sound sentiment of the people," was effectively an appeal to a higher legal or moral authority than positive law. Thus, the judges felt comfortable departing from existing written law relating to punishment when, for example, they felt there was a racial imperative to impose a higher sentence, as in the cases of Leo Katzenberger or the Polish farmworkers. It is striking that several of the defendants in the IMT – notably, Speer – had experienced remorse for their deeds, yet not one of the defendants in the Justice Trial did so.

Was Justice Done?

> "They defiled the German temple of justice...
> The temple must be reconsecrated. This cannot be done in the twinkling of an eye or by any mere ritual. It cannot be done in any single proceeding, or at any one place. It certainly cannot be done at Nuremburg alone."
>
> Opening Statement of Brigadier General Telford Taylor

The defendants in this case, with the arguable exception of Alstotter, were fairly convicted. However, mitigation offered a number of interesting arguments to consider when evaluating the overall fairness of the proceeding.

In his opening statements, counsel for Rothenberger argued that the members of the tribunal must recognize the difficulty of life under a dictatorship. Under circumstances in which arbitrary arrest or dismissal were possible, only the unusually courageous would attempt to counter the system. Most people, apparently including most of the defendants, would therefore lose all initiative and acquiesce in the system, regardless of any personal objections.

This argument would have been stronger were it not apparent that many of the defendants were members of the Nazi Party, and all had been willing to draft unjust laws or willingly rule by analogy. It is striking that there was resistance to the Nazis in other areas of German society, such as the Confessing church, the White Rose, and the Kreisau Circle among Christian groups, and the July 20 conspiracy in the army and the aristocracy. There was no equivalent resistance among the judiciary.[132]

Schlegelberger argued that his actions were strategically designed to mitigate the most detrimental aspects of Nazi rule. He was in constant conflict with the SS, the Gestapo, and the Nazi Party to maintain judicial independence. Thus, by accepting civil jurisdiction over the Night and Fog cases, he prevented victims from being surrendered to the Gestapo for summary execution or immediate confinement in a concentration camp. His draft of the Law Against Poles and Jews intended to maintain at least some semblance of legal process for Poles and Jews. He argued that his suggestion that half-Jews be given the option of sterilization rather than be deported to certain death in the East was the commission of a small evil in order to avoid a greater one.[133]

In his final statement, Schlegelberger argued that he knew that his successors would be far more harmful than he was, and that he had a clear conscience.[134]

Rothenberg made a similar argument. He testified that his lengthy memorandum concerning a Nazi conception of law was ultimately intended to increase Hitler's comfort level with the judiciary so that he would not feel it necessary to end judicial independence.[135]

---

[132] Ibid, 146 has identified only one judge of all the German judges who in fact had the courage to resist unjust laws, but it should be noted that his only penalty was an early retirement at full pension.
[133] Nuremburg, above n 7, 722.
[134] Nuremburg, above n 7, 941.
[135] Nuremburg, above n 7, 498-99.

The tribunal took this argument seriously, particularly with respect to Schlegelberger. However, the tribunal also noted that rather than tempering the demands of the regime, this strategy instead facilitated them. The opinion notes, "If the judiciary could slay their thousands, why couldn't the police slay their tens of thousands."[136] Thus, the tribunal nevertheless felt compelled to bestow severe sentences. However, in the aftermath of the trials, every single defendant was released early, regardless of the severity of the offense or degree of moral culpability. Most notable was Schlegelberger's release in 1951, only four years after the end of the trial.

Although the trial itself accomplished justice, the disproportionately short sentences that the defendants served constituted an injustice, particularly as the commutations of sentence were driven by political expediency rather than legal or moral considerations.

Dr. Martin Luther King Jr. once commented, "the arc of the moral universe is long, but it bends towards justice."

Whether justice was done for the individual defendants in this case – or, for that matter, their victims, who received no restitution and perhaps retribution for their suffering – this trial and the NMT trials in general served larger interests of justice.

The Justice Trial and the other NMT trials exposed the crimes of the Nazis and German society to the world and the German public in a way that was credible and fair.[137] A comprehensive record of the Nazi era exists precisely because these trials afforded defendants a full opportunity to challenge the prosecution's case, present their own witnesses, and introduce documents. Every book and article on the German legal system relies on the record of the Justice Trials. The NMT trials were also a key component of post-war efforts to more explicitly define the laws of war and crimes against humanity. In fact, the trials preceded the 1949 Geneva Conventions, which further defined the laws of war and crimes against humanity, as well as the Genocide Convention. Prof.

---

[136] Nuremburg, above n 7, 1086.

[137] The Office of the Military Government (OMGUS) did conduct intensive public opinion surveys of the German public from 1945-49 on a variety of issues. In polls taken between 1945 and 1946, 79% of the German public thought that the IMT was fair, 55% thought the sentences handed down were just, 21% thought the sentences were too lenient, and 84% stated that they had learned something new from the trial. OMGUS Public Opinion in Germany 1945-49, 31-35.

Boudreau argues above that these legal developments and innovations, whether of historical or positivist origins, help constitute a new law of nations that enables judges to adjudicate future cases involving possible government atrocities. In essence, he adds Blackstone's idea of a law of nations adjudicated by municipal courts to Jeremy Bentham's prevailing positivist paradigm. At the very least, this is consistent with the original intent of the Nuremberg Charter and Trials and provides an opening for judges in national jurisdictions to prosecute these new Nuremberg norms in the future.

So, the cycle of Nuremburg trials is perhaps best understood as part of a general effort to create a new and just world order. Nuremburg was part of an international effort to establish new norms of international conduct and create a rules-based system to govern international conflict, which was further advanced by the Four Freedoms, the Atlantic Charter, the formation of the UN, and the series of post-war treaties defining the laws of war and international humanitarian law, most notably including the Geneva Convention of 1949, the Genocide Convention, and the Universal Declaration of Human Rights. Indeed, the trials created the precedent of personal criminal responsibility that would ultimately lend these treaties more legitimacy. The Justice Trial in particular established the precedent that judges, prosecutors, and legal officials would enjoy no immunities for sham legal proceedings or the misuse of the law for purposes of justifying war crimes or crimes against humanity.[138] (The forthcoming chapter by Oxford-trained Prof. Juan Carlos Sainz-Borgo demonstrates how the Nuremberg category of "crimes against humanity" was possibly *misapplied* by Venezuela's attempt to criminalize the drug trade, and subsequently addressed by that country's court system.)

In the opening of the Justice Trial, Telford Taylor stated in reference to the German legal system, "the temple of justice must be reconsecrated." In fact, by the mid-1960s, Germany was conducting its own war crimes trials.

In *The Eumenides*, the third play in Aeschylus' Oresteia trilogy, ancient goddesses of vengeance called the Furies pursue Orestes, the son of Agamemnon, in order to avenge his murder of his mother. The goddess Athena convenes a trial, which acquits Orestes,

---

138 This precedent has obvious implications if and when the United States ever comes to grips with the use of torture and prisoner abuse by the CIA and military interrogators. These abuses were perpetrated under the purported authority of a series of poorly reasoned legal opinions by a small group of lawyers in the Department of Justice. These opinions were all subsequently withdrawn by the Justice Department. See Senate Select Committee on Intelligence, *The Senate Intelligence Committee Report on Torture* (Melville House, 2014), 7-8.

and the Furies accept the result. Athena then states that a new civilization will result from the replacement of revenge by law.

The post-war treatment of German leadership could have taken many forms, from exile to summary execution to inaction. The trials that did take place documented Nazi atrocities in a manner convincing to all but Holocaust deniers, vindicated the suffering of victims, and established both international standards for fair trials and a useful precedent for future international criminal trials. Most importantly, they helped end the cycle of retribution and violence that threatened to destroy post-war Europe. Although the Justice Trial and NMT trials in general achieved only partial success with respect to individual defendants, they were a material advance in the civilization of the world.

CHAPTER 4

INTERNATIONAL RULE OF LAW AND HUMAN RIGHTS THE ASPIRATION OF AN ESSENTIAL WORK IN PROGRESS

Joaquín González Ibáñez

Before participating in the Nuremberg Trials as the American Chief of Counsel, Robert H. Jackson made the following statement in the spring of 1945, even as Hitler and the Nazi regime in Europe held out in remnants of Germany, including the besieged city of Berlin:

> Our Constitution and our philosophy of law have been characterized by a regard for the broadest possible liberty of the individual. *But the dullest mind must now see that our national society cannot be so self-sufficient and so isolated that freedom, security, and opportunity of our own citizens can be assured by good domestic laws alone.* Forces originating outside of our borders and not subject to our laws have twice in my lifetime disrupted our way of living, demoralized our economy, menaced the security of life, liberty, and property within our country. The assurance of our fundamental law that the citizen's life may not be taken without due process of law is of little avail against a foreign aggressor or against the necessities of war. Either submission or resistance will take life, liberty, and property without a semblance of due process of law...
>
> *But we are at this moment at one of those infrequent occasions in history when convulsions have uprooted habit and tradition in a large part of the world and there exists not only opportunity, but necessity as well, to reshape some institutions and practices which sheer inertia would otherwise make invulnerable*...But we can have nothing in common with the cynics who would have us avoid disillusionment by having no ideals, who think that because they do not believe in anything, they cannot be fooled. *We must keep the faith roughly stated by Lord Chief Justice Coke that even the King is "under God and the law...*
>
> Any United Nations court that would try, say, Hitler or Goebbels would face the same choice. That is one of the risks that are taken whenever trials are commenced. The ultimate principle is that you must put no man on trial under the

forms of judicial proceedings if you are not willing to see him freed if not proven guilty. (Emphasis added.)

Robert H. Jackson,
The Rule of Law Among Nations,
Conference at the American Society of International Law,
Washington, D.C.
April 13, 1945

Introduction

In February 1945, Primo Levi, a Jewish Italian citizen pain-stricken by hunger and illness in the sick bay in Auschwitz, wrote about how he could see from the windows the shadow of a rider entering the extermination camp (*verninstunlager*).[1] That rider wore a soldier's cap with the Soviet Army's red cross, and was on his way to liberate the prisoners. In February 2005, European government leaders from various nations that had taken part in World War II said "*Never Again!*" and expressed the need to strengthen democracy, civil society, and respect for human rights.[2]

The history of the 20th century – and to a large degree, the current century – could well be explained by the horrific World Wars and other conflicts that have occurred, as well as consequent international efforts to strengthen the role of the rule of law to protect freedom, individual human rights, entire peoples, and peace.

Some months before the 1945 London Conference, in which the adoption of the Charter of Military Tribunals created the legal basis for the Nuremberg Trials, the international legalism thesis of Henry Stimson prevailed within the Truman Administration over Morguenthau´s "victors' justice" vision. I agree with Henry Morgenthau´s affirmation that "*[t]he respect which the people of the world have to international law is in direct proportion to its ability to meet their needs.*"[3] That also means that those nations that

[1] P. Levi., *Se questo é un uomo-La tregua* (*If This Is a Man – The Truce*) Einaudi, 1950.

[2] See Joaquín González Ibáñez, "Human Rights and the Rule of Law after Abu Ghraib and the Election of Barack Obama: A European Vision of the Past and Future of the U.S. War on Terror" in *Protección Internacional de Derechos Humanos y Estado de Derecho*, II Volumen obra homenaje a Nelson Mandela, AAVV, director y editor de la obra. Joaquín González Ibáñez ediciones jurídicas, Bogotá, 2009, p. 405.

[3] Morgenthau to Truman, 29 May 1945, *Morgenthau Diary*, vol. 2, pp. 1544-45, cited in Gary J. Bass, *Stay the hand of vengeance.*

do not respect international law and consider themselves unaccountable for their deeds are likely to receive the rejection and disapproval of those who voluntarily submit to the limits and restraints of international law and expect justice and security from its application, as well as from an international legal order that is structured to meet their needs: peace, security, human dignity, and justice.

In view of this, the international rule of law – and specifically, the law of nations, which incorporates international human rights law – is a natural extension of domestic legal jurisdictions dedicated to the principle of a society or societies ultimately ruled by law, not by transient rulers. Such an international rule of law requires judicial enforcement when necessary, which represents the ongoing attempt on the part of the international community to realize its legal, social and moral obligations. This ongoing effort to broaden the scope of domestic and international jurisdictions is evolutionary and thus partially aspirational, reaffirming that the advancement and exercise of full human rights represents one of the most important forms of progress in the human condition. This is especially true because the *progress of the human condition* infers access to the exercise of rights by vulnerable and excluded groups, which typically include women, children, indigenous peoples, poor and marginalized individuals, minorities, and – above all – victims. Human rights are *the rights of the other* and a commitment to the cause of justice.[4]

In his work *On the Rule of Law,* Brian Z. Tamanaha underlined the idea that these questions have been perennial dilemmas for human beings, and that behind injustice, there is a continuous positive process that is the refinement and efficiency of responding to the call against injustice. The answers have been to restore the rule of law and advance its relevance and efficiency for the aspirations of humankind.

> Preventing government tyranny was a concern in ancient Athens, a concern throughout the Medieval Period, and continues to be a concern everywhere today. The nature of limitations will vary with the society, culture, political and economic arrangements, but the need for limitations on the government will never be obsolete. The great contribution to human existence of the rule of law in this sense is that it provides one answer to this need.

---

[4] Joaquín González Ibáñez, "Legal Pedagogy, The Rule of Law and Human Rights: The Professor, The Magistrate's Robe and Miguel de Unamuno" *Journal of Human Rights Law,* 6(1), 2012, p.147, available at <http://www.americanstudents.us/journals/ijhrl/>.

John Ruskin understood human action as an eventual generator of a legacy called civilization. This legacy is measurable in its words, deeds, and arts. Thus, the law applied today, which contains the three elements that Tamanaha has mentioned, will likely be this era's legacy of civility or inequality. Ongoing developments in the present, and those in the legal system in 2012, are definitive for the modern capacity to interpret and assess the current state of civilization.[5]

Yet, once again, the world is presently witnessing the alarming and constant killing of innocent human beings – not only without a proper and immediate response to stop the massacres, but also without the realistic possibility of responding efficiently to the impunity or holding those behind these international crimes responsible.

On February 4, 2012, there was an anti-regime demonstration in the city of al-Qsair, southwest of Homs, where the UN confirmed that Syrian forces had killed more than 200 people, including children and the elderly. At the demonstration, a 12-year-old child held a placard with handwritten letters in an attempt to attract media attention to their fate. It read, "*If you do not help us, we will be killed.*" Hours later, dozens of civilians were killed. It seemed that the world had not believed that child's cry for help, and disbelief was a natural response. It was almost exactly as Elie Wiesel had revealed in his book *Night* when he told the story of a Jewish citizen of his small village in Romania who had managed to escape from a *verningstunglager* (extermination camp), but whose story no one had considered credible until it was already too late for those at Auschwitz.[6]

---

[5] Ibid.

[6] See WIESEL: "I told him that I did not believe that they could burn people in our age, that humanity would never tolerate it (...)" Later on after his release, and for many years, the Auschwitz survivor Elie Wiesel had often recalled the responsibility of survivors as witnesses and keepers of the collective memory: "For the survivor who chooses to testify, it is clear: his duty is to bear witness for the dead and for the living. He has no right to deprive future generations of a past that belongs to our collective memory. To forget would be not only dangerous but offensive; to forget the dead would be akin to killing them a second time." Wiesel, E., *Night*, Hill and Wang, New York, 1985, p.23. In the edition by Hill and Wang quoted here, see the end of book for a copy of his speech as Nobel Peace Laureate in Oslo, 10 December 1986. Also available at http://www.nobelprize.org/nobel_prizes/peace/laureates/1986/wiesel-lecture.html

"This is what I say to the young Jewish boy wondering what I have done with his years. It is in his name that I speak to you and that I express to you my deepest gratitude. No one is as capable of gratitude as one who has emerged from the kingdom of night. We know that every moment is a moment of grace, every hour an offering; not to share them would mean to betray them. Our lives no longer belong to us alone; they belong to all those who need us desperately. (…) Without memory, our existence would be barren and opaque, like a prison cell into which no light penetrates; like a tomb which rejects the living. Memory saved the Besht, and if anything can, it is memory that will save humanity. For me, hope without memory is like memory without hope. (…)

Indeed, in 2012, the world proclaimed once more in reference to Syria, "*Never Again*!" However, is this resolve actually effective and true today? What purpose does international legal machinery serve, and what has it done for victims in Syria? How can all actors, including states, private individuals, and international organizations, be held accountable? With the end of World War II, governments, judges, and statespeople almost universally expressed that the answer seemed to be through the strengthening and enforcement of the international rule of law. This task is still pressing, paramount, and promising, despite the horrific failures of the present time.

I

The Rule of Law

Law is perceived as imperative, and "[i]t seems natural to think of Laws as commands. In doing so, however, we have already begun to theorize about the nature of law (…)."[7] Law incorporates a community's aspirations in terms of its perception of the principles and values necessary to provide dignity, justice, respect, and security to each of its members. Thus, the rule of law is affirmatively "a cultural achievement of universal significance," and likely "the most important political ideal today."[8]

In a conference at the *Center for Public Law*[9] at Oxford University, Judge Tom Binghan listed eight principles that define the generic concept of the rule of law:

a) The law must be accessible and, so far as possible, be intelligible, clear and predictable.
b) Question of legal right and liability should ordinarily be resolved by application of the law and not by the exercise of discretion.

What all these victims need above all is to know that they are not alone; that we are not forgetting them, that when their voices are stifled we shall lend them ours, that while their freedom depends on ours, the quality of our freedom depends on theirs."

[7] LYONS, D., *Ethics and the Rule of Law*, Cambridge University Press, Cambridge, 1993, p. 37.

[8] See TAMANAHA, B.Z., *On the Rule of Law*, Cambridge University Press, 2004, p.1.

[9] See The Rt. Hon Lord Bingham of Cornhill KG, House of Lords, conference of 16 November 2006, full text transcript available at https://www.cpl.law.cam.ac.uk/sir-david-williams-lectures2006-rule-law/rule-law-text-transcript, also published at BINGHAM, "The rule of Law," *Cambridge Law Journal* 67,69, Cambridge, 2007, p. 67-85.

c) The law should apply equally to all, except to the extent that objective differences justify different treatment.
d) The law must provide the necessary human rights protection.
e) Means must be provided for resolving, without prohibitive cost or unjustified delay, *bona fide* civil disputes, which the parties themselves are unable to resolve.
f) Public officers and magistrates at all levels must exercise the powers conferred on then reasonably, in good faith, for the purpose for which the powers were granted, and without exceeding the limits of such powers.
g) Judicial and other complementary procedures must be fair and independent.
h) States must comply with its international law obligations.

In other words, the term "rule of law" now refers to post-World War II innovations in the global legal order that have empowered individuals and other actors in the process of limiting power in domestic and *international spheres.* Since World War II and the herculean effort to destroy the Nazi regime, these legal and political limits are no longer viewed solely within the jurisdiction of a nation state, but must be viewed within the overarching context of the *international* rule of law.

The existence of any domestic society increasingly interacting with international actors with a globalized sphere of economics and relations implicitly assumes and even requires an international rule of law. This is certainly not a new or even original idea; as Dr. Boudreau notes in his preceding article, the classical Roman and later Byzantine civilizations developed the idea of *Jus Gentium* as a law common to all of mankind in order to regulate commerce and interactions with foreigners. At the time, the full scope or location of "all of mankind" was not truly known, so it was largely aspirational to speak of a law common to all of humanity. Historically speaking, this has changed, and as Dr. Boudreau notes, it is possible to speak of a modern law of nations that became fully explicit during and after World War II in the drafting and subsequent enforcement of various declarations, charters, and conventions, such as the Nuremberg Charter, the UN Charter, or the Convention for the Prevention and Punishment of Genocide. As such, the rule of law entails the regulation of mutual intercourse of nations and international contacts and relations of individuals through legal concepts, standards, institutions, and procedures.[10] This is the essence of Dr. Boudreau's argument that the

[10] Charles Rhyner, Opening Statement before Boston conference on World Peace through Law, 27 March 1959, quoted in BINGHAM, T., *The Rule of Law*, Allen Lane Penguin Books, London, 2010, p. 111.

domestic, international, and indigenous courts and judiciaries now have a critical role in the observance and enforcement of the law of nations, a judicial responsibility that can now, when circumstances warrant it, explicitly transcend the limits of a nation state's domestic jurisdiction to include all peoples or individuals under assault by illegitimate state power or terrorism.

As such, the international rule of law is a system that aims to put limits and restraints on governments that, limited by the law, are understood as a formal legality containing the sovereign´s will and the aspiration of justice. Any rule of law is the rule of law and not the rule of man, meaning that legal and political institutions provide a framework for policies throughout time, not just personal and individual figures embodying the state.

In highlighting the importance of the way in which law is adopted, the method by which law enters into force is also relevant. Through the representative of the sovereign in a public, open, and contested way – i.e., a democratic legislative process – there is also a qualitative "threshold" of the law. Anne Ramberg has explained:

> The law must properly incorporate social values including the demand of human rights and international humanitarian law. But not even this is enough. The Rule of Law also requires a proper administration of justice. This in turn mandates a reliable and qualitative court system with well educated and honest judges, prosecutors and advocates.[11]

This idea embraces the concept of legitimacy of a democratic system and the key role of courts and judiciaries of the world in upholding the rule of law. As such, democracy is a system of rule by laws, not by individuals. In a democracy, the rule of law protects the rights of citizens, maintains order, and limits the power of the government. As a consequence, all citizens are equal under the law, and no one should be discriminated against on the basis of race, religion, ethnic group, or gender.[12]

> The international organization created to effectively respond to situations such as the Syrian crisis, sanction perpetrators, and provide relief to victims was conceived during World War II, and the drafting of the Charter of the United Nations

[11]Anne Ramberg quoted at BINGHAM, T., *The Rule of Law*, Allen Lane Penguin Books, London, 2010, p. 171.
[12] TAMANAHA, B.Z., *On the Rule of Law*, Cambridge University Press, City, 2004, p. 141.

commenced in April 1945, even before the war's end. The United Nations, in its Preamble, proclaims its goal:

> ...to save succeeding generations from the scourge of war, which twice in our lifetime has brought untold sorrow to mankind, and to reaffirm faith in fundamental human rights, in the dignity and worth of the human person, in the equal rights of men and women and of nations large and small.

More specifically, Article 3 of the UN Charter states as a main purpose of the organization:

> To achieve international co-operation in solving international problems of an economic, social, cultural, or humanitarian character, and in promoting and encouraging respect for human rights and for fundamental freedoms for all without distinction as to race, sex, language, or religion;

In 2004, 15 years after the fall of the Berlin Wall, UN Secretary General Kofi Annan situated the rule of law at the very heart of the organization´s mission:

> It refers to a principles of governance in which all persons, institutions and entities, public and private, including the State itself, are accountable to laws that are publicly promulgated, equally enforced and independently adjudicates, and which are consistent with international human rights norms and standards. It requires, as well, equality before the law, accountability to the law, fairness in the application of the law, separation of powers, participation in decision-making, legal certainty, avoidance of arbitrariness and procedural and legal transparency.[13]

Yet, even as the UN Charter was drafted, it became apparent that the UNSC would not or could not play a major role in this regard beyond *ad hoc* situation specific cases. There was no room for this in the UNCharter, Chapter VII, *Action with respect to threats to the peace, breaches of the peace, and acts of aggression.* For instance, Russia and China vetoed the UNSC Resolution on Syria in 2012.[14]

---

13 Secretary General Kofi Annan´s Report, 23 August 2004 to the Security Council S/2004/16, 23 August 2004, para. 6.

14 Syria resolution vetoed by Russia and China at United Nations Saturday 4 February 2012 Paul Harris in New York,

As a result, international law scholars, researchers, and observers of violations of the rules of war in the past 50 years have often been poisoned by the Greek myth of Cassandra. Once an observer believes that he or she knows the future occurrence of a catastrophic event from having already seen it repeated in prior conflicts in the last 50 years or even having experienced it firsthand, the observer believes that there is nothing that can be done to stop the event from reoccurring, and particularly that he or she will not be believed when trying to tell others.[15]

Likewise, the evolution of international law since the dilemma of the Doctrine of Humanitarian Intervention after Kosovo[16] and the most recent principle of responsibility to protect[17] has not only failed to demonstrate a capacity to act against grave violations of human rights, but has actually illustrated again that current enforcement of international law often relies on the political decision of the security council members, especially permanent members. A result of this is the foreboding feeling that in Syria in 2012 and elsewhere, one can observe glimmers of the Cold War.

As such, it is becoming quite apparent to nearly all juridical actors or institutions that believe in the rule of law that the *ad hoc* and uncertain current mechanisms for the possible enforcement of international legal obligations are increasingly inadequate in view of the continuing and historic injustices that demand justice and legal accountability.

If political institutions are failing so dismally to provide basic protections to entire peoples under attack, as well as to individuals and their families, then the historic shift to the international rule of law that is already underway must be strengthened and

Martin Chulov, David Batty and Damien Pearse guardian.co.uk, 2012 22.28 GMT. The appalling photo of the children holding the poster from Alessio Romenzi/AFP/Getty:
http://www.guardian.co.uk/world/2012/feb/04/assad-obama-resign-un-resolution

[15] See HOMER, *The Iliad*, Penguin Classics, London, 1991. Cassandra was the daughter of King Priam in *The Iliad.* She warned her father about dreams about the future, and she was doomed to not be believed. She was a cursed prophetess, and her father, King Priam, did not want to believe her when she told him about the consequences of accepting the present of the Trojan horse, which finally meant the fall of Troy.

[16] BAJORIA, JAYSHREE, "The Dilemma of Humanitarian Intervention," Council of Foreign Relations, 24 March 2011, http://www.cfr.org/human-rights/dilemma-humanitarian-intervention/p16524

[17]SG/SM/11701- 15 July 2008, Secretary General Ban Ki-moon Defends, Clarifies "Responsibility To Protect" At Berlin Event On "Responsible Sovereignty: International Cooperation For A Changed World"
http://www.un.org/News/Press/docs/2008/sgsm11701.doc.htm

vigorously pursued. This especially must be done by the various judiciaries in the world, who should not be relegated by political authority to hapless witnesses, like the Greek tragic mask in Picasso's *Guernica*, of the ongoing atrocities in the world. In contrast, this article argues that the independence and efficacy of such domestic, international and indigenous judiciaries are central to a society's legitimacy and ultimate self-determination. This is especially necessary and true of democratic societies.

II

Rule of Law in Democratic Societies: Some Personal Reflections

In the weeks following the violent death of hundreds of innocent people in Syria, professors of international law around the world likely had to strive to develop convincing arguments regarding the purpose of international law and how democracies have implemented a system of international legal order to avoid impunity, provide legal redress, and obtain enduring, court-sanctioned answers to these outrageous crimes.

In view of this, Prof. Fallon has summarized the core structure of the idea and aspirations behind the rule of law: "All understandings of the rule of law share three purposes, or values: the rule of law serves to protect people against anarchy; to allow people to plan their affairs with confidence because they know the legal consequences of their actions; and to protect people from the arbitrary exercise of power by public officials."[18]

Of course, I have tried to avoid cynicism – still believing that most of the work is yet to be done – but it is important to continue posing the right questions about the incapacity to create the spheres of justice, human dignity, and security that appear as the main goals of current international human rights law. There has not yet been another system crafted beyond the rule of law, although it is necessary to acknowledge that "[i]n truth the rule of law is a complex, fragile, and to some extent inherently unrealizable goal."[19] This humble realization must not preclude attempts to achieve that which is humanly possible at the farthest frontier of the international rule of law. The domestic, international, and

[18] FALLON, R. H., "The Rule of Law, as a concept in International discourse," *Columbia Law Review*, I, 7, 1997, p. 97
[19] STROMSETH, J. WIPPMAN, D., BROOKS, R., *Can might make rights?* Cambridge University Press, 2006, p. 57.

indigenous courts and jurisdiction can significantly contribute to obtaining this imperative goal.

The Meaning of Democracy

Democratic societies and states are a logical starting point. They urgently promote the evolutionary and aspirational legal processes leading to the rule of law, such as establishing appropriate jurisdiction or enforcement mechanisms. From a national perspective, an international rule of law is constructed as a process of evolution; individuals and public and private institutions make a difference because of the values, principles, and goals that democratic systems supposedly pursue. The combination of this construction – rule of law and democracy – provides the philosophical and ethical aspiration of international law's improved machinery. In a way, democracy often acts as a gateway to the international rule of law.

Along these same lines, a thorough understanding of human rights in diverse countries is also illustrative. The totalitarianisms are on one side: fascism, communism, and the diverse pseudo-democratic regimes that have dismantled the rule of law and democratic systems and systematically violated people's basic freedoms. On the other side are democracies that, with varying degrees of success, have tried to strengthen democratic institutions by offering a framework of options and opportunities for their citizens and a basis for genuine public liberties.

The pursuit of justice for democratic societies is framed in the construction and reinforcement of the rule of law. Law is a system based on ethical aspirations and common moral values, and it happens to be an intellectual system, or *entelecheia*, that tries to protect spheres of liberty, dignity, and security for people. The instrument in the international domain is now international human rights within the fiduciary law of nations. In short, human rights law is legally binding and obligatory, not an ancillary or incidental characteristic of domestic or international legal orders. As a result, domestic courts, especially those in democracies, have become the primary guardians and, if need be, enforcers of the rule of law, thus ending the unacceptable and politically induced impunity for atrocities such as the one occurring in Syria. Thus, the whole aspiration of achieving international justice for democratic states is fulfilled through the completion and implementation of the international rule of law.

Nowadays, states are the main actors in international relations, forming an international community that has developed out of the creation of a political concept in Europe in the 15th century: the nation state. For most of the modern period, political science and international law has conflated the terms "nation state," thereby perhaps inadvertently contributing to the evolving dominance of the state.

The unfortunate apex of this lopsided and misinformed conflation and evolution of the state was the emergence of the Nazi regime, the abolition of which required a world war. As Prof. Boudreau notes, post-World War II innovations in the international legal order have established the nation within the principle of self-determination (and subsequent decolonization). This post-war development has now increasingly problematized the relationship between the nation and state, given the emergent and empirical definition of the nation or a people as a juridical community that shares a sense of moral and legal obligations to one another. The ulterior idea behind self-determination seems to be that a people, when left to their own powers, are entitled through democratic means to select the best form of government for themselves.

Thus, while recognizing the various ways in which political and legal entities interact, the focus here is on democratic societies and states and identifying the main characteristics that result from an evolution of Western philosophical-political principles and systems derived from the Roman Republic's democracy created 2,500 years ago.[20] This then leads to the challenge of defining a democracy.

---

[20] See MACHIAVELI, N., *Discorsi sopra la prima deca di Tito Livio, Dell'arte della guerra e altre opere,* Rinaldi, UTET, Milano, 2006. It is also interesting to see that the current democratic pattern was conceived in the 6th century BC, during the Roman Republic. M. Sellers has offered a clear and precise analysis of the characteristics of the Roman republican democracy:

"The Origins of Republican Legal Theory

The first self-consciously 'republican' ideology originated in the senatorial opposition to Gaius Julius Caesar, and implies a procedural commitment to certain 'republican' political and legal institutions, usually attributed to Rome's republican constitution of 509-49 BC. The basic desiderata of republican government, as articulated in the republican legal tradition derived from Rome, secure government for the common good through the checks and balances of a mixed constitution, comprising a sovereign people, an elected executive, a deliberate senate, and a regulated popular assembly, constrained by an independent judiciary, and subject to the rule of law. Some republicans would add representation, the separation of powers, or equality of material possessions, to protect the public liberty (libertas) and avoid Rome's eventual descent into popular tyranny and military despotism. Republican liberty signifies subjection to the law and to magistrates, acting for the common good, and never to the private will or domination 'dominatio' of any private master." See M. N. S. Sellers, *Republican Legal Theory. The History, Constitution And Purposes Of Law In A Free State.* 6 Pallgrave MacMillan, New York, 2003. For information on the republic and the Roman democratic model, see Cicero, *De Republica And De Legibus,* (On The Republic And The Laws), 1986.

Legitimate democracies[21] require the following elements:

a) Separation of powers- ensuring checks and balances.
b) Respect for human rights- respecting individual, collective and minority rights.
c) Elections- free, plural and periodical.
d) A sovereign power, represented by the people, composed of a citizens consisting of free men and women with equal rights. Those who form part of that process denote the quality of a given democracy (governance) and the cohesion and inclusiveness of the system.

In particular, it is important to bear in mind the efficiency with which that community, with the full participation of its actors, responds to the demands and needs of citizens (governability). The reduction of institutional and individual corruption remains a basic principal for democracies, as these are a major threat to national sovereignty. Transparency in the functioning and accountability of the acts that institutions and individuals perform is a fundamental aspect of the democratic system.[22]

The existence of the rule of law and accountability requires the pursuit of justice and avoidance of impunity. As the following article by Prof. Juan Carlos Sainz-Borgo evidences, the rule of law is part of system of values, attitudes, and legal spectrum that create a specific society and culture:

> The culture which institutes the rule of law to limit both private and public power consists of a combination of beliefs that law should limit the exercise of power backed up by sufficient behaviour to make it reasonable to think that law in fact does exercise such a restraining function.[23]

Central to this is the independence of the judiciary.

Out of the nearly 200 states in the international community, around 60 are classifiable as democratic, not counting states such as the Russian Federation, Morocco, Egypt, Cuba,

---

[21] See, GONZÁLEZ IBÁÑEZ, J., RAMADAN, H., and RASKIN, J., B., Universidad Alfonso X El Sabio S A B E R E S Social Studies Review, "The Arab Garden And Ground Zero," Revista De Estudios Jurídicos, Económicos Y Sociales, VOLUMEN 6 ~ AÑO 2008, Vol. 6, 2006, ISSN: 1695-631 http://www.uax.es/publicaciones/saberes.htm

[22] See, for example, the case of corruption and its impact on public policies of education by Transparency International, and the impact it creates from both individual and institutional perspectives. See http://www.transparency.org/whatwedo/activity/our_work_on_education, July 2012.

[23] REITZ, J.C, "Export of the Rule of Law" *Transnational Law and Contemporary Problems* vol. 13:429, fall 2003, p.436.

China, etc.[24] Democracies with varying levels of accomplishment have conquered and crafted the rule of law as their genuine product: "(…) the reality is that the existence of the rule of law is matter of degree, with all legal systems being on a spectrum with no rule at all at one end and a complete actualization of the rule of law at the other."[25] This very idea has led the World Justice Project to create a system that might provide an approach of the diverse degree of compliance of 67 countries and different legal systems with the aspirations and goals of the rule of law.[26] It also provides a ranking in alphabetic order and takes into account eight factors that help define a description of the different work in progress of the rule of law. These eight factors are analyzed depending on income group and geographical region and include the following: limited government powers, absence of corruption, order and security, human rights, open government, effective regulatory enforcement, access to civil justice, effective criminal justice, and informal justice.

The interpretation of these factors adopts integrative approach, where the possibility of effective and genuine democracy can be understood as providing the most promising cultural conditions for the exercise of a vastly improved and enhanced international rule of law.

On Legitimacy and the Rule of Law

> "People like myself want not a world in which murder no longer exists (we are not as crazy as that!) … but rather one in which murder is not legitimate."
>
> Albert Camus, *Neither Victims Nor Executioners*

After World War I, the Italian political scientist Guglielmo Ferrero defined political legitimacy as the "invisible genius of the city."[27] According to Ferrero, the main purpose

24 See CIA, *CIA World Fact Report.* US, Virginia, 2005. *at* https://www.cia.gov/library/publications/the-world-factbook/print/us.html This account has not varied dramatically in the past 7 years, and we look with attention at which kind of political system will come out of the Arab Revolution process, and if these changes will spur the activity of individuals who will become citizens as active actors in their political systems.

25 MCCORQUALE, R. "Business, Rule of Law and Human Rights" *The Rule of Law in International and Comparative Context*, British Institute of International and Comparative Law, London, 2010.

26 See the Rule of Law Index produced by World Justice Project available at http://worldjusticeproject.org/rule-of-law-index

27 Guglielmo Ferrero was a disciple of Cesare Lombroso, the inventor of "criminal anthropology," though Ferrero focused afterwards on historical studies and political theory and become one of the most prestigious intellectuals in

of legitimacy is to provide explanations for the actions of governmenst and assure that these explanations will be accepted and recognized peacefully. Legitimacy permits a government to avoid depending on coercion and violence to impose its will and command. The government relationship is founded on the citizen's recognition that certain individuals have a moral right to their obedience, while they feel a duty to give that obedience in return. Where ruler and ruled have agreed on a principle, the government will not fear its subjects. Conversely, as illegitimate governments lack credibility, trust, and consent, they are consistently forced to rely on violence and warfare. This unique relationship between public authority and citizens in a democracy is characterized by a relative absence of fear and coercion.

An appropriate illustration is found in a well-known Latin American example that concerns the way a democratic state legitimizes itself when it pays tribute to the principles and ethical values enshrined in its legal system. It refers to the prologue written by Ernesto Sábato in 1984 in the foreword to the *Argentine National Commission on the Disappearance of Persons Report* (C.O.N.A.D.E.P *Informe Comisión Nacional de Desaparecidos*) during the *dirty war* of the Argentinean dictatorship. Dalla Chiesa was cited as an example of the principles and values that democracies must defend and protect, in both principle and practice.[28]

Sábato tells the story of General Carlo Alberto Dalla Chiesa, general of the Italian *carabinieri*. Dalla Chiesa was an esteemed public official widely known for campaigning against the Red Brigades terrorist group (*Brigate Rosse*) during the 1970s in Italy and also as *prefect* for Palermo for stopping the violence of the Second Mafia War in Italy. In 1982,

---

Europe after World War I. President Theodore Roosevelt nominated Ferrero for a Nobel Prize in Literature for his study of the Roman Republic, a work that presents a radical change from Theodore Mommsen. After 1920, Ferrero became an ardent opponent of Mussolini and had to escape to exile in Switzerland. "The government will be far less frightened of its subjects and of their revolting, knowing that it can count on their voluntary and sincere consent. Being less frightened of its subjects, it will not have to terrorize them nearly as much; less terrorized, the subjects will obey willingly and cheerfully. The principles of legitimacy humanize and alleviate authority, because it is in accordance with their nature to be accepted sincerely, as just and reasonable, by everyone who rules and by the majority, at least, of those who obey. The acceptance of the principles is not always active, willed, and conscious of their deeper meanings. It can be - and frequently is in the masses - a habit more than a conviction, a slothful legacy from the past, a kind of resignation to the inevitable." See FERRERO, G., *The Principles of Power. The Great Political Crises of History*, translated by Theodore R. Jaeckel, G.P. Putnam's Sons, New York, 1941, p. 40. See, the "Introduction" to the Spanish version by Eloy García López, Guillermo Ferrero, *Los genios invisibles de la ciudad*, Tecnos, Madrid, 1998.

[28] See SABATO, E. at the Report of CONADEP, National Commission on the Disappearance of Persons *(Comisión Nacional de Desaparecidos)* available at 1984<http://web.archive.org/web/20031013222809/http://nuncamas.org/english/library/images/linea350.gif> and http://www.desaparecidos.org

Dalla Chiesa was killed in Palermo, along with his wife and their driver, just three months after taking command. In 1978, when the Red Brigades kidnapped Aldo Moro, the President of the Christian Democrat Party (*Democrazia Cristiana*), Dalla Chiesa responded to a suggestion that torture should be used in the investigation of a Red Brigade terrorist arrested a few days before with a statement that was highly contested at the time: "Italy can survive the loss of Aldo Moro. It would not survive the introduction of torture."[29] His unwavering devotion to the rule of law was not in vain.

At the same time, there presumably are already clear international standards for addressing issues such as the aforementioned atrocities that have taken place in Syria; sadly, if anything, the situation there is much worse and more tragic. Evidently, there seems to be no legal norm or convention that restrains many of the combatants. When I first wrote this article in August 2012, the atrocities in Syria were accelerating, and are now continuing in the spring of 2016. Syria is still in flames as this book goes to press. As Prof. Robert Goldman has asserted, in the worst possible scenario of human rights violations, it is now known that justice is a goal in which the means to achieve the goals are as important as the goal itself.[30] This type of abuse of power by states and other actors is also reshaping an atlas of discontented actors in the international arena, as Dominique Moisi has defined in *The Geopolitics of Emotion: How Cultures of Fear, Humiliation, and Hope are Reshaping the World*,[31] where an ubiquitous lack of legitimacy and justice in national and international conflicts diminishes the presence of the international rule of law.

In the increasingly global and interconnected society in which many now live, no policy of democratic states would be sustainable without including active respect, as often expressed by explicit court enforcement actions, for international human rights treaties and international humanitarian law. These principles should not be considered "soft law," but rather as an integral part of law itself, establishing the certain rule of law,

---

29 See *Il generale nel suo laberinto*, published in La Repubblica, Roma, 4 September 1982, http://www.repubblica.it/online/album/ottantadue/bocca/bocca.html

30 Prof. Robert Goldman at WCL-American University made a brilliant and balanced judgment with regards to a breach of the rule of law by the United States as the result of the criminal system created *ad hoc* in response to the September 11 terrorist attacks: "Despite the fact that they call it terrorism, the law of war still applies. We didn't cease applying the law of war in World War II because the SS followed the German troops and committed terrorist acts... If we (Americans) can claim to justify this, our adversaries will say they can do this to us as well." See Sally Acharya, *Law professor defends human rights*, published at American Weekly, 22 March 2005

31 Dominique Moisi, *The Geopolitics of Emotion: How Cultures of Fear, Humiliation, and Hope are Reshaping the World*, Doubleday, New York, 2009.

accountability, and human rights as the heart, mind, and the soul of democratic systems. Because Europeans incited the darkest episodes of humankind, such as World War I, World War II, and the Holocaust, there is a deep belief that strengthening the democratic system depends on the recognition of international rule of law as a binding limit for the respect of individual dignity everywhere, even in the most remote areas of the Earth.

This is especially true in an increasingly globalized period that has witnessed violent threats and a worldwide contest for power and legitimacy. It is also particularly relevant considering that on August 26, 2012, the Syrian regime was accused of killing hundreds in Daraya, and opposition groups claim to have found at least 200 bodies in a Sunni community on outskirts of Damascus – yet, President Bashar Al´Assad's only response to those allegations was "a promise to win at any cost."[32]

This barbaric behavior is unacceptable if there is to be any hope of an effective international rule of law. For such a rule of law to prevail, violators must be held accountable and brought to justice. So, it must be emphasized that the perceived or actual lack of legitimacy and justice among state actors and individuals across the world can be significantly addressed, and even overcome, by an international rule of law that is fully enforced by domestic, international, or indigenous judiciaries that seek to hold state or individual violators or terrorists fully accountable for their atrocities. If this is not achieved, then the totality of past victims will have suffered and died not only unjustly, but also in vain.

This is what fully engaged and interconnected judiciaries can hope to achieve: the observation and necessary enforcement of human rights sanctions and an observance of the law of nations that steadfastly maintains a central focus on the tragic victims of illegitimate and appalling violence. Such judicial safeguarding of the law's legacy is instrumental to any society's legitimacy and ultimate self-determination.

---

[32] See Julian Borger, "Syrian regime accused of killing hundreds in Daraya massacre," 26 August 2012 http://www.guardian.co.uk/world/2012/aug/26/syrian-regime-accused-daraya-massacre See also El pais "La oposición siria denuncia la peor matanza desde el inicio de la Guerra," 26 August 2012 at http://internacional.elpais.com/internacional/2012/08/25/actualidad/1345931724_206892.html

In view of this, I frequently ask myself as a citizen and law professor if our responsibility as humankind is always to improve human conditions, and if law continues to be an effective and necessary means for that end. Progress means real enjoyment of rights, especially for the most vulnerable. If such enjoyment fails, then courts must ensure accountability for this governmental or social failure. This is the only way to validate the claim that a rule of law prevails domestically or internationally.

In Europe, and especially in a country such as my own (Spain) with a limited history of stable democratic periods over the last century, the fight for liberties and dignity starts with the preservation of the culture, principles, rights, and duties that made progress possible in Western life. Since the Enlightenment period and the American and French Revolutions, that system has been based on the rule of law and the preservation of individual and public liberties. A deeper commitment to these values and principles can reassure and re-legitimize democratic systems. Other courses of action jeopardize the achievement of citizenship for all people and the very foundation of democratic political and legal systems.

Since the Enlightenment, Europeans have had an irrational feeling of optimism and a faith in progress. Education has fostered a belief in the transformation and creation of a fairer society with fewer inequalities. That sensation of progress was acclaimed about a century after the French Revolution by some intellectuals of the Second Spanish Republic, which existed before the Spanish Civil War of 1936. Among them was the poet Antonio Machado and his verse, "Today is still the moment/Life is here and now (*Hoy es siempre todavía/ Toda la vida es ahora),*" which contained the spirit of the Enlightenment and self-determination.[33]

Nevertheless, a powerful commitment to the aspiration of justice and concept of non-impunity is imperative, especially after such grave violations of human rights as those this work has described. The idea of *Fiat justitia, el pereat mundos* – "Let justice be done, though the world perish" – is neither a feasible nor realistic situation, at least initially, in countries and communities immersed in the process of transition.

---

[33] See Antonio Machado, *Proverbios y Cantares,* Dedicated to José Ortega y Gasset, Revista de Occidente, n.° III, September 1923. See also "Human Rights and the Rule of Law after Abu Ghraib and the Election of Barack Obama: A European Vision of the Past and Future of the U.S. War on Terror" in *Protección Internacional de Derechos Humanos y Estado de Derecho,* II Volumen obra homenaje a Nelson Mandela, AAVV, director y editor de la obra. Gustavo Ibáñez ediciones jurídicas, Bogotá, 2009, p. 424.

> …accountability processes clearly are having a positive impact in a number of societies, but the effects of these efforts on domestic rule of law have been mixed, complex, and often unclear, and more (…) Whether accountability process have helped to strengthen the rule of law domestically, depends… on their demonstration effects and their capacity-building impact[34]

The current international rule of law contains a set of juridical and moral standards that are chosen through conscience and reason, balancing that which is right with that which is wrong (good and evil). Considering these values and principles, it is crucial to remember that law schools in democratic countries possess a key responsibility to transmit and "embed" in students the belief that the rule of law is one of the most important achievements of humankind. Progress in democracy allows for more freedom and empowerment for individuals, especially those who are weak and in vulnerable situations.

No political and historical commitment in society is more significant than the pursuit of justice. Now, after the fall of the Berlin Wall, "those wise restraints that make mankind free" have prompted reaffirmation of the inherent value of human rights, as apparent in the UN Preamble:

> ... to reaffirm faith in fundamental human rights, (…), and to establish conditions under which justice and respect for the obligations arising from treaties and other sources of international law can be maintained, and to promote social progress and better standards of life in larger freedom, (…) to employ international machinery for the promotion of the economic and social advancement of all peoples.

Failure to adhere to these standards has provoked part of the crisis and crimes in Syria, and it is unclear how long the world must suffer and wait for justice while such atrocities and war crimes continue. History has revealed that the absence of a rule of law that frames relations and provides security, accountability, and the assurance of mutual rights produces continuous cycles of revenge, injustice, inequity, and permanent unrest. Knowing this, Syria should be the last horrific example of human actions without

[34] STROMSETH, J. WIPPMAN, D., BROOKS, R., *Can might make rights?*, Cambridge University Press, Cambridge, 2006, p. 307.

accountability or civilian atrocities without swift and certain judicial enforcement of the rule of law.

III

Epilogue

> Poi mi domandava perché il popolo italiano, prima della Guerra, non avesse fatto la rivoluzione per cacciar Mussolini. Io rispondevo: "Per non dare un dispiacere a Roosvelt e a Churchill, che prima della Guerra, erano grandi amici di Mussolini." Tutti mi guarfavano meravigliati, esclamando: "Funny!". Poi mi domandava che cosa fosse uno Stato totalitario. Io rispondevo: "É uno Stato dove tutto ciò che non è proibito, è obligatorio".
>
> He later asked me why the Italian people, prior to the war occurring, had not started a revolution against Mussolini. I remarked: "They did not start a revolution to annoy Roosvelt and Churchill, because before the war, both were great friends of Mussolini." Everyone looked at me in wonder, and remarked: "Funny." Later, he asked me what a totalitarian state was. I answered, "It is a state where everything that is not labelled as forbidden, is [permissible] and even mandatory.
>
> Curzio Malaparte, *La pelle*

In the final analysis, governments that act in such a way so as to deny the intrinsic importance of any human life cannot do so without insulting their own dignity, and thus violating their basic legitimacy. As such, it is crucial that one is always aware of the approaching "invisible hand" of legal accountability when his or her actions convey such brutal contempt for the intrinsic value of other's lives.

The British Judge Tom Bingham has expressed this sentiment in a definitive manner: "*So it seems to me that observance of the Rule of Law is the nearest we can get to a universal secular religion.*"[35] Rule of law, justice, and commitment go hand-in-hand with the legal and moral

[35] BINGHAM, T., *The Rule of Law*, Allen-Lane Penguin Books, London, 2010, p. 174.

obligations of citizens. The international rule of law has become a spiritual element of democratic societies that aspire to be more just and inclusive and an essential element for achieving developmental goals – or, in other words, a space that offers the options of rights and opportunities. It suggests that the rule of law is an aspiration to dignity that is not exempt from tensions and constitutes one of the clearest elements of a truly civilized and democratic system and society of nations.

I still often wonder whether the evolving nature of the international rule of law is a cultural achievement of universal significance. Following Judge Bingham's metaphor regarding the rule of law as a universal secular religion, we probably have not yet surpassed the "liturgical moment" that represents a simple paragraph that Robert H. Jackson, the American chief prosecutor, pronounced during the second day of the Judgments at Nuremberg in 1945:

> The privilege of opening the first trial in history for crimes against the peace of the world imposes a grave responsibility (...)" and spoke of the Allied "practical effort...to utilize International Law to meet the greatest menace of our times (...)".[36] "That four great nations, flushed with victory and stung with injury stay the hand of vengeance and voluntarily submit their captive enemies to the judgment of the law is one of the most significant tributes that Power has ever paid to Reason.[37]

Will it be the case that our tribute to law is to avoid indifference in the face of injustice, prevent the weakening of our collective memory, and pay respect to the victims of conflicts, such as those taking place in Syria, through international legal protection? Will our tribute be the creation of the necessary policies to avoid impunity? Will that be the legal and ethical threshold of dignity?

Products crafted by human beings that seem to be alive as part of the human experience regardless of time, place, or cultural background are deemed classical works. With

---

[36] Gary J. Bass, *Stay the hand of vengeance*, Princeton University Press, Princeton, 2000, p. 174.

[37] *Opening Statement Before the International Military Tribunal*, Nuremberg, Germany, 21 November 1945. (Emphasis added.)
Available at http://www.roberthjackson.org/

regards to victims, the literature of Primo Levi and Elie Wiesel are perennial reflections for the past and present and a commitment to victims of any conflict.

So, defeat is certain if indifference and oblivion are the prevailing responses to crimes in Syria or elsewhere in the coming months and years. The term *kaputt* is frequently used to refer to an item that is broken, shattered, and ruined. Unconscious thoughts about those killed or seeking refuge have implied voluntary dismissal of the fact that *kaputt* is a word etymologically derived from the Hebrew term kopparoth, meaning *victim*.[38]

I hope humankind will never forget that the concept of justice and dignity relies not only on individuals, but especially on those victims who have been vulnerable and alienated from any chance of hope and opportunity. Their plight is a universal plight. Elie Wiesel's words apply to all:

> Our lives no longer belong to us alone; they belong to all those who need us desperately. (…) Without memory, our existence would be barren and opaque, like a prison cell into which no light penetrates; like a tomb which rejects the living. Memory saved the Besht, and if anything can, it is memory that will save humanity. For me, hope without memory is like memory without hope. (…) What all these victims need above all is to know that they are not alone; that we are not forgetting them, that when their voices are stifled we shall lend them ours, that while their freedom depends on ours, the quality of our freedom depends on theirs.[39]

A legacy of civic commitment and legal culture has been built and strengthened in every corner of the world through civic acts of empathy and encounters toward "the otherness," as Riszhard Kapuscinki has described it.[40] Personally, I have tried to adopt a principle that Prof. Adbullahi Ahmed An-Na'Im has stated and Alberto Moravia has affirmed in his work *The Indifferent 46* (Gli indiferenti): in facing injustice, the only option is to say "no," as to do otherwise is to become an accomplice to injustice itself. I think

38 MALAPARTE, K, Kaputt, Adhelpi edizioni Milano, 2009, p. 280: "Lei conoce l´origine della parola *Kaputt*? É una parola che proviene dall´ebraico *kopparoth*, che vuol dire vittima."
39 Elie Wiesel, Speech acceptance at Nobel Peace Laureate ceremony in Oslo, 10 December 1986, available at http://www.nobelprize.org/nobel_prizes/peace/laureates/1986/wiesel-lecture.htm
40 KAPUSCINKI, R., The other, Verso, London, 2008.

that writer Javier Cercas was right in the closing chapters of *Soldiers of Salamis*[41] when he suggests that maybe being decent *"means learning to say no."*

As such, the international rule of law represents a powerful and legally possible route for the pursuit of justice. Moreover, it maintains a focus on the need to address injustice and fight against impunity. In his work *The Sense of Injustice,* Edmon Cahn interpreted this as part of a human progression: "justice would not be a state, but a process, an action –the active process of remedying or preventing what would arouse the sense of injustice."[42] When facing injustice, the response "is a biologic reaction combining both reason and empathy on the projection of one's self onto others."[43] The sense of injustice forms the basis of law. Heraclitus made this point by stating, "Were there no justice, men would never have known the [its] name." This then recalls the core issue. Since justice and human rights are always "others people's rights," personal empathy and the public and legal enforcement of accountability are key elements in this essential process of fully realizing the international rule of law.

[41] CERCAS, J., *Soldiers of Salamis,* Bloomsbury, London, 2003.

[42] CAHN, E., *The sense of injustice*, New York University Press, New York.1964. quoted by CLARKE, K., M.

[43] CLARKE, K., M., GOODALE, M., *Mirrors of Justice*, Cambridge University Press, Cambridge, 2010, p. 322.

CHAPTER 5

THE INTERNATIONAL CRIMINAL COURT, DRUG TRAFFICKING, AND CRIMES AGAINST HUMANITY: A LOCAL INTERPRETATION OF THE ROMAN STATUTE

Dr. Juan Carlos Sainz-Borgo

The ICC represents the culmination of decades of work by the international community to establish a permanent entity that would prosecute and sanction the worst behaviors of which human beings are capable. This exercise was developed in three stages: (1) the negotiation of the Rome Statute, a comprehensive treaty that establishes a final catalog of international crimes, (2) the establishment of an international criminal tribunal, the ICC, which has the ability to prosecute individuals, and (3) the implementation of a new international organization, the Organization of States Parties, which could monitor the fulfillment of the two previous steps

Given that it was such an ambitious project, the process occurred relatively rapidly after the start of negotiations of the statute, setting a record for how fast the international community managed to build this consensus compared to other courts (e.g. The International Tribunal for the Law of the Sea). This speed may be a sign of the growing maturity of international community and its ability to navigate fundamental challenges, such as establishing a new criminal jurisdiction on a global scale.

As Thomas Boudreau argues in his essay "Law of Nations," the "state-centric" paradigm of international law is no longer an accurate description or adequate explanation of emergent legal development and practices. However, the paradigmatic shift that the establishment of this ICC represents has required state parties to take certain actions that could not be simply limited to the signing of the respective treaty as though it were one of a long list of multilateral obligations and could be solved with the sole approval of the respective legislative powers and international collaboration to ensure compliance with the court's functions. The "state-centric" legal paradigm, broken since World War II, was further shattered by the approval of the Rome Statute, since it forsakes the nation state as the sole owner of international responsibility and compels member states to adapt their criminal systems to incorporate these new features and avoid contradictions among domestic and international systems. The international criminal responsibility of the individual before the ICC represents a profound shift in the development of the international law paradigm. Thus, many states modified their legislation to ensure compatibility with this new legal paradigm, including Argentina, (Ley No. 26.200, January 2007), Brazil, (Projeto de lei No. 301 2007), and Canada (Crimes against Humanity and War Crimes Act 2000). Other states have approved special laws to allow for compliance with these new legal responsibilities without changing any further structure of the legal framework, including Uruguay (Ley Nº 18.026 October 2006) and Germany, with its International Criminal Code.[1]

Yet, a large group of states have neither modified internal laws nor approved special norms, leaving the causal interpretation and jurisdictional reach of the Rome Statute largely limited for now to a case-by-case basis. Even so, enlightening and educational examples can be found of national jurisdictions taking juridical measures to interpret and incorporate the provisions of the statute.

The present article refers to the approval of the Supreme Court of Justice of the Bolivarian Republic of Venezuela judgments that determined drug trafficking-related crimes to be within the definition of crimes prosecuted by the ICC. Both the Criminal Appellate Chamber and the Constitutional Chamber of that court confirmed this decision on several occasions, creating a dangerous precedent for the development of international criminal law and the fight against drug trafficking.

The aim of the article is to analyze this local interpretation from the Bolivarian Republic of Venezuela Supreme Court of Justice and stress the way in which these local decisions, by trying to locally interpret an international treaty, may pose serious problems for the future of the ICC.

The local interpretation

In March 2000, the Supreme Court of Justice of the Bolivarian Republic of Venezuela addressed the issue of crimes against humanity through a decision by the Criminal Appellate Chamber, which the Constitutional Chamber then confirmed. In these decisions, drug-related crimes were qualified as crimes against humanity.

---

[1]Information taken from, International Coalition for the International Criminal Court. http://www.iccnow.org/?mod=romeimplementation&idudctp=20&show=all&lang=en. Accessed July 2012.

There is not an internationally recognized qualification that interprets drug-related crimes or terrorism as crimes against humanity. Article 7 of the Rome Statute does not include such an interpretation in any of its 11 parts, nor do the elements of crimes approved for the Rome Statute.

There is a generous amount of treaties and agreements that demonstrate the will of the international community to eradicate crimes related to drugs. It spans throughout various countries, and its stages and consequences exceed the simple fact that the consumption of a banned product damages a population. However, there is no unanimous qualification of this crime, nor is there consensus within the international community to qualify certain drug-related conducts, such as drug trafficking, as criminal conduct.

This position of the highest Venezuelan court was developed in two clearly defined stages: first, through the decision of the Criminal Appellate Chamber, which referred to elements eminently internal, and second, through the Constitutional Chamber, which used the elements contained in the Rome Statute to validate that decision. This essay briefly reviews both decisions.

In the Criminal Appellate Chamber, the reporting judge, Angulo Fontiveros, approved decision No.359 on March 28, 2000.[2] This decision was related to the case against two Venezuelan citizens who were condemned for the possession of 49.9 grams of cocaine. Fontiveros presented his argument in two great pillars: the constitutional regulation and the theory of legally protected assets.

To begin, the court based its first argument on the eminently constitutional nature of extending the definition of crimes against humanity to include drug-related offenses. The decision cited Articles 29 and 271 of the current Venezuelan Constitution as grounds for its argument, and proposed them as a dialectic unity.

Article 29 of the 1999 Venezuelan Constitution establishes a special description of crimes listed within the same article, to which no statute of limitation is applicable. Thus,

2 http://www.tsj.gov.ve/decisiones/scp/Marzo/359-280300-C99098.htm. Accessed July 2011.

the Constitution ensures victims of those crimes that no passage of time will protect the individuals responsible for those crimes.

This is a breach of the general principle of the statute of limitations. Exceptions must be restrictively interpreted, as general principle of law.

The crimes expressly listed in Article 29 of the Constitution are:

1. Crimes against humanity
2. Serious violations of human rights
3. War crimes

This paper does not further analyze the content of the aforementioned crimes established in Article 29, as such an analysis would not be relevant. However, it is important to clarify that the court's decision took advantage of the lack of definitions for certain concepts, such as crimes against humanity, that could be qualified as open types of crimes to match with Article 271 of the Venezuelan Constitution, which has no direct relation to the Constitution.

With the exception of the war crimes established in the Geneva Convention that form the basis of international humanitarian law, drug-related crimes are not expressly defined as crimes against humanity or considered "serious" human rights violations.

The nature of a serious violation is unclear, as there is no legal definition for this assertion, and jurisprudence of the Inter-American Court of Human Rights and the European Court of Human Rights have not made a scale to evaluate which actions are serious violations and which are less serious.

Moreover, Article 271 of the Constitution of the Bolivarian Republic of Venezuela establishes three direct mandates to the legislative branch.

First, it regulates the general principle of asylum, which is established in Article 69 of the constitutional text. Specifically, it denies the state's protection to people responsible for crimes related to money laundering, drugs, international organized crime, acts against public property of other states, and acts against human rights.

Second, it decrees the non-applicability of the statute of limitations to prosecutions against human rights violations, drug trafficking, or actions against public assets, and establishes seizure of the goods arising from those crimes as an additional penalty for such activities.

Third, it establishes the judicial procedure to be applied in cases provided in this article. Thus, it is important to stress that the Constitution approved but did not integrate all drug-related crimes into Article 69. On the contrary, it describes each criminal basic definition in a specific way. Moreover, it revisits Article 29 and expands the list of crimes that are not affected by passage of time, adding to the list of crimes against patrimony and of drug trafficking, and reiterates violations of human rights.

In my opinion, this interpretation by the Supreme Court threatens legal certainty and the principle that penalties must be lawful as established in Article 1 of the Criminal Code. The decision casts aside the criteria expressed by international criminal law and human rights treaties that Venezuela has signed and ratified, which this essay comments on later. However, at this point it is significant to mention two comments that have been published in Venezuela regarding this matter.

First, the former President of the Supreme Court of Justice, Cecilia Sosa Gomez, has expressed:

> Viewed the arguments content in the decision transcribed we can affirm that the Criminal Appellate Chamber neither has constitutional nor legal basis to support its arguments, except for stressing the seriousness of drug-trafficking crime. Constitutional Articles 29, 271 and 257 at no time mentioned or addressed drug-trafficking crime, defined in the Organic Law of Narcotics and Psychotropic Substances (OLNPS), as a crime against humanity and neither the Rome Statute establishes it as such.[3]

Furthermore, Profs. Jose Malagueña Rojas and Francisco Ferreira have denied that such crimes could have any relation to crimes provided in the Organic Law of Narcotics and

---

[3] Sosa Gómez, Cecilia. (2004) *Crimenes de Lesa Humanidad.* Page 454. En, *Fundación Venezuela Positiva.* (2004) Lesa humanidad. Editorial Gráficas Armitano. Caracas. Translated by the author?

Psychotropic Substances (OLNPS) because the source within international law is completely different and cannot be linked or mixed. [4]

This first part represents the local argument that is subject to debate, as previously mentioned. It only uses domestic legal instruments and does not interpret international law, which happens in the decision of the Constitutional Chamber.

The Reporting Judge of the Constitutional Chamber, Jesus Eduardo Cabrera Romero, has drafted a strong argument in which he defines drug-trafficking crime in a doctrinal way as a crime against humanity and then introduces the example of provisions in the Rome Statute that regulate the matter of crimes against humanity.

The Constitutional Chamber directly interpreted the text of the Rome Statute when it stated that "… Article 7 lists crimes against humanity, and letter K of such law, defines conducts that in the opinion of this chamber encompasses the illicit traffic of drugs." The transcription of Article 7, letter K reads as follows:
"k) Other inhuman acts of similar character intentionally causing great suffering or serious injury to body or to mental or to physical health."

This quotation, directly extracted from the Rome Statute, is a law that, in its context of application and given the human cruelty, adapts to the times; it is the most effective way to remain open to the possibility of new heinous acts, perhaps involving new technologies. In short, the emphasis of the statue is on *actions*, not *substances.*

There are five elements of the crimes included in the annex to the Rome Statute for that article:

1. That the author has caused through an inhuman act great suffering or serious injury to body or mental or physical health.
2. That such act had a similar character as to that of any other act referred to in paragraph 1, Article 7 of the Statute.
3. That the author was aware of the factual circumstances that determined the nature of the act.

[4] Malagueña Rojas, José L. y Ferreira de Abreu, Francisco. (2004) *Los Crímenes de Lesa Humanidad y el Delito de Tráfico de Drogas Ilícitas.* Revista CENIPEC 23. Mérida.

> 4. That the conduct was performed as part of widespread or systematic attack against civilians.
> 5. That the author was aware that the behavior was part of a widespread or systematic attack against civilians or that he had the intention that such conduct was part of an attack of that kind.

None of those five elements can subsume typical premises of drug trafficking or any of its related crimes. Particularly, elements four and five require that offenses be part of a "widespread or systematic attack" against civilians. However, a constitutive element of the crime of drug trafficking by its very nature is that is it selective; it does not seek a general harm to civilians. Its main engine is profit seeking by the drug dealer, and it is not a direct attack on the population. This essay develops this idea later.

Moreover, this interpretation by the Venezuelan Supreme Court of Justice contradicts the general rules of interpretation of international law as established in the Vienna Convention on the Law of Treaties, which is the result of the codification of the International Law Commission (ILC)[5] of the UN. It contains international practices on the subject, such as that explained in Article 31 concerning the need to entirely interpret the treaty, taking into account its objective and purpose.

The object of the Rome Statute, per Article 1, is to establish an ICC to "exercise its jurisdiction over persons *for the most serious crimes of international concern,* as referred to in this Statute." (Emphasis added.)

Thus, this court only tries crimes of the greatest international significance. Article 5 expressly lists: genocide, crimes against humanity, war crimes, and the crime of aggression. Article 7 defines the scope of this crime:

> 1. For the purpose of this Statute, "crime against humanity" means any of the following acts when committed as part of a widespread or systematic attack directed against any civilian population, with knowledge of the attack.

[5] Watts, Sir Arthur. (1999) *The International Law Commission. 1949-1998.* Volume I. y II The Treaties. Oxford University Press. First Edition 1999.

As its general denominator, the article expressly defines that which signatory states have defined as "attack to civilians," which shall be understood as a line of conduct that implies multiple commission of acts mentioned in paragraph 1 against civilians, in accordance with the policy of a state or organization of committing such acts or to promote such policy.

Since the Constitutional Chamber refers to this treaty, it is necessary to quote those interpreting rules presented in this international agreement. Article 22 provides these rules, and to the effects of this paper, number two is highly relevant:

> Crime definition shall be strictly interpreted and shall not be extended or apply by analogy. In case of ambiguity, it shall be interpreted favoring the subject object to the investigation, trial or sentence.

This would suggest that the argument the Constitutional Chamber of the highest Venezuelan court tries to establish does not embody the spirit of the Rome Statute. Moreover, it actually openly contradicts the provisions of the Rome Statute.

Following the Rome Statute, I consider that qualifying drug-trafficking crime as a worldwide scourge that may cause serious harm to the population cannot be framed among the objectives of the ICC as a crime of the greatest gravity and importance for the international community, as evidenced later.

Also, it is important to stress the comments of Profs. Malagueña and Ferreira in the quoted article regarding the argument supporting the decision:

> Premise A: Actions to sanction crimes against humanity have non-applicability of the statute of limitation (Article 29 of the Constitution).
> Premise B: judicial actions towards sanctioning drug trafficking crimes have no statute of limitation. (Article 271 of the Constitution).
> Conclusion: therefore, crimes provided in Article 34 of the Organic Law of Narcotics and Psychotropic substances are crimes against humanity.[6]

[6] Malagueña y Ferreira. Ob. Cit. Page 102.

This line of reasoning of the highest court has, in practice, led regular courts and the Criminal Chamber of the Supreme Court of Justice to dismiss any "prosecuting benefits" that may apply to those involved in any drug-related crime, such as "community service" or home confinement, especially for minors.

Ratification of the Supreme Court's position

This position of the Venezuelan Supreme Court is not isolated. On the contrary, it has been recurrently sustained in multiple ways. For example, the Constitutional Chamber of the Supreme Court of Justice answered a court remedy against the decision of the Appellate Chamber of the Criminal Judicial Circuit of the State of Vargas in August 2003. This occurred slightly less than a year after the decision, which laid the foundations for the binding constitutional interpretation of crimes against humanity and treatment of "benefits during the process," and confirmed their position.

The latest interpretation modified the adopted criteria. However, the Constitutional Chamber subsequently denied such a change, thus creating a great deal of confusion about its application.

Corollary of what has been presented, it is difficult for this chamber to overturn the decision of the Court of Appeals of the Criminal Judicial Circuit of the State of Vargas on December 19, 2002. In this decision, the petition for the court remedy was ruled out of order in *limine litis* for being part of the inadmissibility grounds provided in Article 6.5 of the Organic Law of Court Remedies on Constitutional Rights and Guarantees.

However, this chamber by constitutional mandate urges the Fifth Court of Control of the Criminal Judicial Circuit, State of Vargas, to hold a hearing in the presence of the accused with their respective attorneys and the prosecutor, with the purpose of considering the application of preliminary injunctions replacing the measure involving deprivation of liberty, as provided in Article 244 of the Organic Criminal Procedural Code. Such a mandate is not contrary to decision No.1712/2001 of 12.09, case: Rita Alcira Coy, Yolanda Castillo Estupiñan, and Miriam Ortega Estrada. All measure, coercive, or preliminary injunctions cease when two years elapse without having held trial, and the accused, in principle, are automatically released from the investigated crime.

In the present case, illicit traffic of narcotic and psychotropic substances is a multi-offense crime that injures various legal assets, such as health and life.[7]

To begin, it is important to stress that both the decisions that initiated the involvement of drug crimes by the Supreme Court of Justice – first in the Criminal Court, and then in the Constitutional Chamber – were perfectly aligned in their argument.

However, this new decision changes the line of argument, establishing a great deal of confusion regarding the hierarchy of sources of Venezuelan law, the application of international law in Venezuela, the nature of the Constitutional Chamber, and the monitoring of its criteria by the rest of the republic's courts. However, in its substance, it confirms that the highest body of the judicial branch in Venezuela considers drug-related crimes to be crimes against humanity.

Three years later, the Criminal Appellate Chamber of the same court confirmed its standing in a decision dated December 18, 2006. Again, drug-related crimes are qualified as crimes against humanity through the argument of the two criteria previously presented in the following manner:

> The investigated crimes are related to the traffic and transportation of illicit narcotic and psychotropic substances, so they are pluri offensive because they seriously threaten physical, mental and economic integrity of an unknown number of people. It similarly generates social violence in the areas where such criminal action takes place. In this regard, the Chamber considers such crimes as crimes against humanity, impunity for which should be avoided in agreement with the principles and statements provided in the United Nation Single Convention on Narcotic Drugs (1961); Convention on Psychotropic Substances (1971), and Convention against the Illicit Traffic in Narcotic Drugs and Psychotropic Substances (1988).[8]

It is interesting to note that the decision does not expressly quote the Rome Statute, but in general mixes the will of the international community in rejecting drug trafficking-

---

7 Venezuelan official web site for the Supreme Court of Justice http://tsj.gov.ve/decisiones/scon/Agosto/2398-280803-03-0051. Accessed March 2005.

8 Decision N° 568 Criminal Appellate Chamber, File N° A06-0370 dated 18/December/2006.

related crimes, marking them as crimes against humanity contained within the Rome Statute. In any case, the argument and core of the decision were sustained.

Why drug trafficking-related crimes cannot be considered crimes against humanity

This paper has tried to present some issues that are relevant from the perspective of constitutional law, but at the same time has intended to refer to some aspects that engage with international criminal law.

In this vein, highlighting aspects that contribute to the clarification of the definition of crimes against humanity would be widely useful.

In this regard, drug-related crimes are certainly a worldwide scourge that may cause serious harm to the population. However, it cannot be considered a crime against humanity, nor can it be subsumed under the competence of the ICC as part of the most serious and significant crimes, as defined by the international community.

The Statute of Rome describes the active subject of Article 7, number 2 as a state or organization; it is exceedingly difficult to incorporate the element of crime organizations engaged in drug-related business, even though some drug cartels operate on a regional or global scale. Drug-trafficking crimes described in internal laws and international treaties were approved with the aim of repressing criminal groups or illegal gangs to produce profit. Those are not within the express provisions established by the Rome Statute.

In short, drug trafficking is a multidimensional crime that involves the will of the producer, a trader, and a consumer. However, in no case should it be considered a crime against humanity as suggested by the Constitutional Chamber. In particular, since it also involves a "buyer" who acts with some presumed degree of volition, it cannot simply be construed broadly as a *widespread or systematic attack directed against any civilian population. The reality appears to be more complex, as although a voluntary act of purchase or subsequent recreational use of a drug is potentially harmful, it cannot really be regarded in the same category as an "attack."*

Furthermore, the general definition of "other inhuman acts" is not in agreement with the spirit of the article. Specifically, it is difficult to locate the passive subject, as Magistrate Judge Angulo Fontiveros explained when referring to the legally protected interest. In the same consequence of drug-trafficking crimes, in relation to the drug dependence arising from regular consumption of prohibited substances, there is the individual's own and personal decision. The internal legislator then treats this own free and personal decision of each human being as a disease, but not as a crime.

Therefore, considerations concerning distribution of prohibited substances to the people that frame it as part of a systematic attack or an action that deliberately seeks destruction or to cause suffering to the people are simply not aware of the commercial nature of transactions within the drug exchange in the international market. Moreover, there is a difference between the actions typified by the statute and the conducts prosecuted by the national legislator; most importantly, drug-related crimes have monetary profits as a primary motivation. On the contrary, international crimes have a primarily political objective.

This paper thus considers that the Supreme Court of Justice of the Bolivarian Republic of Venezuela has erroneously applied the concept of crimes against humanity. Furthermore, this misconception may result in legal situations that may affect the foreign policy of the government in the future.

The international fight against drug-related crimes has been permanently informed by the segmentation of the problem: 1. Traditional consumers and growers, 2. Drug-related crimes, and 3. Drug trafficking and money laundering as a more complex and international stage of the crime.

International treaties on this matter have built a broad framework of cooperation that allows each state to adopt the rules most compatible with their national legislation. This is due to the complexity and dispersion of the various activities that compose these crimes. In particular, international relations in this regard have been characterized by the conscious avoidance of creating a supranational body endowed with monopoly powers of investigating and punishing such crimes. On the other side, it is important to remember that states are unilaterally permitted to establish accomplishment levels of cooperation agendas against international crime.

This diversity and complexity displays special aspects in the Americas because the Andean countries are considered to be among the main drug producers in the world. This production of narcotic drugs is closely related to aspects of internal order, ranging from ancestral practices of indigenous peoples concerning the uses of these prohibited or limited substances to free use in some countries, as is the case for the coca leaf in Bolivia and Peru.

In sharp contrast, various situations have been arising in Colombia with regards to different stages of drug trafficking, ranging from drug-related terrorism in the 1980s and 1990s involving Pablo Escobar Gaviria and other infamous characters to the more recent participation of former revolutionary groups, such the Fuerzas Armadas Revolucionarias de Colombia (FARC), in growing and distributing prohibited substances in order to use the resources acquired from this trade to finance the armed conflict. Similarly, in Mexico, groups that control drug distribution are developing a wide display of operations, which prompted former United States Secretary of State Hilary Clinton to compare the country to 1980s-era Colombia.[9]

All these briefly addressed circumstances are part of the sovereignty of each country and the way in which each society manages its problems. However, the qualification of these national crimes as crimes against humanity could provide a basis for international action in resolving internal problems. So, defining the international drug trade as an internal "crime against humanity" could lead to much misunderstanding and tension, and such a construction could easily result in more contentious international relations. Hence, in this regard, there is a very real danger of creating more problems than solutions.

Some conclusions

Local interpretation of international criminal law is becoming a new phenomenon in the global judicial field. Case logs of courts everywhere feature environmental issues, economic negotiations, and contested human rights. In some cases, local interpretation is positive if the objectives achieved are related to the punishment of criminals or avoiding impunity. In other cases, that interpretation could be novel and help to identify a new path for the law, as in the case of the Colombian[10] interpretation of political genocide. This has triggered confrontation among specialists because it opens the criminal definition of the Convention for Prevention and Punishment of the Crime of Genocide of 1948.

---

[9] http://www.queenslatino.com/mexico-esta-como-colombia-hillary-clinton/. Accessed July 2012.

[10] Decision of the Colombian Constitutional Court No. C-177 of 2001

In cases of crimes against humanity, which the Nuremberg Charter first defined, it represents a significant advance of public international law by defining intolerable actions and attacks aimed at civilian populations in order to create a judicial category and ensuing national or international jurisdiction. By doing so, this historic innovation contributes to the prevention of more serious behaviors that affect international communities, guaranteeing punishment and precluding its repetition.

The ICC has been established to try those crimes of which customary consensus among the international community leaves no doubt about the need for their eradication and prosecution. These crimes are genocide, war crimes, crimes of aggression, and a broader category, such as crimes against humanity.

The first paragraph of Article 7 of the Statute of Rome identifies these crimes against humanity, which infringe upon the core values of civilization and may endanger international peace, as the following: murder; extermination; enslavement; deportation or forced transfers; incarceration in violation of the fundamental rules of international law; torture; rape; political, racial, national, ethnic, cultural, or religious persecution; disappearance crime; the crime of apartheid; and other similar acts.

The international community has not yet reached a consensus regarding the inclusion of drug-related crimes in the list of crimes against humanity.

It has been argued here that the decision of the Supreme Court of the Bolivarian Republic of Venezuela to consider drug-related crime as a crime against humanity does not fit the conceptual definition of that crime, or even further, the useful evolution of customary international law and existing treaties in the field. Finally, it could open a gateway to the intervention of international courts in issues such as drugs that have not been solved within national societies, let alone within the international community as a whole.

CHAPTER 6 (I)

AVANCES EN LA JURISPRUDENCIA INTERNACIONAL EN VIOLENCIA SEXUAL CONTRA MUJERES EN CONFLICTOS ARMADOS

ADVANCES IN INTERNATIONAL JURISPRUDENCE ON SEXUAL VIOLENCE AGAINST WOMEN AS CRIMES AGAINST HUMANITY IN ARMED CONFLICT

Baltasar Garzón

INTRODUCCIÓN

Como primera afirmación, se debe convenir en que las últimas décadas han supuesto un sustancial avance en materia del reconocimiento y efectividad de los derechos de la mujer, y específicamente aquellos que ven vulnerados mediante la violencia en el marco de los conflictos armados.

De conformidad a las estadísticas internacionales, por lo menos una de cada tres mujeres ha sido golpeada, forzada a tener relaciones sexuales, o maltratada de alguna manera en el curso de su vida. Esta cifra tiende a aumentar en el contexto de conflictos armados. *"La violencia mundial contra las mujeres es ya otro holocausto"* dijo Ayaan Hirsi Alí al comentar las cifras que se contenían en el Informe elaborado en 2004 por el Centro para el Control Democrático de la Fuerzas Armadas de Ginebra: *"Entre 113 y 200 millones de mujeres de todo el mundo están desaparecidas demográficamente"*

CONTRARIAMENTE A DICHAS ESTADÍSTICAS, LA REFERENCIA PUNTUAL A LOS CRÍMENES DE VIOLENCIA SEXUAL CONTRA LA MUJER EN EL MARCO DE LA NORMATIVIDAD INTERNACIONAL HA SIDO ESCASA HASTA HACE MUY POCO TIEMPO. PESE A EMPEZAR A ESBOZARSE DESDE MEDIADOS DEL SIGLO PASADO, LOS DERECHOS DE LA MUJER EN MATERIA DE IGUALDAD, NO DISCRIMINACIÓN, LA PROHIBICIÓN DE TRATOS CRUELES, A NO SUFRIR AGRESIONES SEXUALES, O A TENER ACCESO A UN RECURSO EFECTIVO[1], HAN

[1] (art. 3 de la Declaración Universal de Derechos Humanos 1948, el artículo 2 del Pacto de Derechos Civiles y Políticos 1966, art. 3 del Pacto Internacional de Derechos Económicos, Sociales, y Culturales, 1976, art. 1 y 2 de la

ESTADO AUSENTES DE LAS RESOLUCIONES DE LOS TRIBUNALES NACIONALES E INTERNACIONALES. EN EL ÚLTIMO SUPUESTO, LA JURISPRUDENCIA INTERNACIONAL DEJA CLARA LA OBLIGACIÓN DE LOS ESTADOS DE PERSEGUIR LOS CRÍMENES DE VIOLENCIA SEXUAL. SIN EMBARGO, NO ES HASTA ÉPOCA RECIENTE CUANDO SU PERSECUCIÓN SE EMPIEZA A HACER EFECTIVA EN ALGUNOS ÁMBITOS. SÓLO CUANDO ESTOS CRÍMENES SE PERSIGUEN COMO DELITOS DEJAN DE TENER CARÁCTER DE DAÑO COLATERAL/INEVITABLE Y PRIVADO Y, SE ASUMEN COMO UNA GRAVE VIOLACIÓN DE DERECHOS HUMANOS, DEL DERECHO PENAL INTERNACIONAL Y DEL DERECHO INTERNACIONAL HUMANITARIO.

HISTÓRICAMENTE, EN NINGUNA DE LAS TRANSCRIPCIONES DE LOS JUICIOS DE NUREMBERG, SE INCLUYERON REFERENCIAS A LAS VIOLACIONES, PROSTITUCIÓN NI A NINGÚN OTRO CRIMEN SEXUAL, Y NI SIQUIERA APARECE LA PALABRA MUJER, A PESAR DE QUE LOS CRÍMENES CONTRA LAS MUJERES FUERON EXTENSAMENTE DOCUMENTADOS. TAMPOCO LA CARTA DE LONDRES QUE CREÓ DICHO TRIBUNAL, APARECE REFERENCIA AL DELITO DE VIOLACIÓN SEXUAL. POR SU PARTE,EN LOS 429 ARTÍCULOS DE LAS CONVENCIONES DE GINEBRA DEL 1949, SÓLO UNA FRASE EN EL ARTICULO 27 DE LA IV PROHÍBE LA VIOLACIÓN SEXUAL Y LA PROSTITUCIÓN FORZADA.

Más increíble aún, es que la Declaración sobre la Protección de Mujeres y Niños en Emergencias y Conflictos Armados de 1974, omite cualquier referencia explícita a la violencia sexual.· En los Protocolos Adicionales a las Convenciones de Ginebra de 1977, que se negociaron con la idea de aclararlas y llenar algunos vacíos, sólo una frase en cada uno explícitamente protege contra la violencia sexual, el art. 76 del Protocolo I, que establece que "*Las mujeres serán objeto de especial respeto y serán protegidas en particular contra la violación, la prostitución forzada y cualquier forma de ataque indecente.*" y el art. 4 del Protocolo II, que establece en el segundo párrafo, subpárrafo (e) que habla de "Los ultrajes a la dignidad personal, en particular el tratamiento humillante y degradante, la violación, la prostitución forzada y cualquier forma de ataque indecente.

El Estatuto del Tribunal Penal Internacional para la Antigua Yugoslavia menciona específicamente la violación como crimen de lesa humanidad de competencia de ese tribunal, más no como infracción de las leyes y costumbres de guerra. Es más, en las

convención sobre la eliminación de todas las formas de Discriminación contra la Mujer, 1979, art.1 de la Convención contra la Tortura y otros Tratos o Penas Crueles, Inhumanos o Degradantes 1984).

primeras acusaciones formales de este tribunal, no se incluyó ni siquiera el delito de violación sexual, a pesar de que el mundo entero había sido sacudido por los reportajes en la prensa de la limpieza étnica que se había practicado en esa república a través del embarazo forzado.[2].

La violencia sexual en escenarios de conflicto armado es uno de los ejemplos más reveladores acerca de cómo el uso de la violencia nunca es neutral al género de la víctima. Se utiliza de forma discriminatoria y haciendo uso de los estereotipos y significados de género para humillar, vencer y controlar al adversario y premiar y cohesionar a su tropa. Algunos de los crímenes de violencia sexual, por su naturaleza sólo se cometen contra las mujeres y niñas, como en los casos de aborto forzoso, el embarazo forzoso o la mutilación de los pechos.

En estos contextos, la violencia contra la mujer es altamente utilizada como herramienta de guerra.

Por medio del cuerpo de la mujer agredida sexualmente, se produce una agresión a la moral de los hombres con quienes la mujer agredida tiene relación de dependencia. En Congo, la destrucción del cuerpo de la mujer en la que se destruyen sus genitales, es una forma indirecta pero de eficacia extrema para destruir la moral del grupo tribal del que la mujer dependa.

Con anterioridad a la década de los años 90 la violación y otros delitos sexuales eran considerados como daños colaterales de las guerras y conflictos armados o bien como atentados al honor de la familia, atentados al honor masculino u ofensas privadas.

Esta tendencia cambia a partir del trabajo realizado por los Tribunales Penales Internacionales para la ex-Yugoslavia y Ruanda, responsabilizando penalmente a los individuos por actos de violencia con base en género y de índole sexual, así como tras la inclusión de varias formas específicas de crímenes de género en el Estatuto de Roma. Asimismo, esta extensión de la implementación de la perspectiva de género en las jurisdicciones internacionales también abarca a los tribunales de carácter

[2] Las mujeres y la Corte Penal Internacional Alda Facio http://www.uasb.edu.ec/padh/revista 1/analisis/aldafacio.htm

regional, como la Corte Inter-americana de Derechos Humanos (Women´s link Worldwide. Crímenes de género en el derecho penal internacional. Guatemala. Agosto 2010).

II

TRATAMIENTO INTERNACIONAL DE LA VIOLENCIA DE GÉNERO.

La violencia contra la mujer en cualquiera de sus formas, se encuentra ampliamente reconocida por el derecho y la jurisprudencia internacional como una forma de discriminación con base al género. Se entiende que una de las causas principales de la violencia es la aplicación de estereotipos de género sobre las mujeres y que, además, la violencia menoscaba o anula la posibilidad para las mujeres de disfrutar y ejercer sus derechos y libertades fundamentales.

A/ La evolución normativa internacional sobre la violencia sexual en el marco de conflictos armados.

A partir de los años 90s, y gracias, entre otros factores, a las organizaciones defensoras de derechos de las mujeres se generó una proliferación de recomendaciones y la adopción de normas puntuales frente a la violencia sexual en el marco del conflicto armado, produciéndose una gran preocupación internacional por la utilización de los delitos sexuales como arma de guerra.

Así, la *Recomendación General 19,* formulada en 1992, el Comité para la Eliminación de la Discriminación contra la Mujer interpretó que el término "discriminación" utilizado en la Convención sobre la Eliminación de todas las formas de Discriminación contra la Mujer ("CEDAW" en sus siglas en inglés) incluía la violencia de género:

> *la violencia dirigida contra la mujer porque es mujer o que la afecta en forma desproporcionada. Incluye actos que infligen daños o sufrimientos de índole física, mental o sexual, amenazas de cometer esos actos, coacción y otras formas de privación de la libertad. La violencia contra la mujer puede contravenir disposiciones de la Convención, sin tener en cuenta si hablan expresamente de la violencia) y la responsabilidad de los estados si no se adoptaban las medidas necesarias para impedir esos actos o para investigarlos y sancionarlos. Así mismo, se enfatizaba sobre*

los peligros que corren las mujeres en caso de guerra o conflicto:

Las guerras, los conflictos armados y la ocupación de territorios conducen frecuentemente a un aumento de la prostitución, la trata de mujeres y actos de agresión sexual contra la mujer, que requiere la adopción de medidas protectoras y punitivas.

Por su parte, el preámbulo de la *Declaración de las Naciones Unidas sobre la Eliminación de la Violencia contra la Mujer,* formulada en 1994, se reconoce que la causa más profunda de la violencia contra la mujer es la subordinación de ésta en la sociedad:
la violencia contra la mujer constituye una manifestación de relaciones de poder históricamente desiguales entre el hombre y la mujer, que han conducido a la dominación de la mujer y a la discriminación en su contra por parte del hombre e impedido el adelanto pleno de la mujer, y que la violencia contra la mujer es uno de los mecanismos sociales fundamentales por los que se fuerza a la mujer a una situación de subordinación respecto del hombre) y se resalta la especial vulnerabilidad de determinados grupos de mujeres, "..como por ejemplo las mujeres pertenecientes a minorías, las mujeres indígenas, las refugiadas, las mujeres migrantes, las mujeres que habitan en comunidades rurales o remotas, las mujeres indigentes, las mujeres recluidas en instituciones o detenidas, las niñas, las mujeres con discapacidades, las ancianas y las mujeres en situaciones de conflicto armado son particularmente vulnerables a la violencia

En el artículo 4 se exhorta a los Estados a actuar:
Los Estados deben condenar la violencia contra la mujer y no invocar ninguna costumbre, tradición o consideración religiosa para eludir su obligación de procurar eliminarla

El Consejo de Seguridad de las Naciones Unidas ha abordado la violencia sexual ejercida contra las mujeres en situaciones de conflicto adoptando diversas resoluciones al respecto:

- En la *Resolución 1325,* adoptada en el año 2000, se pide a los Estados miembros que *incorporen una "perspectiva de género" y aumenten la participación en pie de igualdad de las mujeres en la "prevención y solución de los conflictos" y el "mantenimiento y el fomento de la paz y la seguridad".* Se exhorta también a las partes implicadas en un conflicto armado a que cumplan las leyes internacionales que protegen los derechos de las mujeres y las niñas civiles e incorporen políticas y procedimientos que protejan a las mujeres de delitos de género como la violación y la agresión sexual.

- En la *Resolución 1820*, adoptada en 2008, se pide que *se ponga fin al uso de actos brutales de violencia sexual contra mujeres y niñas como táctica de guerra y a la impunidad de los responsables.* Se pide también a las Naciones Unidas y a su Secretario General que faciliten protección a las mujeres y a las niñas en las iniciativas dirigidas por la ONU sobre seguridad, incluidos los campos de refugiados, y que inviten a las mujeres a participar en todos los aspectos de los procesos de paz.

- En la *Resolución 1888,* adoptada en 2009, se detallan *medidas para aumentar la protección de mujeres y niñas frente a la violencia sexual en situaciones de conflicto*, como solicitar al Secretario General que nombre a un representante especial para coordinar las misiones, envíe a un equipo de expertos en el caso de situaciones que susciten una preocupación especial y ordene a las fuerzas de mantenimiento de la paz la protección de las mujeres y los niños.

- En la *Resolución 1889*, adoptada también en 2009, se reafirma lo expuesto en la Resolución 1325, *se condena la persistencia de la violencia sexual contra las mujeres en las situaciones de conflicto* y se insta a los Estados miembros de la ONU y a la sociedad civil a que tengan en cuenta la necesidad de *proteger y empoderar a las mujeres y a las niñas,* incluidas aquéllas vinculadas con grupos armados, en las actividades programáticas que se lleven a cabo después de un conflicto.

El ESTATUTO DE ROMA de 1998, incluye la violación sexual ya no como una ofensa contra el honor, como está en las Convenciones de Ginebra, sino como un delito tan grave como la tortura, la esclavitud, etc y reconoce de forma explícita que la lista de crímenes sexuales no es cerrada. En el preámbulo se declara que todos los Estados tienen el deber de ejercer su jurisdicción penal sobre los responsables de delitos tipificados en el derecho internacional. En el artículo 6 del Estatuto de Roma, se incluye como crimen de genocidio, la agresión sexual y la imposición por la fuerza de la reproducción; en el artículo 7.1.g, se identifican la violación, la esclavitud sexual, la prostitución forzada, el embarazo forzado, la esterilización forzada o cualquier otra forma de violencia sexual de gravedad comparable como crímenes de lesa humanidad cuando se cometan como parte de un ataque generalizado o sistemático contra una población civil. En el artículo 8, estos actos se tipifican también como crímenes de guerr.

TRATADOS REGIONALES

- En el artículo I de la *Declaración Americana de los Derechos y Deberes del Hombre,* formulada en 1948, se afirma que "[t]odo ser humano tiene derecho a la vida, a la libertad y a la seguridad de su persona". En el artículo V se establece que "[t]oda persona tiene derecho a la protección de la Ley contra los ataques abusivos a su honra, a su reputación y a su vida privada y familiar". En el artículo XVIII de la Declaración se afirma también que "[t]oda persona puede ocurrir a los tribunales para hacer valer sus derechos".

- En el artículo 3 de la *Convención Interamericana para Prevenir, Sancionar y Erradicar la Violencia contra la Mujer (Convención de Belém do Pará), adoptada en 1994, se afirma que toda mujer tiene "derecho a una vida libre de violencia, tanto en el ámbito público como en el privado". En el artículo 4.g se declara que toda mujer tiene derecho "a un recurso sencillo y rápido ante los tribunales competentes, que la ampare contra actos que violen sus derechos [...]".* Según el artículo 7, los Estados Partes deben ejercer la diligencia debida para prevenir, investigar y sancionar la violencia contra la mujer e "[...] incluir en su legislación interna normas penales, civiles y administrativas, así como las de otra naturaleza que sean necesarias para prevenir, sancionar y erradicar la violencia contra la mujer y adoptar las medidas administrativas apropiadas que sean del caso [...]".

- En el artículo 3 del *Protocolo a la Carta Africana de Derechos Humanos y de los Pueblos Relativo a los Derechos de la Mujer en África* (en inglés) (Protocolo de Maputo), adoptado en 2003, se afirma:
Los Estados Partes adoptarán y aplicarán las medidas necesarias para *garantizar la protección del derecho de toda mujer a que se respete su dignidad, así como la protección de la mujer contra todas las formas de violencia, en particular la sexual y verbal.*

- En el artículo 4.a del *Protocolo de Maputo* se impone también a los Estados Partes la obligación de *"promulgar y aplicar leyes que prohíban todas las formas de violencia contra la mujer, incluidas las relaciones sexuales no deseadas o forzadas, ya tengan lugar en público o en privado [...]".* En el artículo 11 se subraya la vulnerabilidad de las mujeres en las situaciones de conflicto armado, y se incluye el siguiente párrafo: Los Estados Partes se comprometen a *proteger a las mujeres solicitantes de asilo, refugiadas, retornadas y desplazadas internamente contra todas las formas de violencia, la violación y otras formas de explotación sexual* y a garantizar que tales actos se consideren crímenes de guerra, genocidio o crímenes de lesa humanidad y que sus *autores sean llevados ante la justicia bajo la jurisdicción penal competente.*

- En el apartado 4 de la *Declaración sobre la Eliminación de la Violencia contra la Mujer en la Región de la ASEAN*, formulada en 2004, los Estados Partes acordaron: Promulgar leyes para *prevenir la violencia contra la mujer* y, cuando sea necesario, reforzarlas o modificarlas; potenciar la protección, curación, recuperación y reintegración de las víctimas y supervivientes, por ejemplo, adoptando medidas para investigar, procesar, castigar y, en caso pertinente, rehabilitar a los perpetradores; e *impedir que las mujeres y las niñas que hayan estado sometidas a cualquier forma de violencia, ya sea en el hogar, el lugar de trabajo, la comunidad, la sociedad o bajo custodia, vuelvan a ser objeto de victimización [...]*

Es especialmente destacable para el caso colombiano, la *Convención Interamericana para Prevenir, Sancionar y Erradicar la Violencia contra la Mujer,* conocida como *Convención de Belém do Pará.* Esta convención -- –que entró en vigor en 1995 y ha sido aplicada en innumerables ocasiones por la Corte Interamericana de Derechos Humanos– tiene carácter vinculante por lo que los estados integrantes de la misma –entre ellos Colombia– tienen la obligación de cumplir con sus disposiciones para prevenir, sancionar y erradicar la violencia contra las mujeres.

A la vez, la protección contra la discriminación basada en sexo, edad, etnia u otra condición está arraigada en el Derecho Internacional de los Derechos Humanos y tiene *carácter de jus cogens*[3]. Señalar en este punto la Convención sobre la Eliminación de todas las formas de Discriminación contra la Mujer ("CEDAW" en sus siglas en inglés) y *especialmente la recomendación general número 12 del Comité para Eliminación de la Discriminación de la Mujer sobre la violencia sexual y la obligación de su erradicación.* Asimismo, el Derecho Internacional de los Derechos Humanos consolida la protección contra la violencia basada en género cometida durante los conflictos armados vía las resoluciones del Consejo de Seguridad y la Asamblea General[4] y la interpretación de tratados a nivel

---

3 Ver: CEDAW. *Recomendación General número 19.* 1992. http://www.un.org/womenwatch/daw/cedaw/recommendations/recomm-sp.htm#recom19
CORTE IDH. *Caso González y otras ("Campo Algodonero") vs. México.* 16 de noviembre de 2009. http://www.corteidh.or.cr/docs/casos/articulos/seriec_205_esp.pdf

4 Resoluciones del Consejo de Seguridad: 1325 de octubre 31 del 2000, 1822 de 30 de junio de 2008, 1888 de 30 de septiembre de 2009, 1960 de 16 de diciembre de 2010. (Ver DOCUMENTO ADJUNTO 1)
Resolución de la Asamblea General: 61/438.
Plataforma de Acción de Beijing de 1995.

internacional y regional. Los tribunales regionales y Comités de Naciones Unidas han adaptado la definición de violación asentada por los Tribunales Penales Internacionales[5].

B/ LA PERSECUCIÓN DE LOS DELITOS DE VIOLENCIA DE GENERO EN EL DERECHO PENAL INTERNACIONAL.

Durante el tiempo en que se mantuvo el conflicto armado en Ruanda, aproximadamente 500.000 mujeres fueron torturadas, violadas, mutiladas y masacradas durante el conflicto de 1 994.[6] Por su parte en Bosnia- Herzegovina, se calcula en más de 60.000 las mujeres y niñas violadas por soldados, policías de forma organizada y sistemática[7].

El Consejo de Seguridad de Naciones Unidas, creó en 1993 y 1994, los tribunales para la Ex Yugoslavia y Ruanda, respectivamente. Por primera vez es tratada la violación como delito de lesa humanidad. A través de sus pronunciamientos, estos tribunales sentaron los precedentes en materia de tipificación y sanción de estos crímenes.

La jurisprudencia internacional sobre violencia sexual a partir de las resoluciones de estos Tribunales y del Tribunal Especial para Sierra Leona han dejado establecido que la violación y las agresiones sexuales pueden constituir en sí mismas genocidio, crimen de lesa humanidad, crimen de guerra y tortura. Así mismo, establece que la violación es un elemento de otros crímenes como la esclavitud sexual y la prostitución forzada.

El genocidio y los crímenes de lesa humanidad poseen el estatus de *ius cogens* e imponen a los Estados obligaciones o deberes no derogables: *obligatio erga omnes*. La violencia basada en género puede constituir el *actus reus(hecho que justifica)* del delito de genocidio o de

---

[5] Ver, por ejemplo: Corte IDH. *Caso Rosendo Cantú y otra vs. México.* 15 de mayo de 2011. http://www.corteidh.or.cr/docs/casos/articulos/seriec_225_esp.pdf
Corte IDH. *Caso Fernandez Ortega y otros vs. México.* 30 de agosto de 2010. http://www.corteidh.or.cr/docs/casos/articulos/seriec_215_esp.pdf

[6]Informe de la Relatora Especial sobre la violencia contra la mujer, sus causas y consecuencias, Sra. Radhika Coomaraswamy, Naciones Unidas. Comisión de Derechos Humanos, 55º periodo de sesiones. Integración de los derechos de la mujer y la perspectiva de género: la violencia contra la mujer preparado de conformidad con la Resolución 1997/44 de la Comisión de Derechos Humanos. E/CN.4/1999/68/Add.4. 21 de enero de 1999.

[7] Informe del Secretario General naciones Unidas 1996, Agresión y violación de mujeres en las zonas de conflicto armado de la ex Yugoslavia. Citado por Roxana Arroyo Vargas y Lola Valladares Tayupanta en Informe Violencia Sexual contra las mujeres. Serie Documentos Jurídicos Año 1.

crímenes de lesa humanidad y por tanto su persecución y reparación es obligatoria en el derecho penal internacional.

La evolución del crimen de violación en la jurisprudencia internacional

El *crimen de violación,* fue el primero en ser reconocido como crimen de lesa humanidad, genocidio o crimen de guerra por la jurisprudencia internacional.

En la actualidad, podemos afirmar que bajo el Derecho Penal Internacional y el Derecho Internacional Humanitario, la prohibición de *la violación y la violencia sexual tienen estatus de derecho internacional consuetudinario.* En la misma línea, en el ámbito del Derecho Internacional de los Derechos Humanos, los tribunales regionales y Comités de Naciones Unidas han adaptado la definición de violación asentada por los Tribunales Penales Internacionales.

La interpretación del crimen de violación ha evolucionado gracias a la jurisprudencia de los Tribunales Penales Internacionales para la ex Yugoslavia y Ruanda, que ha sido posteriormente considerada por el Tribunal Especial para Sierra Leona y la Corte Penal Internacional (CPI). En el caso de los Tribunales Penales Internacionales para la ex-Yugoslavia y Ruanda, *dicha evolución ha girado principalmente en torno a dos elementos constitutivos del crimen de violación, a saber, la penetración y el consentimiento.*

Con anterioridad, se entendía que existía violación cuando se producía penetración vaginal de la víctima, sin su consentimiento, con el pene del agresor.

Estos tribunales han ampliado el concepto de penetración y han establecido en qué casos podemos considerar *per se* que no existe consentimiento de la víctima.

Respecto a la penetración, fue el Tribunal Penal Internacional para Ruanda (TPIR), el que presentó en el caso *Akayesu* una definición de violación novedosa al ampliar, por un lado, los actos de violación a cualquier tipo de penetración corporal, y a la vez a cualquier tipo de invasión corporal no consentida con cualquier tipo de objeto.

Así, en su decisión, el Tribunal explica que "la violación es una invasión física de naturaleza sexual, cometida sobre una persona bajo circunstancias que son coactivas [...] La violación sexual no está limitada a la invasión física del cuerpo humano y puede incluir actos que no suponen penetración o siquiera contacto físico". Esta definición fue posteriormente asumida por el Tribunal Penal Internacional para la ex-Yugoslavia (TPIY) en el denominado caso Celebici. No obstante, este Tribunal dio una nueva definición de violación en el caso Furundzija, donde estableció que los elementos objetivos del crimen de violación son: "i. Penetración sexual, incluso leve:a) de la vagina o ano de la víctima por el pene del perpetrador u otro objeto utilizado por el perpetrador; o b) de la boca de la víctima por el pene del perpetrador; ii. Bajo coerción o fuerza o amenaza contra la víctima o una tercera persona". Este nuevo pronunciamiento generó un amplio debate en torno a la interpretación del crimen de violación, que fue finalmente abordado en la decisión del caso Musema, donde el TPIR analizó las dos definiciones dadas hasta el momento, y determinó que la definición del caso *Akayesu* era preferible a la recogida en el caso *Furundzija*, porque aquella comprendía todas las conductas definidas en esta última.

A pesar de ello, la discusión volvió a surgir con el pronunciamiento del caso Kunarac et al., donde el TPIY adoptó nuevamente la definición del caso Furundzija, pero añadió un nuevo asunto al debate, al analizar la interpretación del consentimiento en los casos de violación sexual. Así, el Tribunal determinó que para que no exista violación, el "[c]onsentimiento debe ser dado voluntariamente, como resultado de la libre voluntad de la víctima evaluada en el contexto de las circunstancias existentes."

"El mens rea es la intención de efectuar la penetración sexual, y el conocimiento de que ello ocurre sin el consentimiento de la víctima". La Sala de Apelación que estudió el recurso interpuesto en el caso Kunarac estuvo de acuerdo con esta definición, y además matizó que "hay factores 'más allá de la fuerza' que podrían dar lugar a un acto de penetración sexual no consensual o no voluntario por parte de la víctima. Un enfoque reducido sobre la fuerza o la amenaza de fuerza podría permitir a los perpetradores eludir responsabilidad por la actividad sexual a la que la otra parte no ha consentido por tomar ventaja de las circunstancias coercitivas sin depender de la fuerza física". La Sala fue más allá y señaló que las circunstancias que daban lugar a los cargos de violación como crímenes de lesa humanidad o crímenes de guerra "serán casi universalmente coercitivas", de manera que "el verdadero consentimiento no sería posible".

Finalmente, el consenso respecto de la definición de violación llegó con la sentencia del caso Muhimana, donde el TPIR señaló que "la definición de Akayesu y los elementos dados en Kunarac no son incompatibles o sustancialmente diferentes en su aplicación.

Mientras que Akayesu se refería en términos generales a una 'invasión física de naturaleza sexual', Kunarac se centró en articular los parámetros qué debería reunir una invasión física de naturaleza sexual para que constituyera violación".

En el caso Kunarac, además de lo dicho deben resaltarse algunos elementos importantes del fallo: se establece que "las formas de penetración sexual forzada infringidas sobre las mujeres con el propósito de interrogar, castigar o ejercer coerción *constituyen tortura* que el acceso sexual a las mujeres ejercido como el derecho de propiedad constituye una forma de esclavitud bajo los crímenes de lesa humanidad"[8].

Frente a la *esclavitud,* la Sala de apelaciones estableció que la esclavitud tiene lugar a través de la explotación sexual de las mujeres y niñas. Considera que para que se configure la misma se deben tener en cuenta factores como "control del movimiento de alguien, el control del ambiente físico, el control psicológico, las medidas tomadas para prevenir el escape, la fuerza, la amenaza, la coerción, la duración, la afirmación de exclusividad, la sujeción al tratamiento cruel y al abuso, el control de la sexualidad y el trabajo forzado[9].

En cuanto al *consentimiento en la esclavitud*, la Sala de Apelaciones aceptó que la falta de consentimiento no era un elemento del crimen que el Fiscal debía probar, porque la esclavitud se basa en el ejercicio del derecho de propiedad y consideraron que en tales circunstancias, era imposible expresar el consentimiento, por lo que era suficiente presumir la ausencia de tal[10].

En cuanto a la *tortura*, la Sala de Apelaciones consideró que está constituida por un acto o una omisión que da lugar a dolor o sufrimientos graves, ya sean físicos o mentales, pero no existen otros requisitos específicos que permitan una clasificación exhaustiva o una enumeración de los actos que podrían constituir tortura [11]. Previamente la Sala de juicio había desechado el argumento de los apelantes que plantearon que el sufrimiento debía ser visible, porque consideraron que algunos actos establecen *per sé* el sufrimiento de las víctimas, y la violación es uno de ellos. La Sala fue más allá y tuvo por probado el sufrimiento aún sin un certificado médico, estableciendo que la violencia sexual daba

[8] Viseur-Seller, Patricia: Gender-Based Persecution, United Nations, Expert Group Meeting on Gender-based Persecution, Toronto, Canada 9-12 Nov, 1997. EGM/GBP/1977.3. 6 de noviembre de 1997.
[9] Sentencia Sala de Apelaciones. Párrafo 119
[10] Idem. Párrafo 120
[11] Idem. Párrafo 129

lugar a dolor o sufrimientos graves, ya sean físicos o mentales. Es decir, una vez que se prueba la violación, se tiene por probado el sufrimiento o dolor severo de la tortura, porque la violación lleva implícito dicho dolor o sufrimiento[12]

Caso Cesic

En este caso el acusado, Ranko Cesic fue investigado por varios cargos entre los que estaba el "asalto sexual" de 2 musulmanes detenidos. Durante el proceso, el acusado aceptó los cargos y fue condenado por el tribunal por crímenes de lesa humanidad por forzar intencionalmente a 2 hermanos musulmanes a realizar sexo oral entre ellos mientras eran observados por otros soldados. Consideró el tribunal que ese tipo de acciones constituye un acto degradante y humillante, contrario al derecho internacional humanitario.

El tribunal valoró la acción como agravada teniendo en cuenta el impacto que las mismas causan a las víctimas y sus familiares al mismo tiempo por haber sido cometidos frente a terceros lo que incrementa la humillación de las víctimas.

Caso Tadic

Miembros de las fuerzas serbo-bosnias que actuaban en el municipio de Prijedor, fue declarado culpable por la Comisión de crímenes de lesa humanidad y crímenes de guerra perpetrados durante 1992. No fue condenado directamente por cometer acto de agresión sexual pero si de participar en una campaña de terror generalizada y sistemática mediante acciones como golpizas, tortura y agresiones sexuales. Pese a que en la acusación original se incluyó el delito de violencia sexual, fue retirado posteriormente debido a que la víctima se negó a declarar.

La sentencia afirma categóricamente que
la violación y el abuso sexual pueden considerarse como parte de una campaña generalizada o sistemática de terror contra la población civil. No es necesario probar que la violación misma fuera generalizada o sistemática sino que la violación constituía uno o tal vez muchos tipos de crímenes, cuyo espectro se cometía de forma generalizada o

[12] Sentencia de la Sala de Juicio, párrafo 205. En: http://www.rnw.nl/informarn/html/act010222_tpicasofoca.html

sistemática e incluía una campaña de terror por parte del agresor

Por su parte, el *Tribunal Especial para Sierra Leona (TESL)* en el caso *Prosecutor vs. Issa Hassan Sesay, Morris Kallon y Augustine Gbao*, conocido como caso *RUF*, considera que *existe violación cuando el acusado invade el cuerpo de otra persona mediante cualquier conducta que resulte en la penetración, por mínima que sea, de cualquier parte del cuerpo de la víctima, utilizando su órgano sexual o penetrando el ano o genitales de la víctima con cualquier objeto o cualquier parte de su cuerpo, siempre que la invasión haya sido el resultado del uso de la fuerza o la coacción.* El Tribunal considera que el uso de la fuerza o su amenaza se producen de tal manera que la víctima sufre un temor a la violencia, la agresividad, la detención, la opresión psicológica o un temor por el abuso de poder, contra ella misma o alguna otra persona, o aprovechando un ambiente de coacción.

Asimismo, en *el Estatuto de Roma* se señala que el consentimiento
no podrá inferirse de ninguna palabra o conducta de la víctima cuando la fuerza, la amenaza de fuerza, la coacción o el aprovechamiento de un entorno coercitivo hayan disminuido su capacidad para dar un consentimiento voluntario y libre
y tampoco cuando la víctima sea incapaz de dar un consentimiento libre. También en el Estatuto del TESL se señala que no podrá entenderse que existe consentimiento cuando la víctima se mantiene en silencio o no pone resistencia a la violencia sexual, y matiza que "la credibilidad, la honorabilidad o la disponibilidad sexual de la víctima o de un testigo no podrán inferirse de la naturaleza sexual del comportamiento anterior o posterior de la víctima o testigo".

Como podemos observar, las definiciones de violación dadas por el TESL y la Corte Penal derivan de las definiciones emanadas de los Tribunales *ad hoc*. Igualmente, las consideraciones en torno al consentimiento son fruto de la evolución de la jurisprudencia de los Tribunales para la ex-Yugoslavia y Ruanda.

En la actualidad, *la violación y las agresiones sexuales pueden constituir en sí mismas genocidio, crimen de lesa humanidad, crimen de guerra y tortura. Igualmente, la violación es un elemento de otros crímenes como la esclavitud sexual y la prostitución forzada.*

C/ Corte Penal Internacional.

Los primeros casos de investigación sobre violencia sexual en el marco de la CPI se han desarrollado frente a la situación de la República Democrática del Congo. Los informes allegados a la Corte se centran en torturas, desplazamiento forzado, reclutamiento de menores y violaciones sexuales. Naciones Unidas estimó que más de 40.000 mujeres y niñas fueron violadas. El caso más avanzado corresponde a la investigación contra Germain Katanga "Simba" y Mathieu Ngudjolo chui, dos líderes guerrilleros de la República Democrática de Congo, acusados de reclutar niños soldado, así como de asesinato, violación y de haber forzado a las mujeres al esclavismo sexual. Su caso es el segundo en llegar a la Corte, y se centra en lo ocurrido en 2003 en Bororo, un pueblo de la región de Ituri, al noreste del país. Según la fiscalía, Katanga y Chui lanzaron allí conjuntamente a sus tropas contra los habitantes y mataron a 200 vecinos. Luego se llevaron al menos a 15 menores para combatir en sus filas. Muchas de las víctimas fueron mutiladas con machetes mientras las mujeres eran violentadas.

Katanga, alias Simba, era el jefe de la Fuerza Patriótica de Resistencia. Pertenece a la etnia lendu, de tradición agrícola, y enfrentada a los hema, dedicada al pastoreo. Chui, también de la comunidad lendu, comandaba el Frente Nacional Integracionista. Luis Moreno Ocampo, fiscal jefe de la CPI, asegura que el conflicto de Ituri, zona rica en oro, "forma parte de la guerra civil que arrasó Congo tras el genocidio perpetrado en la vecina Ruanda en 1994". Después de revisar casi 17.000 documentos, la acusación llamará a 26 testigos. De estos, 21 declararán ocultando su identidad por temor a represalias. Antes de la apertura del proceso, Katanga se mostró "confiado en la imparcialidad" del mismo. En cuando a Chui, se considera "una víctima más[13].

La decisión de confirmación de cargos se dio en septiembre de 2008, y el caso se encuentra en etapa de juicio desde el 24 de noviembre se 2009.

La defensa ha alegado que se está adelantando la investigación por los mismos hechos por en el orden interno por lo cual se debería respetar el principio de complementariedad.

[13] http://www.agenciacna.com/2/nota_1.php?noticia_id=27976

En la decisión de confirmación de cargos por mayoría se encontró suficiente evidencia para confirmar los cargos de crímenes de guerra y de lesa humanidad frente a las acusaciones por violación y esclavitud sexual ocurridas el 24 de febrero de 2003 durante la toma de la ciudad de Bogoro, de forma consciente y conjunta, en el marco de un ataque sistemático y generalizado contra la población civil. En este contexto, la decisión de confirmación de cargos, junto con la decisión de confirmación de cargos en el caso Lubanga son las dos únicas decisiones de carácter sustantivo emitidas hasta el momento por la Corte. En la misma, se abordan por primera vez los elementos contextuales de los delitos de lesa humanidad previstos en el Estatuto de Roma (ER) y en los Elementos de Crímenes (EC), así como los elementos específicos de ciertos delitos de violencia sexual (violación y esclavitud sexual) tipificados en el ER como crímenes de guerra o de lesa humanidad.

Sin embargo en el caso Lubanga, no se ha producido condena por este tipo de delito, a pesar de que lo solicitaba el Fiscal.

D/ JURISDICCIONES REGIONALES

Sistema Interamericano de Derechos Humanos.

El Sistema interamericano de Derechos Humanos también ha generado avances importantes a través de las decisiones de la Comisión y la jurisprudencia de la Corte. En primer lugar la Comisión Interamericana entre 1991 y el año 2000 había identificado ya 14 casos relacionados con derechos sexuales y reproductivos, de los cuales 6 involucraba el uso de la violencia sexual como tortura por parte del Estado. Por su parte la Corte Interamericana ha establecido la responsabilidad de los Estados en casos de esterilización forzada, violencia intra familiar, y tortura con base en la violación sexual.

En lo que respecta a la *Comisión Interamericana, también han sido objeto de desarrollo, los* delitos sexuales y la justicia de género, en forma paralela al desarrollo jurisprudencial referido.

Dicha Comisión, se pronunció, respecto de la violación sexual, en dos Informes: el *Informe sobre Haiti de 1995*: donde sostuvo que los *actos de violencia contra las mujeres califican como delitos de lesa humanidad cuando son utilizados como arma para infundir terror y el Informe s/Perú de 1996*: en donde, luego de definir la *violación sexual como "todo acto de abuso físico y mental perpetrado como acto de violencia", lo calificó como forma del delito de tortura.*

Paralelamente la *Corte Interamericana de DDHH* cuenta a la fecha con dos pronunciamientos relevantes sobre violencia de género y delitos sexuales: *"Castro Castro c. Perú"* (2006) y *"Campo Algodonero c. México"* (2009).

La perspectiva de género se introduce por primera vez en la jurisprudencia de la Corte IDH a través de la sentencia de fondo emitida en la causa "Castro Castro".

La Corte IDH, en el caso citado considera demostrado que durante los conflictos armados internos e internacionales las partes que se enfrentan utilizan la violencia sexual contra las mujeres como un medio de castigo y represión. La utilización del poder estatal para violar los derechos de las mujeres en un conflicto interno además de afectarles a ellas en forma directa puede tener como objetivo causar un efecto en al sociedad a través de esas violaciones o dar un mensaje o lección.

La Corte afirma en sus razonamientos jurídicos (apartado 206) que las mujeres privadas de libertad en el penal Castro Castro
...además de recibir un trato violatorio de su dignidad personal, también fueron víctimas de violencia sexual, ya que estuvieron desnudas y cubiertas con tan solo una sábana, estando rodeadas de hombres armados, quienes aparentemente eran miembros de las fuerzas de seguridad del Estado. Lo que califica este tratamiento de violencia sexual es que las mujeres fueron constantemente observadas por hombres.
La Corte, siguiendo la línea de la jurisprudencia internacional y tomando en cuenta lo dispuesto en la Convención para Prevenir, Sancionar y Erradicar la Violencia contra la Mujer (Belén do Para), consideró que "la violencia sexual se configura con acciones de naturaleza sexual que se cometen en una persona sin su consentimiento, que además de comprender la invasión física del cuerpo humano, pueden incluir actos que no involucren penetración o incluso contacto físico alguno".

Así mismo, la Corte reconoce (apartado 311)
que la violación sexual de una detenida por un agente del Estado es un acto especialmente grave y reprobable, tomando en cuenta la vulnerabilidad de la víctima y el abuso de poder que despliega el agente. Asimismo, la violación sexual es una experiencia sumamente traumática que puede tener severas consecuencias y causa gran daño físico y psicológico que deja a la víctima "humillada física y emocionalmente", situación

difícilmente superable por el paso del tiempo, a diferencia de lo que acontece en otras experiencias traumáticas
Paralelamente, en la causa "Campo Algodonero" la Corte IDH avanza sobre los conceptos vertidos en el precedente citado y establece la responsabilidad del Estado por "haber permanecido indiferente frente a una situación crónica de violencia... ante la existencia de una cultura de discriminación contra la mujer". Para la Corte IDH el Estado es responsable por los actos cometidos por particulares atento su condición de garante respecto del riesgo de violencia basada en género: teoría del riesgo creado (art. 7 de la Convención de Belén do Pará).

A la luz de los antecedentes citados, puede concluirse que la jurisprudencia internacional e interamericana se presenta como un punto de inflexión en el desarrollo de los delitos sexuales como delitos de lesa humanidad, advirtiéndose sólo algunas disidencias al momento de precisar su tipificación: algunos fallos u opiniones postularon su condición de delito de lesa humanidad autónomo, y otros lo valoraron como una forma del delito de tortura.

E/ CASOS CONCRETOS RESUMIDOS EN EL ESPACIO INTERAMERICANO

Caso Fernando y Raquel Mejía vs Perú

Se acusa en el presente caso al Estado Peruano por los hechos ocurridos en junio de 1989 cuando un grupo de militares irrumpió en la residencia de Fernando Mejía Egocheaga y su esposa Raquel Martín; a él se lo llevaron y su esposa fue objeto de violación en 2 oportunidades.

El señor Fernando Mejía fue encontrado muerto 2 días después con signos de tortura, y la señora fue objeto de amenazas e intimidación, que la obligaron a salir del país.

En el caso de la violación, la Comisión Interamericana de Derechos Humanos determinó que se habían cumplido los elementos constitutivos de la tortura establecidos por la Comisión Interamericana para Prevenir y Sancionar la Tortura (Un acto cometido intencionalmente para infringir sufrimientos físicos o mentales, con el fin de castigar o intimidar, y cometido por un funcionario público o instigado por el.), considerándose el abuso sexual como un ultraje deliberado. Estableció que se violan los derechos a la integridad personal (art.5), y al honor y dignidad (art. 11) de la Convención Americana de Derechos Humanos.

Caso Dianna Ortiz v. Guatemala

Dianna Ortiz, era una mujer monja quien denuncio haber sido secuestrada y torturada por agentes del Gobierno de Guatemala en 1989. En varias ocasiones fue violada por múltiples agentes y fue objeto de tortura mediante amenazas, y lesiones como quemada por cigarrillo.
En este caso la Comisión determinó que el trato inhumano que sufrió la Hermana Ortiz en manos de agentes del Gobierno corresponde a la definición de tortura al infringir sufrimiento físico y mental para castigarla e intimidarla por su participación en ciertas actividades y por su asociación con ciertas personas y grupos. Los agentes del Gobierno fueron responsables de las violaciones de derechos de la Hermana Ortiz, quienes actuaban al amparo de su capacidad oficial. El secuestro y la tortura de la Hermana Ortiz corresponden a una pauta de actividades cometidas por el Gobierno de Guatemala en violación a los Derechos Humanos.

La comisión concluyó que el Estado de Guatemala es responsable por violaciones de los Derechos Humanos de Dianna Ortiz a la integridad personal, a la libertad personal, a las garantías judiciales, a gozar de protección para la honra y la dignidad, a la libertad de conciencia y de religión, a la libertad de asociación y a la protección judicial, todos consagrados en los artículos 5, 7, 8, 11, 12, 16 y 25 de la Convención Americana y ha omitido cumplir con la obligación establecida en el artículo 1.

Caso Ana, Beatriz y Celia González Pérez v. México

Las hermanas Ana, Beatriz, y Celia González Pérez y su madre Delia Pérez de González fueron detenidas en 1994 por agentes estatales para ser interrogadas. Una de las víctimas era menor de edad. Por dos horas fueron detenidas, golpeadas y violadas en varias ocasiones por militares. Se denuncia también la violación al deber de investigar por parte del Estado, la falta de castigo a los responsables y de reparación a las víctimas.

Al respecto La Comisión reitera la configuración de tortura en casos de violación y determinó que:

La violación sexual cometida por miembros de las fuerzas de seguridad de un Estado contra integrantes de la población civil constituye en todos los casos una grave violación de los Derechos Humanos protegidos en los artículos 5 y 11 de la Convención Americana, así como de normas de Derecho Internacional Humanitario. Recuerda además que la Convención Interamericana para Prevenir, Sancionar y Erradicar la Violencia contra la Mujer garantiza a toda mujer el derecho a una vida libre de violencia.

La Comisión Interamericana considera que los abusos contra la integridad física, psíquica y moral de las tres hermanas Tzeltales cometidos por los agentes del Estado mexicano constituyen tortura y configuran una violación de la vida privada de las cuatro mujeres y de su familia y un ataque ilegal a su honra o reputación, que las llevó a huir de su comunidad en medio del temor, la vergüenza y humillación.
Según la jurisprudencia internacional de Derechos Humanos, en ciertas circunstancias, la angustia y el sufrimiento impuestos a los familiares directos de las víctimas de violaciones graves de Derechos Humanos configuran adicionalmente una violación del derecho a la integridad personal de aquellos.

En el presente caso, la CIDH estima que el trato que se dio a la madre de las víctimas, Delia Pérez de González, quien tuvo que asistir impotente a la vejación de sus tres hijas por integrantes de las fuerzas armadas mexicanas y luego compartir con ellas el ostracismo de su comunidad, constituye una humillación y degradación violatoria del derecho a la integridad personal que le garantiza la Convención Americana.

La Comisión concluyó que el Estado mexicano violó en perjuicio de la señora Delia Pérez de González y de sus hijas Ana, Beatriz y Celia González Pérez los siguientes derechos consagrados en la Convención Americana: derecho a la libertad personal (artículo 7); a la integridad personal y a la protección de la honra y de la dignidad (artículos 5 y 11); garantías judiciales y protección judicial (artículos 8 y 25). Respecto de Celia González Pérez, el artículo 19 de la Declaración de los Derechos del Niño y todos los artículos relacionados con la obligación general de respetar y garantizar los derechos, prevista en el artículo 1(1) de dicho instrumento internacional. La CIDH establece igualmente que el Estado mexicano es responsable por la violación del artículo 8 de la Convención Interamericana para Prevenir y Sancionar la Tortura.

De otra parte, La Corte Interamericana en sus fallos ha sentado jurisprudencia importante que puede considerarse un avance en la investigación y sanción de delitos sexuales a nivel internacional.

Caso Inés Fernández Ortega Vs. México

Este caso trata tiene como víctima a una mujer indígena, del pueblo Me'phaa (tlapaneco), que fue amenazada, golpeada y violada por tres miembros del Ejército Mexicano, en el estado de Guerrero el año 2002.

En 2004, después de una serie de irregularidades ante las autoridades mexicanas, el caso fue llevado ante la Comisión Interamericana de Derechos Humanos. En 2009, la Comisión presentó una demanda contra México ante la Corte Interamericana de Derechos Humanos, en la que reclamó diversas violaciones a los derechos humanos de Inés Fernández Ortega, su esposo y sus cinco hijos.

El 30 de agosto de 2010, México fue declarado responsable por la violación de los derechos humanos a la integridad personal, a la dignidad, a la vida privada y a no ser objeto de injerencias arbitrarias en el domicilio, en contra de Inés Fernández Ortega. En términos de la Corte "Este Tribunal recuerda, como lo señala la Convención de Belém do Pará, que la violencia contra la mujer no sólo constituye una violación de los derechos humanos, sino que es "una ofensa a la dignidad humana y una manifestación de las relaciones de poder históricamente desiguales entre mujeres y hombres", que "trasciende todos los sectores de la sociedad independientemente de su clase, raza o grupo étnico, nivel de ingresos, cultura, nivel educacional, edad o religión y afecta negativamente sus propias bases"....La Corte, siguiendo la jurisprudencia internacional y tomando en cuenta lo dispuesto en dicha Convención, ha considerado anteriormente que la violencia sexual se configura con acciones de naturaleza sexual que se cometen contra una persona sin su consentimiento, que además de comprender la invasión física del cuerpo humano, pueden incluir actos que no involucren penetración o incluso contacto físico alguno...En particular, la violación sexual constituye una forma paradigmática de violencia contra las mujeres cuyas consecuencias, incluso, trascienden a la persona de la víctima....

La Comisión señaló que la violación sexual cometida por miembros de las fuerzas de seguridad de un Estado contra integrantes de la población civil constituye una grave violación a los derechos humanos protegidos en los artículos 5 y 11 de la Convención Americana. En los casos de violación sexual contra mujeres indígenas, el dolor y la humillación se agrava por su condición de indígenas debido "al desconocimiento del idioma de sus agresores y de las demás autoridades intervinientes[, y] por el repudio de su comunidad como consecuencia de los hechos".

La sentencia condena violaciones a los derechos humanos de su esposo y sus hijos, igualmente establece; que el estado mexicano deberá realizar reformas legislativas a la legislación militar, otorgar becas de estudios a los hijos de Fernández Ortega, pagar una compensación económica y brindar tratamiento médico y psicológico a las víctimas.

Caso Castro Castro vs. Perú (2006)

Este caso se refiere a la masacre desatada durante cuatro días que duró el llamado "Operativo Mudanza 1" en la prisión Castro Castro en el Perú. Los internos de los pabellones 1A y 4B vieron constantemente amenazadas sus vidas por la intensidad del ataque, que implicó el uso de armas de guerra y la participación de agentes de la policía, del ejército y de fuerzas especiales. Se pudo identificar la muerte de 41 reclusos y muchos otros fueron sometidos a tratos crueles y degradantes.

La importancia de este caso radica en que se reconoce el efecto diferenciado que tuvo el accionar militar en las mujeres. Según lo expresa la Corte "la masacre fue inicialmente dirigida contra las aproximadamente 133 mujeres que se encontraban en el pabellón 1-A de la prisión Miguel Castro Castro, con el objeto de exterminarlas, convirtiéndose en blancos singularizados del ataque contra la prisión. Muchas de las internas fueron asesinadas a quemarropa." La Corte también consideró que la desnudez forzada a la que fueron sometidas varias personas internas representaba una forma de violencia sexual y como tal una violación del derecho a la integridad personal.

Caso Campo Algodonero (2009)

La demanda se relaciona con la supuesta responsabilidad internacional del Estado por "la desaparición y ulterior muerte" de las jóvenes Claudia Ivette González, Esmeralda Herrera Monreal y Laura Berenice Ramos Monárrez, cuyos cuerpos fueron encontrados en un campo algodonero de Ciudad Juárez el día 6 de noviembre de 2001. Se responsabiliza al Estado por "la falta de medidas de protección a las víctimas, dos de las cuales eran menores de edad; la falta de prevención de estos crímenes, pese al pleno conocimiento de la existencia de un patrón de violencia de género que había dejado centenares de mujeres y niñas asesinadas; la falta de respuesta de las autoridades frente a la desaparición [...]; la falta de debida diligencia en la investigación de los asesinatos [...], así como la denegación de justicia y la falta de reparación adecuada."

En este caso, la Corte determinó que la desaparición y posterior muerte de tres mujeres en el contexto de discriminación en Ciudad Juarez (mexico) constituía violencia contra la mujer, acudiendo a la Convención Americana de Derechos Humanos y a la Convención Belém do Para.

Caso Rosendo Cantú y otra vs. México. (2010)

Los hechos de este caso se relacionan con la supuesta violación sexual de la indígena Me'phaa Valentina Rosendo Cantú, así como con la alegada falta de debida diligencia en la investigación y sanción de los responsables de los hechos; las alegadas consecuencias de los hechos del caso en la hija de la presunta víctima; la supuesta falta de reparación adecuada en favor de la presunta víctima y sus familiares; la alegada la utilización del fuero militar para la investigación y juzgamiento de violaciones a los derechos humanos, y a las supuestas dificultades que enfrentan las personas indígenas, en particular las mujeres, para acceder a la justicia y a los servicios de salud. La Corte señaló que la violación sexual sufrida por la indígena representa una violación del derecho a la integridad personal, la dignidad personal y la vida privada.

El 8 nov 11 la Comisión Interamericana de Derechos Humanos (CIDH) admitió el caso de tortura sexual de 11 mujeres violadas durante los operativos policíacos del 3 y 4 de mayo de 2006, en Texcoco y San Salvador Atenco, Estado de México.

F/ SISTEMA EUROPEO DE DERECHOS HUMANOS

La Corte Europea de Derechos Humanos también ha determinado que la violación sexual puede constituir tortura, así se pronunció en el Caso Aydin vs. Turquía,
una joven de diecisiete años, que vivía con sus padres en una aldea en Turquía suroriental, de la cual ella nunca había salido. En 1985 se presentaron serios disturbios en esa parte del país entre las fuerzas de la seguridad y los miembros del Partido separatista Kurdo. Turquía denunció que a causa de esta situación habían muerto más de 4.000 civiles aproximadamente y un número similar de miembros de las fuerzas de seguridad.

En este contexto Aydin fue golpeada, y violada mientras a su padre y familiares los detuvieron ilegalmente. Cuando Aydin fue a reclamar por sus familiares, unos guardias la llevaron a un cuarto, la desnudaron y la pusieron en un neumático de carro y le hicieron girar. Luego le golpearon, le lanzaron agua fría a alta presión, le volvieron a vestir y con los ojos vendados fue conducida a un cuarto de interrogatorios, donde un individuo vestido de militar le arrancó las ropas y la violó.

Finalmente el caso llegó a conocimiento de la Corte Europea de Derechos Humanos, la misma que en sentencia pronunciada en Estrasburgo el 25 de septiembre de 1997, sostuvo que la Sra. Aydin había sido sometida a torturas, violada y maltratada mientras estaba detenida por las fuerzas de seguridad turcas, en contra del artículo 3 del Convenio.

En ese caso, el Tribunal consideró que la violación de una detenida por un funcionario del Estado era una forma especialmente grave y aborrecible de malos tratos, de carácter tan grave como para constituir tortura. Además, el Tribunal sostuvo que las autoridades turcas no habían llevado a cabo una investigación completa y eficaz de la denuncia de Aydin que no existían remedios eficaces para resolver su denuncia[14].

La Corte determinó que la violación puede constituir tortura y expresó: (...)La violación de una persona detenida por un agente del Estado debe considerarse como una forma especialmente grave y aberrante de tratamiento cruel, dada la facilidad con la cual el agresor puede explotar la vulnerabilidad y el debilitamiento de la resistencia de su víctima. Además, la violación deja profundas huellas psicológicas en la víctima que no pasan con el tiempo como otras formas de violencia física y mental."

La Corte concluyó que la acumulación de actos de violencia física y mental cometidos en contra de la recurrente, y el acto especialmente cruel de violación a que se vio sometida, son constitutivos del delito de tortura penado en el Artículo 3 de la Convención.

En estos términos concluyo la presente intervención resaltando que la responsabilidad de investigar, castigar y reparar los daños ocasionados corresponde a los Estados. La jurisdicción internacional es complementaria, por lo que se hace necesario, para evitar la impunidad de dichos crímenes fortalecer los sistemas judiciales y de atención nacionales

[14] http://www.unhchr.ch/Huridocda/Huridoca.nsf/0/a193f67c546ae776c1256b730057a340?Opendocument

que permita contrarrestar la impunidad frente a la cual han estado sometidos los hechos de violencia sexual en el marco de los conflictos armados.

G/ LA PERSECUCIÓN DE LOS DELITOS DE VIOLENCIA SEXUAL EN LOS TRIBUNALES NACIONALES.

Las jurisdicciones nacionales empiezan a tomar en cuenta los grandes avances de la jurisprudencia internacional (tanto del DPI como de los Derechos Humanos) en materia de violencia sexual y están conociendo de estos crímenes, creando nueva jurisprudencia, enriqueciendo la existente, todo esto con mira a ofrecer reparación a las víctimas. Algunos antecedentes se encuentran en el Juzgado Central de Instrucción n° 5 de la Audiencia Nacional de España en la investigación de los crímenes de la dictadura argentina y chilena en los caso seguidos por el juez Baltasar Garzón al amparo del principio de Jurisdicción Universal por crímenes de genocidio, torturas, terrorismo y crímenes contra la humanidad. Posteriormente, con más amplitud, deben destacarse varios casos en Argentina y uno más en España, que pueden servir al caso colombiano.

a) *En Argentina* se puede consultar, por ejemplo la sentencia en *el caso N° 2086 y su acumulada N° 2277 contra Gregorio Molina*[15], en la que el tribunal en lo Criminal de Mar del Plata en julio de 2010, establece que, a nivel nacional, ha quedado acreditado en el Juicio a las Juntas y en los informes efectuados por la Comisión Interamericana de Derechos Humanos y la Comisión Nacional sobre la Desaparición de Personas que las violaciones sufridas por las mujeres que se encontraban en los centros clandestinos de detención no fueron sucesos aislados u ocasionales sino que constituyeron prácticas sistemáticas ejecutadas dentro del plan clandestino de represión y exterminio montado desde el Estado y dirigido por las Fuerzas Armadas.

Así mismo añade que, la jurisprudencia internacional es unánime al sostener que los delitos de violación y violencia sexual cometidos contra mujeres en época de guerra o conflicto interno en un país constituyen delitos de lesa humanidad.

En esta dirección se han pronunciado los Tribunales Internacionales, creados para Juzgar los crímenes cometidos en la ex Yugoslavia y Ruanda.

[15] Ver: DOCUMENTO ADJUNTO 2.

El Estatuto de Roma de la Corte Penal Internacional menciona específicamente la violación, la esclavitud sexual, la prostitución forzada y la esterilización forzosa, cuando se cometan en tiempo de guerra o conflicto armado, como crímenes contra la humanidad); *la Resolución en "Actuaciones Complementarias del Centro Clandestino de Detención ARSENALES MIGUEL DE AZCUÉNAGA sobre Secuestros y Desapariciones y conexos"*, el Tribunal, el 27-12-2010 en Tucumán *DECLARA* que los delitos de violación de domicilio, privación ilegítima de libertad con apremios y vejaciones, torturas, torturas seguidas de muerte, abuso deshonesto, violación sexual y homicidio investigados en la presente causa, se habrían perpetrado en el contexto de un ataque sistemático desde el Estado contra una parte substancial del grupo nacional argentino (grupos políticos, políticos militares, y grupos de personas involucradas con la lucha social sin pertenencia política partidaria) a los que se habría identificado como "enemigos" del pensamiento "occidental cristiano" (cfr. Apartado 5.8), lo que configuraría el contexto del *delito internacional de GENOCIDIO*. La violencia sexual acaecida durante la represión es descrita en los siguientes términos: "Durante la vigencia de las leyes de impunidad (1987/ 2004), solo se iniciaron acciones penales por el delito de sustracción y ocultamiento de menores y algunas pocas por apropiación de bienes. *Los delitos sexuales denunciados por las victimas en sus testimonios, no fueron objeto de acción penal habiendo permanecido invisibilizados hasta fechas recientes.*

(Cfr. *Sentencia del Tribunal Oral de Santa Fe en la Causa "Barcos"* (n.43/08) donde se analiza el delito de violación sexual como una forma de del delito de tormento; Sentencia del *Tribunal Oral de Mar de Plata* en la causa "Molina" (n.2086/10) donde se considera probado que en el marco del plan sistemático de represión era habitual que las mujeres ilegítimamente detenidas en centros clandestinos fueran sometidas sexualmente por sus captores o guardianes, afirmando en consecuencia que los actos de violencia sexual no constituyeron hechos aislados ni ocasionales sino que formaron parte de practicas sistemáticas y generalizadas). – Tal situación fue debidamente advertida por el Comité para la Eliminación de la Discriminación contra la Mujer (CEDAW) quien recomendó al Estado argentino que adopte medidas proactivas para hacer públicos, enjuiciar y castigar los incidentes de violencia sexual perpetrados durante la pasada dictadura, en el marco de los juicios por crímenes de lesa humanidad, de conformidad con lo dispuesto en la Resolución 1820 / 2008 del Consejo de Seguridad y que se concedan reparaciones a las víctimas(observaciones finales, 46° Periodo de Sesiones del 12 al 30 de julio de 2010, punto 16).

Por su parte el auto de *procesamiento en el caso del Penal de Villa Urquiza*, de fecha 19-5-2011 establece la comisión de *Torturas agravadas por la condición de género, Violencia de género: Situación de las mujeres detenidas clandestinas durante la vigencia del terrorismo de estado Violación sexual y Abusos Sexuales, y, en particular analiza la* autoría mediata o indirecta, que aparece cuando el agente se vale de otro que actúa pero no comete el injusto sea porque actúa sin tipicidad objetiva, sin dolo, o justificadamente. En el marco de tales conceptos, Roxin elaboró la tesis de que existe otra forma de autoría donde el dominio del hecho se da por fuerza de un aparato organizado de poder, sosteniéndose en que los conceptos usuales no son aplicables cuando se trata de crímenes de estado, de guerra y de organización en los que el determinador y el determinado cometen el mismo delito, siendo decisivo el carácter fungible del último, que puede ser cambiado a voluntad como si se tratara de un artefacto mecánico:

> cuanto más alejado de la víctima y de la conducta lesiva esta el ejecutor, más cerca está entonces de los órganos ejecutivos de poder lo que le proporciona mayor dominio del hecho (Zaffaroni, Alagia, Slokar; Manual de Derecho Penal Parte General, Ediar, 2005, Capítulo 24)

Consecuentemente, conforme la teoría expuesta, para determinar si una persona actuó como autor mediato en virtud de dominio de la organización, es necesario demostrar que el imputado ejercía un cargo y cumplía funciones con capacidades decisorias dentro de la organización, y que en tal condición habría intervenido en los hechos delictivos en tanto estos habrían sido perpetrados

por fuerzas bajo su mando y control efectivo, o su autoridad y control efectivo, según sea el caso", y su responsabilidad deviene "… en razón de no haber ejercido un control apropiado sobre esas fuerzas cuando: a) hubiere sabido o, en razón de las circunstancias del momento, hubiere debido saber, que las fuerzas estaban cometiendo esos crímenes o se proponían cometerlos; y b) no hubiere adoptado todas las medidas necesarias y razonables a su alcance para prevenir o reprimir su comisión o para poner el asunto en conocimiento de las autoridades competentes a los efectos de su investigación y enjuiciamiento (art. 28 del Estatuto de Roma).

Aplicado al caso que nos ocupa, puede afirmarse que los testigos/víctimas que declararon en autos son claros y coincidentes en afirmar que entre 1975 y 1983 habría funcionado en el Penal de Villa Urquiza un lugar de detención en el cual eran alojadas personas secuestradas por fuerzas de seguridad, por motivos políticos o por haber sido calificadas de "subversivas", quienes habrían soportado un trato cruel, inhumano y degradante.

Dicho lugar de detención habría funcionado como un "centro clandestino de detención" administrado y vigilado principalmente por personal del Penal –guardiacárceles-, personal de la Policía de la Provincia, de Gendarmería y del Ejército, y en él se habrían infringido torturas físicas y psicológicas a los que se encontraban allí detenidos, y en algunos casos se habría decidido su muerte.

Para determinar la responsabilidad penal por autoría mediata, corresponde entonces indagar si, atento el cargo y la función que ejercían los imputados y al ámbito donde esta se desarrollaba, puede presumirse que habrían tenido intervención en la comisión de los comportamientos delictivos corroborados en autos, por haber ejercido el dominio sobre los mismos a través del *dominio de la organización*.-

b) En España, en el reciente Auto del Juzgado Central de Instrucción núm. 1 de la Audiencia Nacional (D.P 331/1999) del 26 de junio de 2011, se sienta un precedente único al ser la primera vez que un tribunal nacional afirma que existe la obligación de investigar los crímenes de violencia sexual ocurridos durante el genocidio en Guatemala (1960- 1996).[16] Es necesario destacar también los recientes esfuerzos hechos en Guatemala para investigar y perseguir estos crímenes.

III

CONCLUSIONES

La jurisprudencia internacional sobre violencia sexual desarrollada por los tribunales *ad hoc* de la ex-Yugoslavia y Ruanda, en aplicación del Derecho Penal Internacional, ha conducido a la actual codificación de estos graves crímenes internacionales en el Estatuto de Roma para la Corte Penal Internacional (CPI).[17]

---

16 Disponible en http://www.womenslinkworldwide.org/wlw/new.php?modo=detalle_proyectos&tp=proyectos&dc=22

17 Consultar: Artículo 7 del Estatuto de Roma. http://www.un.org/spanish/law/icc/statute/spanish/rome_statute%28s%29.pdf

A pesar de que la CPI aún no ha emitido ninguna sentencia sobre este tema, en la actualidad tiene investigaciones abiertas por los crímenes cometidos en la República Centroafricana, la República Democrática del Congo, la región de Darfur en Sudán y en Uganda. Estas investigaciones incluyen cargos por esclavitud sexual y violación como crímenes de lesa humanidad y crímenes de guerra.

Es de suponer que esta jurisprudencia, cuando exista, será de particular relevancia pero, mientras, su investigación supone un decidido mensaje sobre el compromiso internacional para con la sanción y persecución de la violencia sexual en conflicto armado. Más aún, los nuevos procedimientos implementados por la CPI para garantizar la participación de las víctimas, también incorporados por las Cámaras Extraordinarias de Camboya, envían un mensaje sobre la necesidad de reparar a las víctimas.[18]

En suma, es evidente que, de acuerdo con la jurisprudencia internacional tanto en el ámbito del derecho penal internacional como de los derechos humanos, existe una obligación de investigar y enjuiciar los crímenes de naturaleza sexual. Así, es el turno ahora de los tribunales nacionales de fortalecer la mentada jurisprudencia en materia de género aplicándola y conociendo de estos crímenes a nivel doméstico. En Colombia, el hecho de que en el proceso de justicia y paz colombiano tan solo se haya pronunciado **una condena** por crímenes de género cometidos en el contexto del conflicto armado (por guerrilla, paramilitares, policía y militares). Esta carencia, después de 6 años, no tiene justificación. El Estado y la justicia colombiana deben afrontar este reto de manera prioritaria e inexcusable. Es una deuda con las mujeres y niñas colombianas que exigen una respuesta firme y decidida por parte de las Instituciones, especialmente la judicial, para hacer efectivo el derecho a la verdad, la justicia y la reparación.

IV. NOTAS: (Chile : informe 2005)

1. "El miedo a la vergüenza social por parte de los hombres, incluidos los jueces, impiden asumir y asimilar ese plus que comporta el desprecio y la humillación de la mujer".

---

[18] SACOUTO, Susana. Victim participation at the International Criminal Court and the Extraordinary Chambers in the Courts of Cambodia: a feminist project? Ver: DOCUMENTO ADJUNTO 5.

2. “Se tenía derecho a la violación, como al cuerpo de la mujer en general; no había nada que constriñera o impidiera actuar contra la misma”. “Era lo lógico”
3. “La violencia de género, puede integrar el delito de genocidio (agresión sexual) si concurre el requisito del propósito de destruir total o parcialmente un grupo nacional, racial, étnico o religioso” (art. 6 ECPI).
4. “En Chile, fue sistemática la tortura mediante agresión sexual en todas las presas, por el hecho de ser mujer. La Comisión Nacional sobre prisión política y Tortura, emitió un informe en 2005 en el que se constataron 3.394 casos de violencia sexual, sin distinción de edades, durante el periodo de represión de la dictadura pinochetista.”

Bogotá a 13 de julio de 2012

CHAPTER 6 (II)

ENGLISH TRANSLATION

ADVANCES IN INTERNATIONAL JURISPRUDENCE RELATING TO SEXUAL VIOLENCE AGAINST WOMEN DURING ARMED CONFLICTS

Baltasar Garzón

Text translated by Keiran Bowtell from Berg Institute

Introduction

The last few decades have witnessed substantial advances in material relating to the recognition and respect of women's rights, and specifically the rights of women who are seen as vulnerable to violence within a framework of armed conflict.

According to international statistics, at least one in three women have experienced battery, have been forced to have sexual relations, or have been physically mistreated in some way during the course of their lives. This figure tends to rise in the context of armed conflicts. Ayaan Hirsi Alí has previously noted, "The world-wide violence against women is already another holocaust," making reference to figures contained in the 2004 report developed by the Center for the Democratic Control of the Armed Forces in Geneva that state, "...between 113 and 200 million women in all the world have disappeared demographically."

It is therefore notable that until recently, there has been little congruency between the aforementioned statistics and specific references to crimes of a violent sexual nature against women in the framework of international regulation. Despite beginning to be drafted from the middle of the 20th century, the rights of women in relation to equality, non-discrimination, the prohibition of cruel treatment, freedom from sexual aggression, or the right to effective recourse[1] have been absent in the resolutions of national and

[1] (Art. 3 of the Universal Declaration of Human Rights, 1948. Art. 2 of the Pact of Civil and Political Rights, 1966. Art. 3 of the International Pact of Economic Social and Cultural Rights, 1976. Art.1 & 2 of The Convention on the

international courts. In the latter case, international jurisprudence has made it clear that states have an obligation to prosecute crimes of sexual violence. However, it has not been until relatively recently that the prosecution of such crimes has become effective in some areas. Only when these offences are prosecuted as crimes do they cease to possess the character of collateral damage or as being inevitable or private in nature. Moreover, only when they are prosecuted are they understood in their own right to be serious crimes against humanity, crimes against international criminal law, and crimes against international humanitarian law.

It is historically significant that not a single declaration made at the courts of Nuremberg included a reference to rape, forced prostitution, or any other sexual crime. The word "woman" does not even appear, despite the fact that crimes against women were extensively documented. Nor does the Charter of London, which created the Nuremburg court, include a reference to crimes of sexual violence. For its part, the Geneva Convention of 1949, with its 429 articles, offers only one phrase (Article 27 IV) that prohibits sexual violence and forced prostitution. The phase which is in concurrence with Ada Facio stated:

> … the Declaration on the Protection of Women and Children in Emergencies and Armed Conflicts of 1974 omits any explicit reference to sexual violence. In the additional protocols of the Geneva Conventions of 1977, which were negotiated with the idea of clarifying them and to fill-in some gaps, only one phrase in each explicitly protects against sexual violence, article 76 of Protocol I, which established that "Women will be the object of special respect and will be protected particularly against rape, forced prostitution and any other form of indecent attack" and in Article 4 of Protocol II, where the second paragraph (subparagraph (e) speaks of "insults to personal dignity, in particular humiliating and degrading treatment, rape, forced prostitution and any other form of indecent attack.
>
> The statute of the International Criminal Court for the Former Yugoslavia specifically mentions rape as a crime against humanity and a competency of the court, not as an offence to the laws and customs of war. Furthermore, in the first formal charges bought before the court the crime of sexual abuse was not even included, despite the fact that the entire world had been shaken by press reports of

Elimination of all Forms of Discrimination against Women, 1979. Art 1 of the Convention Against Torture and Other Cruel, Inhuman and Degrading Treatment or Punishment, 1984).

> ethnic cleansing in this republic, carried out through by means of forced pregnancies.[2]

Sexual violence in scenarios of armed conflict is one of the most instructive examples of how the use of violence is never neutral with respect to the gender of the victim. Sexual violence is used in a discriminatory manner, capitalizing on stereotypes and gender meanings in order to humiliate, defeat, and control the adversary, as well as to reward and foster cohesion amongst troops. Some crimes of sexual violence by their very nature are only committed against women and children. Such is the case with forced abortions, forced pregnancies, and breast mutilation. In these contexts, violence against women is extensively used as a weapon of war.

It is through the bodies of women who are sexually abused that an act of aggression is produced against the men with whom these women form relationships of dependency. In the Democratic Republic of the Congo, the destruction of women's bodies through genital mutilation is an indirect but extremely efficient way to destroy the morale of the tribal group on which the woman depends. A report into gender-specific crimes has noted:

> Before the decade of the 1990's, rape and other sexual offences were considered as collateral damage of war and armed conflicts, or as attacks against the honour of families, attacks against masculine honour or private offences. This trend has changed from the time of the International Courts for the former Yugoslavia and Rwanda, holding individuals criminally responsible for acts of violence of based on gender or with a sexual nature, as well as after the inclusion of various specific forms of gender crimes in the Rome Statutes. Likewise, the implementation of a gender perspective in international jurisdictions also reaches courts with a regional character such as the Inter-American Court of Human Rights.

Women's link Worldwide.
Gender Specific crimes at the International Criminal Court, Guatemala.
August, 2010

---

[2] Women and the International Criminal Court, Alda Facio.
Http://www.uasb.edu.ec/padh/revista1/analisis/aldafacio.htm

International Treatment of Gender-Specific Violence

International law and jurisprudence extensively recognizes violence against women in any form as a type of gender-specific discrimination. It is understood that one of the principal causes of violence is the application of sexist stereotypes[3] to women, and that in addition, the violence infringes upon or annuls the potential for women to enjoy or exercise their rights and fundamental liberties.[4]

The Evolution of International Regulations Regarding Sexual Violence Within a Context of Armed Conflict

Beginning in the 1990s, and partly due to organizations that promote the defense of women's rights, an abundance of recommendations were generated along with the adoption of specific norms addressing sexual violence in the context of armed conflict. This helped foster greater international concern about the use of sexual crimes as a weapon of war.

Along these lines, the Committee for the Elimination of Discrimination against Women (General Recommendation 19, 1992) interpreted the term "discrimination" used in the Convention for the Elimination of all forms of Discrimination Against Women (CEDAW) to include gender-specific violence as the following:

> violence directed against a woman because she is a woman or which affects her disproportionately. It includes acts which inflict damage or suffering of a physical, mental or sexual nature, threats to commit such acts, coercion, and other forms of deprivation of liberty.

Violence against women can contravene dispositions of the convention, taking into account whether or not they explicitly mention violence, and the responsibility held by states if they do not adopt the necessary measures to impede these acts or investigate and

---

[3] The term "sexist stereotypes" is used in order to refer to the social and cultural construction of the characteristics or roles expected of women or men owing to their distinct physical, biological, sexual, or social condition.

[4] "Violence against women is a form of discrimination which seriously infringes upon their rights and liberties in regard to their equality with men." Violence Against Women: General Recommendation No.19 UN Document HRI\GEN\1\Rev.1 at 84 (1994) United Nations Committee for the Elimination of Discrimination Against Women. 11TH Period of Sessions. 1992.

punish them. Likewise, it was emphasized that women are in particular danger in cases of war or conflict:

> The wars, armed conflicts, and occupation of territories frequently lead to an increase in prostitution, sex slavery and acts of sexual aggression against women, which require the adoption of protective and punishing measures.

For its part, the Preamble of the UN Declaration on the Elimination of Violence against Women, formulated in 1994, recognizes that the most profound cause of violence against women is their subordination within society:

> Violence against women constitutes a manifestation of historically unequal power relations between men and women, that has led to the domination of women and discrimination against them by men, impeding their full advancement, and that violence against women is one of the fundamental social mechanisms by which women are forced into a situation of subordination (in respect to men) making special mention of the particular vulnerability of determined groups of women…such as women who belong to minorities, indigenous women, refugees, migrants, women who inhabit remote or rural communities, homeless women, institutionalised or detained women, children, disabled women, elderly women, and women in *situations of armed conflict, who are particularly vulnerable to violence.*

Article 4 urges states to act:

> States should condemn violence against women and not invoke any custom, tradition or religious consideration in order to avoid the obligation to try to eliminate it.

The UNSC has raised the issue of sexual violence against women in situations of armed conflict and has adopted various related resolutions:

- In Resolution 1325 (2000), the council urged member states to incorporate a "gender perspective" and place women on an equal footing in the "prevention and solution of armed conflicts" and the "maintenance and fostering of peace and security." The sides involved in armed conflict were also urged to "obey international laws protecting the rights of civilian women and children, and to incorporate policies and processes that protect women from gender-related crimes, such as rape and sexual aggression."

- In Resolution 1820 (2008), the council demanded an end to all brutal acts of sexual violence against women and children when used as a war tactic, as well as an end to their author's impunity. The UN and its secretary general were also requested to facilitate the protection of women and girls in security initiatives directed by the UN, including in refugee camps, and to invite women to participate in all aspects during peace processes.
- In Resolution 1888 (2009), the council detailed measures to increase the protection of women and girls confronted with sexual violence in situations of conflict. Such measures included a formal request for the secretary general to name a special envoy to coordinate missions, send a team of experts in cases of especially worrying situations, and order peacekeeping forces to protect women and children.
- In Resolution 1889 (2009), content included the reaffirmation of the previous Resolution 1325 and the condemnation of persistent sexual violence against women in situations of conflict. Additionally, member states of the UN and civil society were urged to take into account the need to protect and empower women and girls, including those linked to armed groups, in the programmed activities that are carried out after conflicts.
- The Statute of Rome (1998) now no longer includes sexual violations as offenses against the honor of a person as it is listed in the Geneva Convention, but instead as offenses that are as serious as torture, slavery, etc., and explicitly recognizes that the catalogue of sexual crimes is not closed. The Preamble includes a declaration that all states have the duty to exercise criminal jurisdiction over those responsible for crimes categorized in international law. The Statute of Rome lists the crimes of genocide, sexual aggression, and the forced imposition of reproduction in Article 6 and rape, sexual slavery, forced prostitution, forced pregnancy, forced sterilization, or any other form of sexual crime of a comparable nature in Article 7.1g as offenses to be identified as crimes against humanity when committed as a part of a generalized or systematic attack against the civilian population. Article 8 also categorizes these acts as war crimes.

Regional Treaties

- Article I of the American Declaration of the Rights and Duties of Man, formulated in 1948 affirms, "all human beings have the right to life, liberty and personal security." Article V establishes, "Every person has the right to the protection of the Law against attacks against their honour, their reputation and their personal and family life." Article XVIII of the declaration also affirms, "All people can appeal to the courts in order to exercise their rights."
- Article 3 of the Inter-American Convention for the Prevention, Punishment and Eradication of Violence Against Women (*Convención de Belém do Pará*) adopted in 1994 affirms that every woman has the "right to a life free from violence, in the public and private spheres." Article 4.g states that all women have "the right to uncomplicated and prompt access to competent courts that support them against acts that violate their rights [...]." According to Article 7, the signatory states should practice due diligence in preventing, investigating, and punishing violence against women, and "[...] include in their domestic legislation the criminal, civil and administrative norms, as well as those of any other nature which are necessary for the prevention, punishment and eradication of violence against, and to adopt the appropriate administrative measures where necessary [...]."
- Article 3 of the Maputo Protocol asserts that the signatory states will adopt and apply all necessary measures to guarantee the protection of rights of all women to their dignity, as well as the protection of women against all forms of violence, in particular sexual and verbal violence.
- In Article 4 of the same protocol, the signatory states also recognize the obligation to "promulgate and apply law that prohibit all forms of violence against women, including undesired or forced sexual relations, whether they take place in public or private [...]." Article 11 stresses the vulnerability of women in situations of armed conflict, and includes a paragraph exhorting the signatory states to promise to protect women who request asylum, refugees, and women who are returning or displaced against all forms of violence, rape, and sexual exploitation. Moreover, it obligates signatory states to guarantee that these acts will be considered war crimes, genocide, and crimes against humanity, and that their authors will face the court in a competent criminal jurisdiction.
- In Section 4 of the Declaration on the Elimination of Violence against Women in the Association of Southeast Asian Nations (ASEAN) region formulated in 2004, the signatory states agree to do the following: promulgate laws for the prevention

of violence against women, and when necessary, strengthen and modify them; promote the protection, treatment, and reintegration of victims and survivors, for example by adopting measures for the investigation, prosecution, punishment, and, when pertinent, rehabilitation of perpetrators; and impede women and girls who have been subject to previous forms of violence from becoming objects of victimization again, whether in the home, workplace, community, society, or in custody.

- Of special significance for the Colombian case is the Inter-American Convention for the Prevention, Punishment and Eradication of Violence against Women, known as the *Convención de Belém do Pará*. The Inter-American Court of Human Rights has applied this convention, which entered into effect in 1995, on innumerable occasions. It is binding on those states that form part of that court, including Colombia, and obliges them to comply with its dispositions for the prevention, punishment, and eradication of violence against women.

Simultaneously, protection against discrimination based on sex, age, ethnicity, or other conditions is rooted in international human rights law, and has *jus cogens* status.[5] Also noteworthy is CEDAW, and especially General Recommendation 12 for its reference to discrimination against women in sexual violence and its obligatory eradication.

Likewise, international human rights law consolidates protection against gender-related violence committed during armed conflicts through the resolutions of the security council and general assembly[6] and the interpretation of treaties at a regional and international level. Regional courts and UN committees have adopted the definition of rape established by the international criminal courts.[7]

---

[5] See CEDAW. General Recommendation No. 19, 1992.
http://www.un.org/womenwatch/daw/cedaw/recommendations/recomm.htm#recom19
Inter-American Court of Human Rights. Case of Gonzalez and others ("Campo Algodonero") vs. Mexico. November 16 2009. http://www.corteidh.or.cr/docs/casos/articulos/seriec_205_esp.pdf

[6] Security Council Resolutions: 1325, October 21 2001; 1822, June 20 2008; 1888, September 30 2009; 1960, December 16 2010.
General Assembly Resolution: 61/438
Beijing Platform Action, 1995

[7] See, for example, Inter-American Court of Human Rights. Case of Rosendo Cantú and others vs. Mexico. May 15 2011.
Inter-American Court of Human Rights. Case of Fernandez Ortega and others vs. Mexico. August 30 2010.

The Prosecution of Gender-Related Crimes in International Criminal Law

In 1994, during the persistent armed conflict in Rwanda, approximately 500,000 women were tortured, raped, mutilated, or massacred.[8] In Bosnia-Herzegovina, calculations reveal that soldiers and members of the police force raped more than 60,000 women and girls in an organized and systematic manner.[9]

The UNSC established courts for the former Yugoslavia and Rwanda in 1993 and 1994, respectively. For the first time, rape was treated as a crime against humanity. Through their findings, these courts established precedents in terms of the categorization and punishment of these crimes.

International jurisdiction on sexual violence since the resolutions of these courts and the Special Court for Sierra Leone (SCSL) has established that rape and sexual aggression in itself can constitute genocide, crimes against humanity, war crimes, and torture. Likewise, they have established that rape is an element of other crimes, such as sexual slavery and forced prostitution.

The prevention and elimination of genocide and crimes against humanity possess the status of *ius cogens (*peremptory norm*)* and impose upon states an inalienable obligation or duty: *obligatio erga omnes.* Gender-related violence can constitute the *actus reus (*guilty act*)* of the crime of genocide or crimes against humanity, and its prosecution and reparation is thus obligatory under international criminal law.

The Evolution of the Crime of Rape in International Jurisprudence

The crime of rape was the first to be recognized as a crime against humanity, genocide, or a war crime in international jurisprudence. Today, the prohibition of rape and sexual violence has the status of international customary law under international criminal law and international humanitarian law. Along the same lines in the field of international law

---

8 Report by the Special Rapporteur on Violence Against Women, its causes and consequences, Sra. Radhika Coomaraswamy, United Nation Human Rights Commission, 55th Period of Sessions. Integration of the Rights of Women and Gender Perspective: Violence Against Women, prepared in conformity with Resolution 1997/44 of the Commission on Human Rights. E/CN.4/1999/68/Add.4. January 21 1999.

9 United Nations Secretary General Report 1996, Aggressions and Violations of Women in Areas of Armed Conflict in the Former Yugoslavia. Cited by Roxana Arroyo Vargas and Lola Valladares Tayupanta in Report in Sexual Violence Against Women, Series Legal Documents, Year 1.

and human rights, the regional courts and committees of the UN have adapted the definition of rape that was established by the international criminal courts.

The interpretation of the crime of rape has evolved as the result of the jurisprudence of international criminal courts for the former Yugoslavia and Rwanda. The SCSL and ICC have subsequently considered this jurisprudence. In the case of the international criminal courts for the former Yugoslavia and Rwanda, the aforementioned evolution has focused primarily on two constitutive elements of the crime of rape: the acts of penetration and consent. Previously, it had been understood that rape only occurred in instances of vaginal penetration by the aggressor's penis, and that this took place without the victim's consent.

The aforementioned courts have broadened the concept of penetration and established in which cases one can consider *per se* that there was no consent from the victim.

In regards to penetration, it was the International Criminal Court for Rwanda (ICCR) that presented a new definition of rape in the case *Akayesu*. It did so by broadening the act of rape to include any type of bodily penetration and any type of bodily invasion with any type of object without consent.

In its judgment, the court explained:

> ... rape is a physical invasion of a sexual nature, committed against a person under coercive circumstances [...] Rape is not limited to the physical invasion of the human body and can include acts that don't implicate penetration or even physical contact.

The International Criminal Court for the Former Yugoslavia (ICCY) subsequently adopted this definition in the *Celebici* case. However, the judges incorporated a new definition of rape in the *Furundzija* case, where it was established that objective elements of the crime of rape include the following:

> i. Sexual penetration, including minor penetration: a) of the vagina or anus of the victim with the penis of the perpetrator or any other object used by the perpetrator; or b) of the victim's mouth with the penis of the perpetrator; ii. Under coercion or by force or by use of threat against the victim or a third person.

This new definition generated extensive debate surrounding the interpretation of the crime of rape, which was finally addressed in the ruling for the case *Musema.* In that case, the ICCR analyzed the two definitions that had been given until that time and ruled that the definition in the case of *Akayesu* was preferable to that in the case of *Furundzija*, because the former included all the conduct defined in the latter.

Despite this, the discussion resurfaced with the ruling in the case *Kunarac et al*, in which the ICCY again adopted the definition of the *Furundzija* case. However, it did add a new element to the debate by analyzing the interpretation of consent. Here, the court ruled that in order for rape not to exist, "consent should be given voluntarily, as a result of the willingness of the victim as evaluated in the context of the existing circumstances."

In cases of rape, "the *mens rea* is the intention to carry out sexual penetration, and the knowledge that this will occur without the consent of the victim." The court that studied the appeal lodged in the *Kunarac* case agreed with this definition, and further clarified that "there are factors 'beyond the use of force' that could cause an act of non-consensual or involuntary sexual penetration of the victim." A restricted interpretation limited to the use or threat of force could permit the perpetrator to escape responsibility for the sexual activity by taking advantage of coercive circumstances rather than depending strictly on physical force. The court went further and signaled that circumstances that lead to charges of rape as a crime against humanity or war crimes "will be almost always universally coercive," in a manner in which "true consent would be impossible."

Consensus regarding the definition of rape was finally reached in the case of *Muhumana*, in which the ICCR stated, "the definition given in *Akayesu* and the given elements in *Kunarac* are not incompatible or substantially different in their application. While *Akayesu* refers in general terms to a 'physical invasion of a sexual nature', *Kunarac* centered on the articulation of the parameters within which physical invasion of a sexual nature can be constituted in order for it to be classified as rape."

In addition to the aforementioned elements, the *Kunarac* case also warrants attention considering other important aspects of the ruling. It established that "the forms of forced sexual penetration inflicted upon women with the purpose of interrogation, punishment or coercion *constitute torture*, and that the sexual access to women, exercised as a form of property right, constitutes a form of slavery and therefore a crime against humanity."[10]

In regards to *slavery,* the appeal court established that slavery could occur through the sexual exploitation of women and girls. It considered that, in order to be regarded as such, other factors should also be taken into account, such as "the control of somebody's movement, the control of the physical surroundings, psychological control, measures taken to prevent escape, force, threats, coercion, duration, affirmation of exclusivity, subjugation to cruel treatment and abuse, the control of sexuality and forced labour."[11]

Concerning *consent in case of slavery,* the appeal court accepted that a lack of consent was not an element of the crime that the prosecution must prove because slavery is based on the exercise of the right to property; considering such circumstances, it was impossible to express consent. As such, it was sufficient to presume an absence of consent in these cases. [12]

In regards to *torture,* the appeal court considered that this constitutes an act or negligence that causes pain or serious suffering, be it physical or mental, but that there are not other specific requirements that permit an exhaustive classification or listing of the acts that could constitute torture.[13] Previously, a court had rejected an argument from appealing parties who posed that suffering should be visible, as the court considered that some acts establish *per se* the suffering of victims, and that rape is one of these. The court went further and took the existence of suffering to be already proven without need of a medical certificate, establishing that sexual violence caused pain and serious suffering, be it mental or physical. In other words, once rape is proven to have occurred, it is also considered to be proven that the suffering or severe pain of torture has also taken place by virtue of rape implicitly involving said pain or suffering.[14]

---

10 Viseur-Seller, Patricia: Gender-Based Persecution, United Nations Expert Group Meeting on Gender-Based Persecution, Toronto, Canada 9-12 Nov. 1997. EGM/GBP/1977.3. November 6 2007.

11 Sentence, Court of Appeal, Paragraph 119.

12 Idem. Paragraph 120.

13 Idem. Paragraph 129.

14 Sentence, Court of First Instance, Paragraph 205.

Cesic Case

In this case, the accused, Ranko Cesic, was investigated for various charges, including the sexual assault of two detained Muslims. During the process, the accused accepted the charges, and the court found him guilty of crimes against humanity for intentionally forcing two Muslim brothers to perform oral sex on each other while other soldiers watched. The court considered that this type of action constituted a degrading and humiliating act and thus violated international humanitarian law.

The court considered the action to be "aggravated," taking into account its impact on the victims and their family and the fact that it had been committed in front of a third party, heightening the humiliation of the victims.

Tadic Case

The commission declared members of the Serbo-Bosnian forces acting in the municipality of Prijedor to be culpable of crimes against humanity and war crimes perpetrated throughout 1992. They were not found guilty of committing an act of sexual aggression, but were found guilty of participating in a campaign of generalized and systematic torture by means of such actions as beatings, torture, and sexual assault. Inclusion of the offense of sexual assault in the original charges was subsequently dropped, owing to the victim's unwillingness to declare.

The sentence categorically affirmed the following:

> [R]ape and sexual abuse can be considered as forming part of a generalised and systematic campaign of terror against the civilian population. It is not necessary to prove that the rapes themselves were generalized or systematic but that rape constituted one of numerous types of crimes which were committed in a general and systematic manner, and included a campaign of terror on the part of the aggressor.

For its part, in the case of Prosecutor vs. Issa Hassan Sesay, Morris Kallon, and Augustin Gbao (the RUF case), the SCSL determined that rape exists when the accused invades the body of another person and that conduct results in penetration, as minor as it may be, of any part of the victim's body with his sexual organ, or penetration of the anus or genitals of the victim with any object or part of his body, always being that the invasion has been the result of the use of force or coercion. The court considered that the use of force or the threat to do so causes the victim to suffer from a fear of violence, aggression, detention, psychological oppression, or fear of abuse of power against her or against some other person and exploitation of a climate of coercion.

Likewise, the Statute of Rome states that consent "cannot be inferred from any word or form of conduct of the victim when the use of force, the threat of force, coercion or the use of a climate of coercion, have reduced the victim's capacity to give their consent voluntarily and freely," nor can it be inferred when the victim is incapable of giving free consent. Also, the statute of the SCSL indicates that consent cannot exist when the victim remains silent or does not resist sexual violence, and further clarifies that the credibility, honor, or sexual availability of the victim or of a witness cannot be used to make any inferences about the sexual character of the anterior or subsequent behavior of the victim or witness.

The definitions of rape from the SCSL and Criminal Court derive from definitions that emanate from the courts *ad hoc*. In much the same way, the remarks surrounding consent are fruits of the evolution of jurisprudence of the courts for the former Yugoslavia and Rwanda.

Today, rape and sexual assault in themselves can constitute genocide, crimes against humanity, war crimes, and torture. Similarly, rape is now considered as an element in other crimes, such as sexual slavery and forced prostitution.

The International Criminal Court

The first cases of investigations relating to sexual violence that occurred within the framework of the ICC developed in response to the situation in the DRC. The reports presented to the court centered on cases of torture, forced removal from homes, recruitment of children, and sexual abuses. The UN estimates that more than 40,000 women and girls were raped. The most advanced case corresponds to the investigation of Germain Katanga "Simba" and Mathieu Ngudjolo Chui, two of the guerrilla leaders of the DRC who were accused of recruitment of child soldiers, murder, rape, and forcing women into sexual slavery. Their case was the second to arrive at the court and focused on events that took place in 2003 in Bororo, a village in the region of Ituri in the northeast of the country. According to the prosecution, Katanga and Chui joined forces to launch their troops against the inhabitants of the village, killing 200 people. They later took at least 15 children for the purpose of adding to their ranks. Many victims were mutilated with machetes, while attacking forces raped the women.

Katanga "Simba" was the Chief of the Patriotic Force of Resistance. He belonged to the *Lendu* ethnic group, which maintained agricultural traditions and was in competition with the pastoralist *Hema* ethnic group. Chui, also *Lendu*, commanded the National Integration Front. The Chief Prosecutor at the ICC, Luis Moreno Ocampo, assured that the conflict in Ituri, an area rich in gold deposits, "formed part of the civil war that desolated Congo after the genocide perpetrated in neighbouring Rwanda in 1994." After reviewing almost 17,000 documents, the prosecution called 26 witnesses to the stand, 21 of whom hid their identities for fear of reprisals. Prior to the opening of the case, Katanga stated his "*confidence in the impartiality of the process,*" while Chui considered himself "*yet another victim of the war.*"[15]

The decision confirming the charges was made in September 2008, and the case has been in its trial phase since the November 24, 2009.

The defense alleged that it was bringing forward the investigation of the events because of internal orders, and for that reason, the principle of *complementarity* should be respected.

The majority decision found that there was sufficient evidence to confirm the charges of war crimes and crimes against humanity in relation to the accusations of rape and sexual slavery, which are alleged to have occurred in a intentional and coordinated manner within the context of a systemized and generalized attack against the civilian population on February 24, 2003, during the capture of the city of Bogoro. In this context, the decision confirming the charges together with that confirming the charges in the case of *Lubanga* are the only two decisions of a substantive character emitted by the court until the time of writing. Evidently, this case was the first to engage with the contextual elements of crimes against humanity presented in the Statute of Rome and Elements of Crimes, as well as the specific elements of certain offenses of sexual violence (rape and

[15] http://www.agenciacna.com/2/nota_1.php?noticia_id=27976

sexual slavery) categorized in the Statute of Rome as war crimes and crimes against humanity.

However, it should be noted that there was no conviction given for this type of crime in the *Lubanga* case, despite requests from prosecution.

REGIONAL JURISDICTIONS

Inter-American System of Human Rights

The Inter-American system of human rights has also led to important advances in jurisprudence through the decisions of the commission and the jurisprudence of the court. Firstly, between 1991 and 2000, the Inter-American Commission had already identified 14 cases relating to sexual and reproductive rights, of which 6 involved the use of sexual violence as torture by the state. The Inter-American Court, for its part, has established the responsibility of states in cases of forced sterilization, intra-family violence, and torture based on sexual abuse.

There have also been positive developments in the Inter-American Commission in areas of crimes of a sexual nature and justice for victims of sexism. These have occurred in parallel with the development of the aforementioned jurisprudence.

The abovementioned commission made declarations regarding sexual abuses in two reports: *Informe sobre Haiti de 1995* (Report on Haiti, 1995), which held that acts of violence against women qualify as crimes against humanity when used as a means to spread terror; and the *Informe s/Peru de 1996* (Peru Report, 1996), which defined sexual abuse as "all acts of physical and mental abuse perpetrated as an act of violence" and categorized it as a form of torture.

In parallel, the Inter-American Court of Human Rights has to this date given two relevant sentences regarding sexist violence and sex crimes: *Castro Castro vs. Pero* (2006) and *Campo Algodonero vs. Mexico* (2009).

The gender perspective was introduced for the first time in the jurisprudence of the Inter-American Court of Human Rights in the case of *Castro Castro.* In this case, the court considered it as demonstrated that during domestic and international armed conflict, the opposing parties utilize sexual violence against women as a means of punishment and repression. The use of state power to violate the rights of women in an internal conflict not only affects the women directly, but can also impact society more generally, through such abuses or by sending a message or lesson.

The court stated in its legal reasoning (part 206) that women who were deprived of their liberty in the penal institution *Castro Castro*:

> ...not only received treatment contrary to their personal dignity, but were also victims of sexual violence given that they were kept naked and covered only by a sheet, surrounded by armed men who were apparently members of the armed forces of the state. What qualifies this treatment as sexual violence is that the women were constantly observed by the men.

In following the line of international jurisprudence, and taking into account the contents of the Convention for the Prevention, Punishment and Eradication of violence against Women *(Belén do Para),* the court considered that:

> Sexual violence is constituted by actions of a sexual nature which are committed without the consent of a person, and which in addition to including the physical penetration of the human body can also include acts that don't involve penetration or even any physical contact.

Likewise, the court recognized (311) that:

> ... sexual violations against a detained woman by an agent of the state is an especially serious and punishable act, taking into account the vulnerability of the victim and the abuse of power of the agent. Likewise, sexual violation is an especially traumatic experience that can have severe consequences and cause great physical and psychological harm that leaves the victim "physically and emotionally humiliated", and in a situation that is difficult overcome in time when compared to other traumatic experiences.

Similarly, in the case of *Campo Algodero*, the Inter-American Court of Human Rights added to the concepts evident in the already cited precedent and established the responsibility of the state for having "remained indifferent before a chronic situation of violence... before the existence of a culture of discrimination against women." According to the Inter-American Court of Human Rights, the state is responsible for acts committed by individuals, considering its condition as a guarantee against the risk of sexist violence: theory of created risk (art.7 of the Convention of Belén do Pará).

In light of these cited antecedents, one conclusion is that the international and Inter-American jurisprudence presents itself as a point of inflection in the development of sex crimes as crimes against humanity, making note of only some dissidence at the moment of categorization with some sentences and opinions claiming their status to be one of an autonomous crime against humanity, and others claiming it to be a form of torture.

Summaries of Particular Cases in the Inter-American Judicial Area

Case of Fernando y Raquel Mejía vs. Peru

In this case, the Peruvian state was accused of crimes relating to the events of June 1989, when a group of military personnel entered the residence of Fernando Mejía Egocheaga and his wife, Raquel Martín. He was taken away, and his wife was raped on two occasions.

Mr. Mejía was found dead two days later, with his body displaying signs of torture. Mrs. Martín was subjected to threats and intimidation, obliging her to leave the country.

Concerning this particular case of rape, the Inter-American Commission on Human Rights determined that the elements constituting torture as established by the Inter-American Commission for the prevention and sanction of torture (an act committed with the intention to inflict physical and mental suffering with the purpose of punishing or intimidating, and committed or instigated by a public servant) had occurred, and that the sexual assault was a deliberate offense. The commission established there were violations of the rights to personal integrity (Article 5) and honor and dignity (Article 11) of the Inter-American Convention on Human Rights.

Case of Dianna Ortiz vs. Guatemala

Dianna Ortiz was a nun who denounced having been kidnapped and tortured by agents of the Guatemalan government in 1989. On various occasions, she was raped by multiple agents, subjected to torture by means of threats, and suffered injuries such as cigarette burns.

In this case, the commission determined that the inhumane treatment of Sister Ortiz at the hands of government agents corresponded with the definition of torture, as it involved inflicting physical and mental suffering in order to punish and intimidate the victim for her participation in certain activities and association with certain persons and groups. The government agents, acting in an official capacity, were responsible for the violations of Sister Ortiz's rights. The kidnapping and torture of Sister Ortiz was deemed to be part of a number of activities violating human rights that the Guatemalan government had committed.

The commission concluded that the Guatemalan state was responsible for the violation of Dianna Ortiz's human rights, specifically her personal integrity, personal liberty, judicial guarantees, right to the protection of honor and dignity, freedom of conscience and religion, right to association, and right to judicial protection as consecrated in Articles 5, 7, 8, 11, 12, 16, and 25, respectively, of the American Convention, as well as for the failure to comply with their obligations as established in Article 1.

Case of Ana, Beatriz, and Celia González Pérez vs. México

In 1994, agents of the Mexican state detained the sisters Ana, Beatriz, and Celia González Pérez, as well as their mother, Delia Pérez de González, for the purpose of interrogation. One of the victims was a minor. Over the course of two hours, the military personnel detained, beat, and raped the victims on various occasions. The state was also denounced for neglecting their responsibility to investigate, failing to punish those responsible for the violations, and not compensating the victims.

In this case, the commission reiterated the characteristics of torture in cases of rape, and determined that "sexual violations committed by members of the security forces of a state against members of the civilian population constitute, in all cases, a serious violation of Human Rights as protected in articles 5 and 11 of the American Convention, as well as the norms of international humanitarian law." It also noted that the Inter-American Convention for the Prevention, Punishment and Eradication of Violence against Women guarantees all women the right to a life free from violence.

The Inter-American Commission considered that the abuses that agents of the Mexican state committed against the physical, psychological, and moral integrity of the three Tzeltales sisters constituted torture and a violation of the private lives of the four women and their family, as well as an illegal attack on their honor and reputation, causing them to flee their community due to fear, shame, and humiliation.

According to the international jurisprudence of Human Rights, in certain circumstances, the anxiety and the suffering imposed on the immediate families of the victims of serious violations of Human Rights constitutes an additional violation of the right to the personal integrity of the family members.

In the cited case, the Inter-American Court of Human Rights found that the treatment of the victims' mother, Delia Pérez de González – who had to impotently witness the humiliation of her three daughters at the hands of the Mexican Armed Forces, and later share with them the ostracism from their community – constituted humiliation and degradation, which violated her right to personal integrity as guaranteed by the American Convention.

The commission concluded that the Mexican state violated the following rights consecrated in the American Convention to the detriment of Mrs. Delia Pérez de González and her three daughters, Ana, Beatriz, and Celia González Pérez: personal liberty (Article 7); personal integrity and the protection of honor and dignity (Articles 5, 11); and judicial protection (Articles 8, 25). In regard to Celia González Pérez, Article 19 of the Declaration of the Rights of the Child and all articles related to the general obligation to guarantee rights as stated in Article 1 of this international legal instrument also applied. On the same evidence, The Inter-American Court of Human Rights also found the Mexican state responsible for the violation of Article 8 of the Inter-American Convention for the Prevention and Sanction of Torture.

Additionally, the Inter-American Court has established important jurisprudence through its rulings, which can be considered an advancement in the investigation and sanctioning of sex crimes at an international level.

Case of Inés Fernández Ortega vs. México

This case involved an indigenous woman from the Me'phaa village (Tlapaneco) who was threatened, beaten, and raped by three members of the Mexican Armed Forces in the state of Guerrero in 2002.

In 2004, after a series of irregularities before the Mexican authorities, the case was taken to the Inter-American Human Rights Commission. In 2009, the commission presented a complaint against Mexico in the Inter-American Court of Human Rights, in which it denounced various human rights abuses relating to Fernández Ortega, her husband, and her five children.

On the August 30, 2010, Mexico was declared responsible for the violation of the human rights of Inés Fernández Ortega relating to offences against her personal integrity, dignity, and private life, and for being exposed to arbitrary interference at her home address. In its own words, "the court reiterates that which is stated in the *Convention of Belém do Pará*, that violence against women not only constitutes a violation of human rights," but is also an "offence against human dignity and a manifestation of the historically unequal relations between men and women," which "transcend all sectors of society regardless of class, race, ethnic group, income level, culture, educational level, age or religion and which negatively affects its own foundations." The court, following international jurisprudence and taking into account the contents of this convention, had previously considered sexual violence to be constituted by actions of a sexual nature that are carried out without the consent of a person, that in addition to physical acts to a human body, can also include those acts that do not involve penetration or any physical contact whatsoever. In particular, sexual assault constitutes a paradigmatic form of violence against women, the consequences of which can even transcend the victim herself. *The commission indicated that sexual violations committed by members of state security forces against members of the civilian population constitute a serious violation of human rights as protected in Articles 5 and 11 of the American Convention. In the case of sexual violations against indigenous women, the pain and humiliation is worsened by their indigenous status owing to the "lack of knowledge of the language of the perpetrator, and of the rest of the intervening authorities, and for the rejection by their community which can result from these acts."*

The sentence that condemned the violations of her husband and children's human rights also declared that the Mexican state should commit to legislative reforms concerning the military, concede scholarships to the children of Fernández Ortega, award economic compensation, and provide medical and psychological treatment to the victims.

Case of Castro Castro vs. Peru

This case held in 2006 refers to the massacre that occurred during four days of the so-called "*Operativa Mudanza 1*" in the *Castro Castro* penitentiary in Peru. The prisoners in pavilions 1-A and 4-B saw their lives constantly endangered by the intensity of the attack, which included the use of military firearms and involved the participation of police agents, the army, and special forces. Forty-one prisoners were killed, and many others were subjected to cruel and degrading treatment.

The significance of this case lies in what was identified as differentiated treatment in the military action against women. According to the court,

> The massacre was initially directed against the approximately 133 women who were in the Pavilion 1-A of the *Miguel Castro Castro* penitentiary, and had the aim of exterminating them and turning them into singularised targets in the attack against the prison. Many of the prisoners were shot at close-range. The court also found that instances of forced undressing to which many of the women were subjected also represented a form of sexual violence, and were therefore violations of their right to personal integrity.

Case of Campo Algodonero

This complaint relates to the alleged international responsibility of the state in the "disappearance and subsequent death" of three young women – Claudia Ivette González, Esmerelda Herrera Monreal, and Laura Berenice Ramos Monárrez – whose bodies were found in a cotton field in Ciudad Juarez on November 6, 2001. The state was found responsible for

> ...a failure to adopt the means to protect the victims, two of whom were minors; the failure to prevent the crimes despite the well-known existence of gender-specific violence which had already left hundreds of women and girls murdered; the failure of authorities to respond to the reporting of their disappearance; the failure to conduct due diligence in the investigation of the murders [...], as well as the denial of justice and a failure to provide adequate compensation.

In this case held in 2009, the court found that the disappearance and subsequent death of the three women in the context of discrimination in Ciudad Juarez (Mexico) constituted violence against women, based on the American Convention on Human Rights and the *Convention Belém do Para.*

Case of Rosendo Cantú and other vs. Mexico

The contents of this case, in 2010, relate to the alleged sexual abuses committed against the Me'phaa indigenous woman Valentina Rosendo Cantú, as well as the alleged failure to conduct due diligence in the investigation and punishment of those responsible for the crime, the alleged consequences of the events for the daughter of the presumptive victim, the supposed failure to provide adequate compensation to the presumptive victim and her family, the alleged use of military jurisdiction to conduct the investigation and ruling of human rights violations, and the supposed difficulties that indigenous persons, in particular women, have in acceding to the justice and health systems. The court noted that the sexual violations suffered by the indigenous woman were a violation of the right to personal integrity, personal dignity, and private life.

On the November 8, 2011, the Inter-American Commission on Human Rights accepted the case relating to the sexual torture of 11 women who were raped during police operations on the May 3 and 4, 2006, in Texcoco and San Salvador Atenco, in Estado de Mexico, Mexico.

European System of Human Rights

The European Court of Human Rights has also found that sexual assaults can constitute torture. One example is in the case of *Aydin vs. Turkey*, which involved a 17-year-old girl who had never left the village she lived in with her parents in southeastern Turkey. In 1985, serious conflict between security forces and members of the Kurdish Separatist

Party occurred in this part of the country. Turkey has reported that more than 4,000 civilians died as a result of this situation, and that a similar number of state security forces were also killed.

Within this context, Aydin was beaten and raped while her father and family members had been illegally detained. When Aydin went to ask for her detained family members, some of the guards took her into a room, undressed her, put her in a truck tire, and made it spin. Later, they beat her and hosed her with a high-pressure water hose. They dressed her again, blindfolded her, and took her to an interrogation room, where a man dressed in military fatigues ripped her clothes from her and raped her.

Finally, the European Court of Human Rights viewed the case. In a sentence in Strasbourg on September 25, 1997, the court sustained that Ms. Aydin had been subject to torture, rape, and ill-treatment while detained by the Turkish security forces, acts which are contrary to Article 3 of the European Convention.

In this case, the tribunal considered that the rape of a detained woman by a civil servant of the state was an especially serious and hateful act, and of a character that was so heinous as to constitute torture. Furthermore, the tribunal sustained that the Turkish authorities had failed to carry out a complete and effective investigation of Aydin's complaint and that there were ineffective means for its resolution.[16]

The court determined that rape can constitute torture and expressed,

> ... the rape of a person who is a detained by an agent of the state should be considered especially serious and unusually cruel treatment, given the ease with which the perpetrator can exploit the vulnerability and weakened resistance of his victim. Furthermore, rape leaves deep psychological scars on the victim which don't heal in time as can other forms of physical or mental violence.

The court concluded that the accumulation of physically and mentally violent acts committed against the plaintiff, and the especially cruel act of rape to which she was

---

16 http://daccess-ods.un.org/TMP/6294938.92192841.html

submitted, are constitutive of the crime of torture as punishable in Article 3 of the convention.

The responsibility to investigate, punish, and compensate for the damage caused by crimes of a sexual nature corresponds to the state. The international jurisdiction is complementary, and therefore necessary in itself, in order to avoid the impunity of the aforementioned crimes and strengthen the judicial systems, thus permitting impunity to be countered in the context of armed conflict.

The Prosecution of Crimes of Sexual Violence in National Courts

National jurisdictions have begun to take into account the significant advances in international jurisprudence in international criminal law and international human rights law in matters of sexual violence, and in dealing with these crimes, are creating new jurisprudence and enriching that which already exists. This is all happening with the aim of offering compensation to victims. Some antecedents can be found in the *Juzagado Central de Instrucción no.5* of the *Audiencia Nacional* of Spain in the investigation of crimes committed by the Argentinean and Chilean dictatorships, as pursued by the Judge Baltasar Garzón, and supported by the principle of universal jurisdiction for crimes of genocide, torture, terrorism, and crimes against humanity. Below, other cases in Argentina and Spain are outlined.

a) In Argentina, case No. 2086 and the accumulated case No. 2277 against Gregorio Molina provide an example. Here, the criminal court of Mar de Plata established in July 2010 that, at a national level, it had been accredited in the case of the juntas, and in the reports published by the Inter-American Commission on Human Rights and the National Commission on the Disappearance of Persons, that the violations women suffered while held in secret detention centers were not isolated or occasional cases, but were instead constituted system practices carried out within a secret plan of repression and extermination set up by the state and directed by the armed forces.

Furthermore, the case adds that international jurisprudence is unanimous in sustaining that the crimes of rape and sexual violence committed against women in a time of war or internal conflict of a country constitute crimes against humanity.

The judgments of international courts that have been created for the prosecution of crimes committed in Yugoslavia and Rwanda have also indicated a similar direction. The ICC's Statute of Rome specifically mentions rape, sexual slavery, forced prostitution, and forced sterilization as crimes against humanity when these are committed in times of war or armed conflict. In the resolution of "Complementary Activities of the Secret Detention Center Arsenales Miguel de Azcuénaga and related Kidnappings and Disappearances," the court of Tucumán declared on December 27, 2010 that the crimes of violation of domestic privacy, illegitimate deprivation of liberty under duress and under humiliating circumstances, torture followed by death, indecent assault, sexual assault, and homicide that were investigated in this case had been perpetrated within the context of a systematic attack by the state against a substantial group of the Argentinean nation (i.e. political groups, political military personnel, and groups of people involved in social struggles without belonging to any particular political party) who had been identified as "enemies" of "western Christian" thought (cfr. Annex 5.8). This can thus be characterized in context as the international crime of genocide. The sexual violence which took place during the repression was described in the following terms: "While the impunity laws were still in effect (1987/2004), only penal actions were initiated for the crime of kidnapping a minor and a few for the appropriation of goods. The sex crimes denounced by victims in their testimony were not subject to criminal proceedings, a result of having remained hidden until recent times. *(Cfr. Sentence of the Oral Court of Santa Fe in the Case of "Barcos" (no.43/08) where the crimes of sexual assault is analyzed as a criminal form of torment; Sentence of the Oral Tribunal en the Molina case (n.2086/10) where it was considered as proved that within the context of a systematic plan of repression it was habitual for the women to be illegitimately detained in secret centers where they were submitted to sexual abuse by their captors or guardians. As a consequence, the court upheld that the acts of sexual violence did not constitute isolated or occasional acts but instead formed part of a systematic and generalised practice. Such a situation was accordingly noted by the Committee for the discrimination against Women (CEDAW) which recommended to the Argentinean state that it adopt proactive measures that make public, prosecute and punish the incidents of sexual violence perpetrated during the past dictatorship within a judicial framework that deals with crimes against humanity, conforming with the contents of Resolution 1820/ 2008 of the Security Council, and which concedes compensation to the victims. (Final observations, 46th Period of Sessions of 12th-30th July 2010, point 16.)"*

The commencement of proceedings on May 19, 2011 in the case involving the *Penitentiary Vila Urquiza* established that *aggravated, gender-related torture and sexist violence had been committed in a situation where women were secretly detained during the period of state terrorism and subjected to sexual violence and sexual abuses.* This case in particular analyzes the authorship, indirect or otherwise, that appears when an agent utilizes another who acts, but does not commit the crime himself, whether it be acting without objective authenticity, without malice, or justifiably. In the framework of such concepts, Roxin eleborated the thesis that another form of authorship can exist in which control over the act emanates from the strength of an apparatus of organized power. Roxin also sustained that the usual concepts are not applicable when dealing with crimes of the state, war, and organizations in which the determiner and determined commit the same crime, with the fungible nature of the latter being decisive, noting the possibility for it to be changed at will as if it were a mechanical artefact: *The further away the executor is from victim and the offensive conduct, the closer he is to the executive instruments of power which provide him with greater control over the act.* (Zaddaroni, Alagia, Slokar; Manuel de Derecho Penal Parte General, Edua, 2005, Chapter 24).

Consequently, and in accordance with the theory outlined above, in order to determine if a person has acted as an intermediary author in virtue of the dominance of the organization, it is necessary to demonstrate that the indicted person held a position and fulfilled its functions with decision-making capacity within the organization, and that in such a condition, they would have intervened in the offending acts in so far as these had been perpetrated by forces under their orders and effective control, or their authority and effective control. In accordance with the case, their responsibility exists

> ... as a result of his or her failure to exercise control properly over such forces, where: a) That military commander or person either knew or, owing to the circumstances at the time, should have known that the forces were committing or about to commit such crimes; and b) the superior failed to take all necessary and reasonable measures within his or her power to prevent or repress their commission or to submit the matter to the competent authorities for investigation and prosecution. (Art. 28 Statute of Rome)

Applied to the current case, it can be affirmed that the witnesses/victims who declared at the committal hearings were clear and coincided in asserting that between 1975 and 1983, the Penitentary *Villa Urquiza* operated as a place of detention in which persons who were kidnapped by the security forces for political motives, or because they had been labeled "subversive," were lodged and subjected to cruel, inhumane, and degrading treatment.

The aforementioned place functioned as a "secret detention center" in which physical and psychological torture was inflicted upon detainees, with some cases eventuating in death. Personnel from the penitentiary – including prison guards, provincial police personnel, the Gendarmerie (i.e. military police), and the army – were principally responsible for administering and guarding the facility.

In order to determine criminal responsibility for the intermediary authorship, it is necessary to inquire whether their position and functions and the environment in which these took place can permit the assumption that the indicted person had intervened in the execution of criminal behavior as corroborated in the summary hearing, and had exercised dominance over these through *the command responsibility of the organization.*

b*) In Spain,* the recent proceedings on June 26, 2011 at the Central Court of Instruction No.1 of the *Audiencia National* (D.P 331/1999) set a unique precedent. It was the first time that a national court affirmed an obligation to investigate the crimes of sexual violence that occurred during the genocide of Guatemala (1960-1996).[17] It is necessary to also highlight the recent efforts that Guatemala itself made with regards to the investigation and prosecution of these crimes.

Conclusion

In applying international criminal law, the *ad hoc* courts for the former Yugoslavia and Rwanda have developed international jurisprudence on sexual violence, which has led to the current codification of these serious international crimes in the Rome Statute of the ICC.[18]

Although the ICC still has not delivered a single sentence concerning this particular theme, there are currently several open investigations into crimes committed in the Central African Republic, the DRC, the region of Darfur in Sudan, and Uganda. These investigations include charges of sexual slavery and rape as crimes against humanity and war crimes.

---

17 Available at http://www.womenslinkworldwide.org/wlw/new.php?modo=detalle_proyectos&tp=proyectos&dc=22&lang=en

18 Consult: Art. 7, Rome Statutes. http://untreaty.un.org/cod/icc/index.html

It is understood that this jurisprudence, when it comes into existence, will be of particular relevance. In the meantime, however, the investigation supposes a resolute message expressing international commitment to the prosecution and punishment of sexual violence in armed conflicts. Furthermore, the new processes that the ICC has implemented to guarantee the participation of victims, which the Extraordinary Chambers of Cambodia have also implemented, send a message about the need to compensate victims.[19]

In summary, it is evident that in accordance with the international jurisprudence in the spheres of both international criminal law and human rights, an obligation to investigate and prosecute crimes of a sexual character exists. As such, it is now the turn of national courts to strengthen the aforementioned jurisprudence in matters of gender by applying it and giving greater attention to these crimes at the domestic level. In Colombia, the fact that the current process of justice and peace has only seen one case of sentencing for a gender-related crime within the context of armed conflict (for guerrillas, paramilitaries, police, and military personnel) demonstrates that there are still significant gaps in the prosecution of sexually violent crimes. This deficiency, after six years, is unjustifiable. The state and Colombian justice system should confront and prioritize this challenge and stop accepting excuses; it is the least that can be done to address a debt to Colombian women and girls. It requires a firm and determined response on the part of institutions, especially the judicial system, in order to actualize the right to truth, justice, and compensation.

IV. NOTES (Chile: Report 2005)

1. "The fear of social shame on the part of the men, including the judges, impedes the assumption and assimilation."
2. "There was a right to rape, like a right to the body of women in general; there was nothing to constrain or impede acting against it. It was logical."

---

[19] Sacouto, Susana. Victim Participation at the International Criminal Court and the Extraordinary Chambers in the Courts of Cambodia: A feminist Project?

3. Gender-based violence is a crime of genocide (sexual aggression) if it concurs with the requisite that its aim is to totally or partly destroy a national, racial, ethnic, or religious group (Art. 6) Rome State of the ICC.
4. In Chile, torture through sexual aggression was systematic for all female prisoners on the basis that they were women. The National Commission on Political Imprisonment and Torture released a report in 2005 that documented 3,394 cases of sexual violence, without distinction in ages, during the period of the Pinochet dictatorship.

CHAPTER 7

REFLECTIONS FROM A WITNESS OF SPANISH MAGISTRATE BALTASAR GARZÓN

Joaquín González Ibáñez

"By confronting the past...we can gain access more easily and more directly to the World around us. To understand the thought of yesterday allows us to change the thought of today, which in turn influences future acts."

The Imperfect Garden, Svetan Todorov

Victims and International Human Rights Law

In the prologue of *Arguably*, his last collection of essays, Christopher Hitchens reflects on the meaning of maturity. He writes that maturity arrives when we stop interpreting life as simply the principles we have, and instead see it as the experiences that make these principles vivid and meaningful in the world.

For professors who research and teach in the field of international law and human rights, the constant balancing of principles and experiences is the essence of our working lives. However hard the lessons that we learn from our experiences may be, we are always in a state of maturing and transforming our principles through experience. Much of this intellectual and existential growth for us takes place in Spain and Latin American countries, places to which we travel frequently in order to work with magistrates, prosecutors, police, the armed forces, and in post-graduate courses with university professors. We go there to promote a stronger consolidation of international standards of human rights and to preserve the rule of law. (...)

Epilogue

In February 2012, the same month of the massacre in the Syrian town of al-Qsair and two months before the massacre of Houla, I decided – not in a rhetorical fashion, or as part of an intellectual exercise – to attend the proceedings of a High Court of Justice and sit on the bench beside the professor and lawyer Manuel Ollé Sesé. I had come to know

Baltasar Garzón by collaborating with him on a book that I had edited concerning victims and the protection of human rights. I believe that the launching of legal proceedings and subsequent writs Magistrate Garzon had ordered, which related to crimes against humanity that the Francoist regime committed during the civil war and post-war period, are in accordance with the law. They stem from crimes against humanity and the obligation to recognize and compensate victims, regardless of how much time has passed, who committed the crimes, or where they took place. International human rights law after 1993 is unequivocal in the jurisprudence and resolutions of human rights organizations such as the UN Human Rights Committee, and the Spanish Courts (Audiencia Nacional) have exercised jurisdiction in cases of crimes against humanity and genocide that occurred in Pinochet's Chile, Guatemala, and Argentina, among other places. (...)

That Tuesday, during the testimony of the four witnesses that took place throughout the day, the magistrate presiding over the proceedings required, without any limitations, that the witnesses respond in depth to the questions posed by the lawyers for the defense and prosecution. When the witnesses began to speak, I realized that I was not in Case A, B, C, or by any other name, but instead was simply in the case of *victims*, each and every one of them, and I obstinately recorded in my notebook a quote by Walter Benjamin that had come to mind: "For the victims, the state of emergency is permanent."

I noted the phrases and expressions that I had read and listened to in previous hearings of mass violations of human rights in Chile, Argentina, Columbia, Perú, Guatemala, and El Salvador. The syntax was indistinguishable, and the subject and action seemingly identical; the only variation was in the names of the places and people involved. After hearing direct testimony from a woman from Navarra, a man from Cordoba, a Catalan, and a man from Valladolid, I comprehended that although the accents of the people and scenes of the crimes had changed, the narrative has remained constant. The same terrifying narrative and sequence of criminal events have taken place on both sides of the Atlantic.

I remembered the demands for civic and human spaces that had lain dormant within my memory. I took notes, my handwriting changing as I listened to the testimony: *"... they were... they are people..." "...out of fear we never decided to act... and I came to the high court looking for Justice..."* and above all, when one of the witnesses – a man of my father's age, born during the Civil War – stated with an unwavering voice, "... *I am the son of a missing person and all my life I have been conditioned by this fact.*"

And so, before the session ended, my mind was filled with ideas.

...I began to think that the rule of law is an aspiration to dignity that is not exempt from tension, and which constitutes one of the clearest elements of the democratic system. I remembered what I had witnessed in Leuven University 20 years before, when Andrea Canalis and some fellow students from Italy had begun to cry when they received the news of the assassination of Judge Giovanni Falcone at the hands of the Sicilian Mafia on May 23, 1992. Their tears of defeat and shame sprung from the vision of Falcone, a man who understood justice and law as a civic and moral commitment to the construction of a more equal and integrated society, but whom the mafia had just silenced. His belief in the betterment of the human condition can be measured in the transformational value of ideas and civic commitment that create the rights and laws in a democracy:

> Men come and go, but ideas remain, and remain with their implicit moral tensions, that will continue to walk shoulder to shoulder with other men ("*Gli uomini passano le idee restano restano le lore tensioni morali, continueranno a caminare sulle gambe di altri uomini*").

I began to think that the international rule of law – specifically, international human rights law represents an attempt on the part of the international community to realize an ethical and moral aspiration. This aspiration reaffirms that the advancement and exercise of human rights innately symbolizes one of the most important forms of progress in the human condition, especially because the *progress of the human condition* means access to the exercise of rights by vulnerable and excluded groups, normally women, children, indigenous peoples, poor and marginalized people, minorities, and above all, victims. Human rights are *the rights of the other* and a commitment to the cause of justice.

Furthermore, I thought in the manner of Isaac Newton that to have his vision of human rights and victims, professors, jurists, and citizens must stand upon the shoulders of giants who have allowed us to see and understand these new horizons. I myself have learned from people, such as Baltasar Garzón, of their commitment and deeds, as well as from the men and women of the High Court, the Supreme Court, and the Constitutional Court of Spain, not only because they are men and women of law, but also because in their work – through their rulings, resolutions, and sentences – they are also the men and women of justice, who have incorporated a new opportunity for victims within a new legal framework.

I thought of my friends and colleagues with whom I work on both sides of the Atlantic to promote and defend this vision of the law that has constituted a revolution in our time. Of course, we know that revolutions always seem impossible until the moment in which they become inevitable. This revolution of human rights has left us with a legacy, and the current world order confirms the statement of Prof. Fabián Salviolli that "[h]uman rights have come in order to disrupt, and they have come to stay.

John Ruskin understood human action as an eventual generator of a legacy called civilization. This legacy is measurable in its words, deeds, and arts. The law applied today, which contains the three elements mentioned by the above writer, is also likely to be our legacy of civility or inequality. New developments in our legal system in 2012 are definitive for the ability to interpret and assess our civilization.

Again, with melancholic reservations, Spanish citizens must resume with strengthened character the task of weaving a fabric of tolerance with regard to some aspects of the *res publica* and institutions. These words are likely to attract critics, either for their lukewarm defense of the magistrate Baltasar Garzón, or for lacking profound respect for the decisions of the Supreme Court and being legally inconsistent. However, they are words that simply attempt to sanction that which makes us more civil, impartial, and competent as a democratic country, and which is otherwise known as the rule of law. The argument I sustain here is an attempt to vindicate the actions of a civil servant in the prosecution of the alleged crimes against humanity during the Francoist dictatorship. It is an argument that upholds the belief that Judge Garzón's investigation demonstrated a coherent, truthful, and legally defensible interpretation of the rule of law under the existing legal system.

In the case of Spain, the writer Javier Cercas has authored a balanced article titled "The Left and the Transition"' (La izquierda y la transición- El País, March 4, 2012) where he has argued that the political transition in the case of Spain, although successful in many aspects, has suffered from lack of an honest format of transitional justice. In his article, Cercas states:

> And so it is that (in 2012) instead of doing what should have been done to resolve the scandal that is the existence of ditches filled with the bodies of the dead- instead of paying with funds from the public treasury so that the dead could be exhumed, identified and buried with honour- we have painted over the situation with a law (Ley de Memoria Historica, 2007) … It is unreasonable because it never has been; in 1978 maybe it wasn't practical- or simply it wasn't possible- to exhume the dead; in 2012 it is appalling that they continue to be buried where they have been left.

The Copernican Turn in Favor of Victims

As an avid reader of literature, I have learned to try not to dwell on the biography of the writer, but instead on the quality and transcendence of the work. Spain is a generous and caring country, but one where fraternal hatred can prevail, and where some are happily toasting in the public domain while others feel humiliated and violently wronged by the resolution of the Supreme Court. In Spain, it is of the utmost importance that people understand what really matters: the anonymous and silent effort of civil servants. Their work legitimizes the legal system, from the Trial Courts (*Juzgados de Instrucción*) to the Supreme Court (*Tribunal Supremo de España*). Moreover, they still have unfinished work, which includes the task of guaranteeing due process and access to justice for all, and *not merely the right to a process* that dilutes the expectations of citizens, to whom the current events in our tribunals are proving especially difficult to understand. This is especially the case for citizens who are victims. Primo Levi claimed the necessity of a public space for the commemoration of victims, the case being that the contempt they experience is multiple: first when they are murdered, and once again when they are forgotten. It is a sad paradox that the case against Baltasar Garzón has been the only opportunity our democracy has provided in which the victims have had a voice in a judicial setting. We cannot forget that the aforementioned Copernican Revolution arrived in legal culture precisely because the victims – those who are most vulnerable and obscure – have become the epicenter of the legal universe.

CHAPTER 8

THE GLOBAL AND REGIONAL IN THE RESPONSIBILITY TO PROTECT: WHERE DOES THE AUTHORITY LIE?

Bernard Ntahiraja

Introduction

On May 20, 2011, delegates of an African Union (AU) *ad hoc* high-level committee on their way to Tripoli were refused "permission" to land on the Libyan territory – not by the Libyan government, nor the then-armed wing of the National Transitional Council (NTC), but by a UN commission in charge of the implementation of the 1973 UNSC Resolution on Libya. The delegates were carrying a mandate from the AU with respect to the ongoing conflict in Libya.[1] Observers saw the incident as a humiliation for Africa and its continental organization. However, placing the incident into its broader context reveals the complex relationships between the world organization and regional organizations with regards to the implementation of the Responsibility to Protect (R2P). The AU is not an example because the incident happened in Africa, but rather because Africa is the continent that has by far counted the highest number of regional peace and security mechanisms and missions.[2]

Both the Charter of the UN and the evolving doctrine of the R2P recognize the role of regional actors in building peace and security. Indeed, the UN alone cannot achieve peace and security, which underscores the importance of regional organizations. The relationship between the UN and regional organizations becomes all the more complex when enforcement action is involved, i.e. when military, political, or economic measures are applied against the will of the state concerned. A (perhaps overly) simplistic approach would be to vigorously and literally enforce Chapters VII[3] and VIII[4] of the UN Charter,

---

[1] Wiliam Davison and Oudaa Marouf, "African Union Panel is Denied Permission to Land in Libya," http://www.bloomberg.com/news/2011-03-21/african-union-negotiating-committee-is-denied-permission-to-land-in-libya.html at 20 August 2012.

[2] The logical explanation might be that Africa also counts the biggest number of conflicts. According to one non-profit organization, there were 10 active armed conflicts in Africa during 2011 alone. "Conflict Descriptions," Project Ploughshares, http://www.ploughshares.ca/content/conflict-descriptions at 20 August 2012.

[3] United Nations Charter, Chapter VII: Action with Respect to Threats to the Peace, Breaches of the Peace, and Acts of Aggression, United Nations, http://www.un.org/en/documents/charter/chapter7.shtml at 20 August 2012.

which give primacy to the organ of the UN in charge of peace and security: the UNSC. Taken together, they *subordinate* regional organizations to the UNSC.

Some authors have argued that the charter regime no longer applies, instead claiming that the UNSC has *delegated* its power to use force to regional organizations, and that the latter can take and implement enforcement measures *autonomously*. There is even a theory that sees the UN and regional organizations as coexisting under two parallel regimes: the *charter system* establishing the supremacy of the UNSC and the *operational system* recognizing that, depending on the issues at stake, enforcement action without UNSC authorization may be lawful.[5]

The point of this paper is not to definitively declare what constitutes the law. It is not to "adjudicate" and identify which of the above theories is correct. On the contrary, it is to highlight the legal uncertainty characterizing the issue. While still acknowledging the supremacy of the UN Charter in affairs under Article 103,[6] this paper argues that a valid interpretation of the charter must take into account the evolutions that took place after the 1945 constitutive conference. The article demonstrates how the most official document establishing the R2P so far – the World Summit Outcome Document[7] – missed the point by simply and literally stating the charter rule as the exclusive legal reference for the issue enforcement action. An opportunity to contribute to the progressive development of international law was lost in a way that is likely to undermine the R2P agenda.

---

4 United Nations Charter, Chapter VIII: Regional Organizations, United Nations, http://www.un.org/en/documents/charter/chapter8.shtml at 20 August 2012.

5 M. Hakimi, "To Condone or Condemn-Regional Enforcement Action in the Absence of the Security Council Authorization," *Vand Journal of Transnational and International Law* (2007) *volume, page #*.

6 "In the event of a conflict between the obligations of the Members of the United Nations under the present Charter and their obligations under any other international agreement, their obligations under the present Charter shall prevail." Charter of the United Nations, Art. 103, http://www.un.org/en/documents/charter/chapter16.shtml at 20 August 2012.

7 2005 World Summit Outcome, United Nations, paras. 138-140, http://daccess-dds-ny.un.org/doc/UNDOC/GEN/N05/487/60/PDF/N0548760.pdf?OpenElement at 20 August 2012. ("Each individual State has the responsibility to protect its populations from genocide, war crimes, ethnic cleansing and crimes against humanity. This responsibility entails the prevention of such crimes, including their incitement,
through appropriate and necessary means. We accept that responsibility and will act in accordance with it. The international community should, as appropriate, encourage and help States to exercise this responsibility and support the United Nations in establishing an early warning capability.")

The author of this paper is aware that, contrary to a widely shared belief, R2P is not synonymous with enforcement action. Use of force against a sovereign state remains a difficult proposition, even under modern international law. Theoretically, it is a measure of last resort under both the charter and R2P. Understandably, it is the most controversial form of intervention. This paper discusses enforcement action from the perspective of the AU-UN relationship. It also briefly addresses other aspects of that complex relationship, such as possible disharmonies in approaches to conflict management. These disharmonies center on the UN's preference for military action as opposed to the AU's preference for political solutions for a conflict. Theoretically, the reverse situation is possible for other regional organizations working with the UN.

This article begins by examining the pre-R2P state of affairs, with particular reference to the charter rule. This part of the paper underscores that the literal interpretation of the relevant provisions, especially Article 53,[8] has been consistently challenged in both law and practice. Part II of the article analyzes whether the R2P doctrine has had any impact on the relationship between the UN and the AU. Part III, the shortest, briefly analyzes the issue of contradicting strategies between the UN and regional organizations. A conclusion ends the paper.

I

ENFORCEMENT ACTION AND THE RELATIONSHIP BETWEEN THE UN AND REGIONAL ORGANIZATIONS UNDER THE CHARTER.

The letter of the charter

The framers of the UN Charter had foreseen the need to involve what they called regional "agencies" or "arrangements"[9] in the maintenance and restoration of international peace. They dedicated the entirety of Chapter VIII of the charter to that issue. The latter makes a clear distinction between political and military approaches to

[8] United Nations Charter, Art. 53, http://www.un.org/en/documents/charter/chapter8.shtml at 20 August 2012.

[9] See e.g., United Nations Charter, Art. 33(1), http://www.un.org/en/documents/charter/chapter6.shtml at 20 August 2012 ("The parties to any dispute, the continuance of which is likely to endanger the maintenance of international peace and security, shall, first of all, seek a solution by negotiation, enquiry, mediation, conciliation, arbitration, judicial settlement, resort to regional agencies or arrangements, or other peaceful means of their own choice.")

conflict management or resolution. For political and diplomatic intervention, the UN and regional organizations do have equal power. Priority is even reserved for regional actors. When the action does not involve use of force, priority is given to regional arrangements or agencies. Article 52, paragraph 2 of that instrument states:

> The Members of the United Nations entering into such arrangements or constituting such agencies shall make every effort to achieve *pacific settlement* of local disputes through such regional arrangements or by such regional agencies *before referring them to the Security Council.*[10] (Emphasis added.)

However, when force is to be used, the UNSC seems to be the supreme and unique power holder. Therefore, interventions by regional organizations at least need authorization. Paragraph 3 of Article 53 of the charter clearly states:

> The Security Council shall, where appropriate, utilize such regional arrangements or agencies for enforcement action under its authority. But *no enforcement action shall be taken under regional arrangements or by regional agencies without the authorization of the Security Council.*[11]

The delegates at the 1945 San Francisco Conference focused closely on the use of force. Abuses of military power were still fresh in the collective memory of delegates, who aspired to prevent history from repeating itself. Thus, one of the key principles of UN membership is to refrain "from the threat or use of force against the territorial integrity or political independence of any state, or in any other manner inconsistent with the purposes of the United Nations."[12]

The issue was taken so seriously that even the two admitted exceptions, self-defense and enforcement action, are strictly submitted to the UNSC's control. Self-defense is legal only until the UNSC has had the opportunity to take action itself.[13] Entities undertaking self-defense measures are also obliged to report to the UNSC. As for enforcement

---

[10] http://www.un.org/en/documents/charter/chapter8.shtml at 20 August 2012.
[11] Ibid. (Emphasis added.)
[12] United Nations Charter, Art. 2(4), http://www.un.org/en/documents/charter/chapter1.shtml at 20 August 2012.
[13] See e.g. United Nations Charter, Art. 51, http://www.un.org/en/documents/charter/chapter7.shtml at 20 August 2012.

action, the UNSC is responsible for placing its imprimatur on its use, which only happens when other measures "would be inadequate or have proved to be inadequate."[14]

It is commonly accepted that the charter's prohibition on using force, except in the two aforementioned cases, applies not only to nation states, but also to regional arrangements.[15] The question is which actions those organizations can legally take without bypassing the charter. Like states acting individually, regional arrangements do have some legal powers, but the UNSC strictly controls their action. The primacy that Chapter VIII gives the UNSC reflects the compromise made at the San Francisco Conference, which featured heated debates concerning the proper relationship between the bodies of the UN on the one hand, and regional arrangements created separately from the UN on the other. The delegates in San Francisco ultimately agreed to allow regional arrangements to act in self-defense without obtaining UNSC authorization, but to require such authorization for enforcement actions.[16] Security Council control in this area was considered necessary to prevent isolated regional arrangements from acting without global accountability or regard for the global interest in international peace and security.[17]

According to a certain doctrine, when the UNSC authorizes a regional organization to use force in cases other than self-defense, the latter is merely given permission to act on the behalf of the former.[18] This does not, however, mean that the UNSC could also delegate ultimate control of military operations to the organization engaged in it. This would arguably amount to a complete abdication of powers and would undermine the centralized nature and institutional structure of the charter in the context of international peace and security.[19] Furthermore, the UNSC cannot legally delegate that power, being itself a delegate of the UN member states: *delegatus non potest delegare.*[20] It is therefore a duty of the UNSC to maintain control of regional organizations that it has authorized to act militarily.

---

[14] United Nations Charter, Art. 42, http://www.un.org/en/documents/charter/chapter7.shtml at 20 August 2012.
[15] Above n 5.
[16] Ibid.
[17] Ibid.
[18] De Wet, E., "The relationship between the Security and regional Organizations during enforcement action under chap VII of the United Nations Charter," *Nordic Journal of International Law* (2012) 71, 1-37.
[19] Ibid.
[20] Ibid. at 11.

De Wet has argued that the prohibition of open-ended mandates to regional organizations in matters of international peace and security is dictated by the fact that centralization of the use of force is the cornerstone of the charter.[21] Thus, with the exception of those undertaken for self-defense, military interventions by regional organizations have to be authorized by the UNSC. They are otherwise illegal, even in cases of gross and systematic human rights violations.

Politically speaking, challenging the exclusive authority of the UNSC has been viewed as a challenge to the UN, and even worse, as weakening international law:

Those who challenge or evade the authority of the UN as the sole legitimate guardian of international peace and security in specific instances run the risk of eroding its authority in general and also undermining the principle of a world order based on international law and universal norms.[22]

Does this orthodox view prevail unquestioned? Does literal interpretation of the charter tell the whole story? A review of state practice and its recognition by the international community suggests that it does not.

Pre-R2P challenge to the literal interpretation of the charter

Long before the emergence of the R2P doctrine and questioning of the exclusive authority of the UNSC by regional organizations, the challenge from within the UN was a reality. In 1950 and 1956, the UNGA took the "United For Peace Resolutions" and sent military missions in Korea and Egypt, respectively.[23] The UNSC was in a deadlock following the decision of the former Soviet Union to exit after the admittance of Taiwan to the UN. Interestingly enough, the UNGA never claimed to have legally taken over the UNSC's power. Officially, its support to the mission was a kind of political and moral substitute to the legal blessing that would have come from the UNSC. This conveyed the message that even in the absence of UNSC endorsement and with the UNGA's power only recommendatory, an intervention that takes place with the backing of a two-thirds

21 Above n 18.
22 Garth Evans, "The Responsibility to Protect," *NATO Review*, http://www.nato.int/docu/review/2002/issue4/english/analysis.html at 21 August 2012.
23 United Nations, http://untreaty.un.org/cod/avl/ha/ufp/ufp.html at 21 August 2012.

vote in the UNGA would clearly have powerful moral and political support. However, most of the challenges are found in the practice of regional organizations, such as the Economic Community of West African States (ECOWAS), the Organization of American States (OAS), and the North Atlantic Treaty Organization (NATO).

In 1990, the ECOWAS undertook an enforcement action to establish peace in Liberia. The organization did not obtain UNSC authorization and did not attempt to justify the action in terms of the charter system. Literally speaking, this could have been viewed as a brutal violation of the charter. Nevertheless, the international community reacted positively. Hakimi has noticed that, for months, the UNSC simply ignored the conflict in Liberia, as well as the fact that ECOWAS had taken an unauthorized enforcement action. He has further observed that when the council finally considered the issue for the first time in January 1991, and later in its Chapter VII resolutions, it commended ECOWAS for its efforts to establish peace in Liberia without mentioning the authorization requirement of Article 53.[24]

Some scholars have interpreted the UNSC's commendations to constitute retroactive authorization for purposes of Article 53. This interpretation is convenient because it places the international response to the Liberian conflict within the legal framework of the UN Charter. However, it is not completely accurate. In fact, the UNSC did not authorize any enforcement action. Resolution 788, frequently cited by scholars holding those views, invoked the council's Chapter VII authority, but did so only to impose the arms embargo, not to authorize the use of military force as well. Moreover, there is some evidence that the failure to authorize the use of force was deliberate. Western diplomats at the UN were prepared to authorize only political action, and not military action, in Liberia. Thus, the fact that the UNSC commended ECOWAS for its multifaceted efforts to establish peace in Liberia does not translate into UNSC authorization for the enforcement action *per se*. Even if it did, the UNSC's "authorization" in November 1992 would not explain the failure of the international community to enforce the charter system for the two years leading up to that point.[25] Military intervention in Liberia by ECOWAS took place without any authorization by the UNSC, but no one – not even the UNSC – regarded it as unlawful. On the contrary, almost the entire international community praised it. The situation of ECOWAS in Liberia is not an isolated case.

---

[24] Above n 5.
[25] Ibid.

In 1962, 28 years before ECOWAS intervention in Liberia, the United States and other members of the OAS had imposed quarantine on Cuba to prevent it from receiving missiles from the Soviet Union. The quarantine was an enforcement action without UNSC authorization, but most other states tolerated or even supported the action. The states that openly supported the quarantine acted as if it raised no issues under the charter system.[26]

There is no question that the quarantine constituted the threat or use of force under international law. Notably, neither the United States nor the OAS attempted to justify the quarantine in terms of self-defense.[27] Some scholars argued that the quarantine was not prohibited under Article 2(4). Others argued that the quarantine was a lawful act of self-defense based on the understanding that deployment of nuclear weapons in Cuba constituted either an effective "armed attack" for purposes of Article 51, or an imminent threat of armed attack for purposes of the doctrine of anticipatory self-defense. These arguments are not absurd, but they require interpreting the charter in a way that is inconsistent with the security framework it originally established. As Prof. Riesman and Andrea Armstrong explain:

> The United Nations Charter's prescription with respect to the use of force is essentially binary: either a use of military force is in self-defense, as that concept is conceived in the Charter, in which case it is lawful, or it is not, in which case it is unlawful. As for the right to resort to military measures in self-defense, it materializes only when the state invoking it has suffered an "armed attack," a stricture that does not even extend to the *Caroline* doctrine of anticipatory self-defense.[28]

It is not particularly interesting to note with regards to both these interventions that the involved organizations (OAS and ECOWAS) did not request authorization from the UNSC prior to their military operations; this is merely a fact. Rather, the most interesting legal lesson from those cases is that these interventions have been met with welcome and praise, even by the UN organ in charge of peace and security. This is more than a

26 Ibid.
27 Ibid. at 17.
28 Ibid.

political statement; it is a legal seal of approval. It suggests the development of a customary rule. ECOWAS in Liberia and the OAS in Cuba are just cases,[29] but how this custom can coexist with the charter rule is another issue.

Hakimi has argued that two distinct legal systems govern enforcement action by regional arrangements. The charter text reflects one system that major international actors have publicly endorsed. The second, more nebulous system is based on expectations and demands in the absence of UNSC authorization. Under this second system, the international community may discreetly tolerate a deviation from the charter rule depending on the substantive interests at stake, the circumstances surrounding the lack of authorization, and the characteristics of the acting regional arrangement. However, these three factors require further explanation.

What should we understand by the substantive interests at stake, the circumstances surrounding the lack of authorization, and the characteristics of the acting regional arrangement?

According to Hakimi, which interests the international community deems sufficient enough to warrant "unauthorized" use of force largely depends on context. The international community is notoriously fickle in protecting international norms. Major actors sometimes believe action is appropriate in order to cease a humanitarian crisis, prevent an incident of nuclear proliferation, or eliminate terrorist havens. The international response in any particular case thus depends on the context in which these norms are implicated and the extent to which they conflict with other interests.

As a general matter, however, the international community is more likely to acquiesce to an unauthorized enforcement action when the interests being satisfied relate in some way to the maintenance of international peace and security. The use of force to maintain international peace and security is an established component of the international legal process and is provided for in the UN Charter. Although the charter also requires that such actions obtain UNSC authorization, the failure to fulfill this requirement does not eliminate the weight of the substantive interest.[30]

29 Above n 5.
30 Ibid.

With respect to the circumstances surrounding the lack of authorization, the first relevant observation is that regional arrangements presumably forgo the authorization requirement of Article 53 because they expect not to obtain authorization. However, the circumstances in which such authorization is forgone will vary widely and influence the international response. For example, it matters whether and in which way the UNSC is seized of the matter when the regional arrangement acts. It also matters whether the regional arrangement takes steps to involve the UNSC or attempts to circumvent the council altogether. Finally, it is significant why UNSC authorization would not be forthcoming. Therefore, international actors will likely analyze the situation differently if they view a permanent member as being intransigent based on motives unrelated to the issue at hand than if they believe there are legitimate reasons for the council not to authorize the use of force.[31]

As for the characteristics of the regional arrangement, the international community will consider, for instance, whether that arrangement has any connection to the target of the action, and whether it is subject to any controls. First, the international community is more likely to tolerate a deviation from Article 53 in cases where the regional arrangement has a unique connection, usually based on geography, to the subject of the action. Regional arrangements are understood to have a strong interest in addressing threats that originate within their own regions, and they often have the tools necessary to respond quickly and effectively. Therefore, it is acknowledged that regional arrangements may be better suited than the universal organs of the UN to address local threats to peace and security. This is particularly the case when the regional arrangement acts against one of its own member states. In that event, the targeted member state may be deemed to have "bought into" the regional regime within which the regional arrangement acts.[32]

It might appear obvious that regional organizations can only act against their own members; however, the truth is that this is not always the case. The NATO campaigns in Kosovo and Libya suggest caution. The scope of this article does not allow for further inquiry into the distinction between the "regional arrangements or agencies" the charter mentions in Chapter VIII and regional defense organizations, such as NATO or the

---

[31] Above, n. 29.
[32] Ibid.

former Warsaw Pact. It suffices to mention that the latter are formed mainly for self-defense purposes against external aggressions.

Debates preceding the adoption of the R2P doctrine indicated expectations of more flexibility in the law of use of force. However, predictably, the controversial nature of the issue obliged promoters of R2P to proceed with caution. To gain consensus, the document of the new framework chose to reassure the most conservative states in order to obtain their approval. The exclusive authority of the UNSC was reaffirmed despite repetitive and consistent challenges, as previously mentioned.

II

THE RESPONSIBILITY TO PROTECT AND THE SECURITY COUNCIL'S EXCLUSIVE POWER TO AUTHORIZE ENFORCEMENT ACTION

The 2004 World Summit Outcome Document: A restatement of a fallacy

In the debates regarding the UN reform in 2004, the World Summit officially took up the concept of R2P. Its definition, justification, pillars, and implementation policies are part of the outcome document of the summit. [33] The legal value of that report, and thus of the R2P, is beyond the scope of this article.

Much like the charter did with respect to international peace and security more than 60 years ago, the R2P framework recognizes that the collaboration between the UNSC and regional organizations is necessary, and even inevitable. On the issue of discussion here, i.e. military intervention, the report of the summit provides:

> We are prepared to take collective action, in a timely and decisive manner, through the Security Council, in accordance with the Charter, including Chapter VII, on a case-by- case basis and *in cooperation with relevant regional organizations as appropriate*, should peaceful means be inadequate and national authorities manifestly fail to

[33] Above n 7.

> protect their populations from genocide, war crimes, ethnic cleansing and crimes against humanity.[34] (Emphasis added.)

The report avoided, in very clear terms, any possible ambiguity about the meaning of the word "collaboration" between the UNSC and regional organizations, as far as enforcement action is concerned. It literally cited the report of the International Commission on Intervention and State Sovereignty (ICISS), as completed and submitted to the UNGA three years before. It states:

> The Commission is in absolutely no doubt that *there is no better or more appropriate* body than the Security Council to deal with military intervention issues for human protection purposes. It is the Security Council which should be making the hard decision in the hard cases about overriding state sovereignty.[35] (Emphasis added.)

Although the commission assumed that standpoint, admittedly reflecting the international consensus at that time, it was aware of the shortcomings of the UNSC. It even recognized that there was a legitimacy issue to confront. Its conservative position was apparently the only way to reassure states that were afraid of possible imperialist agendas hidden behind the noble R2P concept. It thus stated:

> If international consensus is ever to be reached about when, where, how and by whom military intervention should happen, it is very clear that *the central role of the Security Council will have to be at the heart of that consensus*. The task is *not to find alternatives to the Security Council as a source of authority*, but to make the Security Council work much better than it has.[36]

The World Summit entirely ignored the *contra legem* customary rule that was developing at that time. Even worse, it failed to take stock of the law that regional organizations had developed, nor did the final report take into consideration the strong reactions to ICISS proposals on that issue that those organizations had submitted to the UNGA prior to the summit, such as that from the AU.[37]

---

[34] A. Ademola, "The African Union and the Responsibility to Protect,", in J. Hoffmann & A. Nollkamper (eds) *The Responsibility to Protect: From Principle to Practice* (2011), 119.
[35] Ibid at 222.
[36] Ibid.
[37] Above n 7.

African Union law and the centralization of use of force

The Constitutive Act of the African Union and its additional protocols

In 2002, a "revolution" took place in the law and politics of the African Continental Organization. The context was the creation of the AU. The defunct Organization of African Unity (OAU) had been established in 1963 with the main aim of preserving the independence of new states and politically supporting the African peoples that were still under colonization or apartheid. Therefore, it is not surprising that the organization established in its charter and based its policies on the two principles of *sovereign equality of all member states* and *non-interference in the internal affairs of states.*[38] The strong affirmation of these two principles arose not only out of fear of European imperialism, but also partly out of the desire of larger members of the OAU to allay the fears of smaller members, who were concerned that they would be overwhelmed by greater force in frontier disputes.

As respectable and relevant as they might have sounded at the time, the above principles prevented the OAU from acting in the prevention and management of intra-state conflicts. In the 21st century, strong claims of democracy and human rights made it necessary to rethink state sovereignty in Africa. As far as security is concerned, tragedies like the Rwandan genocide made it impossible to continue admitting that states could act in any way they wished inside their borders. It is in this context that Article 4(h) of the Constitutive Act[39] established "the right of the Union to intervene in a Member State pursuant to a decision of the Assembly in respect of grave circumstances, namely war crimes, genocide and crimes against humanity" as one of the key principles with which the union must function in accordance. This was saluted as a shift from *non-interference to non-indifference.*[40] From a legal perspective, this shift is significant because it happened even before the adoption of the R2P concept by the 2005 World Summit, and explains why the AU is often referred to as a pioneer of the R2P.[41] According to Ademola, no

[38] Moller, B. "The African Union as a security actor: African solutions to African problems?" Working Paper, Crisis States Research Center, LSE DESTIN (2009), www.eprints.lse.ac.uk at 20 August 2012.

[39] Constitutive Act of the African Union, Government of South Africa, http://www.au2002.gov.za/docs/key_oau/au_act.pdf at 21 August 2012.

[40] P. Williams, "From non-intervention to non-indifference: The Origins and development of the African Union's security Culture" *African Affairs* (2007) volume, page #.

[41] E. Luck, "The United Nations and the Responsibility to Protect," *Policy analysis brief* (2008).

single international organization had ever legally provided for humanitarian intervention in its treaty prior to the advent of the AU.[42]

The other reason for the relevance of the AU law in the R2P discussion is the broadness of the triggering events it admits. In fact, the initial list made by the Constitutive Act – genocide, war crimes, and crimes against humanity – has been expanded by the 2003 Maputo Amending Protocol to include "serious threats to legitimate order." This phrase is believed to mean military coups or other attempts at overthrowing a legitimate government.[43] Attempts to mitigate absolute sovereignty in democracy-related matters have also materialized in the adoption of the 2007 African Charter on Democracy, Elections and Governance, which explicitly referred to the causal link between unconstitutional changes of government and insecurity, instability, and violent conflict in Africa.[44]

Including the fight against unconstitutional change in the R2P agenda is characteristic of the breadth of the new framework of the AU. It is worth mentioning that the AU is not actually "(re)inventing the wheel" in Africa. In 1990, the ECOWAS sent a force the Economic Community of West African States Monitoring Group (ECOMOG) to Liberia with the mandate to restore law and order and cultivate the necessary conditions for free and fair elections.[45] Involvement in obviously domestic politics is no longer anathema in African regional law and politics. When compared with the heated debate about regime change as part of the "global" R2P agenda, one can simply conclude that visionaries (or imperialists, as the case may be) are not typically the ones labelled as such.

Although the letter of Article 4(4) clearly highlights that the AU has recognized the right to intervene in the aforementioned situations, the actual extent of that "right" has been subject to debate. The ambiguity lies in the degree of autonomy the union has in the exercise of that "right." In other words, can the union decide to use force without the authorization of the UNSC? Or can it act and wait for an *ex post facto* authorization? Scholars like Ademola have argued that the union only has the power to use political means.[46] This would fall perfectly within the peaceful mechanisms recognized by Article

42 Above n 34.
43 Above n 40.
44 African Union, African Charter on Democracy, Elections and Governance at 21 August 2012.
45 Above n 18.
46 Above n 34.

52 of the UN Charter. The author believes that the AU founders did not actually want to grant the union the power to autonomously use force. The argument is based, according to the author, on an analysis of both charter provisions and the history and political context of the reform. This view can be criticized in many respects. Its main weakness is its lack of realism. Stating that the "revolution" the drafters of the Constitutive Act wanted was limited to political and diplomatic interventions is to forget the aim of the R2P intervention: preventing or stopping war crimes, genocide, crimes against humanity, and ethnic cleansing. It seems that a strategy totally exclusive of military action is not likely to achieve that goal. Whether military action without authorization by the UNSC would still be lawful is another question. The AU thoroughly considered this issue during the Ezulwini conference.

The Ezulwini consensus: A "declaration of independence" from the Security Council?

In 2005, at Ezulwini in Swaziland, African states discussed methods for dealing with the UNSC authorization in the implementation of R2P. They adopted a document that is still referred to as the "Ezulwini Consensus."[47] The consensus states that the authorization for the use of force by the UNSC should be in line with the conditions and criteria proposed by the High Panel on Threats, Challenges and Change created by the UN Secretary at that time, Kofi Annan. The high-level panel had in fact identified five criteria or conditions that should guide the UNSC's decision as to whether or not to authorize a military intervention: seriousness of threat, proper purposes, last resort, proportionality, and balance of convenience. The Ezulwini Consensus agrees with those criteria, but strongly states that their interpretation by the UNSC should not undermine the responsibility of the international community to protect civilian people at risk of the aforementioned crimes.[48] The supports the conclusion that the AU accepts the primacy of the UNSC for military operations, but only insofar as the council behaves responsibly, i.e. in a way that does not undermine the ability of the international community to discharge R2P.

[47] Document available at Responsibility to Protect, http://www.responsibilitytoprotect.org/index.php?option=com_content&view=article&id=34 at 21 August 2012.
[48] Above n 34.

However, even at Ezulwini, the AU has never had the illusion that the UNSC would ever apply these conditions in a manner that would guarantee that African lives would not be lost due to the misbehavior of UNSC politics. Precedents of the UNSC's extremely costly inaction in African conflicts, particularly during the 1994 Rwandan genocide, have left many Africans understandably disillusioned about leaving the implementation of R2P to the exclusive charge of the UNSC, especially with respect to the use of force to halt or avert humanitarian disasters. That is the reason why the AU decided as a precaution at Ezulwini that although it recognizes that the authorization from the UNSC is required for a military intervention to be legally valid, such approval could be granted *after the fact* in circumstances requiring urgent action.[49] The union thus reserved for itself the right to act first and then seek retroactive approval as the situation might warrant. The signal Ezulwini had given was that the AU does not regard Article 53(1) of the UN Charter, under which regional organizations are obligated to seek UNSC authorization for their enforcement actions, to be always applicable. The legal and political question of Ezulwini was a kind of dilemma that the AU decided to solve. According to Ademola, the choice was between leaving everything to the UNSC and risk doing nothing, and taking steps towards protecting human lives prior to worrying about compliance with legal obligations.[50] The AU chose the latter.

Although the document of the Ezulwini Consensus does not mention it literarily, the decision was presumably based on the hope that the UNSC would retrospectively validate the interventions. However, from the perspective of an intervener, there is a contradiction in recognizing that the authorization of the UNSC is required for the legality of the intervention while simultaneously stating that the authorization can be granted afterwards, *après coup*. This seems to put the UNSC in front of a *fait accompli*, and it is uncertain which consequences would arise if the authorization would be refused afterwards. In sum, for a regional organization rooted in the good faith of its members, there is no practical difference between stating that authorization can come afterwards and arguing that it is not required at all.

Article 4(h) of the Constitutive Act of the AU and the Ezulwini Consensus are clearly at odds with the letter of Article 53 of the UN Charter. A rigorous interpretation of the latter suggests, in fact, that authorization must be given prior to intervention. However,

---

[49] Ibid.
[50] Ibid.

the question is whether or not they can still be lawful. Article 103 of the UN Charter stipulates:
In the event of a conflict between the obligations of the Members of the United Nations under the present Charter and their obligations under any other international agreement, their obligations under the present Charter shall prevail.[51]

Hakimi would give an affirmative answer to the above question.[52] As previously highlighted, he has proposed that legality no longer equates to consistency with the charter.

Levitt has claimed that Article 4(h) of the AU Constitutive Act and its interpretation by the Ezulwini Consensus do not actually violate Article 103 of the UN Charter. He has based his point on the fact that the UNSC, acting under Chapter VII of the UN Charter, has retrospectively authorized African regional interventions taken under the authority of hardened regional customary law that has been modified into treaty. He specifically refers to operations that the ECOWAS had undertaken in Sierra Leone. He therefore concludes that Article 103 of the UN Charter seems to create an exception for African intervention treaties. According to him, it cannot be argued otherwise, unless one accepts that the UNSC violated Article 103 in retrospectively authorizing those interventions to which he refers – a difficult claim to make given the discretionary power of the UNSC in that matter.

Levitt's argument is fantastical from a formal point of view.[53] The problem with its reasoning is that the author does not take into consideration the fact that, in order for the UNSC to grant an *ex post facto* authorization to an intervention, the "regional law" in accordance to which the intervention was decided is indifferent. It is an "internal affair" for the organization. Rather, what matters is whether the UNSC would have allowed the intervention *ex ante*, according to the provisions of the charter and with regard to the facts of the situation. If the council determines that it should have, but did not do so because of its own shortcomings, then it grants the *ex post facto* authorization. The function of that authorization is then to validate an already legal intervention, as far as

---

51 United Nations Charter, United Nations, http://www.un.org/en/documents/charter/chapter16.shtml at 21 August 2012.

52 Above n 5.

53 Levitt, J. "The Peace and Security Council of the African Union: The known unknowns," *Transnational Law and Contemporary Problems* (2003) 109, 109-137.

the substantial motives are concerned. On the contrary, if the council deems that it would not have given authorization, for instance because the grounds for intervention are absent, the fact that the intervention has already taken place in accordance with "regional law" does not change anything, and the intervention is declared illegal. This is the weakness of Levitt's argument. When the UNSC grants *ex post facto* authorization to a military intervention undertaken by a regional organization, the authorization is not to be seen as a declaration that the "regional law" according to which the intervention was first decided is in conformity with the charter, nor does it guarantee authorization for similar interventions in the future. The power of the UNSC is discretionary, and it exercises this discretion on a case-by-case basis.

Furthermore, a doctrinal trend suggests that because Article 103 is addressed to states and not to international organizations, and since the latter are not signatories to the UN Charter, their use of force without UNSC authorization to implement R2P does not contravene Article 103.[54] The argument might look a bit hypocritical; it sounds as if it were possible for states to escape collectively from obligations that they individually assume under the UN Charter. As far as use of force is concerned, this cannot happen, as the relevant provision here (Article 53) directly targets regional "arrangements or agencies," not individual states. However, the argument does have some relevance. It recalls that there is no rigid hierarchy in existence within the sources of international law, and therefore enables the entry of customs that might contradict, at least slightly, the letter of the UN Charter.

Political realities support the claim that regional organizations do have independent power to use force. One such reality is the inaction of the UNSC. Kofi Annan, the former UN Secretary General, once warned:

> If the collective conscience of humanity ... cannot find in the United Nations its greatest tribune, there is a grave danger that it will look elsewhere for peace and for justice. If the Council – and the five permanent members in particular – fail to make the Council relevant to the critical issues of the day then they can only expect that the Council will diminish in significance, stature and authority.[55]

---

[54] Above n 34.
[55] Press Release: Secretary-General Presents his Annual Report to the General Assembly, United Nations, https://www.un.org/press/en/1999/19990920.sgsm7136.html at 21 August 2012.

The logic of the argument is that if the UNSC does not want regional organizations to use force, it can prevent them from doing so by acting itself, taking Chapter VII measures. Ironically, the Ezulwini Consensus viewed the UNSC's exclusive authority in exactly the same way the R2P doctrine views state sovereignty. For a state, sovereignty implies responsibility, and in this case, the willingness and ability to protect its citizens and inhabitants against genocide, crimes against humanity, war crimes, and ethnic cleansing. Applying the same rule to the UNSC begs the following question: why should the council always claim exclusive authority to authorize enforcement action when it does not necessarily comply with its R2P duties? Just as a state that does not comply with its R2P duties forfeits all or part of its sovereignty, so should an exceedingly passive UNSC be obliged to bear other actors who intervene to protect individuals in danger.

A conservative counterargument is that this contravenes the spirit of the charter with respect to the functioning of the UNSC. De Wet has argued that the international community cannot demand the council to justify its non-adoption of military measures. According to him, in the case of enforcement action, the charter system is based on an "opt in" procedure, rather an "opt out" one. Thus, the UNSC only has to justify its engagement in military action, and may not be forced into a situation where it has to justify its inaction. The veto power of the five permanent members reflects this.[56] That counterargument is unconvincing precisely because the doctrine introduces the notion of "Responsibility." It is erroneous to envision the UNSC only as a power holder; it is also a responsibility bearer.

The misuse or abuse of the veto power by permanent members offers another source of legitimacy to attempts to override the exclusive authority of the UNSC. Today, it is deemed unconscionable that one veto can override the rest of humanity on matters of grave humanitarian concern. Of particular concern is the possibility that needed action will be held hostage to unrelated political interests of one or more of the permanent members.

The consultations that led to the adoption of the R2P framework included a suggestion of a "code of conduct" for the use of the veto with respect to actions necessary to stop or avert a significant humanitarian crisis. The idea was essentially that in matters where its vital national interests were not claimed to be involved, a permanent member would

[56] Above n 18.

not use its veto to obstruct the passage of a resolution that would otherwise obtain majority approval. The concept would have been similar to "constructive abstention," an expression used in that context in the past. This was identified as the most pragmatic way to prevent the veto power from sabotaging entire R2P project.[57] Promoters of this idea knew that it was unrealistic to expect a timely amendment to the charter, so far as the veto power and its distribution were concerned. The adoption by the permanent members of a more formal, mutually agreed upon practice to govern the R2P situations in the future would have been a salutary development. During the 2005 summit that led to the adoption of the World Summit Outcome Document, which defined the R2P, it was suggested to include that agreement in the final document. However, the United States rejected the proposal.[58]

Apart from its inaction, the UNSC has been criticized for its unprincipled implementation of the global security system. This has a particular significance for Africa. The indignation of African states towards entrusting the UNSC with exclusive responsibility to protect peoples derives from a history of costly disappointments and betrayal at the hands of the notoriously selective priorities of the UN. Unprincipled application of collective security has prompted African states to openly defy some UNSC decisions. For instance, the OAU's Assembly of Heads of State and Government adopted the Ouagadougou decision, which mandated its members to disregard the UNSC sanctions imposed on Libya pursuant to the Lockerbie Affair.[59]

Another argument is that the proximity of regional organizations to conflict areas adds to their legitimacy to intervene. At Ezulwini, African heads of states and governments thought it was imperative that regional organizations in areas close to conflicts be empowered to take action since the UNGA and UNSC are often far from scenes of conflicts and may not be in a position to fully appreciate the nature and development of conflict situations.[60]

---

[57] Andy W. Knight and Frazer Egerton, *Routledge Handbook of the Responsibility to Protect* (2012), 99-100.

[58] Above n 34.

[59] Ibid.

[60] Ibid.

Smartly circumventing the charter: Extending the definition of self-defense

Depending on the level of integration, states cede parts of their sovereignty and bestow relatively important powers to the regional organizations of which they are members. Ceding part of one's sovereignty is in itself a sovereign act. The charter cannot forbid it, even if it concerns military action. In fact, the ECOWAS member states did it in 1999. In order to avoid possible controversy that could result from interventions similar to that undertaken in Liberia a decade earlier, they adopted a protocol authorizing the ECOWAS to take enforcement actions in any member states without their consent. Since then, ECOWAS has applied the protocol on several occasions, including repelling Faure Eyadema's unconstitutional ascendancy to the Togolese presidency after the death of his father, and imposing arms embargoes on Guinea and Niger in 2009.[61]

Since consent is given in a treaty, the intervention arguably cannot qualify as enforcement action. The argument does not survive scrutiny, though. It is worth keeping in mind the difference between consent given to a specific intervention and consent given once and for all in a treaty. The latter does not alter the enforcement character of the operation.

As the above developments clearly reveal, the conflict between the UNSC and regional organizations mostly concerns the power to use force. However, conflict may also arise regarding the means of intervention. In other words, the regional organization's approach might be to peacefully seek political solutions to the conflict, while the UNSC might think force is the only option. This scenario happened in Libya between the AU and the UNSC.

III

CONFLICTING APPROACHES TO PROTECTION

At the very beginning of the insurrection in Libya, before the incendiary declarations of Muhamar Kaddafi promising hell to the rebels, the AU had established a high- level *ad*

[61] Ibid.

hoc committee on Libya. On March 10, 2011, the committee received a mandate articulated primarily in three points:

1. To engage with all the parties in Libya and continuously assess the evolution of the situation on the ground;
2. To facilitate an all-inclusive dialogue between the Libyan parties on the appropriate reforms to be carried out; and
3. To engage AU's partners, in particular the League of Arab States (LAS), the Organization of the Islamic Conference (OIC), the European Union (EU) and the United Nations, to facilitate Coordination of efforts and seek their support for the early resolution of the crisis.[62]

The committee immediately recognized the Libyan people's aspiration to democracy, political reform, justice, peace and security, and socio- economic development, as well as the need to ensure that these aspirations would be fulfilled in a peaceful and democratic manner.[63] It never supported any side openly. The African action it called for revolved around the following elements:

i. the immediate cessation of all hostilities;
ii. the cooperation of the concerned Libyan authorities to facilitate the diligent delivery of humanitarian assistance to the needy populations;
iii. the protection of foreign nationals, including African migrant workers living in Libya; and
iv. dialogue between the Libyan parties and the establishment of an inclusive transition period, with the view to adopting and implementing the political reforms necessary for the elimination of the causes of the current crisis, with due consideration for the legitimate aspirations of the Libyan people for democracy, political reform, justice, peace and security, as well as socio-economic development.[64]

---

62 Communique of the 265th Meeting of the Peace and Security Council (10 March 2011), Mathaba, http://www.mathaba.net/news/?x=626177 at 21 August 2012.

63 Looking at the Libyan political landscape and practices of that time, it is not clear that peaceful political voices calling for change would have even been heard. However, in calling for a peaceful political process, the AU was simply and faithfully applying the Charter on Democracy and Good Governance, to which Libya is a party. Above n 44.

64 Press Release: Visit of the African Union High-Level ad hoc Committee on the situation in Libya to Tripoli, African Union (10 April 2011), http://www.au.int/en/sites/default/files/Communique%20Libya%20_eng_%2010.4.pdf at 21 August 2012.

However, that agenda survived only on paper. By applying the UNSC Resolution 1973, NATO refused access to the Libyan territory to the AU committee that was flying to Tripoli to start contacts in view of the implementation of that roadmap. The "*no fly zone*" component of the resolution cannot justify the decision, as its logical targets were Libyan military aircrafts and their possible supporters. The real reason was that the AU's political approach was in open conflict with the NATO and UN military strategy. When the committee was finally allowed to enter Libya, it was too late. The NATO bombing had created a military context in which one side of the belligerents was no longer interested in negotiations.[65]

The Libyan case exemplifies that the statement identifying use of force as the last option is merely theoretical. It does not have the same meaning in practice for the UN as for the AU. According to Thakur, the UN's eagerness to use force should not be surprising. Basing his judgment on history, he has stated that the UN was neither designed as nor expected to be a pacifist organization. In fact, the origins of the world organization lie in the anti-Nazi wartime military alliance among Britain, the United States, and the Soviet Union.[66]

Proud of its Kenyan experience with Kofi Annan during the 2008 post-elections violence (an episode still believed to be the first application of the R2P), the AU had dreamed of achieving the same success in Libya: preventing the worst without using force. However, it ultimately did not happen like that. Whether the AU's proposed approach would have been the most effective is another question. The case simply highlights that the conflict between approaches in the implementation of the R2P is likely to happen again. In such a situation, determining which organization has the last word requires much more than a literal reading of the charter rule.

Conclusion

This article has examined the relationship between the UN and regional organizations in the implementation of their R2P duties. Although it has also discussed possible conflicts

[65] K. Apuuli, "The Principle of 'African solutions to African Problems' under the spotlight: The African Union (AU) and the Libya Crisis," journal title (year) volume, page #.
[66] R. Thakur, "Libya and the Responsibility to Protect: Between Opportunistic Humanitarianism and Value-Free Pragmatism," *Security Challenges* (2011), 13-25.

between approaches to protection by regional organizations and by the UN, the predominant focus was on power distribution with respect to enforcement actions. The article has highlighted that recent state practice has challenged the charter rule that regional organizations can only engage in enforcement action with UNSC authorization. Based on an analysis of the practices of the OAS and the law and practice of the AU and other African sub-regional organizations like the ECOWAS, this article has argued that the challenge to the exclusive power of the UNSC to authorize enforcement action started long before the emergence of the R2P as a policy or norm. It has also highlighted that those challenges cannot be seen as violations of international law because they seem to be accepted, even by the UNSC itself. However, this paper has refused to view charter rules as mere legal niceties. Instead, it has argued that the letter of the charter is no longer exhaustive with regards to the law of use of force. Although the UN Charter remains relevant, neglecting the internationally accepted practice of regional organizations is shortsighted. The former UN secretary general characterized the R2P as "an evolving norm of International Law."[67] It is questionable whether the same can be said of the authority of regional organizations to *autonomously* conduct all their R2P duties, including enforcement action.

67 Public Conference in the University of Ottawa on the 10th anniversary of the adoption of the R2P.

CHAPTER 9

A PRAGMATIC APPROACH TO THE HUMAN RIGHTS AND MULTILATERAL TRADE LINKAGES

Professor Mihir Kanade

Introduction

The modern recognition of international human rights largely emerged, as Prof. Boudreau stated earlier, out of the agony and ashes of World War II. The linkages between human rights and multilateral trade have been a subject of considerable debate in the last decade or so. The emergence of the World Trade Organization (WTO) in 1995 as the nodal agency for multilateral trade in goods and services led to its intrusion into many issues that had not previously been considered to be normally in the domain of trade policy.[1] These included areas such as intellectual property rights and sanitary and phyto-sanitary measures. Over the past few years, this intrusion has highlighted various tensions caused by overlapping international obligations of states under different legal regimes and international forums. Human rights in particular merit special concern, as states have undertaken through numerous international treaties under the auspices of the UN to respect, protect, and fulfill human rights. The International Covenant on Economic, Social and Cultural Rights (ICESCR) in particular requires states to pursue policies and strategies aimed at the realization of the right to food, health, shelter, education, work, and social security for every individual.

In the face of these human rights obligations, it is imperative that international trade policies be framed in a manner that would, at the very least, not violate the former, and in fact further them. All members of the WTO have ratified at least one core international human rights treaty.[2] Thus, states face the dual task of not only adhering to their commitments under both sets of law, but also harmonizing the same so as to avoid a breach of one by the other.

---

[1] Sampson, Gary (2005) – *The WTO and Sustainable Development*, P. 4, UNU Press, Tokyo.
[2] Dine, J and Fagan, A (2006) – *Human Rights and Capitalism*, P. 228, Edward Elgar Publishing, Cheltenham.

However, states have adopted international trade policies under the WTO that have raised serious human rights concerns, with scholars from civil society[3] and at least one early report from the UN[4] itself branding the WTO as a "veritable nightmare" for the human rights of citizens in the Third World. Backlash against economic globalization centers on the adverse effects that the opening up of markets and the trade policies of dumping, subsidizing, and distorting liberalized trade mete out to third-world countries. Even so, the adoption of a "human rights clause" in the WTO agreements has been met with severe resistance from developing countries themselves, primarily because they see its incorporation as a proxy for inflicting neo-colonialist policies upon them and an underhanded means by which developed countries could impose trade barriers.[5]

The purpose of this paper is to provide a pragmatic perspective to the linkages between human rights and multilateral trade. There are two primary reasons why the approach presented in this paper has been self-labeled as the "pragmatic approach." As for the first reason, the starting point for this approach is based on a complete bypassing of the oft-cited critical argument that liberalized trade in general has not led to or cannot lead to economic growth, and is therefore resultantly bad for human rights. Undoubtedly, some critics of the liberalized trade system have cast doubts over its efficacy in generating economic growth;[6] however, the fact of the matter is that the opening up of markets is now an irreversible process inasmuch as states are legally bound by WTO agreements for a substantial amount of multilateral trade (indeed, the proliferation of preferential trade agreements has only fortified this proposition). States have invested way too much in transitioning to the liberalized trade regime, both structurally and economically, to permit any retraction now. Whether skeptics like it or not, for good or for bad, protectionism is a bygone option, unless specifically permitted by the WTO agreements in exceptional circumstances. Pragmatism, therefore, demands that discussions of multilateral trade-human rights linkages bear that in mind.

---

3 Tandon, Yash (1999) – "The World Trade Organization and Africa's Marginalization," *Australian Journal of International Affairs*, vol. 53, No. 1 (1999), P. 83-94.
4 United Nations: Economic and Social Council (2000)- *The Realization of Economic, Social and Cultural Rights: Globalization and its impact on full achievement of human rights*, E/CN.4/Sub.2/2000/13, Para 15
5 Kolben, Kevin (2006) – "The New Politics of Linkage: India's Opposition to the Worker's Rights Clause," *Indiana Journal of Global Legal Studies* (2006), P. 225-259
6 Joel R. Paul (2003) – "Do International Trade Institutions Contribute to Economic Growth and Development?" *Virginia Journal on International Law* 44 (2003-2004), P. 283-340.

The second reason is concerned more with the approach to finding solutions to problems related to linkages. Criticisms of WTO policies vis-à-vis human rights have been so severe that critiques have tended to brand the WTO itself as an antagonist to human rights.[7] Therefore, proposed solutions have varied from complete abolition of the WTO itself[8] to an entire overhaul of WTO processes by making human rights a central purpose of the same.[9] The fallacy with most of these arguments lies in the fact that human rights – although indeed affected by international trade policies – are so affected in many and varied ways. Some of them are directly a result of inadequacies in the WTO policies, and therefore warrant a human rights-based approach. However, there are also some human rights which, despite succumbing during the process of opening up markets, are not directly caused by WTO obligations of states. As such, they deserve to be addressed in a different manner. A holistic, all-inclusive approach to problems that are inherently distinct cannot be the solution. The WTO is primarily a trade institution, and there is no merit in attempting to convert it into a human rights institution, especially in light of the UN's role as the specialized international institution bearing responsibility to promote human rights on the global level. The need, however, is to find approaches that ensure that WTO processes do not adversely affect existing legal obligations to recognize and enforce human rights.

In this factual matrix, it is necessary to provide effective solutions and clearly fix responsibility on states, the UN, and the WTO system to jointly and separately take action, as well as to hold them accountable for addressing human rights concerns without venturing into the "beggar-thy-neighbor" policies that protectionism entails. Therefore, this paper attempts to deconstruct the broad ways in which multilateral trade under the WTO affects human rights, and then examines the pragmatic approaches through which both sets of obligations can be harmonized without disturbing the fundamental ethos underpinning both the WTO and the UN. The stress is on approaches, rather than on specific solutions.

---

7 Op. Cit. FN 4

8 Freedom Socialist Party & Radical Women (1999) – *Abolish the WTO: Capitalist trade can never be free or fair*, http://www.class.uidaho.edu/gjmarchive/pdf/Images%20to%20upload/WTO%2099/wto20/wtop113099f.pdf (Retrieved on 14/08/2012)

9 3D_Trade - Human Rights - Equitable Economy - Dommen, Caroline (2004) – *The WTO, International Trade and Human Rights*, available at http://www.3dthree.org/pdf_3D/WTOmainstreamingHR.pdf (retrieved on 14/08/2012)

The approaches of the UN and the WTO

The "scourge of war" evidenced by the world, both during and in the immediate aftermath of World War II, witnessed the prelude to a "New World Order," according to which the new post-war international order was to rest on four pillars: peace and human rights on the one hand, and trade and finance on the other.[10] The first two pillars of peace and human rights were conceived to be developed and implemented by a global intergovernmental institution to be known as the UN. In order to develop and implement the other two pillars of trade and finance, the two Breton Woods Institutions – namely, the International Monetary Fund and the World Bank – as well as the *de facto* predecessor of the WTO, The General Agreement on Tariffs and Trade, 1947 (GATT 1947), were established by the participants of the Breton Woods Conference of 1944.[11]

Before focusing on the complex interactions between the obligations of states under the UN and WTO, it would only be apt at this juncture to briefly highlight two essential facts – one historical and the other legal – a proper understanding of which is a *sine qua non* for an intelligible appreciation of this topic.

The first issue concerns the historically different approaches that the UN and WTO have adopted in their functioning – the human rights-centric approach of the UN and the economic approach of the WTO - despite both organizations having some common objectives. Since its inception, the UN has incorporated a human rights-centric approach, not only in the UN Charter and other human rights treaties, but also in the functioning of its various subsidiary organs.[12] Meanwhile, like its predecessor, the GATT 1947, the WTO has followed a predominantly economic approach based on the theory of liberalization of trade, as evident from the Preamble of the WTO Umbrella Agreement.[13]

---

[10] Possel, Jens (2008) – "A Human Rights approach to 'sustainable development' within WTO," in *Developing Countries and the WTO,* Edited by Sampson, G. and Chambers, B., P. 192-228 at P.192, UNU Press, Tokyo.

[11] Idem

[12] For instance, see the founding documents of FAO, WHO, UNICEF, UNCTAD, UNHCR, etc.

[13] Petersmann, Ernst-Ulrich (2008) – "The development objectives of the WTO: State-centered versus human rights approaches," in *Developing Countries and the WTO,* Edited by Sampson, G. and Chambers, B., P. 169, UNU Press, Tokyo.

This difference in the approaches of these two institutions since their inception offers a strong indication of why the two legal regimes of trade and human rights have developed more or less independently from one another, as opposed to within an interdependent and integrated system. This dichotomized development has resulted in a rather ambivalent situation for states, since they are legally bound to both regimes. At the UN, states adopt (or at least are required to adopt) a human rights-based approach in compliance with their human rights obligations under the UN Charter and various human rights agreements. In the same breath, under the auspices of the WTO, these very states adopt a predominantly economic approach in order to promote their own economic growth. The ambivalence in approaches results in a problem only when either set of obligations leads to undermining the obligations cast under the other. In other words, if certain policies that states adopt under the WTO result in undermining human rights, then these states are actually breaching their human rights commitments in favor of their trade commitments.

However, it must be stressed that despite the distinct approaches states have adopted for the two organizations, both in fact share some common objectives. Article 55(a) of the UN Charter provides that the UN shall promote higher standards of living, full employment, and conditions of economic and social progress and development. These are the very same expressions present in the Preamble of the WTO Umbrella Agreement, which reads as follows:

> The Parties to this Agreement,
> *Recognizing* that their relations in the field of trade and economic endeavor should be conducted with a view to raising standards of living, ensuring full employment and a large and steadily growing volume of real income and effective demand, and expanding the production of and trade in goods and services, while allowing for the optimal use of the world's resources in accordance with the objective of sustainable development, seeking both to protect and preserve the environment and to enhance the means for doing so in a manner consistent with their respective needs and concerns at different levels of economic development,[…]
>
> Agree as Follows:

This only emphasizes that although these organizations were established separately with specialized mandates, they were never intended to develop in such remarkable isolation from each other. On the contrary, their establishment sought to obtain a unified international social order based on respect for human rights, sovereign equality of states, and international cooperation in trade and finance.

There are satisfactory reasons why these two regimes ought to have developed in a mutually reinforcing manner. The fields of human rights and trade are interdependent, and in many cases overlapping. The fulfillment of human rights, including both civil and political on the one hand, and economic, social, and cultural on the other, depend on the generation of wealth and availability of resources, which result from trade. For instance, the exercise of the right to vote, effective functioning of judiciaries, the right to food, clothing, and shelter, and the right to health each require resources, and are thus dependent in part on the successful implementation of trade policies. Similarly, a healthy population with necessary basic amenities, medicines, access to justice, and effective governance are all prerequisites for a successful multilateral trading regime. Apparently, one cannot exist without the other, especially in the context of today's globalized world.

The second issue that warrants clarity is the legal debate on the *interpretation* of WTO rules vis-à-vis human rights treaties. The Vienna Convention on the Law of Treaties, especially Article 31(3)(c) thereof, recognizes the rule of "Harmonious Construction" of international laws, or the rule of "Systemic Integration."[14] Quite logically, the interpretative principle of harmonious construction conveys that WTO rules must not be interpreted in a manner that infringes upon human rights obligations under UN treaties. However, it is important to remember that the principle does not entail that human rights provisions should be used to supplement or add a human rights obligation to an existing WTO provision. Furthermore, human rights provisions cannot be used to diminish the operation of provisions under the WTO.[15] In other words, even if it is found that certain human rights are breached as a result of the *omissions* in WTO agreements, the agreements cannot be added or diminished with human rights obligations under UN treaties by way of interpretation. This fact is significant because

[14] United Nations: International Law Commission (2006) – *Conclusions of the work of the Study Group on the Fragmentation of International Law: Difficulties arising from the Diversification and Expansion of International Law*, available at http://untreaty.un.org/ilc/guide/1_9.htm (retrieved on 14/08/2012)

[15] Marceau, Gabrielle (2006) – "WTO Dipute Settlement and Human Rights," in *International Trade and Human Rights*, Edited by Abbott, F. et al., P. 215, University of Michigan Press, City. This prohibition of "filling in the gaps" in a provision of law by reading in extraneous requirements flows from the doctrine of *casus omissus*. See Art. 3(2) of the Dispute Settlement Understanding for the interpretative limits on the DSB.

the latter half of this paper argues that WTO rules generally do not violate human rights laws *per se*. To a large extent, WTO laws do limit the policy space that states have in order to ensure human rights at home; however, that lack of policy space cannot be expanded by recourse to rules of interpretation of treaties. The solution lies elsewhere.

There is yet another preliminary legal issue that warrants attention. Article 103 of the UN Charter explicitly states, "in the event of a conflict between the obligations of the members of the UN under the Charter and their obligations under any other international agreement, their obligations under the UN Charter shall prevail." Now, Article 55(3) of the charter dictates that the UN shall promote "universal respect for, and observance of, human rights and fundamental freedoms for all without distinction as to race, sex, language, or religion." Article 56 is a pledge by all member states that they will "take joint and separate action in co-operation with the organization for the achievement of the purposes" set forth in Article 55. As a result, it has been argued that by virtue of Article 103, the human rights obligations of states as enshrined in Articles 55 (3) and 56 of the UN Charter enjoy a hierarchical superiority over the obligations of the same states under any other treaty law,[16] including WTO law. A natural corollary from this argument follows that in the contingency of a WTO obligation being incapable of interpretation in a manner consistent with a human rights obligation, the former must be superseded by the latter because of the latter's hierarchical superiority in the normativity of international law.[17]

However, this proposition may not be quite accurate. The obligation that the charter imposes on states under Article 56 is the obligation to "take action" for achievement of all of the purposes mentioned in Article 55, including those related to human rights. In other words, the *operative part* in Articles 55(c) and 56 regarding the charter obligation on states for the purposes of Article 103 is the obligation to "take action." Taking action means that states are required to take steps towards achievement, which is quite different from ultimately achieving results. It signifies that states are obliged to work on the means (taking of action) by which they will achieve the ends (purposes set forth in Article 55).

---

[16] Loukaidēs, Loukēs G. (1995) – "Chapter 10," in *Essays on the Developing Law of Human Rights*, P. 220, Martinus Nijhoff Publishers, Dordrecht.

[17] Federation of International Human Rights (2005) – *Understanding global Trade and Human Rights*, P.1, available at http://www.un-ngls.org/orf/FIDH.pdf (retrieved on 14/08/2012)

Thus, irrespective of whether the purposes set forth in Article 55(c) are promotional in nature or are more than that, the obligation on states is still that of taking action.

Importantly, the charter leaves it to the discretion of states to determine by which means they would achieve the purposes set forth under Article 55. They are required to to take action using their governance space to achieve the ends in the manner deemed effective and appropriate by the state. In determining their own means, states generally have a variety of options available, including legislative, administrative, judicial, institutional, or budgetary means.[18]

The obligation to "take action" is clearly not the same type of obligation that states have under the International Covenant on Civil and Political Rights (ICCPR), ICESCR, any of the other seven core human rights treaties, or even regional human rights treaties, because under these instruments, the obligation extends beyond "taking action" to actually achieving results. In fact, the very emergence of human rights treaties is an expression of states "taking action" to achieve the purposes set forth in Article 55. Given that the obligation under the UN Charter is one of taking action, it is now important to situate that in the context of Article 103. In order for the charter obligations to prevail, it is important that there be a conflict with a non-charter obligation. Therefore, given the specific nature of obligations under the charter with respect to human rights, in order for a conflict to arise it is necessary for the non-charter obligation to either negate the ability of states to "take action" or put serious restrictions on the same. However, as evidenced above, given the wide array of choices states have in terms of "taking action," such a "conflict" occurs in an extremely narrow set of circumstances. Even if a non-charter law eliminates one manner of taking action to promote or achieve a particular human right, it still would not be in "conflict" if there are other ways of taking action that are available to the state to achieve the same result. Surely, the policy space of states would shrink due to the elimination of one of the options to "take action"; however, there still would not be a conflict.

In any case, even if a legal primacy of human rights obligations presumably exists, it would be crucial to indicate what that entails. Article 103 would supersede *obligations existing* under WTO agreements with human rights obligations under the UN Charter.

---

[18] Stoll, Tobias (2012) – "Article 56," in *The Charter of the United Nations: A Commentary*, 3rd edition, volume II, P. 1604, Oxford University Press, City.

However, if it can be shown that human rights obligations are undermined as a result of *absence of obligations* under WTO Rules, Article 103 may not have application at all. This is indeed the case, as there is no obligation existing in any WTO agreement that requires states to violate human rights. Indeed, several WTO laws do create environments that limit the policy space states have to adequately address their human rights concerns; however, that varies somewhat from arguing that WTO obligations of states are in conflict with their human rights obligations.

Yet, this does not mean that WTO rules and policies may legitimately violate human rights. To wit, WTO obligations surely cannot undermine human rights obligations of states, but not because of a presumed hierarchical superiority of the latter under Article 103. They cannot do so simply because states have undertaken both sets of obligations under two different institutions, and therefore cannot operate at either one in a manner that undermines the other.

With this backdrop, this paper now analyzes the various manners in which human rights are affected while interacting with the process of trade liberalization under the WTO.

Deconstructing multilateral trade-human rights linkages

Although there is widespread concern and recognition amongst different actors regarding the adverse effects of trade policies on human rights, there is no general consensus on how to address human rights issues related with trade. While some have argued that the WTO, being primarily a trade organization, should not be overburdened with the additional task of handling human rights,[19] others have claimed that the WTO has both moral but legal responsibilities to make policies that protect and promote human rights.[20] This difference of opinion has also manifested in various solutions proposed to tackle the issue. One suggestion is strengthening the UN human rights monitoring bodies,[21] which do not enjoy the same judicial authority that WTO dispute

[19] Eres, Tatjana (2004) – "The limits of GATT Article XX: a back door for human rights?" in *Georgetown Journal of International Law*, Vol. 35, No. 3 (2004), P. #. Also, see Op.Cit. FN 1

[20] Howse, Robert and Mutua, Makau (2000): *Protecting Human Rights in a Global Economy: Challenges for the World Trade Organization*, International Center for Human Rights and Democratic Development, available at http://www.dd-rd.ca/site/_PDF/publications/globalization/wto/protecting_human_rightsWTO.pdf, (retrieved on 14/08/2012)

[21] Zagel, Gudrun (2005) – "WTO and Human Rights: Examining Linkages and Suggesting Convergence," International Law Development Organization (IDLO), *IDLO Voices of Development Jurists Paper Series*, Vol. 2, No. 2 (2005), P.20

settlement bodies enjoy. Other solutions include developing a human rights-based approach to the WTO,[22] which involves the whole gamut of proposed reforms, ranging from incorporation of a "social clause" in WTO agreements,[23] to changing the objectives of the WTO itself by situating human beings as the central subjects of international trade rather than mere objects,[24] to conducting human rights impact assessments of trade policies,[25] to changing the judicial approach of the dispute settlement mechanism.[26] However, in almost all proposed solutions, there appears to be a collective dealing of all human rights issues affected by trade, in that the various facets of human rights that trade undermines have been treated as a single issue that deserves a common solution. The truth is very much to the contrary. International trade affects human rights in various ways, directly and indirectly, and no single one-size-fits-all formula can be devised to address the multiplicity of ways in which WTO policies affect human rights. This calls for a pragmatic deconstruction of these different linkages, and this deconstruction, in turn, needs a rational basis for doing so.

Some of the most visible examples of human rights concerns arising out of multilateral trade comprise issues such as lack of access to medicines, subsidies granted in one part of the world affecting livelihoods of producers in another part of the world, trade in products that affect health, and disregard for labor standards in order to benefit from comparative advantage, amongst others. When it comes to human rights of the citizens of a state, the principal international legal obligation to respect, protect, and fulfill those

---

22 Robinson, Mary (2000) – "Making the Global Economy Work for Human Rights," in *The Role of the World Trade Organization in Global Governance,* Edited by Sampson, G., Chapter 10, P. 209-222 at P. 218, UNU Press, Tokyo. See also Op.Cit. FN 10.

23 Sterling, Patricia (1996) – "The Use of Trade Sanctions as an Enforcement Mechanism for Basic Human Rights: A Proposal for Addition to the WTO," *American University Journal of Law and Policy,* Vol. 11 (1996), P. 1; Sutherland, Johanna (1998) – "International Trade and the GATT/WTO Social Clause: Broadening the Debate," *Queensland University of Technology Law Journal,* Vol. 14 (1998), P. 83.

24 Op.Cit FN 13

25 United Nations: *Economic, Social and Cultural Rights: The Right of Everyone to the Enjoyment of the Highest Attainable Standard of Physical and Mental Health,* Report of the Special Rapporteur Paul Hunt, Addendum: Mission to the World Trade Organization, 1 March 2004, E/EC.4/2004/49/Add.1, para. 53.

26 Petersmann, Ernst Ulrich (2008) – "Human Rights, International Economic Law and Constitutional Justice," *EJIL,* Vol. 19 (2008), P. 769. In this article, Petersmann argues that the human rights revolution imports into WTO dispute settlement a conception of constitutional judicial review. For a critique of Petersmann, see Howse, Robert (2008) – "Human Rights, International Economic Law and Constitutional Justice: A Reply," *EJIL,* Vol. 19, No. 5 (2008), P. 945-953. Also, see Irish, Maureen (2011) – "Special and Differential Treatment, Trade and Sustainable Development," *The Law and Development Review,* Vol. 4, No. 2, Article 5 (2011), P. #, arguing for adoption of a teleological approach by the DSB.

lies on the state concerned. Therefore, it is obvious that states must have adequate "space" to adopt and implement appropriate "policies" for respecting, protecting, and fulfilling human rights. Their ability to do so can be seriously jeopardized if this "policy space" is limited due to external factors, including multilateral trade rules. Because WTO laws are legally binding on all states, and because the WTO has a comparatively more robust dispute settlement mechanism than other regimes in international law, they can also shape the limits of the policy space that states have in adopting appropriate domestic laws for promoting human rights. In some instances, WTO laws indeed do limit this policy space, whereby they create a limiting environment for states to take protectionist trade measures to safeguard human rights. Examples include WTO laws on subsidies, access to medicines, and trade in products that may affect health, amongst others. The solution for these problems clearly lies in amending WTO laws and processes that limit policy space of states to fulfill their human rights obligations.

On the other hand, there are some instances in which WTO laws do not necessarily limit policy space of states to fulfill their human rights obligations. Instead, states do so voluntarily in order to take maximum advantage of the liberalized trading system. Examples include lax labor standards adopted by several states in order to benefit from cheap labor, and thereby gain comparative advantage on the global market. In this instance, the WTO laws do not create any sort of limiting environment for states to safeguard the labor rights of their workers. On the contrary, they create a permissive environment for states to be able to violate labor rights. It is obvious that solutions for problems created by those WTO laws that limit policy space of states and those that do not cannot be one and the same, and there is a need to deconstruct these linkages. The basis of this framework enables categorization of the linkages between multilateral trade and human rights under two broad divisions.

Trade laws that do not limit policy space of states with respect to their human rights obligations:

This category concerns human rights that are not directly affected by actions of states in *compliance* with their WTO obligations, but are willingly or unwillingly neglected in the process of liberalization in order to benefit from comparative advantage. In other words, these are cases in which addressing human rights concerns does not require WTO agreements to be amended, tampered with, or even revised. As stated above, in this instance, WTO laws do not limit policy space of states to deal with the particular human rights issue at all. This category predominantly includes labor rights, as well as all other contextually associated human rights, such as gender and child rights.

Many developing states undermine core labor standards set under the International Labour Organization (ILO) and other human rights treaties (including working conditions, minimum wages, right to unionize, equal remuneration, prohibition of child labour, gender equality, etc.) in order to gain comparative advantage for their products on the world market. For these countries, low wage labor and unrigid working standards constitute their comparative advantage on the global scale since they result in a higher turnover of products and services at lower costs than those prevalent in developed countries. As a result, the incentive for maintaining the status quo with relation to these human rights violations includes much more than the obligations under various human rights treaties related to labor standards. In the process, labor rights of actors within developing countries are severely and aversely affected.

Two reasons can be ascribed to this situation within the WTO context. Firstly, the existing provisions of WTO agreements do not create any obligations for member states to abide by their labor rights commitments under the ILO conventions and other treaties. On the contrary, in the specific instance of labor rights, WTO rules indirectly prohibit any distinctions made between products manufactured without labor rights abuses and those manufactured by violating labor rights standards. For instance, the principle of most favored nation treatment enshrined under Article I of the GATT dictates that member states cannot discriminate between trading partners while imposing import tariffs for any reasons whatsoever, including on grounds of labor rights abuses in the exporting country, if the products are "like."

According to GATT jurisprudence, the likeness of a product is determined through the quality, function, and end-use of the product, tariff classification, and consumer habits and preferences.[27] As the process and production methods (PPMs) do not usually influence the quality of the product and the other aforementioned criteria, a different treatment due to PPMs is not allowed if the quality of a product is the same.[28] In the

[27] World Trade Organization, Dispute Settlement Body: *Japan - Customs Duties, Taxes and Labelling Practices on Imported Wines and Alcoholic Beverages*, (L/6216 - 34S/83), GATT Panel Report, 10 November 1987, para. 5.6; Also, see *European Communities – Measures Affecting the Prohibition of Asbestos and Asbestos Products* (WT/DS135), Appellate Body Report, adopted on 5 April 2001, para. 101

[28] Op. Cit FN 21, at P. 14

Tuna Dolphin II case, a differentiation between tuna that was caught with dolphin-extruding devices and tuna that was caught without protecting dolphins was prohibited, as there was no difference in the "likeness" of the products with regards to the identified criteria.[29] Arguably, a similar situation occurs concerning labor rights issues, such as minimum wages or forced overtime work. There is actually no precedence in WTO jurisprudence with direct respect to whether products manufactured by labor rights violations are "like" those manufactured without. However, based on existing jurisprudence on defining "like products," similar conclusions are reliable. Since the quality, function, end-use, tariff classification, etc. of products manufactured by violating labor rights are generally the same as those produced without violating them, a state cannot prohibit the import of such products through an import ban or additional tax, as it would violate Articles III or XI of GATT.

Furthermore, Article XX of GATT allows a state to take certain measures to protect some non-economic concerns, such as human, plant, or animal life, but only if these protections are required to be put in place within their jurisdiction. There are similar analogous provisions in other WTO agreements as well, and they are dealt with later in this paper. As a rule, WTO jurisprudence does not permit a state to take protectionist measures in response to human rights violations in another country. The first *United States – Tuna case* explicitly rejected measures with extraterritorial effects imposed by the United States to protect dolphins outside their jurisdiction.[30] In the *Shrimp-Turtle case*, the import ban the United States imposed on shrimp from other countries that were netted without turtle-extruding devices was held valid by the appellate body on the grounds that sea turtles are migratory species and are found in territories where the United States has jurisdiction.[31] This restriction on extraterritoriality principally seeks to address the concerns of developing countries that developed countries might start imposing their own unilateral standards as a proxy for protectionism.[32] Apart from this fear of neo-colonialism, there are sound policy reasons for excluding extraterritoriality from Article

[29] GATT 1947: *United States - Restrictions on Imports of Tuna* (DS29/R), GATT Panel Report, circulated on 16 June 1994, para. 5.9

[30] GATT 1947: *United States - Restrictions on Imports of Tuna* (DS21/R - 39S/155), GATT Panel Report, circulated on 3 September 1991 (not adopted), para. 5.25

[31] World Trade Organization, Dispute Settlement Body: *United States - Import Prohibition of Certain Shrimp and Shrimp Products* (WT/DS58), Panel Report, circulated on 15 May 1998, paras. 133, 164. However, it did not fulfill the criteria of the chapeau of Art. XX, as the conservation measure was again too restrictive.

[32] Op.Cit. FN 21, at P.16

XX of GATT and analogous provisions in other WTO agreements. This has to do with the stability of the multilateral trading system itself. If exceptional protectionist measures based on extraterritoriality are allowed, then there is a grave danger of the system sliding down a slippery slope, which may be termed "extra-extraterritoriality." For instance, if an import ban by the United States on products from China is permitted because companies in China are violating labor rights, this is an instance of extraterritoriality. This is because the United States would have imposed the measure not to protect the rights of United States citizens in the United States, but to protect the rights of Chinese workers in China. Thus, if this were permitted, then by that logic, China could impose an import ban on United States products, because United States companies may be violating labor rights – not of United States citizens in the United States, nor of Chinese citizens in China, but of Ecuadorian citizens in Ecuador, where such companies may be operating. This is not an instance of extraterritoriality, but of extra-extraterritoriality, which could lead to an utterly dysfunctional multilateral trading system in which every state can impose import bans on products from virtually every other country for proxy reasons.

As a result, the concept of "like products" together with the prohibition on trade-related human rights measures with extraterritorial effects have caused some labor rights issues in developing countries to be ignored by such countries.

There is a second reason why WTO laws do not incorporate a specific "social clause" or "labor clause" that may allow states to impose import bans on states that allow labor rights violations. This reason - indeed a very potent one - is the vehement opposition of developing states themselves to the incorporation of such clauses in WTO agreements, which would make it incumbent upon members to adhere to strict labor rights standards in the course of their multilateral trade. First is the fear of neo-colonialism discussed earlier. Second, developing countries argue that better working conditions and improved labor rights arise through economic growth. Thus, sanctions imposed on countries with lower labor standards would merely perpetuate poverty and delay improvements in workplace standards.[33] Moreover, experience has shown that trade-related human rights measures aimed at changing human rights policies often do not have their intended

---

33 World Trade Organization: *The WTO, Misinformation*, available at http://www.wto.org/english/thewto_e/minist_e/min99_e/english/misinf_e/03lab_e.htm (retrieved on 14/08/2012)

effect and, on the contrary, aggravate the situation.[34] History has demonstrated that the imposition of certain human rights and social standards from the outside has almost always been a failure, and those that suffer the most due to such external sanctions are the victims of such abuses themselves.[35]

In this context, it is evident that a stalemate of sorts exists with regards to addressing the labor rights abuses indirectly permitted by states as a result of participation in the process of trade liberalization under the WTO. Therefore, the crucial questions become: How should the international community approach this problem? Should the WTO bear the brunt of addressing human rights abuses under this category?

In searching for an answer to these questions, it must be kept in mind that the abuses under this category are not a direct result of member states complying with their WTO obligations. The WTO rules do not require states to be lax on labor standards for their own workers. In other words, WTO laws do not create a limitation on the policy space that states have for enhancing labor standards domestically. There is, therefore, no real conflict between WTO laws and human rights laws in this category of linkages.

This is precisely what distinguishes this category from the second category discussed below. Violations of labor and associated rights, unlike other linkages, are *not* due to provisions of WTO agreements. They arise because states do not follow their human rights and ILO obligations, and instead breach them. In other words, there is no need to amend GATT or General Agreement on Trade in Services (GATS) to make it illegal for states to violate labor rights. These obligations already exist under labor rights instruments, and must be followed in any case. When advocates talk about countering these violations of labor rights through the inclusion of "labor clause" in WTO agreements, they are really seeking the creation of enforcement mechanisms for labor rights through the WTO, an organization created for a completely different purpose, rather than through the body that was created to deal with the issue of labor rights: the ILO. It is true that the provisions of GATT or GATS do not declare products manufactured through violations of labor rights illegal. However, that does not make the

---

[34] Bal, Salman (2001), "International Free Trade Agreements and Human Rights: Reinterpreting Art. XX of the GATT," *Minnesota Journal of Global Trade*, Vol. 10 (2001), P. 62-108, at P. 64.

[35] Stern, R.M. and Terrell, K. (2003) - *Labor Standards and the World Trade Organization*, at P. 8, available at http://www.fordschool.umich.edu/rsie/workingpapers/Papers476-500/r499.pdf (retrieved on 14/08/2012)

violation of labor rights under ILO instruments legal; they are illegal anyway. Simply making them illegal under the WTO will not make the violations *more* illegal. As such, WTO agreements do not really require amendment to hold states accountable for labor rights violations.

It is apparent that not much can be achieved by thrusting additional responsibility on the WTO to address this category of human rights abuses. The WTO clearly does not have the mandate, resources, or expertise to follow up on these issues. This job can be best done by the ILO itself, and must not be transferred to the WTO. For instance, nothing prevents UN agencies, including the ILO, from asking states to enforce the labor standards set by various treaties while conducting trade as per WTO rules; in fact, it is their job to do so. As Zagel has explained, "if the human rights community wanted the enforcement of standards through trade restrictions, this would have been established through the existing human rights instruments, not in an entirely different organization - whose task is to promote free trade."[36] The UN and its specialized agencies are charged with advancing human rights, and a case can be made that these institutions should be strengthened and provided with the resources they need to carry out their tasks successfully so that the WTO does not have to deal with the wider agenda that it now seems to be acquiring.[37] Unfortunately, many of the relevant UN treaty bodies (e.g. ICESCR, Human Rights Committee) and charter bodies (e.g. Human Rights Council) do not have the enforcement mechanisms necessary to effectively hold state actors to their obligations.[38] As such, the approach for this category should really be to strengthen the UN human rights system and ILO mechanisms rather than to additionally burden the WTO.

Referring back to the theme of pragmatism that this paper emphasizes, the approach urged above is also necessary because amending GATT Article XX to incorporate a new "labor clause" is an extremely complex process. Article X of the Agreement Establishing the WTO requires a consensus to be built within the Ministerial Conference, or a two-thirds majority in its absence, for even tabling the amendment proposal for consideration by the members. It is highly unlikely that a proposal for amending Article XX or

[36] Op. Cit. FN 21, P. 20

[37] Op. Cit FN 1, at P. 11

[38] International Federation for Human Rights (2005) – *Understanding Global Trade and Human Rights*, Report No. 432/2, available at www.fidh.org/IMG/pdf/wto423a.pdf, at P. 8-9 (retrieved on 14/08/2012)

analogous WTO provisions to include a "labor clause" would capture a two-thirds majority at the WTO under the prevailing circumstances. Given the stance that various states have adopted, the possibility of such incorporation is practically nil. It would in fact be more pragmatic to advocate for amending the ILO Constitution in accordance with Article 36 thereof in order to implement strong enforcement and supervisory mechanisms. Advocacy strategists must realize that it is a significantly easier process to amend the ILO Constitution than to amend a WTO agreement.

Trade laws that directly limit policy space of states with respect to their human rights obligations:

This category concerns human rights violations that result directly from the inadequacies in WTO agreements and corresponding trade policies adopted by members of the WTO. These cases result in limits to the policy space that states have for attending to their human rights obligations. This issue is intrinsically connected with the process of liberalization itself in that opening up markets in terms of specific WTO agreements, entails major structural changes within a society, which in turn yields human rights implications. Although structural changes of this kind inevitably occur within any economy throughout its normal course of evolution, globalization tends to have both an accentuating and distorting effect on structural changes.[39] Because WTO agreements necessitate these structural changes, it is imperative that these agreements are framed in a manner compatible with human rights.

It has become commonplace for critics to argue that existing WTO rules contravene human rights. However, a closer scrutiny would suggest that it is not the WTO rules *per se*, but *inadequacies* within them that lead to human rights violations. If trade laws limit policy spaces of states to adequately manage human rights concerns at home, it is due to existing WTO laws that create such a limiting environment for states – not because WTO provisions are directly contrary to human rights law. This can be tested with three illustrations, which are by no means exhaustive, but are useful to highlight the distinction between the misplaced argument that WTO rules violate human rights and the correct position that inadequacies within WTO rules result in limiting policy spaces of states to satisfactorily fulfill their human rights obligations.

---

[39] United Nations, Economic and Social Council (2004) – *Study on Policies for Development in a Globalizing World: What can the Human Rights Approach Contribute*, E/CN.4/Sub.2/2004/18 of 7 June 2004

An example is the harmful effect of inadequate WTO policies enshrined under the Dispute Settlement Understanding (DSU) relating to economic compensations. This example is borrowed from Shahin's work,[40] albeit in a different context and to raise a different argument. Cotton is a strategic crop for the four least developed Western and Central African (WCA) countries: Burkina Faso, Benin, Mali, and Chad. As over 90% of the cotton produced in this quad is for export, cotton accounts for up to 75% of export earnings, and is thus vital for poverty reduction strategies in these countries.[41] However, plagued with extreme poverty and malnutrition, these countries are fighting against illegal cotton subsidies by the United States and European Union, who have continued to provide billions in subsidies for domestic producers, dumping overproduced cotton at 61% below the cost of production between 1997 and 2002.[42] These cotton subsidies by these two entities have resulted in a substantial reduction in cotton prices, from an average of $0.72 USD per pound to $0.42 USD per pound in 2001 and 2002.[43] Until today, such a collapse has unabatedly wreaked havoc upon the already fragile economies of these countries and generated substantial losses in their hard currency earnings.

Article 6 of the ICCPR guarantees the right to life. Similarly, the ICESCR guarantees the right to work to all human beings, including the universal right to the opportunity to make a living through work that has been freely chosen or accepted, as well as the right to just and favorable conditions of work (Articles 6, 7). The illegal subsidies by the United States have infringed upon these rights of farmers in WCA countries. However, in the event that the four countries were to approach the Dispute Settlement Body (DSB) as complainants challenging the illegal subsidies, there is no way in which they could be compensated reasonably for their losses, thereby permitting violating states (in this case, the United States) to adopt "hit and run" practices.[44] This is because financial

---

40 Shahin, Magda (2008) – "The Cotton Initiative," in *Developing Countries and the WTO: Policy Approaches*, Edited by Sampson, G. and Chambers, B., P. 41-61, UNU Press, Tokyo.

41 Goreux, L (2004) – *Prejudice Caused by Industrialized Countries Subsidies to Cotton Sectors in Western and Central Africa*, available at http://www.fao.org/es/esc/common/ecg/306/en/Goreux_Prejudicef.pdf (retrieved on 14/08/2012)

42 3D-->Trade—Human Rights—Equitable Economy & Ethical Globalization Initiative (2004) – *US and EU Cotton Production and Export Policies and their impact on West and Central Africa: Coming to grips with international human rights obligations*, www.3dthree.org/en/page.php?IDpage=27&IDcat=5, (retrieved on 14/08/2012)

43 Oxfam (2002) – *Cultivating Poverty: The impact of US cotton subsidies on Africa*, available at http://www.oxfamamerica.org/publications/cultivating-poverty (retrieved on 14/08/2012)

44 Georgiev, Dencho and van der Borght, Kim (2006) – *Reform and Development of the WTO Dispute Settlement System*, P. 42, Cameron May, London. The authors describe the practice of states to blatantly violate WTO provisions for the entire period until implementation of DSB judgments as "hit and run" practice.

compensation falls outside of the WTO mandate, and is thus not a permitted solution for the aggrieved party. As Shahin rightly indicates, under Article 22 of the DSU, compensation can be granted to the successful litigant by only two instruments. Firstly, this can be done by offering supplementary concessions for other products. This mechanism cannot apply to these four countries because they only have a few other exports, which in most cases already receive preferential access on account of special and differential treatment. Secondly, customs tariffs can be increased on imports by these four countries. This is also of little use to these nations, as it is likely to backfire on their consumers. Moreover, these countries do not import sufficiently from the United States to offset their loss in cotton exports. The only way in which cotton producers from WCA countries can be compensated for their incursion of severe losses is through economic compensation, which is not provided for by the DSU.

A perfunctory perusal of the aforesaid discussion might lead to the initial conclusion that the existing provisions of the DSU are in violation of human rights. However, closer scrutiny reveals that this is not so. The legality of a provision is tested on the content it does include, not that which it omits. The provision under consideration actually permits compensation by way of tariff modifications, and therefore cannot be said to violate human rights *per se*. Serious human right issues are inured for the four WCA countries by that which is absent from the provision – *the inadequacies* – namely, economic compensation. This is an example of how WTO laws can limit the policy space that the WCA countries have in order to attend to their obligations to protect the human rights of their citizens.

Similarly, one of the oft-cited arguments of a WTO law breaching human rights relates to the provisions of the Agreement on Trade-Related Aspects of Intellectual Property Rights (TRIPS) in the context of patenting of pharmaceutical products by drug companies in the developed world, which results in predatory prices beyond the reach of the poor in the Third World. This is again a misplaced argument. None of the existing provisions of the TRIPS agreement by itself can be said to breach human rights, including the right to health. There are, after all, certain waivers that have been incorporated into the original text of the agreement by virtue of the Declaration on the TRIPS Agreement on Public Health in November 2001,[45] and later by virtue of the so-

[45]World Trade Organization: WTO Document No. - WT/MIN(01)/DEC/2 dated 20/11/2001 – adopted on 14/11/2001

called "August 30 Decision."[46] Thus, these provisions consist of procedures for compulsory licensing and contain certain waivers for the benefit of public health in developing and least developed countries. If testing these provisions on their explicit content, no argument can be raised that they contradict the human right to health. The waivers may be inadequate to address the right to health (Article 12 ICESCR) and right to life (Article 6 ICCPR) of third-world citizens, as perhaps evidenced by the fact that, to date, only Rwanda has formally taken benefit of the existing waivers by notifying the WTO.[47] However, even then, the existing waivers being in the nature of flexibilities to the strict patent regime cannot be said to violate human rights *per se*. When critics say that provisions of TRIPS agreement are harmful to public health concerns of the Third World – and in most cases, rightly so – they really mean that lack of additional waivers or flexibilities, i.e. *the inadequacies*, lead to human rights concerns. Thus, there is a need for more safeguards, and if there were certain additional flexibilities that are presently absent, then some of the human rights concerns of third-world countries could be addressed more efficaciously. It is the lack of these additional flexibilities that limit the policy space that states have in order to attend to their obligation to protect and fulfill the human right to health and life.

The second example of how human rights are directly affected by provisions of WTO agreements through limited policy space of states is Article XX of GATT, a provision that has already been discussed above in a different context. This is related to the rigors of trade rules to take measures affecting human rights *within* one's own borders. As discussed while engaging with the first category, WTO agreements prohibit extraterritorial measures to protect human rights. However, insofar as territorial measures are concerned, Article XX of GATT lists specific public policy reasons that justify deviation from GATT principles. Those directly relevant for trade-related human rights measures are protection of public morals (paragraph a) and protection of human, animal, or plant life or health (paragraph b). In addition to fulfilling the requirements of the specific policy goals, the protective measure must satisfy the general requirements of Article XX ("chapeau"), i.e. it must comply with the principle of non-discrimination, and must not constitute a disguised restriction to international trade. The purpose of the

[46] World Trade Organization: WTO Document No. WT/L/540 and Corr.1, 30/08/2003.

[47] World Trade Organization: http://www.wto.org/english/tratop_e/trips_e/public_health_notif_import_e.htm (retrieved on 14/8/2012), whereby Rwanda notified its intention to import the triple-combination AIDS therapy drug, TriAvir, under compulsory licence from Canadian drug company, Apotex, Inc.

requirements in the chapeau is to avoid abuse of the exceptions of Article XX. Demonstrating that the requirements of the chapeau have been fulfilled is generally a difficult task, and existing case law regarding environmental matters and public health concerns indicates that the DSB has thus far been quite restrictive in its jurisprudence. For instance, in the *Brazilian Retreaded Tires case*,[48] Brazil's action to impose a global ban on its import of retreaded tires under Article XX(b) on the grounds that they affect the right to health of its citizens was challenged by the European Union. Brazil was forced to grant exemption from its global import ban to the members of the MERCOSUR[49] (a regional trade agreement between Brazil, Argentina, Paraguay, and Uruguay), who had successfully obtained the said exemption in a judicial proceeding before the MERCOSUR Tribunal. The challenge by the EU thus proceeded on the grounds that Brazil had applied the import ban to the EU in a manner that constituted arbitrary or unjustifiable discrimination and a disguised restriction on international trade within the meaning of the chapeau of Article XX, since it excluded MERCOSUR members. It did not matter that Brazil did not even want to exempt the MERCOSUR members from the global ban, and was instead forced to do so by a judicial tribunal; the DSB accepted the contentions of EU by adopting a strict interpretation of the chapeau, despite agreeing with Brazil that the ban on import of retreaded tires had a nexus with protection of public health.

The only case in which the DSB accepted an action by a state under Article XX(b) as valid is the *EC – Asbestos case*.[50] In that case, the DSB did uphold the right of France to impose an import ban on substances containing asbestos on the grounds of protecting public health. The DSB also held that France's action satisfied all the requirements incorporated under the chapeau to Article XX. This signifies the difficult for a state to take measures under Article XX to protect the human rights of its citizens, particularly the right to health. In other words, the chapeau and clauses of Article XX create a seriously limiting environment for states to have the policy space to address human rights concerns.

48 World Trade Organization, Dispute Settlement Dispute: *Brazil – Measures affecting import of retreaded tyres*, DS/332, Appellate Body Report adopted on 17/12/2007.
49 MERCOSUR is a Spanish acronym for Mercado Común del Sur.

50 World Trade Organization, Dispute Settlement Body: *European Communities – Measures Affecting the Prohibition of Asbestos and Asbestos Products* (WT/DS135), Appellate Body Report, adopted on 05/04/2001, para. 101

Other WTO instruments, such as the Sanitary and Phytosanitary (SPS) Agreement (Article 2), Technical Barriers to Trade (TBT) Agreement (Article 2.2), and GATS (Article 15), also contain similar provisions permitting states to derogate from their trade commitments in order to protect human health and safety, provided there is strict fulfillment of certain requirements. An illustration under the SPS Agreement is the *Hormone Beef Case,*[51] in which the United States and Canada challenged the EU action of imposing a ban on the import of hormone-treated beef before the DSB. While the EU contended that it had imposed the ban in order to protect the health of its citizens on the basis of perceived adverse effects of hormone-treated beef, the United States and Canada argued that the requirement under Article 5 of the agreement to conduct a prior risk assessment of the effect of hormone-treated beef on human health was not fulfilled. The appellate body observed that, although there was evidence of genuine anxieties concerning the safety of hormone-treated beef, the EU ban could not be sustained since it was not based on a risk assessment, as Article 5 requires.

This case again confirms the fact that WTO agreements do permit states to make certain deviations from their trade obligations in order to protect human health and safety within their territories, but the provisions operate in a manner that does not serve the purpose of creating such flexibilities. The policy space of states that the introduction of the exception clauses sought to safeguard is actually quite limited, as empirics have indicated.

It is clear from all three examples above that some WTO rules clearly impede states and their policy spaces in ways that do not allow them to take the necessary measures to sufficiently address the human rights concerns of their citizens.

In instances where the inadequacies of WTO rules curb policy space, can the DSB intervene and expand the policy space by way of interpretation? As evidenced, the rule of harmonious construction does not permit adding or diminishing WTO provisions with human rights obligations by way of interpretation. Indeed, filling the absence of necessary provisions in WTO agreements is not an interpretative function that the DSB itself can assume. Thus, even if the provisions of WTO agreements are not complete

---

[51] World Trade Organization, Dispute Settlement Body: *European Communities – Measures Concerning Meat and Meat Products (Hormones),* DS/47 and DS/48, Appellate Body Report, adopted on 13/02/1998

enough to respect, protect, and fulfill human rights, the rules of interpretation do not permit the DSB to insert human rights obligations into WTO provisions in order to address the inadequacies and expand the policy space of states.

Unfortunately, states have tended to compartmentalize their legal commitments - on the one hand as WTO members, and on the other as states party to human rights treaties under the UN. The rhetoric and policy disconnect between these areas has led most states to disregard their binding human rights obligations while pursuing trade negotiations.[52] The position of the WTO itself has long been dominated by the "watertight compartment's view,"[53] i.e. the WTO is a trade organization, not a human rights organization. Diplomats and judges from the WTO have a longstanding preference for avoiding human rights discourse in WTO bodies.[54] Additionally, states themselves do not agree to read human rights treaty obligations exogenous to these WTO agreements into such agreements, hence the opposition to incorporation of a human rights clause.

Where, then, does the obligation of states to address this lack of policy space lie? There is clearly a deadlock, and therefore a need to find a pragmatic argument that warrants states to consider human rights concerns at all stages of WTO processes, including pre-negotiation, negotiation, and trade policy review. This could ensure that WTO rules do not unjustly limit this policy space, and that states remove any unjust limitations. However, this lack of policy space has to be addressed not by the DSB's interpretative process, but by some other established procedure.

This approach warrants a search within the WTO Umbrella Agreement itself for an obligation upon states to respect, protect, and fulfill human rights. If such an obligation not exogenous to WTO agreements does not exist, then it provides legitimacy to the argument that states must take human rights into consideration while acting at the WTO as a matter of internal WTO obligations. It would also validate arguments that human rights must be the central purpose of international trade, as opposed to purely economic interests. Therefore, the point of departure would be to acknowledge that trade and

---

[52] Op. Cit FN 17, at P.4

[53] United Nations: *Economic, Social and Cultural Rights: Mainstreaming the Right to Development into International Trade Law and Policy at the World Trade Organization,* Robert Howse, 09/06/2004,
E/CN.4/Sub.2/2004/17, para. 20

[54] Op. Cit. FN 13, at P. 180

economic growth are not ends in themselves,[55] but rather a means to promote human rights.

This link can be found in the Preamble of the Umbrella Agreement, which incorporates "sustainable development" as one of its principal objectives. Thus, the WTO's mandate is clearly to frame all trade policies and agreements in a manner that would achieve sustainable development. In other words, trade policies and agreements cannot be counterproductive to the very institutional objective of achieving sustainable development. It is well established that this concept encompasses three general policy areas: social development, economic development, and environmental protection. This has been reiterated by several UN texts and many World Summit outcome documents.[56]

Right to Development as a Human Right

At the same time, the 1986 Declaration on the Right to Development by the UNGA has also recognized the right to development as a human right.[57] The declaration was adopted by a vote of 146 to 1 (the United States opposing), with 8 abstentions. The preamble of this declaration states that development is a comprehensive economic, social, cultural, and political process, which aims for the constant improvement of the well-being of the entire population and of all individuals on the basis of their active, free, and meaningful participation in development, as well as in the fair distribution of benefits resulting therefrom. This definition of the term "development" is relatively elastic, but nevertheless a people-centered approach to the meaning of development.

It is also in line with the work of Amartya Sen, who has explained development as the expansion of freedom of choice for human beings, both in terms of "processes that allow freedom of actions and decisions, and the actual opportunities that people have, given their personal and social circumstances."[58]

Article 1(1) of the declaration proclaims that "the right to development is an inalienable human right by virtue of which every human person and all peoples are entitled to

---

55 Op. Cit. FN 17, at P.1

56 United Nations, World Millennium Summit (2005): GA Doc. No. A/60/L.1, available at http://www.unep.org/greenroom/documents/outcome.pdf (retrieved on 14/08/2012)

57 United Nations, General Assembly: *Declaration on the Right to Development*, GA/41/128 of 4/12/1986, available at http://www2.ohchr.org/english/law/rtd.htm (retrieved on 14/08/2012)

58 Sen, Amartya (1999) – *Development as Freedom*, P. 17, Oxford University Press, City. See also United Nations, Economic and Social Council: *The Legal Nature of the Right to Development*, E/CN.4/Sub.2/2004/16 of 01/06/2004

participate in, contribute to, and enjoy economic, social, cultural and political development, in which all human rights and fundamental freedoms can be fully realized." The human person is the central subject of development, and should be the active participant and beneficiary of the right to development [Article 2(1)]. Various provisions of the declaration oblige states to frame policies that would propagate and further the human right to development of their citizens.

What follows from the aforesaid provisions is that the right to development is a self-standing right. At the same time, it is a composite of all other internationally recognized rights and freedoms. There are strong arguments today that the human right to development has become part of customary international law, and states are obliged to ensure the same to their citizens. The *opinio juris* of states is evident from the fact that 146 countries voted in favor of the declaration. Furthermore, states have consistently and emphatically reiterated thereafter that the right to development is an inviolable human right.[59] States also confirm the same in their practice by acting extensively and uniformly in virtually all fields of international law according to the principles set out in the 1986 declaration.[60] The millennium development goals and unequivocal commitment to them by states in their domestic policies is an eloquent example of this. Undoubtedly, skeptics have raised arguments that the "right to development" is not yet a part of customary international law, and being incapable of judicial enforcement is therefore not legally binding upon states; as such, it is not a human right at all. However, this argument is fallacious because it erroneously equates human rights with legal rights. In order to be recognized as a human right, the same need not necessarily be a legal right capable of judicial enforcement.[61] There is no doubt, therefore, that the right to development is a human right. The dispute regarding its legally binding nature as part of international human rights law is ongoing, but it is neither important nor decisive in the context of the present analysis. Assuming that there is no legal obligation on states to fulfill this right to

---

[59] Vienna Declaration and Programme of Action, World Conference on Human Rights, 48th Session (1993), UN Doc. A/CONF.157/23(1993)

[60] Op. Cit. FN. 10, at P.199. Also for a detailed analysis of the right to development as customary international law, see Aleinikoff, Thomas Alexander and Chetail, Vincent (2003) – *Migration and International Legal Norms*, P. 260, T.M.C. Asser Press, The Hague. See also Bedjaoui, Mohammed (2008) – "The Right to Development," in *International Human Rights in Context*, Edited by Steiner et al., P. 1447, Oxford University Press, City, for the extreme proposition that right to development is a *jus cogens* norm.

[61] See Sengupta, Arjun (2002) – "On the Theory and Practice of the Right to Development," *Human Rights Quarterly*, Vol. 24 (2002), P. 837-889 at P.859, where he explains that in order to be a human right, it is not necessary that it be also recognized as a legal right. See also Nickel, James (2007) – "Human Rights as Rights," in *Making Sense of Human Rights*, P. 22-34, Blackwell Publishing, City.

development as a self-standing right, there can be no doubt that, by virtue of the very nature of this right also being an amalgam of all other undisputed human rights, states are legally obliged to respect, protect, and fulfill at least the components thereof, and hence in effect, the very right itself.[62] In any case, there can be no doubt that by virtue of the declaration and individual state practice, this human right at minimum qualifies to be a political and moral obligation of states. This minimum position is sufficient for the purposes of the argument presented here.

The right to development and sustainable development

The concept of the right to development incorporates the notion of sustainable development and each of its three pillars. Similarly, sustainable development is inherently wedded to human rights, and cannot be fulfilled without also satisfying the *specific* human right to sustainable development. One cannot survive without the other, as they are interdependent and mutually overlapping. This is irrespective of whether the right to development is part of customary international law and therefore a legal obligation, or whether it is merely a political or moral obligation. In a report prepared for the Office of the United Nations High Commissioner (OHCHR) in 2004, Gutto has rightly noted that the right to development very well includes the notion of sustainable development, and that the former actually translates as the "right to sustainable development."[63]

Bringing WTO into the Picture

It is within this factual matrix that the link between human rights and trade can be found through the objective of "sustainable development" in the WTO Agreement itself, and not in extraneous human rights treaties. States are obliged to take human rights into consideration when operating at the WTO because the *institutional objective* of the WTO to ensure sustainable development, as enshrined in its preamble, mandates so. Human

62 See United Nations, Economic and Social Council: *Study on the current state of implementation of the Right to Development*, E/CN.4/1999/WG.18/2, Arjun Sengupta, Independent Expert on the Right to Development, 27/07/1999. In this report, Sengupta describes the right to development as a vector, wherein the vector itself is a self-standing human right; at the same time, the vector is also composed of all other human rights. Therefore, in order for states to improve the right to development, it is important that at least one of the components of the vector is enhanced, while none of the others deteriorates.

63 United Nations, Economic and Social Council: *The Legal Nature of the Right to Development*, E/CN.4/Sub.2/2004/16, Gutto, Shadrack, 01/06/2004.

rights are inextricably linked to development, while development is inseparably linked to trade. It may be worthwhile to note, in particular, the provisions of paragraph 3(3) of the 1986 declaration, which mandates states to realize their rights and fulfill their duties in such a manner as to promote "a new international economic order" based on sovereign equality, interdependence, mutual interest, and cooperation among all states, as well as to encourage the observance and realization of human rights. This clause in particular is of the utmost significance in that throughout the Uruguay round of negotiations around the same time, and while establishing the WTO almost a decade later, states were aware that they had committed to establishing a "new international economic order" in terms of the conceptions of paragraph 3(3) of the 1986 declaration.

In sum, the concept of the right to development suggests that the "appropriate" development strategy is one that conforms to the international human rights framework. Identifying this link of development between the human rights regime and the international trade regime culls out a pragmatic approach, which should rest to calm all opposition from states for bringing exogenous human rights treaties into WTO processes.

Now, it is necessary to acknowledge that this human right to development approach does not permit any party to make a claim before the DSB that the trade policies of another party are illegal because they breach the human right to development. This is because the obligation of states to formulate WTO policies with the aim of furthering the human right to development is borne in the concept of sustainable development as enshrined in the Preamble of the WTO Umbrella Agreement. Canons of interpretation of treaties do not accord the same value to preambles as they do to substantive provisions themselves. A substantive provision can be breached, as well as challenged before the DSB. On the other hand, the role of the preamble is limited to the interpretation of WTO agreements, i.e. only to provide context for interpreting substantive provisions. However, the fact remains that the Preamble of the WTO Umbrella Agreement asserts the purposes and objectives of the WTO in no uncertain terms; therefore, even if the same cannot be enforced through the DSB, states are obliged to take them into consideration while negotiating and acceding to WTO agreements. Similarly, if any inadequacies are found in the existing agreements whereby human rights concerns remain unprotected, or if the policy space of states to adequately deal with their human rights concerns is found lacking as a result of WTO obligations, the objective of sustainable development obliges states to remove them by subsequent negotiations. Given this position, this human right to development-based approach needs to be incorporated at all stages of the WTO process, including the stages of pre-negotiation, negotiation, and trade policy review.

To put this into context, the inadequacies in the DSU relating to economic compensations and in the TRIPS Agreement relating to additional waivers need to be rectified by way of negotiations, because the objective of sustainable development obliges so. Similarly, the lack of policy space created by the manner in which Article XX of the GATT operates must be removed, as the objective of sustainable development also obliges so. One way to avoid the negative impacts of trade regulations on the human rights situation in member states is through a "human rights impact assessment" of WTO agreements, policies, and decisions. At the very least, human rights impact assessments facilitate an informed negotiation and trade policy review process at the WTO. This mechanism has been explored before and, as such, is not developed in this paper.[64] The purpose here is to clearly identify this second category and find a pragmatic approach to addressing it. The approach essentially calls for undoing the limiting environment that some WTO laws create with respect to the policy space of states to address their own human rights concerns. States need to do so because the institutional objective of the WTO is sustainable development, which cannot be achieved without ensuring the respect, protection, and fulfillment of all human rights. This revisitation of the WTO provisions that limit policy space of states cannot be done by the DSB, but must be done collectively by states themselves at the WTO. They need to do so as part of their international law obligations by negotiating amendments to the already existing WTO laws. Similarly, while negotiating new WTO agreements, states must essentially take into account the impacts that trade laws may have on their policy space to address their human rights concerns.

Conclusion

In conclusion, it may be said that economic globalization in general and liberalization of trade in particular are irreversible processes. Barring global catastrophes, such as world war or climate change, these processes are here to stay, and in my judgment, there is

[64] For a detailed analysis of HRIA methods, see http://www.humanrightsimpact.org/introduction-to-hria/hria-tutorial/introduction/ (retrieved on 14/08/2012). See also Harrison, James and Goller, Alessa (2008) – "Trade and Human Rights: What does 'impact assessment' have to offer," *Human Rights Law Review*, Vol. 8, No.4 (2008), P. 587.

simply no option to backtrack now. All WTO members have invested massively in creating structural changes to their economies in order to adhere to the new world order. India, China, Brazil, and South Africa are eloquent examples of developing countries that benefit from the liberalized trading regime in general. However, it is a fact that these countries, along with other developing countries, also face significant human rights challenges in adjusting to this relatively new multilateral trading regime. The right to employment, work, and health, amongst others, are casualties in the process for many of the poorer states. Even so, states have legally bound themselves to the liberalized trading regime on the economic logic that these casualties should be transitory, and eventually comparative advantages would adjust themselves, along with the citizens working within these economies. In view of the probably irreversible nature of liberalization, a pragmatic approach is needed to handle the complex multilateral trade-human rights linkages. Therefore, the appropriate manner in which to address these concerns is through a human right to development approach, as discussed above. There is growing literature oriented towards this approach, and methods for embedding this culture in the WTO to ensure its permeation through all processes should be the vision for further action. Human rights impact assessments provide a helpful starting point in this context; however, other means could also be developed. In the same breath, it is important to realize that the complexities and multidimensional nature of multilateral trade-human rights linkages should not be a concern of states under only the WTO. The deconstruction of these linkages carried out in this paper has demonstrated that, in some areas, the UN – and in particular, its specialized agency, the ILO – must also assume this responsibility. Pragmatism mandates that the development of methods to address concerns arising from these linkages must occur within the existing systems themselves. Thus, cooperation from all actors involved in these linkages - the states, the UN, and the WTO - is inevitable for the coexistence of both the human rights regime and the international trade regime. In the past few years, the UN, WTO, and Bretton Woods institutions have taken steps to constitute annual high-level meetings comprised of representatives from all institutions to work progressively towards achieving their respective mandates.[65] This is another apt starting point, and it acknowledges that addressing the issue of multilateral trade-human rights linkages demands a pragmatic approach. This is ultimately the only way to fulfill the solemn objectives enshrined in the preambles of both the UN Charter and WTO Umbrella Agreement without these

---

[65] See for more information World Trade Organization: *The WTO and United Nations*, available at http://www.wto.org/english/theWTO_e/coher_e/wto_un_e.htm (retrieved on 14/08/2012)

institutions condemning each other or states compartmentalizing their international law obligations into two separate camps in complete isolation from each other. In contrast, the pragmatic approach proposed here could ensure international integration and linkages between the existing legal obligations of states with regards to both the WTO and human rights.

CHAPTER 10

PARADIGMS LOST AND FOUND? THE EMERGENT INTERNATIONAL LEGAL ORDER

Thomas Bourdreau

Paradigm Lost? State-Centric International Law

Historical events in and after World War II resulted in a virtual revolution in the current international legal order, which became much more differentiated, complex, and pluralistic. Summarizing the information in Chapter 1, the most noticeable changes were subsequent innovations in the following:

a) Legal and specifically fiduciary norms, duties, and obligations, as well as other relationships between the nation and the state, resulting in a modern law of nations that relevant courts should further interpret, develop, and apply when necessary;

b) New legal limits on state authority to unilaterally legitimate violence by the state, except, in cases of self-defense against *armed attack*, as stated in Article 51 of the UN Charter. If a state blatantly violates this, post-war legal innovations ensured, if necessary, domestic or international prosecutions for war crimes to end the age of impunity for leaders so that *nemo judex in sua causa* or literally, "no-one should be a judge in his own cause";

c) One way to prevent the state from being the "judge of its own actions," such as with armed attacks or aggression, is the Nuremberg Charter's (1945) innovation of providing for international legal jurisdiction over individuals accused of crimes committed in the name of the state, especially when domestic jurisdiction fails or is unable to do so;

d) The historic and legal recognition of the right to self-determination, which a group possesses prior to actual statehood; the establishment of this principle in the Atlantic Charter (1941) first, and then the UN Charter, led to the historic wave of decolonization around the world after the war;

e) The advent of international human rights regimes and other legal protections designed, in large part, to prevent state or sub-state oppression and violence against human beings either as individuals or groups. The evolving International Bill of Human Rights or Raphael Lemkin's pioneering efforts to successfully create the Convention on the Prevention and Punishment of Genocide (1948), as discussed in Chapter 1, are examples of these profound legal innovations;

f) Perhaps least expected is the increasing obsolescence of the past legal and political belief that the juridical concept of "domestic jurisdiction" was an almost impermeable barrier. After the horrors of World War II, this once nearly unchallengeable defense by states is now proving to be a highly porous boundary that no longer prevents other governments or courts from judicial or other interventions to protect the domestic populations of an offending state;

g) As mentioned earlier, the strengthening of universal obligations or common and shared jurisdiction concerning legal obligations in wartime or military occupations, including war crimes and crimes against humanity. The pioneering "Martens Clause" is one older example of this principle; more recently, the shared obligations of the high contracting parties found in common Article 1 of the 1949 Geneva Conventions are further critical examples of such joint or "common" legal obligations, which can be adjudicated in international, regional, national, or indigenous courts;

h) As argued in Chapter 1, the creation of a new public law of nations that includes the traditional fiduciary legal order concerning the global commons, which can and will evolve in the future, as does almost any other legal order. These profound changes simply cannot be accommodated, without reductionist simplifications, in the old paradigm of international law consisting largely of norms, agreements, or recognized practice between sovereign states.

Since World War II, legal scholars have struggled to capture and define the nature and scope of these legal innovations,[1] spurred by massive deaths of human beings across

---

[1] For instance, there are various alternatives proposed by Ruti Teitel, (2013) *Humanity's Law*, Oxford University Press, Reprint edition (May 1, 2013); Anne Marie Slaughter's "New World Order"; The emergence of the Responsibility to Protect (R2P) doctrine, as well as the revival of natural law theories within international law advocated by Jeremy

much of the globe that culminated in the unparalleled horrors of the Holocaust.[2] Such unimaginable atrocities and human losses demanded political, moral, and legal prescriptions and condemnation, coupled with the immense popular demand that such a war never be faced or fought again.

So, even as the war was waged and the human costs of the war continued to escalate, the Allied powers promised in the Moscow Declaration in 1943 to establish a new international organization, the UN, to help preserve the peace and protect human rights after the war was won. (Such an organization was clearly implied, but due to President Roosevelt's fear of the isolationist influence back home, it was not made fully explicit in the Atlantic Charter back in 1941.)[3] Much blood was spilled between the Moscow Declaration and the near end of the war in the spring of 1945. As a result, a war-weary world looked to their wartime leaders and battled tested diplomats gathering in San Francisco in late April 1945 to forge the new Charter of the UN that would sustain wartime promises to forge a better world in which such a war could never occur again. Hopes were high; as one American paratrooper in France wrote to his congressman, "We can win this war but you must win the peace."

This is why almost the entire world was watching the commencement of the UN drafting convention in San Francisco in April 1945, including Pvt. Joe Polowsky and his comrades in a United States Army patrol driving that morning through German-held territory to the River Torgau. This patrol was, in essence, the most advanced Allied troops from the West in Europe.[4] The diplomats and statesmen opened the drafting convention for the UN Charter on April 25, the same day that Pvt. Polowsky and his comrades linked up with the Soviets on the Elbe River, deep in the heart of Germany. Despite the dangers, Polowsky and his comrades were keenly aware of the opening of

---

Waldron and others. Alternative paradigms include post-war legal developments being described by David Scheidermann and Ernst Petersman as the new international "Constitutionalism" in economic matters. Finally, there is the new paradigm offered here of a new law of nations. Thanks to Prof. Jose Alvarez for these references.

[2] See: PETER LONGERICH [2]See PETER LONGERICH, *HOLOCAUST: THE NAZI PERSECUTION AND MURDER OF THE JEWS*. (Oxford Univ. Press Inc., 2010). See: Anthony D'Amato,* Human Rights as Part of Customary International Law: A Plea for Change of Paradigms, 25 Ga. J. Int'l & Comp. L. 47-98, Fall, 1995 /Winter, 1996. This essay is a partial answer to Prof. D'Amato excellent challenge and groundbreaking article.

[3] The isolationists were a formidable domestic factor in American politics until Pearl Harbor. See, for instance: Lynne Olson, (2013) *Those Angry Days: Roosevelt, Lindbergh, and America's Fight Over World War II, 1939-194, passim.* MANFRED JONAS, (1989) *Isolationism in America 1935-1941* [Paperback] (Imprint Pubns, 1989). Also: WAYNE COLE, *Roosevelt and the Isolationists, 1932-1945.* (Univ. of Nebraska Press, 1983, 698 pp.)

[4] See "The Law of Nations" (2012) J.Juris p. 285-352, as well as Studs Terkel, *The Good War: An Oral history of World War II* (1997) The New Press, Reprint edition.

the UN drafting convention on the same day, several thousand miles away. It was an auspicious beginning. While the drafting of the UN Charter continued for several months, the war progressed to its bloody conclusion – first in Europe, and finally in the Pacific.

When coupled with the Nuremberg Charter, the end result of the San Francisco Drafting Convention – the Charter of the UN – marks a virtual watershed in the evolution and development of international law. As already mentioned, these are the "twin offspring" of World War II, as described by General Telford Taylor earlier. In particular, the UN Charter is really a hybrid document, consisting of both treaty and trust law, since its drafting was clearly one of the wartime promises the Allied powers had made to help mobilize the millions of people needed to win. As such, trust law is obviously a source of international law and binds states as a basic condition of their legitimate authority. With these critical changes to the old paradigm of international law first defined by Bentham, something much greater, more diverse, and more pluralistic arose from World War II and post-war legal innovation in international law. Since the drafting and adoption of the Nuremberg and UN Charters, as well as other resulting legal conventions or documents emerging out of World War II, legal scholars and practitioners have struggled to define a new *and accurate* paradigm of the international legal order that accurately reflects and describes this new and living legal landscape.[5]

Even so, international consensus over any new or controlling definition of the new international legal order is likely to be difficult to obtain and emerge only gradually. These difficulties will potentially be compounded, since any such plausible paradigm *must first and foremost describe and explain international law as it has actually and historically developed.* Jurisprudence ignores history at its own peril, and must rediscover the powerful impact of the actual, not simply the abstract, on the living law. [6] This "historical grounding" is critical, especially if the peoples of the world are to finally enjoy the rights so dearly earned during the horrors, Holocaust, and immensely costly battles of that worldwide war.

---

[5] See: *supra*, ftnote 1. The final paradigm may well prove to be a fusion of some or all of these efforts….
See for example, Edgar Bodenheimer, (1974) *Jurisprudence: The Philosophy and Method of the Law.* (Harvard Univ. Press, 1974).

Specifically, the idea that Bentham's paradigm of the international legal order consisted largely of "agreements or practice by states" requires significant expansion and must be historically grounded in the profound legal developments that have occurred since his death. As evidenced in Chapter 1, (Please disregard the following deletion of chapter 1>) the historical and legal innovations and developments triggered by World War II helped to define and describe a new paradigm based upon the fiduciary nature of the Allied powers' wartime declarations and promises *to their own and other peoples of the world.* In this regard, it should be noted that the British philosopher John Locke describes governments as simply trustees that must preserve the rights of the people who are both the trustors and beneficiaries of this fiduciary arrangement.[7] Locke's ideas provide crucial insight to the actual history of the war: namely, that the Allied governments became the enduring trustees of these "promises made" once the war was finally won.

Every principle of domestic law insists that solemn promises, however general, that are made in *good faith* to others who then consent and act upon these pledges, must be kept. The great jurist Prof. Oscar Schachter has stated that "good faith" is a binding principle of international law as well. Thus, the peoples of the world have now become the beneficiaries of the resulting fiduciary obligations created by the declaratory and promissory statements of the Allies concerning the purposes of the war. In short, the people or "nation" assumed extraordinary importance in these promissory statements, declarations, and charters that had been made during wartime. As in Chapter 1, the terms "people" or "nation" are definable here as a "jural community" in which members have shared moral and legal obligations to each other, as well as a communal consensus concerning the appropriate dispute resolution mechanisms to be used among them, such as the courts. As such, the depth and extent of these shared legal and moral obligations can be empirically tested. (See Michael Barkun's classic book *Law without Sanctions* (1968) for an elaboration of this definition of a "jural community" found first in the anthropological literature.) During and after World War II, such nations took on new meaning and significance in international law.

---

[7] JOHN LOCKE, SECOND TREATISE OF GOVERNMENT (C.B. Macpherson ed., Hackett Publ'g reprt. 1980). *See also* A. JOHN SIMMONS, ON THE EDGE OF ANARCHY: LOCKE, CONSENT, AND THE LIMITS OF SOCIETY (Princeton Univ. Press reprt. 1995). Finally *see*: WILLIAM EBENSTEIN, GREAT POLITICAL THINKERS: PLATO TO THE PRESENT 120 (Holt, Rinehart & Winston 4th ed. 1969). Locke's definition of property that includes one's life, liberties, and what we would today construe as rights.

Specifically, in their promissory declarations, the Allies appealed to their own and other nations, as well as to the conquered, colonial, or neutral peoples of the world, to make the sacrifices necessary to win the war. As such, the people or nation can no longer be regarded as purely a passive presence, or described merely as a "population" in international law. These promises made to the peoples of the world in such dire times of mortal danger must be honored. Future domestic, international, and indigenous courts' decisions will have to determine when and how the Allied promises made to millions of their own and other peoples can be construed or constructed as implied, executive, and enduring trusts or fiduciary norms and duties that belong to the people or nations of the world, not the state.

This actual historical account differs from Locke's *Treatise* in significant ways. Most importantly, Locke believed that the people themselves take the initiative, once they have left the state of nature via the social contract, to create a government as a fiduciary trust. As such, Locke's theoretical scenario differs from the historical circumstances surrounding governments during World War II, in which they initiated the promissory declarations and documents that were effectively made to their own and other peoples. These provided the "seeds" of the "promises to keep" by governments and courts that were to later grow and flourish if the war was first won. If so, as in Locke's theoretical scenario, the people of the world become both the *trustors and beneficiaries* of the resulting fiduciary obligations, duties, and norms that this essay has characterized as a new law of nations.

Modern human rights law has its origins in these same legal developments, especially in the fiduciary promises made by governments to their own and other peoples during the darkest times of the war. The UN Charter, a treaty binding on states, partially redeemed these promises by recognizing human rights on the international level. Coupled with the Atlantic Charter, also cited and "subscribed to" in the Declaration of January 1, 1942,[8] these promissory documents were the very beginning of the law of nations that was, with the coming victory, to reach its partial fulfillment in the Charter of the UN.[9] In particular, the Atlantic Charter recognized the right of peoples to self-determination as a war aim of the Allies. The Nuremberg Charter afforded added rights and protections to peoples defined as a group, if attacked. Due in part to these developments, which were

[8] See "Law of Nations," (2012) J.juris 285 44.

[9] See "Law of Nations," *supra*,.

forged in the agony of the greatest war in human history, the law of nations emerged as an *independent legal order that now, among other things, represents a law common to humanity and governs the relationships between the state or government and its own and other peoples.*

As such, the people or nation and its courts, as an independent jural community or civil society, are the new *imperium et imperii,* or ultimate source, as well as the beneficiaries of the norms of self-determination, human rights, and collective security in international affairs. Most importantly, and as mentioned earlier, the idea that other states or judicial institutions *cannot intervene* in the domestic jurisdiction of an offending state no longer legally "excuses" a state from outside international or judicial scrutiny. Simply stated, domestic courts cannot surrender their common and shared jurisdictions over the law of nations to the servile excuse that the case presents a nonjusticiable political question. Furthermore, as Prof. D' Amato and other legal scholars have noted, many of these developments – especially in human rights – are now entrenched in customary international law as well. For instance, modern international human rights regimes have much of their origins in the new fiduciary norms that governments recognized during the war. In the future, it will be the task of individual courts and different domestic, international, regional, or indigenous jurisdictions to give these legal norms and protections continual, if not greater, life and meaning when applied to new and complex challenges confronting individuals or groups as a whole, especially if they are under violent attack by states, substate actors, or terrorists.

In short, the World War II legal developments unquestionably resulted in a profoundly significant seismic shift in the legal landscape of international law or related norms, obligations, and relations. In his book *The Structure of Scientific Revolutions*, Thomas Kuhn describes such profound changes as "paradigm shifts" in the prevailing worldviews of the theorists, scholars, and practitioners in a particular field.[10] The preceding analysis throughout this chapter argues that, in effect, the old paradigm of "state-centric" international law is simply inadequate to describe the historical and legal developments ushered in by World War II. Indeed, the old paradigm is metaphorically "lost at sea" and cannot seem to find the necessary maps to accurately navigate back to a safe harbor in the profoundly changed coastlines and landscape of the new legal world.

[10] See: Kuhn, T.S. *The Structure of Scientific Revolutions*. Chicago: University of Chicago Press, 1962

Blackstone and Bentham: The Oxford Opposites on the International Legal Order

At such a moment, it is possibly very helpful, or even necessary, to remember the defining characteristics of the old paradigm or map of international law. Specifically, this requires asking and briefly exploring the question: How did the prevailing paradigm or "map" of international law as consisting largely of "agreements between states" originate? In his book chapter on Blackstone and Bentham, Mark Janis has tried to answer this by conducting a remarkable study on the competing versions of William Blackstone and Jeremy Bentham in late 18th century England concerning the nature of the international legal order.[11] Janis highlights that in the period from 1765 to 1769, the great English jurist William Blackstone wrote his famous legal *Commentaries*, in which he defined the law of nations as one that *municipal courts could engage in and decide upon*:

> The law of nations is a system of rules, deducible by natural reason, and established by universal consent among the civilized inhabitants of the world;[1] in order to decide all disputes, to regulate all ceremonies and civilities, and to insure the observance frequently occur between two or more independent states, and the individuals belonging to each.[2]This general law is founded upon this principle, that different nations ought in time of peace to do one another all the good they can; and, in time of war, as little harm as possible, without prejudice to their own real interests.[3] And, as none of these states will allow a superiority in the other, therefore neither can dictate or prescribe the rules of this law to the rest; but such rules must necessarily result from those principles of natural justice, in which all the learned of every nation agree: or they depend upon mutual compacts or treaties between the respective communities; in the construction of which there is also no judge to resort to, but the law of nature and reason, being the only one in which all the contracting parties are equally conversant, and to which they are equally subject.[12]

[11] Mark Janis, 2010, *America and the Law of Nations*, Oxford: Oxford University Press, p. 1-15; Also see: Willem Theo Oosterveld, The Law of Nations in Early American Foreign Policy: Theory and Practice (2015), Brill Publ.

[12] Blackstone, BOOK 4, CHAPTER 5, OF OFFENSES AGAINST THE LAW OF NATIONS. QUOTED IN JANIS, *OP. CIT.*, P.9

In Blackstone's definition, the law of nations includes and applies equally to "states," "individuals," "nations," and "all contracting parties." This defines the subject matter of the law of nations in large "broad-strokes," with potentially expansive application. Most importantly, later in the same passage he gives a critical role to the "common law," which often requires the courts or a "municipal" or domestic court in adjudicating key aspects of the law of nations. This is an essential component in a modern law of nations as well, and so far seems to be happening through the diffusion of legal norms across national jurisdictions rather than any pure adherence to a doctrinaire definition of "international law." However, rather unfortunately, Blackstone then emphasized the uncertain role of "natural reason" in deducing and discerning the role and reach of the law of nations. In fairness, by doing so, Blackstone was simply trying to follow in the footsteps of past influential jurists, such as Suarez, Wolff, and Vattel.[13]

Yet, by doing so, and by attempting to establish the origins of the relevant law in "natural reason," Blackstone's resulting definition of the law of nations lacks any historical specificity, and more importantly, any limiting legal precision. Specifically, his system of law is guided by the law of nature and "natural reason" – not by actual historical legal developments, actual texts, historic charters, or promissory declarations. Posed in this way, Blackstone's definition of the law of nations seems rather vague and all-inclusive. As a result, a perceptive Oxford student listening to one of Blackstone's lectures – the young Jeremy Bentham – was intensely dissatisfied with Blackstone's definition. Trained as a lawyer (though he never practiced), Bentham believed that relations between states and nations needed greater clarification and reform.

So, perhaps unsurprisingly, only 20 years later in 1789, David Bentham coined the term "international law" and defined it in the following, highly rigorous terms: "There remain, then, the mutual transactions between sovereigns, as such, for the subject of that branch of jurisprudence which may be properly and exclusively termed international…"[14]

---

[13] *IBID.*, BLACKSTONE SPECIFICALLY STATES: "therefore the law of nations (wherever any question arises which is properly the object of its jurisdiction) is here adopted in its full extent by the common law, and is held to be a part of the law of the land." ALSO SEE: T. Hochstrasser (Editor), (2003) P. Schröder, (Editors). *Early Modern Natural Law Theories: Context and Strategies in the Early Enlightenment* (International Archives of the History of Ideas Archives internationales d'histoire des idées) [Hardcover]. Springer; 2003 edition.

[14] Janis, supra, ftnote 11, p 13; also see: Bentham, Jeremy (1789). *An Introduction to the Principles of Morals and Legislation.* London: T. Payne.

Bentham perceived his new contribution in terms of a reformist agenda that he aspired to apply to law in general; the happiness or greatest good for the greatest number could be obtained when the sovereign's right to rule was recognized. Thus, ensuring the rule and authority of the sovereign could presumably preserve domestic peace most effectively.[15] Yet, in defining international law in this way, Bentham has totally rejected the relationship between the sovereign with its own and other peoples as a source of needed regulation, let alone law, and thus exempts this critical relationship, including the colonial one (perhaps unwittingly), from judicial review.

The problems with this definition of international law were almost immediately apparent; for instance, because of Bentham's definition, customary law instantly became an "orphan child" of international law, since it clearly is not often the initial result of a simple agreement between sovereigns, except in a secondary and derivative form as "state practice." Yet, when customary law is relegated to merely a state practice, this unfortunately results in a greatly diminished and deformed definition since so many rich and enduring examples of customary law have existed among peoples, princes, or the "powers and principalities" prior to states or statehood, and still exist despite the advent and ensuing "state practice" of total war in the 19th and 20th centuries.

So, in contrast, customary law is best understood as a traditional practice of the people that is subsequently "recognized" or tolerated by an empire, kingdom, or – later – a state. For instance, I would argue that customary law concerning the protection of ambassadors, places of worship, the wounded or imprisoned, or even hospitals or schools, do not disappear simply because state practice, terrorists, or both have seen fit to increasingly slaughter such protected individuals or decimate such protected places with increasing regularity, ferocity, and self-righteousness. In short, when left stranded under Bentham's conception of international law, customary law all too often becomes simply that which fits into the eye of the beholder.[16]

Yet, even as an "orphan," customary law is still recognized as a main source of international law, and the first of what Thomas Kuhn has called evidence of an episodic

---

[15] Janis, *op. cit.*, p. 10-20.

[16] See, for instance, Anthony D'Amato, "Trashing Customary International Law" *The American Journal of International Law*, Vol. 81, No. 1 (Jan., 1987), pp. 101-105

exception, in this case in the Benthamite paradigm of international law; there will be many more…

Nor is there any room in Bentham's definition for the role or rights of the people on an international plane, *unless* agreed upon by power-seeking sovereigns or states. Hence, if strictly adhering to Bentham's definition, human rights are essentially given or "recognized" *only* by the state, a clearly unacceptable practice or idea, except perhaps to dictators.[17]

Furthermore, the whole idea of trusts or solemn promises between a government and its own and other people as a source of international legal obligations also becomes "impossible" *by definition*, even though most law-abiding jurisdictions around the world would recognize and respect such solemn promises made within a domestic society as a legal and "fiduciary" obligation. Most importantly, after Bentham, the "people" or nation became purely a passive presence in the definition of the state or international law, and had minimal independent legal recognition until the subsequent upheavals and wars of the 20th century.[18]

Finally, and most importantly at the time, is that Bentham's conception and definition of "international law" had, perhaps unintentionally, an enormous global import in terms of legitimating European control of its colonies. As Anthony Anghie argues in his book *Imperialism, Sovereignty and the Making of International Law*, international law as defined by Bentham and further shaped by John Austin was uniquely suited to favor the Europeans in their "colonial confrontation" with the peoples in the rest of the globe.[19]

---

[17] A Stalin would probably be very happy with such a definition, and would never agree with the reasoning of say, a Jefferson, or for that matter, Locke. See, for instance, Leo Strauss, *Natural Right and History* (University of Chicago Press, 1965).

[18] Jeremy Bentham ordered his body embalmed, and his head set upon a tray after this death; his embalmed "presence" still graces a closet at the University of London, which he helped to found. I simply suggest that his definition of international law is—in view of historical developments since his death-- as disembodied now as well.

[19] Anthony Anghie, (2004) *Imperialism, Sovereignty and the Making of International Law* (University of Cambridge Press, 2004).

Also: Dirk Moses, (2008) *Empire, Colony, Genocide: Conquest, Occupation and Subaltern Resistance in World History* Berghahn/Oxford (editor). Finally, see: CARL SCHMITT, NOMOS OF THE EARTH IN THE INTERNATIONAL LAW OF JUS PUBLICUM EUROPAEUM (G.V. Ulman trans., 2003).

20 See Janis,[Janis! Thanks] supra, ftnote 11; Also see: See CARL SCHMITT, surpra Also see: Julian Waterman, Thomas Jefferson and Blackstone's Commentaries, 27 Ill. L. Rev. 629 (1932-1933) Finally, see the magnificent HOMI K. BHABHA (1994) "Of Mimicry and Man: The Ambivalence of Colonial Discourse," in THE LOCATION OF CULTURE, 85-92. Prof. Bhabha's idea of the Europeans colonizing and policing even the once-autonomous

In particular, the rebellious American colonies at the time were directly influenced by and even quoted Vattel and Blackstone in their rationale for independence.[20] For the European colonial powers jealously guarding their vast colonial acquisitions overseas, this simply would not suffice. The American Revolution was undoubtedly a warning, if not a wake-up call, concerning the importance of failing to grant legal power and legitimacy to groups of peoples, such as colonies or their limited provincial legislatures designed to provide immensely limited "self-government." An alternative and more limiting definition had to be found if further colonial uprisings were to be legally delegitimized and outlawed from the very beginning of any future potential or real unrest. So, Bentham's limiting and scholarly definition soon found favor and acceptance in most of the ruling courts and capitals in Europe, and slowly but surely elsewhere as well.

In short, as Anthony Anghie and others have argued, prevailing normative narratives had to fit the political practices of profit and power valued by the emergent European colonial states; in particular, international law conceived as narrowly as Bentham had – as the law created by sovereign states – privileged the political practices of European states, which were then subjecting most of the global "peoples" to colonialism, and made their colonial power and jurisdiction more absolute.[21] Oppressing or exploiting an entire people – the essence of colonialism – then became a matter of "domestic jurisdiction" and not subject further to other "states." Thus, this paradigm of concentrated state power and control lasted until the "nation state" reached its murderous and extreme expression in Hitler's Germany.

In short, Bentham's "state-centric" definition of international law proved to be highly "utilitarian," at least for European colonial powers, during the subsequent years that represented the height of European colonial empires overseas. As such, this convenient "colonial" definition of "international law" largely persisted even beyond World War I until the advent of the Nazi state and consequent outbreak of World War II. The ensuing massive crimes of the Nazis against their own and others peoples that

---

peripheries of other cultures through contrasting narratives and implicit normative frameworks is fascinating, and to the point.

[21] Ibid., ftnotes 19 and 20, supra

culminated in the unimaginable terror of the Holocaust has forever shattered – or, at least, it should have – the prevailing paradigm of international law as only those obligations and agreements voluntarily accepted or "practiced" between states.

In this regard, as Chapter 1 has illustrated, President Roosevelt deliberately ensured such an anti-colonial outcome to the war when he insisted on this point as a preeminent war aim in the Atlantic Charter, which became the condition for entry of the United States into World War II. By the president's deliberate design, this moment – August 1941, when the Atlantic Charter was signed and the United States was still at peace – became the real beginning of the end for European colonial empires. This guaranteed that after the war, the peoples or nations of the state could no longer be simply a mere matter of "domestic jurisdiction." Practically every legal innovation of World War II and afterwards aimed to recognize the rights of peoples to "self-determination" and the saliency of human rights, end the unilateral use of force, and thus ensure the impossibility of such legal reification of state power, which reached its horrific apotheosis in the Nazi regime.

So, Bentham's definition has a compelling simplicity that was compatible with the times and seemed to suffice for decades until the emergence of the lawless Leviathan of Nazi Germany, which sought to do all actions to its own or other peoples under the fake, and indeed profane, pretenses of "legality." When World War II began, the Nazis waged an unprecedented, massive war on domestic "populations," including their own people and especially Jewish Germans and other Jews, under Hitler's devastating occupation. Simultaneously, the Nazis waged war *upon entire peoples* that they had captured, culminating in the murderous Holocaust, which subsequently horrified the world and the fighting Allied soldiers who liberated skeletal survivors from the death camps.[22]

In view of the unprecedented agony and horror of the war, international law could not regard the people or nation as simply passive presences merely within the domestic jurisdiction of a sovereign state. Many of the legal innovations made during and after the war were intended precisely to protect such civilian populations, as well as punish the perpetrators who had attacked them. Thus, a people or nation, as well as individuals,

[22] See supra, Footnote 2 {not 3}—my mistake—again!}. For instance, on a personal note, when I was quite little, I had a friend, Peter Hewitt, whose father had liberated a death camp while the latter was a captain in the US Army in Europe during World War II. My friend's father had trouble sleeping at night, and would never talk to us about what he saw—though we were all very proud of his service, though we did not quite understand why or what happened at the time, as we now do, or try to understand the vast, murderous magnitude of the Holocaust....

now have an enduring and inviolate standing under international law – as they imperfectly did in Blackstone's conception concerning the law of nations.

Many of the post-war legal innovations and developments were implemented with this goal clearly in mind; for instance, Raphael Lemkin's near-solo and heroic efforts towards the prevention and punishment of the crime of genocide that have been discussed above are a profound case in point.[23] So, in view of actual historical developments during World War II, *a necessity arose for an adequate definition of international law that incorporates and protects the peoples of the world from the violence of their own or other governments, and from terrorists or other substate actors.* The rights of the people or nation, as well as the human rights of the individual, could no longer be sidelined or ignored; *in particular, the legal obligations and relationships, duties, and norms that a government creates when it makes solemn promises to its own and others peoples simultaneously must now be recognized as part of international law.* It was the vast and utter agony of World War II that birthed the public law of nations as a fully emergent legal order. This obviously complicates the once-simplified international legal landscape that Bentham's definition of international law conveniently provided to European colonial powers. In the wake of World War II, a more accurate definition of this new international law is clearly needed to account for the profound and complex legal developments during and after the war that are established within the state and between nations and their governments. In view of this, and with due diffidence to Occam's razor, the simplest answer may not be the best, as modern algorithms attest; in particular, too much would be omitted and lost through the continued acceptance of Bentham's overly exclusive definition of international law as consisting of only those agreements between sovereign states. This simply is not accurate anymore in view of the legal innovations, developments, and realities that have occurred since Bentham and the

---

[23] See: Convention on the Prevention and Punishment of the Crime of Genocide, Dec. 9, 1948, 78 U.N.T.S. 277 (entered into force Jan. 12, 1951) *available at* http://www.hrweb.org/legal/genocide.html; *see also* JOHN COOPER, RAPHAEL LEMKIN AND THE GENOCIDE CONVENTION (Palgrave Macmillan 2008). HERBERT HIRSCH, GENOCIDE AND THE POLITICS OF MEMORY. Chapel Hill: University of North Caroline Press, 1995). Finally, *see*: IRVING LOUIS HOROWITZ, GENOCIDE: STATE POWER AND MASS MURDER (Transaction Books, 1976). Raphael Lemkin is a hero of humanity; the Genocide Convention is largely the result of his lifelong efforts to outlaw mass killings, an effort he began as a Polish lawyer under the League of Nations. He finally succeeded in 1948 at the United Nations, though unbelievably, in a terrible and cruel irony, much of his own family perished in the Holocaust during World War II. He worked for the United States government during World War II and at Nuremberg to account for Nazi war crimes. In tribute, I devote almost an entire chapter to this remarkable man in my forthcoming book, *Law of Nations, Legal Order in a Violent World.*

1780s, during the European colonial era that was to finally die in the agony and aftermath of World War II.

Paradigm Found? The International Legal Order

As argued above, a new, fully explicit and evolving fiduciary law of nations came into being with the hard-earned victory of the Allies in World War II, the greatest war in human history. The legal innovations that occurred or culminated during this bloody period almost completely shifted the sole sovereign center of magnetic force in the international legal order from the state to include the nation, group, and individual. As the war and its historical and legal aftermath made clear, neither the individual nor the "nation" could be excluded any longer from international law and its protections.

Because of this decisive expansion of international legal norms, *the current international legal order must be able to incorporate the competing visions of Bentham's state-centric law and Blackstone's earlier emphasis on subjects besides the states; Blackstone also emphasized the authority of municipal or domestic courts to adjudicate the "law of nations." Specifically, Blackstone states:* "therefore the law of nations (wherever any question arises which is properly the object of its jurisdiction) is here adopted in its full extent by the common law, and is held to be a part of the law of the land." (The common law in England is interested by courts throughout the land.) According to Blackstone's definition of the law of nations, courts did not automatically hide behind the servile shield *of a* nonjusticiable political question. Under a modern and renewed law of nations like that proposed in Chapter 1, courts must weigh each unique case on its own legal merits.

A partial synthesis of these two men's visions is possible, and in view of historical and legal developments, even necessary. Since "states" as such seem to be permanent fixtures, Bentham's and Blackstone's seemingly incompatible versions of specific roles for domestic judicial decision must be integrated into a new paradigm and practice of international law. Such a paradigm must include the actual historical and legal evolution of the international legal order during and after World War II; in particular, the creation or recognition of international law can no longer be defined simply in terms of "states," thus evading a historically adequate and legally accurate definition of the international legal order as it now exists. As the essay "Law of Nations" has stated, the new law applies broadly to entire peoples or nations, directly to individuals, in terms of human rights or liability (i.e. Nuremberg), and to states. Thus, if any individual attacks another individual, group, or a nation, he or she can be liable and tried for war crimes and, if the facts so indicate, be charged with crimes against humanity or peace as well. These innovations simply do not "fit" into Bentham's conveniently "colonial" conception of inter-state law, except as ancillary or almost historically accidental events. As the authors have tried to argue throughout this volume, such an antiquated understanding of international law is simply no longer adequate or accurate for the current world.

In particular, Bentham's definition of international law no longer explains the profound legal protections given to groups, such as in the Nuremberg Charter and trials, or to individuals, as expressed in the very first article of the UN Charter, which recognizes human rights, and subsequently reflected in the development of the International Bill of Human Rights.[24] In contrast, the fiduciary law of nations clearly and consistently recognizes such peoples or nations as preeminent, invokes punishment for any individuals attacking any other individuals, peoples, or nations so defined, and establishes it an international crime of the first import. There is simply no legal consistency in Bentham's conception of international law concerning these issues – existing as essentially agreements between sovereign states – unless one limply argues that such protections, rights, duties, and punishments are essentially *gratis*, or agreed upon as *gifts* of the state.

So, at the very least, there are now *twin poles in international law:* the state and the nation coexisting in an often-uneasy alliance that is sometimes nearly seamless, and other times actually torn asunder by growing abuses, aggression, and even atrocities by the state when it violently attacks its own or other peoples. In fact, much of the violence in the

---

[24] See Janis, supra, ftnote *11*, p 12-3.

**See* Universal Declaration of Human Rights, G.A. Res. 217A at 71, U.N. GAOR, 3d Sess, 1st plen.mtg., U.N. DOC A/810 (Dec. 12, 1948); *see also*: JOHANNES MORSINK. THE UNIVERSAL DECLARATION OF HUMAN RIGHTS ORIGINS, DRAFTING AND INTENT (Bert B. Lockwood, Jr., ed., Univ. of Pa. Press 1999); *see also*: MARY ANN GLENDON, WORLD MADE NEW: ELENOR ROOSEVELT AND THE UNIVERSAL DECLARATION OF HUMAN RIGHTS. Random House Trade Paperbacks; 1st edition (June 11, 2002). Finally, see: WILLIAM R. SLOMANSON, FUNDAMENTAL PERSPECTIVES ON INTERNATIONAL LAW (Wadsworth Publ'g Co. 6th ed. 2010) (1990) which provides an excellent overview and summary concerning the contents of the International Bill of Human Rights Law. Also see: UN GA resolution A/RES/543(VI). Also see D'Amato, supra, ftnote 2; In short, human rights are no longer nonjusticiable political questions.

world today is internal to the state; some or all of its people may rise up against the government and state and thus launch a civil war. These conflicts too now have international protections. The actual legal, political, and diplomatic history of World War II is decisive in this regard; the demand for a new definition of international law is a belated acknowledgment of this need to recognize the *actual historical political, military, and legal realities and developments of that war.* The atrocities committed in World War II, culminating in the Holocaust, simply had no precedent or parallel in modern human history. As such, the survivors of that war attempted to construct enduring international structures and innovative court procedures, which were reviewed earlier in this journal in the essay "Law of Nations" (2016), for legal protections and interventions to preclude the recurrence of such horrible events. The emergence of a public and fiduciary law of nations was an unintended, but perhaps inevitable result of these historic events.

In short, there is an entirely new international legal landscape that requires a new conceptual map – a new paradigm – in order to navigate and adjudicate successfully in domestic and international jurisdictions. Because of this, the time is overdue to reframe the explanation of this new and complex international legal order, its sources, and its ensuing judicial practice out of Bentham's rather narrow definition of "international law."[25] So, the term "international legal order" is used here rather generally to indicate that these new norms, relations, and practices are generally intended to apply to much more than the traditional conception of international law. In this sense, it is an expansive, pluralistic, and certainly nonexclusive term, which indicates that the focus is beyond state-centric law and the many uniquely local matters of *domestic* jurisdictions.

Influenced in part by the work of Hatfield and Weingast, the new international legal order can be generally defined here as a public regulatory process that is supervised by a decentralized enforcement regime (the domestic courts, the ICJ, the ICC, and in the final analysis, by the UNSC) that shares four attributes: a) *normative classifications of behavior that have originated in and been historically developed by independent domestic, regional, indigenous,s or international courts, jurisdiction,s or actual national practice*; b) in turn, such normative classifications are historical and cultural products of a *public reasoning process* that originates at the domestic or international level; to be fully public, such a process is always open and subject to both individual and legal interrogation, including judicial review; c)

Compliance comes out of a pre-existing social and procedural consensus that obedience is in the best interests of and sanctioned by the parties and peoples actually involved, as reflected in traditional or legislative action; d) and *wrongful actions carry a specified penalty* of some sort, which can be addressed through a series of decentralized enforcement mechanisms ranging from further self-restraint or sanctions to the formation of criminal investigations to even – in the most serious and deadly disputes – collective security actions by the UN.[26]

In short, this is law within a legal order that is not primarily defined in terms of negative sanction or coercion. Many people, if not most, want to obey their domestic law in order to further their own life goals and ambitions, as well as to safeguard their family or property. In other words, people follow the law because they want to, and see it as part of their inherent moral code and social obligations. Prof. Michael Barkun has stated the following in his classical study, *Law Without Sanction: Order in Primitive Societies and the World Community*:

> In summary, then, the utilization of coercive sanctions is hemmed in by limitations: by the insufficiency of resources, the ambiguous relationship with deterrence, and by the minority character of deviance…Two important consequences follow from these considerations. First, coercive sanctions need not be the mainstay of the law in as much as the vast number of social interactions never seem to invoke them or to be due to their presence. To limit law solely to instances in which sanctions are applied…is to reduce it to social pathology. *Second,*

26 There are, of course, a variety of competing definitions, of a domestic or international "legal order"; see, for instance, HANS KELSEN, (2009) A PURE THEORY OF LAW, The Lawbook Exchange, Ltd. (June 30, 2009). Despite what I consider the severe shortcomings of Kelsen's theoretical approach, I want to pay homage to his tireless work, even as World War II waged, to bring Nazi warlords and criminals to justice. For a contrasting definition of legal order, see Claudio Grossman & Daniel D. Bradlow (1993) "Are We Being Propelled Towards a People-Centered Transnational Legal Order?" in *American University International Law Review* Volume 9, Article 1. Also see Philip M. Moremen, National Court Decision as State Practice: A Transnational judicial Dialogue? N.C. J. InT'L&COM.REG 259 (2006); Finally, see Anne Marie Slaughter, A Global Community of Courts, 44 Harv. InT'L L.J. 191(2003).] Rather than solve here the contrasting assumptions of these various definitions, I am using, with revision, the best criteria that I have encountered concerning what constitutes a legal order, established by Gilian Hadfield and Barry Weingast in their article, "What is Law: A Coordination Account of the Characteristics of a Legal Order." *Harvard Journal of Legal Analysis*, March 2011.

> *the [social and] procedural consensus upon which sanctions are based is perceived to be ideologically and perhaps temporally prior to the use of force.*[27]

According to Michael Barkun, in order for law to exist, there must be *a pre-existing social and procedural consensus involving a complex calculus of self-interest and tacit collective consent.* So, the international legal order is not defined mainly or merely by the presence or absence of legal coercion mechanisms; instead, its main characteristics are normative narratives that are often uniquely developed in specific cultural and historical contexts that contain an indigenous, national, or regional *public reasoning process* subject to interrogation and review. These normative narratives and public reasoning processes reflect a deeper pre-existing *social and procedural consensus* found among almost all peoples, groups, or even states, which often ensures compliance to a legal order without constant or even recessed coercion. This may help explain why, in view of strong social forces for compliance, "most law is followed most of the time," as Louis Henkin so simply yet eloquent states.[28]

At the same time, there is always a criminal element in domestic or international affairs. Any subsequent legal violations or criminal behavior of law is often dealt with through coercive mechanisms that enhance, *but never ensure*, compliance with the law, or punishments for such behavior on either the domestic or international levels. In particular, the international legal order is a polycentric system of differing jurisdictions, normative classifications, public reasoning, and a decentralized enforcement regime that allocates and often coordinates a lawful penalty for actual criminal and unlawful behavior, either by a state, corporation, or individual. For instance, the ICC issued arrest warrants for President al-Bashir of Sudan, which the United States supported and will enforce if the *ad hoc* opportunity presents itself despite not really recognizing the court. In short, the sanction of criminal behavior cannot be the key characteristic of a legal order if such sanctions are too often inconsistent, evaded, or simply not applied.

27, MICHAEL BARKUN, LAW WITHOUT SANCTION: ORDER IN PRIMITIVE SOCIETIES AND THE WORLD COMMUNITY. Yale Univ. Press. (1968). p. 64. Prof. Barkun has been an invaluable teacher and colleague. (Emphasis added.)

28 IBID. See Louis HENKIN, HOW NATIONS BEHAVE 47 (2d ed. 1979) (emphasis omitted).(omit0, Also see his: *The International Bill of Rights: the Covenant on Civil and Political Rights*, (New York: Columbia University Press, 1981). Finally, to understand better the complex phenomenon of obedience, which has many causes besides coercion, see GENE SHARP. (1973) THE POLITICS OF NONVIOLENT POLITICS, PART I, POWER AND STRUGGLE. Porter Sargent Publishers (June 2, 1973) (Vol. 1)

Hence, as in the case of domestic deviance or crime, the reality of ineffective lawful coercion exists in any meaningful and effective legal order. In fact, the law is never totally effective or ensured, even in the so-called most "advanced" domestic societies. For instance, many murders go unsolved, and thus murderers go free in the United States all the time. Hence, the important factor in this regard is the legally sanctioned *possibility or even the increasing probability* of coercive enforcement. Since World War II, this possibility has increased slowly and painfully in the international legal realm, though in most instances there is the possibility of UNSC or ICC intervention and action.

Yet, as Prof. Barkun has noted, what is decisive is not the presence of coercion, sometimes avoided, in any jurisdiction; rather, the critical component of an effective legal order, or law, is the *a priori socially shared consensus* to create, operate, and support a juridical system that includes norms, duties, responsibilities, or sanctions that are, as Prof. Barkun so eloquently states, "*temporally prior to the use of force*" in any legal jurisdiction. In the first instance, this is true of both an international legal order and a domestic one.

In view of this, there are a variety of possible and plausible rival hypotheses concerning the most accurate paradigm needed to explain World War II and post-war legal innovations and developments. Any such paradigm must be able to articulate the *ascendency of the people or nation as a whole in relationship to the state* as now subject to and protected by international law.

Furthermore, since World War II, the international legal order has increasingly interpenetrated domestic jurisdictions in a variety of novel, yet indispensable ways, from trade agreements and administrative law to human rights and *erga omnes* norms. Thus, there are now a variety of domestic or indigenous jurisdictions, and even subsidiary legal orders – each with its own privileged normative classifications of behavior, public reasoning, and enforcement mechanism – within the overall and composite phenomenon of the post-World War II international legal order. In short, it is somewhat obvious that an almost radically new form or "paradigm" (in classical Greek "paradigm" means "form" or "pattern") of international law has emerged out of the agony of World War II and its aftermath.

Yet, defining such a new paradigm is not an easy task, since the war yielded essentially an entirely new and complex international legal order, which continues to develop today, decades later. So, a preliminary paradigm is ventured here not as a definitive final definition, but as a necessary and overt starting point to advance the debate concerning a new definition of international law that is based upon actual historical events, not held hostage to merely scholarly speculations or outdated definitions. In this regard, it is important to note that international norms now simply do not derive from the legislative process or state agreements; they also evolve out of humanity's proud yet painful historical journey through unchartered times, with all its wars, tragedies, victories, bravery, and often unexpected voices, such as President Roosevelt, who near the very beginning of World War II called for self-determination, greater recognition, and respect of basic rights for all peoples if – as the very first words of the UN Charter express – "We the Peoples" first won the war.

As such, the new international legal order is a composite and global phenomenon that incorporates the world's various jurisdictions, and in which the promissory and normative narratives of momentous historical events can and are distilled into lasting legal codes, fiduciary duties, or documents that can and do differentially diffuse into a single nation's courtroom by inclusion of a now-obligatory norm into its domestic jurisdiction. This is especially true of the fiduciary norms, relations, duties, and obligations that emerged during World War II as a result of the Allied powers' solemn promises to their own and other peoples that finally were victorious in the war. These promises, however generalized and inchoate at the time, must become promises kept. In the post-World War II world, this now particularly becomes the critical role and responsibility of the judiciary and courts, which can give concrete legal meaning to the emergent and evolving norms of the law of nations that now governs the manifold relationships between a government and its own and other peoples.

Thus, Blackstone's understanding of the law of nations as one in which domestic or "municipal courts" could and should adjudicate, as was occurring in England and other common law systems at the time, is critical and relevant in this new international legal order and must be recognized in theory and respected in practice. In fact, as the great Judge Garzon's indictment of Pinochet in Spain has illustrated, this is already in motion. At the same time, Bentham's definition of international law should not be simply discarded. First, his definition of law as that which is agreed to between sovereigns is highly accurate of the interstate legal order that still very much exists; World War II by no means changed this reality of international life. Since the Treaty of Westphalia in 1648, states have consistently made agreements or treaties, often short-lived, and will reliably continue to do so in the future. So, state-making law is still a critical component of the international legal order; this is simply a fact of current international relations. The new international legal order simply builds upon this state-founded basis as a means of expanding the normative protections and legal responsibilities to nations and individuals as well. By doing so, the implicit political and legal tensions between the nation and the state are now fully manifest, explicit, and – most importantly – legally regulated.

So, with the development of the law of nations as a consequence of World War II, the traditional dichotomy between public and private international law gives way to a more realistic and *pluralistic* international legal order *in which three types of international law, or distinct legal orders, dynamically interact and conflict within and increasingly across domestic jurisdictions* (See Figure 1, infra.) These three legal orders can be conceptualized, or re-conceptualized, as the following: a) the public law of states, or more generally, *Jus inter Gentes*; this is the legal order that embodies and preserves Bentham's definition of law; b) the public law of nations, or "international law." In this sense, it is truly an inter-*national* law, or *Jus Gentium,* and is clearly not *jus inter gentes*, or simply law between states; c) private international law or transnational private law, also described as the "conflicts of laws," which deals with the laws governing private interests in an increasingly globalized world.

Thus, the narrow term of international law should be enlarged and replaced by the general term of the international legal order. Within this, there are three pluralistic, macro, and often-contested legal orders that can be conceptualized, including the role of the courts at the intersection of three Venn diagrams, as follows:

Figure 1: The Public Law of Nations, which now governs the relationship of governments and states to their own and others peoples, interacting within a pluralistic International Legal Order.

THE PUBLIC LAW OF STATES: The first of these international legal orders is conceptualized here as consisting of public law of states, or perhaps more accurately, "public inter-state law." These include formal treaties signed and approved by sovereign nation states, as the Vienna Convention on the Law of Treaties has defined and elaborated upon, as well as between nation states and indigenous peoples within or between domestic jurisdictions.[29] This order thus recognizes the lawmaking capability, sanctified by Bentham, between mostly sovereign European states.

At the same time, it is important to note that these treaties clearly are not, or historically have not been, consistently controlling among these same sovereigns. For instance, several native and sovereign American Indian nations have scores of treaties with the French, Spanish, English, and United States governments; most of these are observed only in the breach but are still on the books, and hence binding if a state's word or bond in treaty law is or will be worth more than the paper on which it is printed. Ironically, the rights of indigenous peoples throughout the world as sovereign nations have only relatively been recognized on an international plane by the UN.[30] Under Bentham's prevailing paradigm, these indigenous nations have obviously had or have little to no ability to "make law." Under the law of nations, this possibility must once again be seriously entertained, especially since most indigenous peoples now live within the jurisdiction of a traditionally defined state and enjoy the hard-fought and -won rights promised by the Allies during the war.

THE PUBLIC LAW OF NATIONS can also be defined here as true "international law." This fiduciary law of nations now governs the relationship of governments to their own and other peoples and enunciates the entitlement of such nations to human rights, self-determination, trusteeship, and collective security, among others, as embodied in the Charter of the UN and other post-war documents. In particular, the modern law of nations limits and sharply curtails the unilateral violence that a government can legitimately use against its own or other peoples, as the UN or Nuremberg Charters, the Convention on the Crime and Punishment of Genocide, or the subsequent international human rights regime can attest. By doing so, the emergence of the law of nations resulted in a fundamental realignment of the legal relationship between the nation and

---

[29] The Vienna Convention on the Law of Treaties (VCLT) is itself a treaty, and specifies what constitutes a treaty. See United Nations, *Treaty Series*, Vol. 1155, p. 331. It was adopted on 22 May 1969 and opened for signature on 23 May 1969. For a partial record of treaties made with native peoples, see: DONALD FIXICO (2007)
Treaties with American Indians: An Encyclopedia of Rights, Conflicts, and Sovereignty (Google eBook), ABC-CLIO

[30] See: Allen, Stephen, The UN Declaration on the Rights of Indigenous Peoples: Towards a Global Legal Order on Indigenous Rights? (May 7, 2009). *THEORIZING THE GLOBAL LEGAL ORDER*, A. Halpin & V. Roeben, eds., Hart Publishing, 2009. Also: United Nations adopts Declaration on Rights of Indigenous Peoples United Nations News Center, 13 September 2007. Also see:Aprueba ONU declaración de derechos indígenas *El Universal,* 13 September 2007.

the state, terms that are usually conflated in legal lexicon. In view of this, there is an increasingly important and problematic *legal relationship between a nation or nations and the state* that actually does, or purports to, represent and protect its people under the relevant and respective domestic and international legal orders.

This public law of nations as a legal order **first and foremost incorporates and consists** of *Jus Gentium,* or "Laws…common to humanity," to be adjudicated by domestic, international, regional, or indigenous courts, and includes common domestic prohibitions against murder, assault, theft, and the like. Yet, on a larger scale, these include the legal regimes recognizing and maintaining the global commons, the shared and collective norms embodied in international diplomacy, and the hybrid treaty and trust norms embodied in the UN Charter, including its general recognition of human rights, self-determination, and the prohibition on the use of unilateral force by states in all cases but self-defense against armed attack. The inclusion of the global commons, such as the Earth's oceans and atmosphere, can play an important role in combatting climate change in the future. Chapter 1 briefly discusses and elaborates upon this possibility, as does the Appendix in this book.

This public law of nations also includes critical protections for the following: for entire peoples against torture, terrorism – a growing scourge of the "modern" world – or other forms of attack from their own or other governments; universal jurisdiction; customary international law; and domestic human rights law. In view of this, the term "international law" can also accurately describe this public law of nations. In fact, this is more accurate with regards to the original meaning of "national," which derives from the Latin *nationem* (nominative *natio*) and means birth, origin; breed, stock, kind, species; race of people, tribe, literally "that which has been born." Or, to put it more bluntly, a people, *peoples, or nations are naturally born,* while states are subsequently social constructions and often somewhat artificially created. So, this is simply transforming Bentham's use of the word "international" to describe this emergent legal order, which actually engages with the rights – fiduciary or otherwise – of living nations, as well as of the groups or individuals within it.

This descriptive transformation also restores and recognizes again, in part, the work and ideas of Vattel, Blackstone, and others, whose understanding and use of the law of nations included a role of the municipal or domestic courts; the courts and country's recognition and practice of the law of nations was largely vanquished by Bentham's state-centric definition of "international law," which helped to legally legitimate the prevailing colonial international legal order.[31] During and after World War II, this state-centric legal order, *alone*, actually vanished but then reappeared, at this current time it is slowly but surely being replaced by the post-war international legal order that recognizes the domestic court's role in upholding the public law of nations, or current international law. The faithful and *a priori* observation of these laws provides the only legal foundation for the lawful basis of political authority in any state.

Simply stated, in view of the horrors and Holocaust in World War II, it is no longer possible to consider the "people" to be merely a passive, almost ancillary presence in the legal definition of a state. After World War II, the protection of peoples – both entire nations and individuals – became a paramount purpose of this international legal order.[32] These are the rights, powers, and "property," defined in terms of the Lockean meaning of the word (above) to include life and liberty, of the peoples of the world.[33] Preserving the lives, rights, and liberties of its people is unquestionably the main purpose of a state, and not simply to preserve or expend its own power, especially at the expense of its people. When a state questions or violate these fundamental purposes of its existence, then it is the responsibility of its own courts or those of other national, regional, or international jurisdictions to uphold and enforce the rule of law.

The fiduciary foundations of this law as an enduring trust is found in the very origins and nature of its content; as mentioned earlier, it now fully realizes the aspirations of the ancient idea of the "law of nations," traditionally conceived of in Justinian *Institutes* as a law "common with all of humanity," and now also includes the fiduciary norms or duties that emerged out of World War II and its immediate aftermath.

Justinian was also the first to define and champion the concept of the public trust, which here is generally characterized as the global commons in recognition of its international significance and application. So, as part of a public law of nations, a fiduciary law of

---

31 See Anthony Anghie, (2004) *Imperialism, Sovereignty and the Making of International Law* (University of Cambridge Press, 2004. Also see: JANIS, supra, ftnotes 151 and 152.

32 See Boudreau, Law of Nations (2016) J. Juris 285. Also see Phillip Jessup (1948) excellent book *A Modern Law of Nations* in which he anticipates the profound paradigm shift occurring, though he dismissed the utility of the Justinian idea of *Jus Gentium* to describe some or all of these developments. He also alleges these developments are *de lege ferenda,* or still in the future of what the law ought to be. (Reprinted: Orth Press (March 15, 2007)

33 LOCKE, SUPRA, NOTE 7: Locke's definition of property includes one's life, liberties, and what we would today construe as rights.

nations that is "common to all of humanity" is fully consistent with and incorporates the traditional fiduciary legal status of the global commons. In more modern times, this is also morphing into the "Common Heritage of Humanity."[34] This, in fact, resolves another inconsistency of Bentham's definition of international law, since states cannot claim a global commons that belongs to all, though some still do. Most importantly, this now applies to the Earth's atmosphere as a global trust, an issue that may help decide the fate and future of the Earth, if there is to be one {See Proposal in the Appendix}. As such, this is where the term "public law of nations," which includes that which is owned by all, now truly applies, as it interacts by necessity with the other spheres of the international legal order. At the same time, this understanding of the global commons is fully consistent with the fiduciary law of nations as outlined in this book. For this reason, as stated before, the enduring reality of international trusts should now be belatedly recognized and considered a primary source of international law.

The legal inheritance of World War II now belongs to all peoples and individuals around the globe. By agreeing to and accepting the UN Charter, which consists (as seen in Chapter 1) of both trust and treaty law, newly created states are recognizing their obligations as trustees to apply this law to their own peoples as well. Ironically, this even includes the former Axis nations, all now in new or reconstituted states. It is up to each nation's domestic jurisdiction, first and foremost, to interpret and apply this law of nations now available as a universal birthright.

In particular, a fiduciary law of nations is not a "Western concept" in that it owes its origins, in part, to deep aspirations around the world for self-determination, human rights, and an end to colonialism, a goal that the Atlantic Charter and other solemn declarations in World War II had promised. In short, the colonial concept of international law, perhaps unwittingly pioneered by Bentham, is now clinically dead as the sole or even dominant explanatory paradigm of the international legal order. In contrast, every domestic or indigenous jurisdiction now has a unique role to play in the development, interpretation, and application of the evolving public law of nations, or true international law.

---

[34] JUSTINIAN, see: Moyle, J.B. *The Institutes of Justinian.* Translated into English with an Index. Fifth Edition. Oxford: Clarendon Press, 1913. viii, 220 pp. Reprinted 2002 by The Lawbook Exchange, Ltd. LCCN. Also see: Baslar, Kemal. *The Concept of the Common Heritage of Mankind in International Law.* Dordrecht, The Netherlands: Martinus Nijhoff, 1998.

With the great success of decolonization, the public law of nations anticipates and incorporates a diversity of legal cultures now interacting within the international legal order. Each post-colonial court is free to incorporate those aspects of the law of nations most needed or appropriate for its unique jurisdiction; for instance, the article by Dr. Juan Carlos Sainz-Borgo earlier in this book eloquently illustrates how the Venezuelan court rejected the legal norm of "crimes against humanity" to characterize the drug trade. This essay brilliantly depicts how each domestic jurisdiction may choose to either incorporate or refuse the fiduciary legal inheritance of all nations from World War II. For this reason, this legal order is called the public laws of nations and reflects the extraordinary diversity of local, national, or regional jurisdictions; in other words, the era of the exclusively sovereign or state-centric international law as a distinctly European creation is over.

In fact, the modern law of nations can be argued for and justified on a variety of historical, judicial, jurisprudential, and even positivist grounds. Chapter 1 has already briefly reviewed the grounds for a historical and juridical law of nations that allows, and even requires, international, regional, domestic, and indigenous courts to adjudicate the norms, duties, and obligations of the law of nations that resulted from the greatest war in human history. From a jurisprudential perspective, this text has argued that governments can and do make solemn pledges or promises that become the enduring and now-recognized legal legacy of the people; this is especially true, as evidenced, when governments make such solemn promises *and commitments to their own and other peoples simultaneously*. Such promissory declarations made in times of mortal peril must be keep in good faith if the peoples so promised had acted upon them to the point of sacrificing their own lives so that their nations and governments could endure. Promises offered under such solemn circumstances are promises that create fiduciary legal norms, obligations, and duties that must be enforced and, hence, are "promises to keep."

The positivist grounds are simply revealed in that some of the promissory statements and declarations made by the Allied powers in World War II were partially redeemed later by treaties or conventions that required explicit state consent. For instance, nearly all states in the world have approved the UN Charter as binding treaty law. At the same time, the hybrid nature of the charter, which Chapter 1 has described as consisting of both treaty and trust law, is because the promises made and expressed in the charter with fiduciary foundations in the wartime promises of the Allies, have yet to be fully enacted or fulfilled, and thus take on the character of an executory trust.*

Furthermore, modern legal scholars have argued that national court decisions can be considered examples of state practice, or positivist law. For instance, citing the growing "cross pollination" between national judiciaries, Prof. Philip M. Morement has analyzed how courts may constitute state practice for the purpose of the formation of customary international law. He has emphasized that the term "national court" is synonymous with "municipal court decision[s]" as well. It will be interesting to see if courts will increasingly accept such judicial decisions as evidence of customary state practice in the future.

In short, the international, regional, national, domestic, or indigenous courts of the world must ultimately determine the legal origins and full scope, application, and extent of the law of nations in the future. Specifically, within the constitute documents, declarations, and events that help create a modern law of nations, current and future courts or judiciaries can find the key ingredients – depending on the unique legal evolution and history of each jurisdiction – of the legally binding elements of a binding executive, express, implied, constructive, public, or other trust, as well as ensuing fiduciary duties, obligations, norms, or rights enjoyed by their own and other peoples. In view of the subsequent sacrifices, costs, and consequences among the Allied peoples of the world to win World War II, these solemn promises made in good faith by the Allied governments can only be construed as "promises to keep," thus creating a binding fiduciary order that is now part of the public law of nations.

So, as argued here, the public law of nations, or true international law, is in fact a robust and fully operational international legal order justiciable by the relevant courts that is constantly interacting with, complimentary to, and often contesting the public law of states as well as the third major legal order, which is now briefly examined.

The third legal order is also known as "private international law," or "conflicts of law." This is the law that attempts to govern or regulate the conduct of businesses and other

* This section inspired and influenced by Ms Brittany Foutz, a talented graduate student in international law.

private interests across boundaries, often resulting in a "conflict of laws" at best, and jurisdiction shopping for the best law at worst. This law has an enormous role, for better or worse, in the increasing neoliberal globalization of the world's economies. In view of the emergent development of globalized economies, the concomitant and profoundly interrelated issues of worker's rights should be globalized and legally recognized as well. In particular, such rights should include President Roosevelt's Four Freedoms, especially the freedom from want, and include an end to child labor, safe working conditions, a decent minimum wage, health insurance, paid holidays, and limited weekly work hours. As one of the key architects of the post-war world, Roosevelt raised the issue of free trade with Churchill in their first meeting, which resulted in its inclusion in the Atlantic Charter. President Roosevelt's vision of a free and fair deal for all is or should be a cornerstone of economic globalization, which now seems more like a new order of feudalism. *If not promptly and adequately addressed, these pressing issues of ending child labor, a decent minimum wage, decent and safe work conditions, health coverage, and paid holidays could be increasingly recognized as basic and universal human rights for anyone working in an evolving human rights regime, and thus come under the jurisdiction of the law of nations as well. As such,* bitter social, political, and judicial contests are surely coming in this regard in the future—if there is one.

Besides failing to protect workers' rights, the most significant weaknesses of private international law is its inability to legally recognize or meaningfully protect the Earth's environment, especially local ecologies, or provide distributional justice – the latter being a concern for Western philosophers since Aristotle's time....[35]

At the same time, it is vitally important to humankind to unshackle the entrepreneurial spirit and power of individual people, as well as the nation as a whole, in order to create necessary wealth and thus produce the very substances and sustenance of our daily lives. So, there is a precious and precarious balance to strike in private international law. Yet, since the primary focus of this article has been between public state law and the law of nations, not much more can be said here about this key legal order. Even so, a

[35] Distributional justice was a concern for Aristotle in his *Politics* and *Ethics,* but apparently not during our "Enlightened Age." See, for instance, his *Nicomachean Ethics*, trans. T.H. Irwin, Introduction. Hackett Publishing Company (Indianapolis: 1999). Also see *The Aristotelian Ethics: A Study of the Relationship between the Eudemian and Nicomachean Ethics of Aristotle,* (Oxford, 1978).

contribution from Prof. Mihir Kanade in this volume engages with the critical juncture between the law of nations and human rights with private international legal order.

At the center of the international legal order is the world's judiciaries, as well as those general principles of law that are, as the great jurist Prof. Oscar Schachter has asserted, characteristic of any legal system as such. These include the general principles cited earlier, such as "good faith," concerning the creation of legal obligations out of political discourse and promises.[36] Such general principles also include new fiduciary general principles created out of the agony of World War II concerning *erga omnes* norms, etc.; these go beyond this essay, but are discussed in my forthcoming book.

These three orders of law dynamically diffuse into and interact with each other, yet each often operates within a distinct legal sphere. Thus, the entire international legal order is pluralistic in nature, and not necessarily monist or dualist.[37] *Most importantly, within this pluralistic legal order, there is a plurality of jurisdictions rather than a single overarching "world law."* In this regard, each court and judge – within his or her own local, national, or international jurisdiction – serves in a unique role of deciding which legal norm applies, and which do not or are irrelevant to the case. In other words, as Michael Barkun has stated, "[t]he world is not a one-law world, fervent wishes to the contrary notwithstanding; it is a world of 'diverse' public orders."[38]

Thus, the cumulative international legal order consists of a variety of interacting domestic, regional, indigenous, and international legal jurisdcitions, each involving unique normative narratives and public reason processes. The international legal order as a whole is thus characterized by any or all regional, domestic, or institutional legal orders that interact with those of other peoples or nations. Such interactions may be intermittent, and thus short term, or may be continuous, global, and expanding. Some of these legal interactions may be limited to two or three states, while others involve entire

---

[36] See the great Prof. Schachter's ideas in this regard at e.g., RICHARD CRAWFORD PUGH, OSCAR SCHACHTER & HANS SMITH, INTERNATIONAL LAW: CASES AND MATERIALS 283-85 (Louis Henkin ed., West Group 3d ed. 1993).

[36] OSCAR SCHACHTER, INTERNATIONAL LAW IN THEORY AND PRACTICE, 178 Rec.des Cours 120 (1982-V)..

[37] WILLIAM R. SLOMANSON, FUNDAMENTAL PERSPECTIVES ON INTERNATIONAL LAW (Wadsworth Publ'g Co. 6th ed. 2010) (1990), which provides an excellent overview and analysis concerning the evolution of human rights law since World War II

[38] BARKUN *LAW WITHOUT SANCTION: ORDER IN PRIMITIVE SOCIETIES AND THE WORLD COMMUNITY.* Yale Univ. Press. (1968). Prof. Barkun has been an invaluable teacher and colleague. Here, I am defining the nation or nations legally as a "jural community," usually in relationship to a state, a concept that can be empirically tested, or falsified, though it is an admittedly elusive concept in daily discourse or the social sciences.

regions or even span the globe. Courts must ultimately decide the scope and limits of each legal order.

Consistent with this, the primary international legal orders that are truly global in scope are the public law of states, the public law of states or true "international law," and the private international law. The great legal and political contests to come will of course be between state law and authority versus the public international law. Such clashes and contests are inevitable since, as illustrated, the peoples and nations of the world have inherited the law of nations as their birthright and legal inheritance as a result of the Allied victory in World War II. This fiduciary law of nations, in turn, now provides lawful conditions for the foundation and legitimate existence of the state.

In particular, if a government becomes largely lawless or criminal and fails to observe the law, or actively violates fiduciary norms or court decisions, then the rights return – as envisioned by John Locke and the American founding fathers – to the nation and the people. Their first recourse to such perceived or actual injustice should be through the national courts. In turn, states that fail to uphold public international law so reframed and defined are still to be regarded as *de facto* states in terms of power and control; yet, they cannot be termed *de jure* states, and their leaders should be held accountable if they continually violate either domestic or international norms and obligations concerning the fiduciary law of nations and consequently threaten the safety, security, human rights, or even lives of all the people under their jurisdiction. If domestic courts fail to act, then the right and responsibility recurs to courts in other countries or to the ICC, which is the international court of last resort.

Specifically, as the Pinochet case initiated by the great Spanish magistrate Baltasar Garzon has illustrated, *independent courts in other lands must address and indict the most egregious breaches of law*. At first, such pioneering judges can expect to be lionized and vilified, even in their own country, as this volume's eloquent and insightful essay by Prof. Joaquin Gonzalez Ibanez on the trial of Judge Garzon in Spain has demonstrated. Yet, as time progresses and judges indict more war criminals, the price of pioneering the international enforcement of law should lessen, and ultimately cease. This is because the sizeable mass of often impoverished and downtrodden humanity instinctively recognizes its judicial champions, such as Judge Garzon, as its first and final guardians against rampant terrorism, illegal state violence, and tyranny.

In summary, because of post-war innovations in international law, a pluralistic international legal order has emerged in the wake of World War II that consists of the traditional state-centric intergovernmental law or the public law of states, private international law, and a transformed "international law" that includes a new fiduciary law of nations common to the whole of humanity. How these different legal orders diffuse across their "borders" and interact in the future is a fruitful subject for further research. Current trends suggest that the domestic and differential diffusion of fiduciary and international norms across and within different jurisdictions will increase, strengthening the scope and significance of the international legal order in the future.

The Law of Nations and Global Legal Pluralism

The concept of "global legal pluralism" accurately captures this phenomenon of a diverse and multifaceted international legal order.[39] However, it is imperfect for three reasons. First, global legal pluralism is a more complex phenomenon than simply the domestic diffusion of international norms across a number of different types of legal entities, such as courts, jural communities, or transnational jurisdictions. This is much more than a simple conceptualization as a "conflict of laws." This phenomenon is occurring at a much larger magnitude *between entire legal orders*, as well as between and within transnational or domestic jurisdictions. Thus, there are sometimes compatible and often competing levels of complexity in the multifaceted interactions between entire legal orders that contribute to global legal pluralism. Several scholars in the field have recognized this initial complexity and brought this phenomenon to the world's attention, beginning (I believe) with Sally Falk Moore's pioneering early essays and continuing with Sally Engle Merry's impressive work in the past two decades.[40] The emergent pluralistic

[39]There is a rich and rewarding literature on the growing phenomenon of global legal pluralism. See, for example, the many publications of Sally Engle Merry, who (along with Sally Falk Moore) pioneered the idea in the 1980s. Her latest contribution is "International Law and Sociolegal Scholarship: Towards a Spatial Global Pluralism," in a special issue, *Law and Society Reconsidered,* in the journal *Studies in Law, Politics and Society*, vol. 41 149-168, 2008. Also, see H.H Koh (1996) "Transnational Legal Processes," *Nebraska Law Review*, 75, p.181. Finally, for an insightful restatement of the literature on this phenomenon, see Paul Schiff Berman (2007) "Global Legal Pluralism" at Princeton: Program in Law and Public Affairs, Accepted paper Series, paper No. 08-001. Prof. Berman develops an excellent "procedural paradigm" of global legal pluralism that describes the transnational or domestic diffusion of legal norms across national, and often competing, jurisdictions. Finally, for the impact on the judiciary, see Slaughter, *Judicial Globalization*,, 40 VA J INT,L L. 1103 (2000).

[40]See, e.g., Sally Falk Moore, Legal *Systems of the World: An Introductory Guide to Classifications.*" (Leon Pipson & Stanton Wheeler eds., 1986). Also see: Sally Engle Merry, Legal Pluralism, 22 L & SOC'Y REV. 869, 870 (1988). Finally see *e.g.* Berman, as well as Kol at *supra* note 38.

reality is a key reason why comparative legal research must become a critical part of any legal education or scholarship.

Second, every court and jurisdiction is historically and culturally unique. Specifically, different cultures, jurisdictions, and even political histories often critically influence what is incorporated into a nations's jurisdiction, and what is omitted. Thus, every domestic or national jurisdiction is distinctly situated and developed, and is contoured by its own historical, legal, and even geographical features. My colleague Juan Carlos Sainz-Borgo has eloquently developed and illustrated this idea earlier in this volume. He conclusively demonstrates that each national court must be able ultimately to decide the law, and specifically if the resulting norms from World War II apply in each unique circumstance or case.

At the same time, the domestic diffusion of legal norms shared among differing national jurisdictions is unquestionably occurring, if not accelerating, and is thus a significant phenomenon. However, more is at work than this sharing of domestic decisions or norms among judiciaries. In this regard, *it becomes important to discriminate more precisely between the types and processes of legal interactions that are occurring between legal orders, jurisdictions, and international, regional, domestic, or indigenous courts.* Specifically, these processes of interactions can be generally characterized as the *domestic, transnational, or differential diffusion of norms into differing legal orders,* as well as into national or transnational jurisdictions. Domestic or transnational diffusion occurs when national or transnational courts refer to one another's cases and normative culture or incorporate those laws "common" to legal systems into their own decisions. These are, in essence, the laws common to humanity. This type of diffusion is the focus of much of the literature on global pluralism, and results in what Paul Berman seems to describe in his excellent essay on global legal pluralism as a "procedural pluralistic paradigm."[41]

Differential diffusion is characterized by the incorporation of the World War II fiduciary norms that are now a precondition for legitimate state authority. Third, then, there is now a new hierarchical and historically determined dimension to international law due to the unique nature of certain fiduciary and often non-derogatory norms that constitute an important part of the modern law of nations. Specifically, such hierarchical legal norms

[41]BERMAN, *supra* note 38.

consist of the wartime and post-World War II fiduciary law of nations, including norms and laws against torture, war crimes, crimes against peace, and crimes against humanity. These new and hierarchical norms result in a complex process of judicial incorporation, which is described here as differential diffusion.

Furthermore, the post-World War II fiduciary norm is essentially below – or more accurately, begins below – the threshold of traditional interstate treaties. The original promises and solemn declarations that the Allied powers made in the early desperate days of World War II frequently resulted in eventual treaties after the war was won, and thus often became (as argued above), like the UN Charter, hybrid agreements consisting of both state-centric or treaty and trust law. Yet, the origins of the trusteeship relationship forged in the crucible of world war began *within the state, as a matter between the mortally threatened government and its own and other peoples.* As such, the resulting trust – often consisting of contested fiduciary rights, interests, and relationships, such as human rights – are or should be self-executing *within* the nation's own boundaries and judiciary. This is currently an especially contested issue in the United States, despite its role as one of the primary architects of the new post-war legal order.

In theory, this is largely a vertical process that occurs when international fiduciary norms, such as the *jus cogens* or relatively "new" *erga omnes* (1970) norms, are actually recognized, incorporated, and adjudicated in international, regional, domestic, or indigenous tribunals.[42] Yet, due to the factors outlined above – the differing types of diffusion and the uniqueness of every legal culture and jurisdiction – such differential diffusion is not simply a causal consequence of the public law of nations. These processes of diffusion – domestic or transnational, as well as differential – occur slowly or rapidly during specific historical periods, especially after wars. Hence, such diffusion occurs episodically, since some jurisdictions are more receptive at a particular time to incorporating law from other jurisdictions. In short, such differential diffusion occurs on a case-by-case basis, and can

[4242]See MAURIZIO RAGASZZI, *THE CONCEPT OF INTERNATIONAL OBLIGATIONS ERGA OMNES* (Oxford U Press, 2000). Also, see M. Cherif Bassiouni, 1998. "International Crimes: *Jus Cogens* and *Obligatio Erga Omnes*," *Law and Contemporary Problems* 59: 63-74. The concept of *Jus Cogens* predates World War II, yet events during the war gave it added urgency, although it still suffers from legal imprecision. *See* CHRISTOS L. ROZAKIS, *THE CONCEPT OF JUS COGENS IN THE LAW OF TREATIES*, (North-Holland Publ'g 1976); see also Carin Kahgan, *Jus Cogens and the Inherent Right of Self Defense*, 3 ILSA J. INT'L & COMP. L. 767 (1997). Finally, see Vienna Convention on the Law of Treatises, May 22, 1969, U.N. Doc. A/CONF 39/27

See, e.g., supra note 9. Belgium v. Spain - Barcelona Traction, Light and Power Company, Limited (New Application: 1962) - Judgment of 5 February 1970 - Second Phase - Judgments [1970] ICJ 1; ICJ Reports 1970, p 3; [1970] ICJ Rep 3 (5 February 1970)

be profoundly influenced by the unique legal culture of each jurisdiction, society's relative respect for the rule of law, which can fluctuate even within so-called "advanced' legal cultures, and prevailing power politics. For instance, there was an extraordinary growth in the law of nations during and immediately after World War II, which only ended with the advent of the Cold War between the United States and the former Soviet Union. In current times, one can unfortunately anticipate a real political resistance to the domestic incorporation of hierarchical and fiduciary norms as a result of the pressing threats of terrorism, war, and the "crisis slide"' into both group and state barbarism that is characterized by the increasing attacks on civilians during this emergent age of extremes.

Yet, in such times, the rule of law is the greatest safeguard, though still precarious. Fortunately, the often-quiet legal processes of domestic or differential diffusion are continually occurring as the result of increasing globalization, facilitation of communication (such as the Internet), and sophistication and networking of legal elites.[43] These new "vertical" norms of the fiduciary law of nations include, but are not limited to, *erga omnes* and *jus cogens* norms. The UN Charter prohibition on the unilateral use of military force except in cases of self-defense against "armed attack" is a case in point. Every country's judiciary should be prepared to enforce such legal norms and, if need be, punish transgressors of the basic rule of law upon which – and only upon which – legitimate state authority is established.

This places added and urgent emphasis on the teaching and use of comparative research methods in the legal profession. Otherwise, it is probable that American international legal scholars will largely quote and talk to other American legal scholars, European legal scholars will quote their own peers, and so on down the line in rather insular conversations that are based upon state- or culture-centric scholarship concerning the international legal order. In view of this, there is a need to truly internationalize the profession of international legal studies and *begin to apply international legal norms and principles to one's own and other leaders.* Those who are true scholars can and will do this; those who cannot will simply criticize from the safety of academia, or continue to comment on micro issues of the law. Yet, the judges and judiciaries of the world are much more active, assertive, and certainly not shy; thus, the hope of applying the hard-

[43]Slaughter, "*Judicial Globalization*," supra, note 68.

fought and won legal norms of the new international legal order rests first in their able and experienced hands. As such, judges are the first and final guardians of the international rule of law.

In short, there are now complex and pluralistic *vertical and horizontal* dimensions concerning the differential diffusion of fiduciary legal norms into domestic jurisdictions due to the advent of World War II charters, norms, and subsequent legal innovations. As demonstrated, these developments created a law of nations applicable to the whole of humanity, or at least common to most nations and peoples of the world.[44] In certain cases, these new fiduciary legal norms, such as the adjudicated crimes of Nuremberg as examples of *erga omnes* norms, can and do preempt domestic legal norms. Such "vertical" and increasingly "common" legal norms resulted from the fiduciary promises and pacts of the Allies during or immediately after World War II; these can and are being incorporated, without being described as fiduciary norms, into domestic jurisdictions through judicial interpretation and legislative or executive action.[45] These vertical norms perhaps show the greatest promise now for establishing an enduring international rule of law throughout the world.

The vertical nature of differential diffusion is also due to collective or shared obligations to enforce the law of nations. A central characteristic of the *corpus juris* adopted during and after World War II is the fiduciary and even *collective commitment* to maintain or restore international peace and security. This collective obligation, meaning first and foremost a *shared* commitment, is simply the converse of the charter's legal limits on the unilateral legitimation of political violence, especially since it is coupled with legal obligations embodied within the UN Charter to enforce collective security measures and sanctions. Hence, the charter's system of collective security, especially in combination with the Nuremberg Charter and other post-World War II conventions that *legally limited a state's sovereign right to legitimate unilateral political violence*, constitutes the core of a new law of nations and international fiduciary legal order.

[44]This assertion of a vertical element in international law contradicts the excellent and now-famous article by Richard Falk, "International Jurisdiction: Horizontal and Vertical Conceptions of legal order," *Temple Law Quarterly*, 32 (1959), p. 295-320. Falk's excellent article reflects the current and now-conventional wisdom concerning the horizontal jurisdiction of international legal order(s). I am suggesting that this is not entirely accurate, especially if national, transnational (regional), or international courts provide remedies to violations of *erga omnes* norms and other fiduciary norms. Judge Garzon's indictment of Pinochet is simply one example.
[45]See Koh, supra note 114.

Specifically, evidence of these fiduciary, shared, and – as described here – vertical legal norms and obligations in the modern law of nations is most dramatically reflected in the collective and non-derogatory enforcement aspects of fundamental legal norms, such as the Nuremberg Charter, various human rights regimes, and wartime protections for civilians and the sick, wounded or shipwrecked, as well as UNSC actions calling for collective security. For instance, the four Geneva Conventions (1949) recognize and even require enforcement actions by "the high contracting parties." As such, the norms of the Geneva Convention, the so-called "Law of Geneva," have arguably become customary law as well and, as such, should become enforceable in any court of law.[46] There is also the common obligation of all signatory states as expressed in the famous Martens Preamble to the 1907 Hague Convention on the Laws and Customs of War on Land.[47]

In human rights law, contemporary legal prescriptions concerning individual rights and protections are, in the words of the International Court of Justice, *obligatio erga omnes*: owing by and to all humankind.[48] Regional international courts are recognizing these non-derogatory obligations as well. For instance, in two recent path-breaking advisory opinions, the Inter-American Court of Human Rights held that the remedies of *amparo* and *habeas corpus* are among "the judicial guarantees essential for the protection of rights" made *non-derogable* by Article 27(2) of the American Convention.[49] Domestic courts within a state's jurisdiction can now follow the lead of these regional courts.

In view of this, a more accurate empirical description of the vertical legal nature of post-World War II law is to fundamentally distinguish between the nature of specific legal contractual, state-centric, or treaty obligations and fiduciary obligations that result from the modern law of nations. Such a distinction imperfectly parallels the legal distinction found in classical Roman jurisprudence between *obligatio civilis*, defined as

> ... obligations engendered by formal contracts, or from such portions of the *Jus Gentium* as had been completely naturalized in the civil law, and *obligatio praetoriae*, or

[46] See supra, ftnote 7. Also, see Theodor Meron, The Martens Clause, Principles of Humanity and the Dictates of Public Conscience, 94 AM. J. INT'L L. 78 (Jan. 2000).
[47] Ibid.
[48] See, e.g., ICJ's Barcelona Traction Case. ICJ Rep. 1970,
[49] Advisory opinion OC-8/87 of 30 Jan. 87. Also see LAURENCE BURGOQUE-LARSEN, *THE INTER-AMERICAN COURT OF HUMAN RIGHTS: CASE LAW AND COMMENTARY.* (Oxford Univ. Press, 2011).

> obligations established by the Praetor in the exercise of his jurisdiction that exists under the law of nations.[50] In short, the existence of the *Jus Gentium* as a whole was often a precondition for the exercise of this type of jurisdiction by a "judge" – in this case, the Praetor. His authority only existed under the consensually created law of nations as a whole; in fact, its *rasion d' etre* was due to the multiple and often competing norms and jurisdictions within the Roman Empire. So, if Romans or "foreigners" wanted to trade and conduct business in Rome, they had to recognize the a *priori* authority of the law of nations, which included a third-party judge who would exercise jurisdiction, and even discretion, in order to settle disputes peacefully. The point is that the authority of *obligatio praetoriae* came directly from the existence of the *Jus Gentium*, or law of nations as a whole, rather than from any specific decree from another ruler, "sovereign," or empire.

Although the parallel is imperfect, the comparison between classical and contemporary definitions concerning legal obligations in international law is revealing; like the classical conception of *obligatio praetoriae*, there are legal obligations embodied in the unique *corpus juris* recognized after World War II that derive from the law of nations as a fiduciary legal order, not solely from subsequent consent of the state or specific parties. In particular, a a modern law of nations should distinguish between specific state obligations that arise from express or implied state consent and fiduciary obligations that arise out of collective, non-derogatory legal norms that are *a precondition for the exercise of legitimate state authority.*[51] The argument here is essentially that states are only "legitimate" to the extent that they follow the law of nations, including the UN Charter, as an executory, constructive, public, or implied trust, resulting in the first instance from the Allies' World War II promises to their own and other peoples if they first fought and won the war.

If such obligations or norms are violated, including international prohibitions against initiating war, war crimes, terrorism, or torture, then it is preeminently the role of the courts throughout the world to enforce their government's collective or shared commitment to the law by holding potentially culpable leaders or actors accountable. As mentioned earlier, the full weight of domestic or international adjudication should now

---

[50]See, e.g., *supra*, note 74.

[51]See, e.g., supra note 9. In the early Roman Republic, only one praetor was established. As commercial trade with foreigners increased, a second praetor was established to handle suits in which one or both parties were foreigners (*Jus Gentium*). The original office was renamed *praetor urbanus*, and the new office was called *praetor peregrinus*.

equally apply to those, including state or substate actors or individuals, who commit terrorist acts that involve the killing of innocents, either through disproportionate or excessive use of force or wanton disregard for innocent civilian life. In particular, terrorism – the attacking and resulting death or injury of innocent civilians, either deliberately or in wanton disproportionality often obscenely justified as "collateral damage" – seems to be a growing way of life for renegade individuals, groups, and even states as a whole.

In this regard, the cruel calculus of proportionality in any armed conflict is significant. If a state or substate actor claims the right to kill 100 or more civilians in return for the death of one or several of its own – a practice condoned by the Nazis – then a war crime has almost unquestionably occurred and must be investigated with the purpose of possible prosecution to the full extent of the law. Otherwise, the retaliatory state of substate actors become a savage victim of their own protest, and commit what they profess to be fighting. In fact, terrorists seem to recruit in the rubble of their victims' overreactions, and so the vicious escalatory cycles of violence and counterviolence, especially against civilians, seemingly continues and intensifies in this emergent age of extremes.

So, terrorism is defined inclusively here, without mitigating exceptions, as actual attacks (regardless of "intent" or "justification") *against innocents, especially those protected by law from armed hostilities*, including women, children, babies, the elderly, patients, or civilians in or near hospitals, places of worship, and UN or Red Cross/Crescent facilities. In view of this, terrorism can be defined as both state-sponsored, -condoned or -conducted acts or attacks of terrorism by governments – in short, state terrorism – as well as substate actors and groups or demented individuals. In essence, civilians are now the frontlines of any armed dispute, as in the Middle East, Africa, or Afghanistan, and this is simply unacceptable.

In view of the growing atrocities of the modern world in this emerging age of extremes, international, regional, national, and indigenous courts must seek reliable evidence and, when warranted, indict those individuals responsible for such violent atrocities. *The terrible era of state or individual impunity for killing innocent civilians and other war crimes must end,* or the world could slip into a new and deeper dark age from which only more blood, bones, and ruins will emerge. As Gideon Gottlieb once stated, the "decline of our civilization may well be measured by reference to the growing gap between professed human ideas solemnly affirmed in international instruments and the growing brutalization of civilians in armed conflict."

So, in particular, these fiduciary norms must be applied to the most powerful states, and not simply to marginalized or defeated leaders. Lest hegemonic hubris infect the very fabric of international law, both the victors and the vanquished – as Chief Prosecutor Robert Jackson so eloquently stated during the first Nuremberg Trials – must be held accountable in war. In the final analysis, the international, national, domestic, and indigenous judges and courts of the world can and must act to end the current age of impunity and restore, at minimum, the incredibly fragile foundations of a livable world without fear under the rule of law.

Yet, substantial military powers continue to trample upon weaker powers, and millions of innocent civilians are subsequently caught up in the maelstrom. This is true, for instance, for the United States' invasion of Iraq, where there is compelling evidence that the war was launched despite no hostile or armed action by Iraq towards the United States; in fact, much of the supposed information used to justify the war was allegedly fabricated, or later proved false.[52] United Nations weapons inspectors were already in the country, had extraordinary access, and found no evidence of weapons of mass destruction (WMDs); the Iraqi regime was already effectively a prisoner of the rigorous international inspection regime. In fact, when the issue was brought before the UNSC in the fading winter of 2003, the council rejected the United States' claim for any justification to attack. However, the United States government proceeded anyway, attacking Iraq soon after despite a lack of any real *casus belli* and facing large-scale domestic and unprecedented global protests.[53]

---

[52]See, e.g. JOSEPH WILSON. *THE POLITICS OF TRUTH: INSIDE THE LIES THAT LED TO WAR* (CARROLL &GRAF, 2004). Amb. Wilson also published the famous op-ed piece: "What I Didn't Find in Africa," *New York Times*. (July 6, 2003). Also, see MICHAEL ISIKOFF AND DAVID CORN. *HUBRIS: THE INSIDE STORY OF SPIN, SCANDAL, AND THE SELLING OF THE IRAQ WAR* (Crown, 2006). For a study done by a premier former U.S. intelligence official, see PAUL PILLAR, *INTELLIGENCE AND U.S. FOREIGN POLICY: IRAQ, 9/11 AND MISGUIDED REFORM.* (Columbia University Press, 2011). Finally, see Greg Thielmann, The Cost of Ignoring UN Inspectors: An Unnecessary War with Iraq, Arms Association Now, a blog by the Arms Control Association. March 5, 2013

[53]This controversy over who has the proper authority to use military force was an example of "authoritative ambivalence," a phenomenon consisting of the institutional conflict within the UNSC between the unilateral and collective legitimating of force that I first described in "Legitimating Military Force and Collective Security: The Emergent Role of the Security Council in the Post-Cold War World." PARC WORKING PAPER * 31 Program on the Analysis and Resolution of Conflicts, The Maxwell School, Syracuse University, February 1994. The US's failed

In short, this war was a violent and unprovoked attack against a state, and as such constitutes a "crime against peace," a criminal category first defined in the Nuremberg Charter. Furthermore, during the war, ample photographic evidence in the public domain arose that demonstrated that the United States used torture, such as with the infamous Abu Ghraib prison photos. Considering this, all of those responsible, and especially the civilian leadership in Washington, D.C., should be held accountable in a national or international court of law for subsequent war crimes as well. In fact, the net should be cast much wider than at Nuremberg, where only the most prominent leaders were placed on trial, while their senior assistants or subordinate policy makers all too often went free or received symbolic sentences. The same mistake cannot be made again in the future.[54] Political leaders, their key aides, and their civilian lawyers who launched this war should be prosecuted to the fullest extent permitted by international law.

Such prosecutions, when legally warranted, would give needed additional life to the "twin offspring" of the war enunciated earlier by General Telford Taylor, the United States prosecutor during the later Nuremberg Trials. As he states above, if the UN system of collective security fails, then the Nuremberg Charter and subsequent trials

---

attempt to get the UNSC to approve its planned war in Iraq is simply the latest and most dramatic example of authoritative ambivalence, a phenomenon that has characterized many of the UNSC debates, especially since the end of the Cold War. I hope that this will also be a chapter in my forthcoming book, if ever completed, *The Law of Nations*. Quoting Chief Justice Jackson at Nuremberg: "I must [try], as Kipling put it, 'splash at a 10-league canvas with brushes of comet's hair.'"

[54] There was a symbolic conviction from a Malaysian "War Crimes Tribunal," but its contents and perpetrators – largely limited to Bush, Cheney, and Rumsfeld – are too narrowly construed. Other senior officials and aides to President Bush, Rumsfeld, and Vice President Cheney should be scrutinized as well for their possible involvement in the "planning, preparation, initiation or waging of a war of aggression,"—Nuremberg Charter, chapter 1, *supra*, at note 4. Witnesses are readily available; see *e.g.* Interview with Col. Lawrence Wilkenson, *Democracy Now* with Amy Goodman, Aug. 30, 2011), as well as for the subsequent war crimes that resulted from the initiation of this unjustified "preventive" war upon Iraq. In fact, the Machiavellian and moral motives seem to coincide for those within the U.S. government and population who opposed the attack on Iraq and argued against the war. The logic seemed clear and compelling. First, *terrorists such as al-Qaeda recruit in the rubble of their victims' overreactions*; so, any war would end up strengthening the *al-Qaeda*, the primary threat to U.S. interests. Second, since the primary opponent of the US after 9/11 was al-Qaeda, an attack on Saddam Hussein's secular Iraq - a regime that hated al-Qaeda for its own reasons – would destroy a self-policing buffer against the terrorist group, however despicable Hussein was personally. Third, such an attack would remove the primary opposition to Iranian expansion in the area, and thus strengthen Iranian hegemony in post-war region. Such advice was obviously ignored. Now, some of the same individuals from the former Bush Administration are urging another military confrontation, or even "preventive" war in Syria with Russia and Iran, indicating that there is no learning curve, let alone moral restraint, among certain policymakers from the tragedy of Iraq. See e.g., Wilson; Pillar, *supra* note 128. Also, see "The Burden of Proof: Two Former CIA Analysts Talk About The Lies behind Iraq War," HTML format, Thomson Gale Publisher, May 2006. Finally, e.g.: Ray McGovern AND Doug Rawlings, "Addressing U.S. Intelligence on Iraq and Iran." Audio Book. Radio Free Maine, Nov. 10, 2006.

were meant to be the next step to ensure that those suspected of violating international peace and security would be brought to trial. In short, *a collective or shared obligation means that, if one court fails to act, others are still obligated to do so in order to bring those guilty to justice, especially when erga omnes norms are involved.* If anything, Nuremberg conveys that *no one is now immune from the consequences of their decisions or actions*, even – *or especially* – *when* acting for a government. The basic elements for this new legal order consist of the fiduciary norms, obligations, sanctions, and institutions created by this World War II *corpus juris.*[55] Applying international legal sanctions simply to the leaders of developing, third-world, or African countries is simply not sufficient or acceptable any longer. In an ethnocentric world, selective suffering or blame is often morally troubling and suspect; all human beings bleed a deep red when wounded or killed in unprovoked or unjustified attacks, and their attackers must thus be held accountable, regardless of race or nationality, even if they are viewed as somehow privileged or powerful. In particular, highly developed states are still very much on the warpath, and their leaders must be held accountable as well for unwarranted and murderous attacks. This is necessary for both state leaders and leaders of terrorists groups when they violate the laws of war and peace and kill innocent civilians. This is especially true when there is obviously no "armed attacks" (Article 51) against their own nation or state, and yet they still go to war against an uninvolved state or a powerless people As explained, this seems to be the case for the unprovoked attack on Iraq, so those that fomented and initiated this war should be brought into a court of law in the near future to examine legal evidence for and against their unprovoked attack.

In other words, the very fabric of a state's legal legitimacy is determined by its observance of the law of nations, especially the new fiduciary and *erga omnes* norms, not only in relation to other states, but now first and foremost to its own people as well. Thus, it is ultimately the responsibility of a nation's own judiciary to ensure that its government and state respect and observe the law. This is admittedly a rare and difficult task. However, failure to do so passes this right and shared responsibility to other national or international judiciaries, who then have the responsibility and authority under universal jurisdiction to bring those guilty of violating the law of nations, war crimes, crimes against peace or humanity, and other fiduciary norms to justice. As Prof. Gonzales Ibanez of Spain has argued so eloquently, the apparent age of impunity for

[55] See, Law of Nations (2012) J. Juris. 285. Many thanks to Mr. Edwin Njonguo for sharing this critical idea and insight about the Afrocentric nature of ICC indictments up until now.

leaders suspected of or indicted for war crimes and other grave offenses against humanity must end, and thus fulfill the promise of the UN and Nuremberg Charters.

The so-called Chilcot Report regarding Prime Minister Tony Blair's decision to commit troops from the United Kingdom is an insightful starting point that is illustrative of the type of critical introspection that a country must conduct after a supposedly "optional" or "preventive" war.[56] Yet, Blair was merely following the lead of his ally, the United States. So, in sharp contrast with the United Kingdom, it is simply astounding that there was a lack of any similar official or legal inquiries or indictments in the United States, even by the international legal profession, concerning the Bush Administration's decision to launch a war that resulted in death or lifelong injury for thousands of American soldiers and hundreds of thousands of Iraqis, as well as a now largely destroyed or decimated state and society and the resulting emergence of Islamic State of Iraq and the Levant (ISIL). Such legal introspection and adjudication of the war in a court of law that allows for the assembly of all evidence and public argument in a painful but necessary cross-examination is essential in a society such as the United States, which claims to be governed by the rule of law.

Conclusion

"Making Gentle the Ways of the World"

The Hope of Aeschylus

The purpose of this chapter is to present, in a brief outline, the jurisprudential argument for the law of nations within a pluralistic international legal order. This argument has, by necessity, required a somewhat archeological and inevitably inadequate excavation into the theories and thinking of Bentham and his professorial predecessor, Blackstone. The resulting paradigm proffered here of the modern international legal order must be ultimately measured by the number of episodic exceptions and blind spots that it addresses or fills in Bentham's outdated understanding of international law, i.e. as basically agreements between states or of recognized state practice. As such,

[56] The Report of the Iraq Inquiry was published on 6 July 2016. Sir John Chilcot's public statement can be read at http://www.iraqinquiry.org.uk/.

jurisprudence is not concerned with the "is" and the "ought"; it is ultimately concerned with articulating the most accurate and plausible "rival hypothesis" to new facts, historic developments, and subsequent legal innovations. So, this paradigm offered here of a public law of nations within a robust international legal order is the beginning of this quest. If it fails in whole or in part in this regard, the challenge then is to define and develop a better one that more fully explains post-World War II legal innovations and other evidence, including the glaring "exceptions" created and now fully recognized (see paragraph I of this chapter) to Bentham's state-centric international law.

Undoubtedly, there are be those who will continue to believe, like Voltaire's Prof. Pangloss, that Bentham's conception of international law is the "best of all possible worlds." In contrast, this book has tried to demonstrate the inadequacy of this antiquated paradigm through analyses of exciting and evolving legal developments with regard to a new paradigm of international law.

To put it bluntly, Bentham's conveniently colonial conception of international law should have perished with the post-war period of decolonization and subsequent slow but inexorable liberation of formerly colonized peoples that was promised by the Atlantic Charter and Roosevelt's Four Freedoms within all of the European and American former colonies.

Yet, as mentioned earlier, individual governments or states often attempt to hoard as much power and control as possible. As a result, there is and will continue to be an intense competition within and between these three legal orders of the public, the private, and the fiduciary law of nations concerning which legal norm or norms should prevail, especially in cases involving human rights, the environment, or war crimes. The abject failure for any such judicial review or scholarly condemnation within the United States concerning the Bush Administration's unilateral decision to attack Iraq in the spring of 2003 has been cited as a glaring example of the current age of impunity that can and must end if there is any hope of a world governed by the rule of law.

As such, in contrast to the old paradigm of international law, this new paradigm of the international legal order provides, if not requires, a vital new role for these domestic, indigenous, regional, and international courts, as well as other jurisdictions, in upholding the new fiduciary law of nations as the basic legal precondition of legitimate state authority. Only a truly independent and fully respected judiciary can achieve this. Therefore, it is ultimately the duty of current courts or those in session in the future – whether domestic, regional, indigenous, or international – to decide if the promissory declarations and documents produced by the Allied powers in World War II can or should be construed as an implied, constructed, executive, or other type of trust under the constraints of accepted legal interpretation or practice. Given the evidence cited above, as well as the declarations, speeches, and documents left unexamined here during this period, I believe such a legal decision is inevitable. In this sense, such an independent judiciary is a high mark of self-determination, and thus a true measure of a state's sovereignty. The independence of the judiciary, in turn, can be measured by this simple maxim: "When the courts decide, the nation – and government – abide."

Unfortunately, history is too vivid and rich with recurring examples of states becoming ravenous beasts or lawless Leviathans in constant search of more power and control. Under the new international legal order, the lawful power of the state can be checked, limited, and preserved in the first instance by its strict observance of inter-state and international law, as embodied in the UN Charter. However, if future atrocities, acts of terrorism, armed conflicts, or even inter-state wars arise, the appropriate remedy becomes, when necessary, the domestic, indigenous, regional, or international jurisdictions and judges of the world prosecuting the individuals or leaders who initiated such irreversible horrors. As such, the differing jural communities throughout the world and their courts – if the latter are truly independent – will consistently provide the most significant safeguard for peace, human rights, human liberty, and a strengthened international legal order.

CHAPTER 11

REFLECTIONS ON A REVOLUTION IN INTERNATIONAL LAW: TRENDS AND THE SECOND BOUNCE OF THE BALL

Professor Brian Polkinghorn

As managing editor of this book, I have read, analyzed, and edited the chapters contained in the previous pages. In view of this, I thought that it would be useful to reflect upon, summarize, and share my thoughts as I finish up the delightful duties of editing. I write these reflections not as a lawyer, but as a scholar-practitioner of conflict intervention, who must grasp legal frameworks in order to effectively assist combatants or disputants in many of the places mentioned in the previous chapters, such as Bosnia and the Middle East. As such, I have witnessed firsthand the ravages of unresolved protracted conflicts and war. Humans are capable of unimaginable horror against other people, and so it is encouraging and enlightening to read these chapters and see glimmers of hope that, even in a highly complex world, there may be a revolution of sorts where the outcome is the development of coordinated legal structures relating to crimes against humanity. In view of my personal experiences in these areas of the world, I agree with the main theme or assumption of this book that there is no higher calling than the prevention of war. So, I share the following comments as my own personal and professional reactions to and reflections on the previous chapters.

Before proceeding to a reflection of the unique contributions and overarching themes throughout this book, I need to caution the reader with a few provisions. The first is the whole notion of what it means to be a nation within the global political world. As we know, nations rarely overlap perfectly with the state – the main unit of political organization. Consider Africa, for example, and how it was partitioned by colonial geographic dynamics wherein decisions were made on another continent based on, among other things, strategic positioning on a global scale. If we superimpose a map of nations – or for that matter, other means of group identification – on top of the state map of Africa, we quickly grasp the contradiction and source of inherent identity-based conflict. Having the nation become the focus of the interaction among people in a state-dominated political format therefore imposes, at least in part, a geopolitical challenge. To his credit, Prof. Boudreau limits the scope of his inquiry to the "increasingly important and problematic *legal relationship between a nation or nations and the state*, which actually does

– or purports to – represent and protect its people under the relevant and respective domestic and international legal orders [Second Paragraph of Essay]."

In this sense, Prof. Boudreau is primarily concerned with the legal relationship between a nation or nations and a state that *already exists*, calling for a more active role for the judiciary within such an established jurisdiction. In short, his concern is with the legal relationship between the nation or nations and the 193 states that currently exist within the international order, signified by membership in the UN. Yet, in my opinion, such a "clean cut" application may not always be possible, and parties or self-proclaimed "nations" seeking statehood may claim such status based, in part, on the emergent law of nations.

Second, even when nations move to assert their rights within a given state system or through the use of international institutions such as the UN, it produces a completely uneven set of outcomes that makes it difficult, under the direction of legal precedence, to provide guidance when other nations assert similar claims. It is evident how East Timor, Kosovo, and South Sudan effectively asserted national interests and rights through international institutions in order to obtain autonomy or a new status of statehood. At the same time, though, national interests are being used for nefarious reasons, such as in Crimea, Ukraine or Georgia. A brief glimpse at each of these should highlight concerns to keep in mind when balancing out the positive impact of the law of nations on the larger global equilibrium. Ethnic Russians in the Crimea most likely welcome reunification with Russia, as they were once a part of Russia. Ethnic minorities, some of whom claim that the Soviets stacked the population with Russians as a means of control, claim a historical precedence to the region. This competing narrative for territorial control of resources and political hegemony is in motion around the world, with current hot spots being Israel-West Bank and the recent aggressive moves of the Chinese in the Spratly Islands, among other places.

Ukraine, some argue, is a continuation of the Crimea crisis, and this is accurate to some extent. In this instance, ethinic Russians in Ukraine are making the same claim to autonomy, but the distinction here is that they live within the recognized borders of Ukraine. This poses problems for countries that have treaties with Ukraine, world institutions, and – for that matter – world order. For instance, if East Ukraine were to forcefully cede from Ukraine and world leaders took no action in response, then there could be a surge of national minorities around the world interpreting this as recognition of national rights and launching a revolution or some form of crisis. The potential for internal strife within the state system can and will remain high if the relationship between nations within the state are not addressed on a case-by-case basis.

In other words, it is necessary to recognize that there is a vast array of state-to-nation relationships that are shaped by historical, political, economic, and other dyanmics, which can serve as a cauldron of creative yet conflicting considerations causing the very conflicts that the international rule of law is intended to prevent. This is especially true for situations in which factual oppression and subjugation exists or arises. The Apartheid system in South Africa, the indigenous people of Australia, and American Indian nations all provide cautionary tales of regrettable past deeds. Isolating people of other nations in Bantustans and reservations is a physical reminder of the "us-versus-them" mindset. It also forces control through physical isolation. In the United States, the relationship between the federal government and tribal nations is one of subjugation, or more precisely, of international relations among unequal partners. There is therefore a need to careful consider the unintended consequences of nations asserting their needs and rights in the existing state-dominated system.

Finally, as more groups assert national lay claim to territory and natural resources through various arenas and methods, there is a need, generally speaking, to be diligent and mindful of the meaning of nations, how they are formed, and – most importantly – recognized by other groups. When a group of people collectivizes and makes a claim of national status, it has to be evaluated through some set of rules or guidelines, which are often developed by some other group. Take, for instance, the difference between those that have coveted recognition versus unrecognized American Indian nations in the United States. Those that are formally recognized by the federal government have an incredible status advantage over others, and can assert their needs and rights in ways that unrecognized groups simply have no legal, political, or social means to do. Some have argued that the means of recognition is unfair and ignores a wider range of ideas for defining nationhood. Others have said that there needs to be parameters to effectively obstruct groups whose sole purpose is to gain nation status for economic means, and not to preserve the nation from which they come. One example is tribes that have emerged that have not historically been accounted for, but wish to build a casino. Then, compare this group to another American Indian nation that has a documented history of at least several hundred years, and has entered into treaties and had many interactions with other groups. The question becomes where to draw the line on recognition, and how that line moves over time to expand and contract the definition of a nation on a state scale and, if ever possible, a global scale. Prof. Boudreau argues that indigenous peoples often have or are entitled to their own traditional judicial processes and even court systems, which now, with recent actions and declarations of the UN, deserve domestic and international recognition.

In practical terms, these issues remain unsettled and provide a rich source of conflict. Therefore, the focus must remain on the ability of nations to play a more dominant role in intra-state and inter-state affairs, while showing due diligence to the unintended consequences that this may have locally, regionally, and globally on the status quo.

The First Bounce of the Ball

Cause and effect relationships are the basic for all logic. When we throw a ball and it is struck by a bat, we can – if in the right position – see where the ball is heading, and where it might even land. That is strategic advantage, simply explained. Knowing the direction of a ball, political movement, or change in a market provides time to assume the position, metaphorically speaking, to "catch" the ball or take advantage of the change. This is the mindset to adopt while reviewing the chapters in this book so that by the end, we may have an idea where all these fantastic changes are leading.

Perhaps as an oversimplification, I would summarize this book as a bold attempt to demonstrate the contested nature of multiple legal orders interacting in view of the revolutionary developments that occurred in international law during and after World War II. Prof. Boudreau specifically articulates and discusses the modern "law of nations" as part of a newly emergent international fiduciary legal order. In this regard, Boudreau is fond of quoting his professor and mentor Michael Barkun's words in his classic book *Law Without Sanction*: "[t]he world is not a one-law world, fervent wishes to the contrary notwithstanding; it is a world of 'diverse' public orders."

Taking inspiration from Prof. Barkun's insight, Boudreau argues in his keystone chapter that there are actually three macro international legal orders interacting in a contested and sometimes complimentary way in international law today. When taken together, these interactions of entire legal orders, consisting of the readily recognized public "state-centric" international law, private international law, and newly emergent and evolving fiduciary international law, constitute a highly dynamic pluralistic international legal order. Boudreau is correct in thinking that these orders are constantly interacting, diffusing, or even colliding into one another, resulting in constant legal contest on the macro and micro scale concerning which specific law will prevail. Indeed, determining which legal order will dominate within and between states can be viewed as a problematic concern, or for others, a natural evolution in state-system relationships.

Before going further, I should divulge that I am a personal friend and close professional colleague of Prof. Boudreau, who wrote the first chapter "Promises to Keep: The Law of Nations and the Post-World War II International Legal Order." I am very familiar with his work in the area of conflict analysis and resolution, including his pioneering work on the epistemology of violent human conflict, which begins, as he notes, with the elemental "epistemic encounter" between two human beings or groups of human beings who seek to destroy each other's existence. Based upon this epistemic framework, his subsequent work on "multiplex methodologies" and the "rehumanization" of those who have been demonized and dehumanized in violent human conflict has made a valuable and unique contribution to our shared field of conflict analysis. I have worked with him on several pieces relating to the rehumanization of the enemy other, and we have lamented the lack of legal institutions that can support, the framework where victims can go to assist them in restitution and perhaps recovery, to some degree. Thus, his work in international law, his field of special interest and expertise, can be viewed as an elaboration of his earlier work in the field of violent human conflicts. His interest in the "law of nations" comes directly from his behind-the-scenes, yet very real efforts to help the Bosnian people during the three years of the Balkans war (1992-1995). He even had a former student in the office of Assistant Secretary of State Richard Holbrooke when, as Prof. Boudreau has stated, "they decided to unleash him" [Holbrooke]. Prof. Boudreau thought that Holbrooke — given his extraordinary combination of talents, intellect, and iron will – would end the war in three months, and it was. Some would say the war ended just as Holbrooke wanted: like a bulldozer (Holbrooke) leveling the playing field. My one concern with Holbrooke's approach is that he assumed the role of a power negotiator, meaning he brought with him the force of the United States military and all United States institutions to bear on the process. This led to an outcome, but the subsequent implementation and enforcement produced suboptimal results.

In my judgment, Prof. Boudreau's chapter on the "law of nations" is a ground-breaking, if not revolutionary, contribution to the fields of international relations and international law; his chapter occupies a unique intersection of historical and contemporary jurisprudence. He essentially posits that the fiduciary international "law of nations" emerged from the "agony and ashes" of World War II. Specifically, he first argues that the Allied nations made a series of solemn declarations and promises in good faith to the Allied, conquered, colonialized, and neutral peoples of the world during World War II. Second, fiduciary obligations, duties, and norms were created when the millions of the Allied, conquered, and colonized peoples of the world expressly or tacitly consented to these promises, as evidenced by their subsequent service in helping to defeat global fascism. Third, he asserts that it is the preeminent role of present and future national or international judges, courts, and tribunals to ascertain the extent and nature of these fiduciary obligations and duties accepted by governments, and made possible by their people's subsequent service and sacrifices in order to win the war. I know that to him, this seems self-evident and obvious in light of the actual historical context and evidence that resulted from the Allies' promissory declarations and individual statements throughout the war. Yet, it admittedly was not self-evident to me at first, or probably to some of his readers. There have been plenty of promises and laws made on the international stage during wars that have been subsequently broken or reneged on once those wars concluded. Yet, I now find his argument convincing, if not compelling, and even unique.

I know that Prof. Boudreau is not fully convinced that scholars schooled in the current "hegemonic" state-centric international law paradigm accept his new paradigm and the resulting pluralistic complexity in international law or relations. Thus, the reaction will understandably attempt to reduce the fiduciary international legal order to existing legal frameworks of state-centric law. Alternately, scholars and others may revert to stereotypical thinking and characterize his innovations in simplistic slogans, such as consisting of a "monist" world law, or applicable only within "domestic jurisdictions" of states. Many will likely deny that a fiduciary "law of nations" can exist, though Prof. Boudreau eloquently argues that this is ultimately for current or future courts to decide. These are real concerns that cannot be argued away without a clear framework upon which to discuss the role of nations within the state-dominated system. His chapter, and this book, begins the conversation on how that framework might look.

Indeed, I think this chapter – and the entire book, for that matter – is written for judges who are pondering the controlling law, each alone in his or her study, as these yet-unnamed judges struggle with very real cases and individuals in their national or international jurisdictions. It is also written for citizens and legislators to ponder, but I am more curious to know what judges in the trenches think of the ideas expressed herein. Prof. Boudreau seems to think that the fully explicit international fiduciary legal order will be recognized, first and foremost, by a globalized judiciary, with some accepting for now an international fiduciary legal order while others retreat into a seemingly safe, yet (if Boudreau is right) incomplete paradigm of international law. He has cited to me in private conversations the section in the book the *Structure of Scientific Revolutions* in which Thomas Kuhn believes that the "old guard" scholars will simply have to die out before the new paradigm is accepted. Until then, there is an interesting dynamic tension between pluralists and state-centric or sovereign-rights schools of thought. It is uncertain what will happen, but I suspect that within the next 20 to 30 years there will be a rigorous exchange, even mixing, of ideas – which is the way it should be. In this regard, Prof. Boudreau believes that once you see an old problem from a new angle, then that which was once thought to be only "X" can now become "XYZ," or even "WYC," inspiring a new synthesis, and such a process may occur in the years ahead with the "law of nations."

Indeed, I think that Prof. Boudreau underestimates the ability of the now-global academy of scholars to accept or even teach supposedly radical new ideas. Admittedly, a state-centric international law or international relations is still very much present, and typically serves us well; yet, a fully explicit international fiduciary legal order based upon the global commons, the "law of nations," and even customary international law can be seen *as a natural evolution* of the existing state-centric paradigm, and not so difficult to grasp or accept.

Finally, as someone who has travelled extensively through war zones across the globe, I have seen up close the vast human devastation caused by supposedly "limited" or "low intensity" war. I am thinking of my work in Nepal, Israel-West Bank, Myanmar, and Bosnia, where slow-grinding conflict digs deep trenches between people. In view of these personal experiences, I fully support Prof. Boudreau's call for individual accountability for initiating war, when warranted, and for any subsequent war crimes. In the current absence of individual governments' willingness to observe the compelling norms of obligatory compliance with international prohibitions against the initiation of war, the legal enforcement of individual accountability may be the most effective short-term method to deter such wars from occurring in the first place.

Given this, I do not believe as Prof. Boudreau does that the war in Iraq was an unnecessary war of aggression, and that as such, the architects of this war in the Bush

Administration, as initiators of the invasion, should be prosecuted for war crimes. I also do not believe the Obama Administration's exit plan left the country in any improved state, and arguably made the situation even more unstable. If what happened during the 17-month "rush to war" was indeed a faux pretext for engagement, then the leaders of several allied countries – along with several in Arab countries – would all be held to account for reasons that they believed to be credible causes of action at the time. He and I both agree that Saddam Hussein was a despicable leader who essentially waged war upon his own people for decades. Yet, he disagrees that the war was necessary and a last resort, while I believe that a renegade government headed by someone like Saddam Hussein (or Muammar Gaddafi or Kim Jung Un, for that matter) was always a threat to international peace and security, as illustrated by his invasion in the early 1990s of his neighbors Kuwait and (lest people forget) Saudi Arabia. Hussein therefore needed to be confronted using a variety of political means, sanctions, boycotts, divestiture, and other means to deter his behavior. More recently, one might argue the same point about Muammar Gaddafi and the Obama Administration's participation in the military invasion in the Libyan Civil War. He and I also have personally and publicly supported the United States troops engaged in combat in Iraq; Prof. Boudreau has even had one member of his extended family deployed there, so this is a position that he and I do not take lightly, and we have honorably agreed to disagree on some points regarding specific areas of engagement. Such disagreements should be expected, as Prof. Boudreau argues in the last section of his chapter, in a world characterized by a diverse pluralistic international legal order. Differences are positive, and one would hope to find honest discourse from them – and perhaps even the "third way."

The next essays in this collection show, in fact, how evolutionary attempts to apply fiduciary or new norms by courts can be so contested and complex in a pluralistic international legal order that now characterizes post-World War II international law. The contested nature of the new norms began immediately at the Nuremberg Trials, and has continued to the present day; specifically, Prof. Tara Helfman's chapter: "Francis Biddle and the Nuremberg Legacy: Waking the Human Conscience" first illustrates the contested nature of judicial decisions and application of the controlling law. For the research of this article, Prof. Helfman plunged into the historic Syracuse University Bird Library's Nuremberg and Francis Biddle Collection.[667] Prof. Helfman begins her essay by

[667] Now found on file as well at http://library.syr.edu/digital/guides/b/biddle_f.htm. at the Library's Special Collections Research Center (SCRC)

noting that her chapter reveals that "the members were acutely aware that the proceedings at Nuremberg represented an important pivot point in the history of international law, and that they managed the proceedings accordingly. Biddle knew that far more was at stake at Nuremberg than the fate of the 22 Nazi defendants on trial. The future of international criminal law was also in the tribunal's control." Prof. Helfman makes it quite clear that Nuremberg was a major game changer for international law and relations.

Prof. Helfman then proceeds to describe the judges' own thoughts and deliberations as they struggled with the momentous task set before them, as well as specific legal dilemmas: first, *what to do* with the Nazi warlords after all surviving members of Hitler's inner circle were captured; second, whether the Nuremberg Charter was an exercise in *ex post facto* law rendering, its results suspect or even illegal. Prof. Helfman reviews the competing considerations of policy, principle, and law to demonstrate how the first question was answered. The Allies eventually agreed upon a trial rather than summary execution, partly due to military considerations of pursuing a peaceful occupation of Germany without creating martyrs, and partly to place the Holocaust and other Nazi atrocities in the courtroom for the world to see.

Secondly, the Allies struggled with the sheer enormity of the Nazi crimes, especially the Germans' genocidal assault against the Jews, gypsies, Poles, and others deemed unfit to live in the "Third Reich." As Prof. Helfman notes, at "the heart of the crimes to be confronted at Nuremberg was, as Winston Churchill called it, 'a crime without a name.'[668] Rafaël Lemkin named it 'genocide.'"" Prof. Helfman notes how this question was directly yet subtly addressed through commentary submitted to the tribunal that *ex post facto* law is a condition of domestic jurisdiction, and that no such principle had yet been established by sovereign states in international law at the time of the trials. Until one was, this legal principle could not be considered binding for sovereign states. Furthermore, and perhaps more importantly, one cannot really criminalize on the international level that which, prior to the actual crime, one *could not even conceive of being committed*, especially against an entire people, as in the Nazi Holocaust. Yet, as Prof. Helfman highlights, the Nuremberg "crimes against humanity" were military criminal code and law "writ large." In view of this, there could be no doubt that these actions

---

[668] Quoted in William Schabas, *Genocide in International Law* (2000) 14.

were wrong, and the magnitude of the "crime without a name" — previous to the Nuremberg Charter — could not and should not go unpunished.

In other words, the fiduciary international legal order that Prof. Boudreau articulates and discusses was born in the cauldron of contested and competing legal, historical, and even military forces. There is no smooth, "yellow brick" road to the implementation of the Nuremberg and post-Nuremberg principles of fiduciary international law; every step of the way was, and will be, challenged and contested. Prof. Helfman has dramatically demonstrated in original and compelling research how the contested nature of the new international norms were argued in the judges' chambers, even as the trial progressed. In fact, the Biddle papers are full of conversations and disagreements among the judges concerning the ultimate outcome of the trial. For Prof. Boudreau, such judicial reflection, analysis, and contested considerations are the very essence of lawmaking, especially when a new fiduciary legal order is being born.

The next article by the Hon. Stephen J. Sfekas entitled "Taming the Furies: The Justice Trial at Nuremberg, 1947" picks up where Prof. Helfman's article leaves off – namely, at the subsequent trials of Nazi leaders at Nuremberg after United States Justice Jackson completed the first trial and departed for the United States. In this article, the judge elaborates upon the legal evolution of the Nuremberg Charter during its actual application at the subsequent trials. His research reveals several critical aspects of these trials that are often overlooked in international law. First, as he ably states, "Taylor felt that the Justice Trial would be of particular interest to judges and lawyers because of the anomaly that judges and prosecutors of one country were trying judges and prosecutors from another country for crimes committed within the judicial process.[669] Indeed, German judges and justice officials were tried on German soil, in many cases for crimes against German citizens for acts of injustice apparently sanctioned under German law.[670]

Indeed, this trial can best be interpreted as an attempt to establish universal standards of justice." Given this, Judge Sfekas ask three key questions: a) Was the trial procedurally fair?; b) Was the trial substantively fair?; c) Was justice, in fact, done? Noting that the Nazi defendants had more procedural rights at Nuremberg then United States citizens had at the time, the judge determines that the trials were in fact fair and just, thus setting

669 Taylor Final Report at 169.
670 *Id.*

a critical foundation for possible subsequent trials of accused war criminals, even on their own soil. In particular, he notes how the criminal category of "crimes against humanity," which was designed to protect civilian populations against violence by their own or other governments, began to take on a life of its own during these trials, as some Nazi defendants were charged with solely this offense. The next two chapters analyze the misapplication of this now-independent criminal category (Sainz-Borgo) or the appropriate application (Garzon) by the respective judiciaries to novel situations in order to more effectively protect civilians in times of war. According to Boudreau, these and other Nuremberg innovations that are now contained within the law of nations invite, if not require, such experimentation and evolutionary legal application. Only in this way will the purposes and principles of the Nuremberg Charter and other fiduciary norms of law of nations receive full observance.

The next chapter by Juan Carlos Sainz-Borgo entitled "The International Criminal Court, Drug Trafficking, and Crimes against Humanity" provides a local example of how these new norms of Nuremberg are "differentially diffusing," as Prof. Boudreau would claim, into domestic jurisdictions. Specifically, Prof. Sainz-Borgo challenges the Venezuelan Supreme Court's recent attempt at incorporating the Nuremberg criminal category of "crimes against humanity" into the domestic jurisdiction of Venezuela as an anti-drug trade provision. In a pluralistic legal order, there will be no simple solution and no single and proven way to apply such international norms; each unique national jurisdiction will likely struggle, in view of its own legal and cultural history, with how to apply these norms. As Prof. Sainz-Borgo cites, even the unique geography of the Andes nations plays a significant role in how the court should interpret, incorporate, and apply international norms. In this case, he concludes that the Supreme Court's efforts to incorporate international norms, such as the Nuremberg criminal category of "crimes against humanity," is misguided in relation to the Venezuelan drug trade and would cause more problems than it solves. I completely agree with his claim that "drug-related crimes are certainly a worldwide scourge that may cause serious harm to the population. However, it cannot be considered a crime against humanity, nor can it be subsumed under the competence of the ICC as part of the most serious and significant crimes, as defined by the international community." In essence, there are limitations to the evolving "law of nations" as they encroach upon domestic law, not simply because of sovereignty issues, but for the plain and simple explanation of lack of applicability. Likewise, the application of "crimes against humanity" in domestic law was not likely intended for misuse as a potential smoke screen for the elimination of domestic political rivals, which could easily become a natural consequence of the application seen in Venezuelan courts.

The next chapter by Prof. Berrnard Ntahiraja of Rwanda continues with this theme, illustrating the difficulty of trying to apply new post-Nuremberg norms of "responsibility to protect" (typically abbreviated as R2P or PTP, depending upon one's legal culture). The point of his chapter is not to declare what the law definitely is, not is it to "adjudicate" and say which of the theories is the right one. As he states, "[o]n the contrary, it is to highlight the legal uncertainty characterizing the issue." He first notes that African states were developing such a doctrine well before its modern incarnation as a post-2004 World Summit declaration. In an interesting analysis of the post-World War II tension between the unilateral and collective legitimation of military force, Prof. Ntahiraja indicates that, in lieu of UNSC action in a specific issue, regional organizations *can and should* authorize the use of military force as a last resort in cases requiring humanitarian intervention. He pointedly argues that the UNSC's inaction can cost lives, as African states have learned in some tragic places in recent decades. So, a major theme of his chapter is to analyze enforcement action and the use of force from the perspective of the relationship between the AU and the UN. As such, it is an invaluable addition to the rather slight attention usually given in powerful capitals to regional arrangements and their potential role in maintaining international peace and security.

Prof. Ntahiraja notes that, in the first instance, regional enforcement might be preferable, and that

> the international community is more likely to tolerate a deviation from Article 53 in cases where the regional arrangement has a unique connection, usually based on geography, to the subject of the action. Regional arrangements are understood to have a strong interest in addressing threats that originate within their own regions, and they often have the tools necessary to respond quickly and effectively. Therefore, it is acknowledged that regional arrangements may be better suited than the universal organs of the UNa to address local threats to peace and security.

In the case of Libya, he seems to argue that the reverse occurred, stating that UNSC Resolution 1973 inadvertently "allowed" NATO to prevent the delegates of the AU from seeking a peaceful resolution to the pending threat of a bloodbath by Gaddafi forces within the context of the UNSC resolution. Thus, he argues for a vigorous role in humanitarian interventions in the future for regional organizations; this could be a substitute strategy for those who want to see the R2P doctrine fully mature in the future as a non-military option before the UNSC finally throws down the gauntlet.

The next chapter by Prof. Mihir Kanade, Director of the Human Rights Center at the University of Peace, concerns the contested nature of merging trade and human rights regimes. First, Prof. Kinade notes that modern international human rights regimes are a direct outgrowth of World War II legal developments and innovations. He then cites the specific example of the World Trade Organization (WTO) and argues that the implementation of human rights can occur, and even strengthen, within the context of the existing WTO. In particular, he explains that encouraging "sustainable development" is one of the goals in the Preamble of the founding "Umbrella Agreements" of the WTO. At the same time, the UNGA in recent years has identified sustainable development as an important human right independently of trade agreements. As such, he argues that these areas of overlap provide a common ground in which both human right norms and trade agreements can be linked and prove to be mutually beneficial, rather than polar opposites.

This article illustrates that once again, the potentially contested nature of merging different legal norms and obligations, especially those that derive from entirely distinct legal orders, can be complementary and mutually supportive, rather than simply "zero sum" and competitive processes. Thus, this example has critical implications for judges in the future who seek to merge the norms of differing legal orders into a coherent and complementary whole. The legal community must also be alert to the unintended application and consequences of employing "competing" legal orders to issues of national rights and obligations. This topic is the subject of another book.

Future Trends: Short Term vs. Long Term

On the United States legal front, there are many examples of temporary fads (such as the prohibition of liquor) and current trends (gay marriage) to evidence that even in the law – the backbone of social order – there is development, experimentation, modification, and elimination. When considering the development of laws that bind states via treaties, it is quite easy to see how the current state system operates to make this happen.

The question raised here is whether or not, in situations, events, or activities focusing on human rights or crimes against humanity, the unit of analysis – the "state" – is the appropriate measure, or if the international legal order should evolve to emphasize and experiment with the "nation" as well. Given the current structure of international law, this will be an admittedly difficult task to consider, much less execute. It is uncertain if this endeavor is merely a temporary idea that will be absorbed into the current legal order, or if it is a genuine trend that will fundamentally alter the existing legal paradigm and restructure some areas of international law. The answer will take time to develop, but evidence to date suggests at least some movement in discussing this radical shift in thinking. The honest and most alarming aspect of such an idea is the direct confrontation of existing state *sovereign rights* and *constitutional limitations*. Addressing both concerns is imperative if legal scholars are to ever have a decent chance of successfully building such a binding "law of nations."

The question is, given this new paradigm presented by Prof. Boudreau, how can or will it develop in the future? Will it produce, at best, some minor modifications in the international legal order? Will it evolve into a trend as national voices, and especially the courts, become more prominent? Will there be the predictable productive tensions, or will this somehow evolve in a completely unique manner that scholars have not contemplated? One cannot know for certain, but there are many questions to ponder – some of which go "over the horizon" and involve looking into future unknowns.

The Second Bounce of the Ball

It is one thing to predict the next evolutionary moves in the development of international law as conceptualized by Prof. Boudreau's "law of nations" construct. Taken together, the insights, lessons, and warnings convened throughout this book provide a strong framework for the reader to begin the strategic process of "getting in the right place to catch the ball." Knowing where processes are likely to end up allows us to more adequately consider the variables that shape the eventual outcome. However, it is another thing altogether to seriously consider all potential paths and real obstacles that may arise. There are several ways to examine what may lie ahead. First, we must consider obvious roadblocks and other challenges. Would the eventual and delicate balance between an evolving international legal structure pose a credible threat to member state sovereignty, in that it might lead to the subjugation or weakening of domestic laws within participating states? Would a "law of nations" on matters relating to crimes against humanity supersede indigenous laws that, by treaty, would threaten a state's ability to regulate its own citizens? What about constitutional restrictions or challenges? Would the development of a "law of nations" somehow backfire and provide a catalyst for rogue and despotic regimes to use it as a vehicle to oppress their own people? If so, will this lead to resistance from many quarters — from democratic countries to despotic regimes? Would a "law of nations" serve to destabilize legitimate but vulnerable states that are struggling with indigenous terrorist groups, or those bent on inciting the collapse of the state? Prof. Boudreau would argue that such terrorist groups have no legal legitimacy, especially if they have not first exhausted all domestic and international legal avenues; few to none do this, or even try.

Second, we must examine the inconspicuous and unintended consequences of a poorly conceived path that could arise during the evolution of the "law of nations." Consider, for example, the worst-case scenario of an inexperienced, theoretically focused, and ideologically driven political leader who may be able to see that there could be some good that can come from such an order, but who has no realistic experience or clue about accomplishing it (or, worse, sees it as a benefit to one group at the expense of another). Now, setting motive aside, this situation has the potential to lead to outcomes that are serious, yet not immediately obvious. If a "law of nations" is misunderstood, then it could easily be ill-framed, perhaps using an outdated or discredited ideological lens, which could mean the grounding of the law can lead to future problems. In other words, poor leadership that ignores legal scholarship and precedent has a tendency to propagate an ineffective framing of issues, which typically yields more challenges. Likewise, failure to identify non-obvious consequences and properly frame the issues can lead to the growth of more ill-advised paths, which can produce more unintended consequences. Caution and time are critical in the evolution of any complex social arrangement.

There are several methods for identifying potential inconspicuous challenges, but two in particular are considered here. The first entails the consideration of several counterfactual experiments, such as envisioning the consequences had Roosevelt and Churchill not developed the Atlantic Charter – including how the world would look geopolitically today, and how that would impact the development and functioning of a "law of nations." Another possible question would be, "what would the legal order look like today if the Allies decided to simply execute the Nazi leadership, rather than undertaking the Nuremberg trials?" One might also consider the role of specific leaders by envisioning possible scenarios that could have unfolded had Hitler had not risen to power. Counterfactual exercises force the contemplation of alternative historical paths that allow for the recognition and appreciation of actual history, the forces that were in place, and the dynamics within that historical context, and how they led to the trajectory of the world today. Another related method is to focus on the future, envision as many scenarios as possible, and consider the range of outcomes. This might help evolve the focus on the intended functioning of international law.

From this, it is possible to consider non-obvious and unintended consequences. Regardless of the source of trouble – be it poor leadership decisions, poorly written language, or poor execution of the law – every effort must be made to identify these potential roadblocks early and prevent them from becoming engrained in the evolutionary process. Here, remarkably, one can learn from people who live and work in the private sector. Regardless of how one might view members of the business world, they do provide several creative and entrepreneurial means for solving old problems with new ideas, which can be instructive to this discussion. Creative thinking requires seeking the non-obvious and taking advantage of it when possible. Social evolution is predicated on creative thinking and, I argue, the entrepreneurial spirit. Indeed, much of the success of conflict intervention and the resolution of protracted conflicts comes, whether one wants to make the connection or not, from a business mindset of meeting needs. There is no reason why this entrepreneurial spirit cannot be employed in the evolution of law.

Finally, if all goes well and there comes a time for a version of the "law of nations," then we have to consider the "second bounce of the ball." This is another way to say that we must examine not just long-term consequences, but also the more important idea that there is an over-the-horizon, second-generation method of thinking. For instance, back in the late 1970s and early 1980s, as baby boomers were just beginning to enter middle age, the United States experienced a health craze that social institutions just were not prepared to effectively manage. Those who predicted this typically "cashed in" on the "first bounce of the ball" by opening gyms, health food stores, and fitness clubs. That is fine, as they were directly and effectively fulfilling a pressing social need. Now, going one step further in this trajectory reveals that few had thought about what would come next; after all these people had gotten into shape, what else would they need as they aged? My point is that very few have anticipated the aging cycle of baby boomers, who by now seem to be discovering their own mortality as though this was occurring for the first time in human history. They did not really anticipate the second bounce. Ideally, the evolution in international law would not make the same mistake.

The whole notion of the "second bounce of the ball" requires one to think through the entire trajectory and over the horizon to identify the unthinkable, unforeseen, and unexpected – i.e., the fuel from which opportunities arise – and develop a plan now on how to steer this trajectory in order to prevent a collision with problems, or if that will inevitably occur, find potential remedies before it happens so that the evolutionary or developmental plan can continue on course. If there is to be a real evolution, a paradigm shift that replaces the "old problem-solving methods" with new, innovative, or novel methods, then there must also be an accompanying focus on second-generation thinking and outcomes.

As a word of caution, we must realize that great ideas sometimes flounder in the laboratory because the inventor does not know how to get the product to the market, or conversely, the leader with a brilliant idea fails because he or she gets too far out in front of his or her people, who become unable to see the path and outcome and thus refuse to follow. In the case of a "law of nations," we see a large, complex, slow-moving, and new paradigm that can only be adequately framed and addressed if the political class allows it, legal scholars embrace it, and – most importantly – nations reject the notion of placing value only on the immediate moment or the next six months or so. If nations and their courts internalize the idea, psychologically accept it as their own trajectory, and act as trendsetters, then a new and unexpected international law may evolve in the future.

Made in United States
Orlando, FL
04 November 2026

90209907R00222